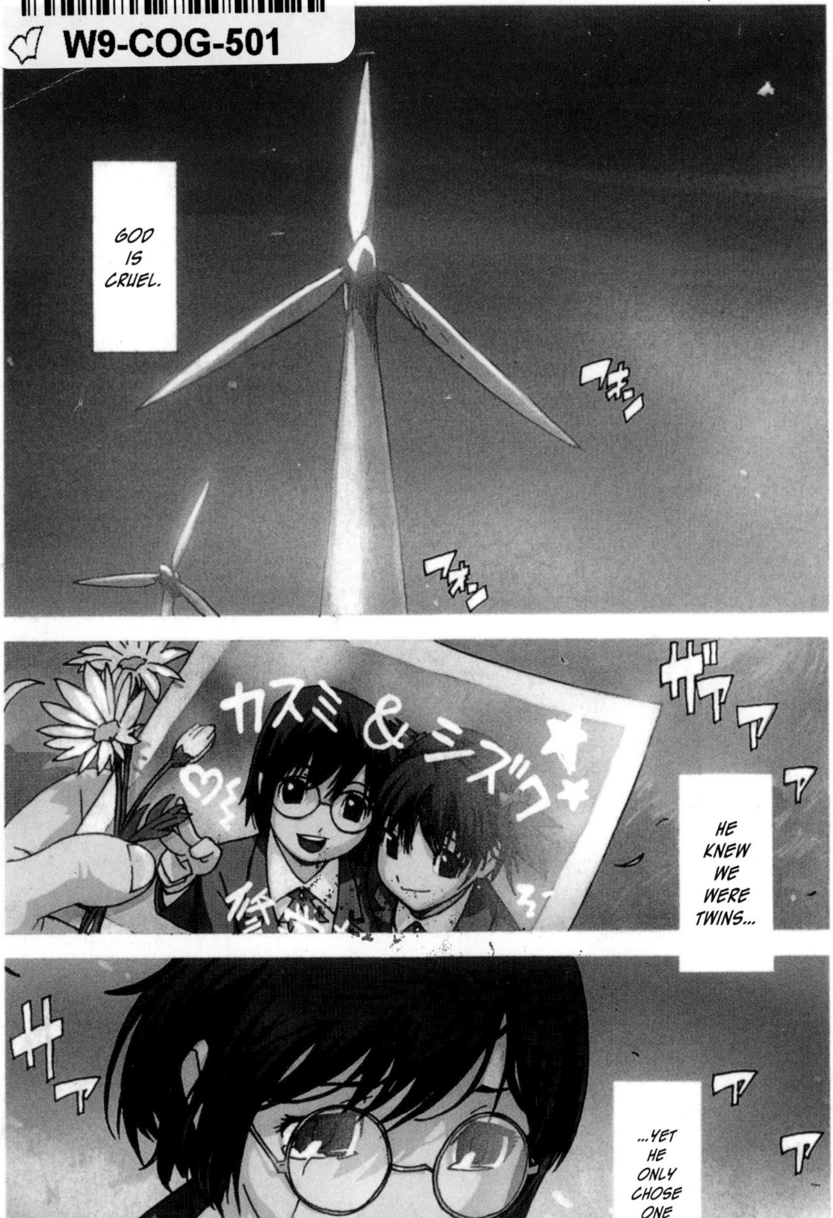
フォン
フォン
GOD IS CRUEL.
ザァァァ
HE KNEW WE WERE TWINS...
カスミ & シズク
サァァ
...YET HE ONLY CHOSE ONE OF US.

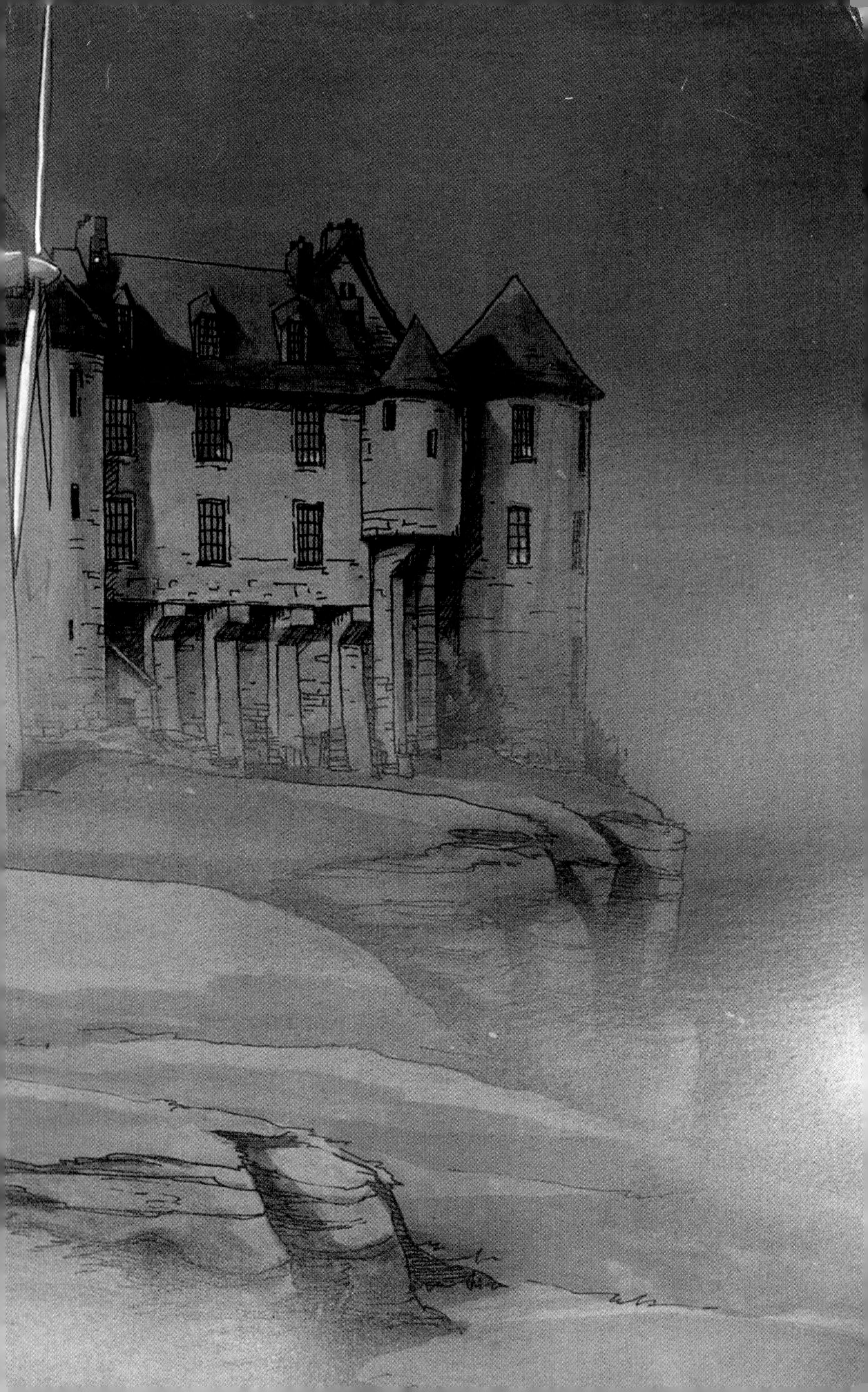

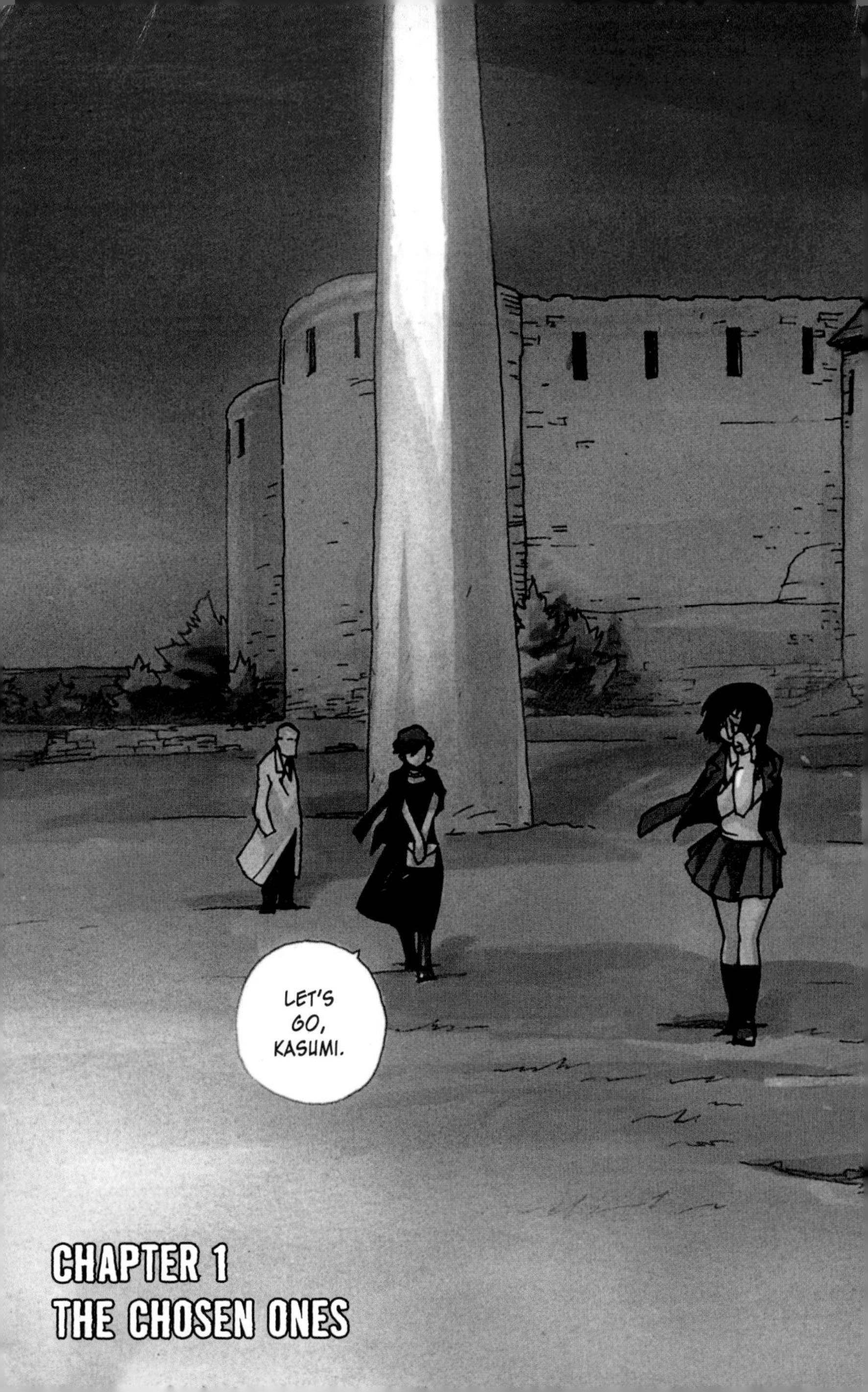
LET'S GO, KASUMI.

CHAPTER 1
THE CHOSEN ONES

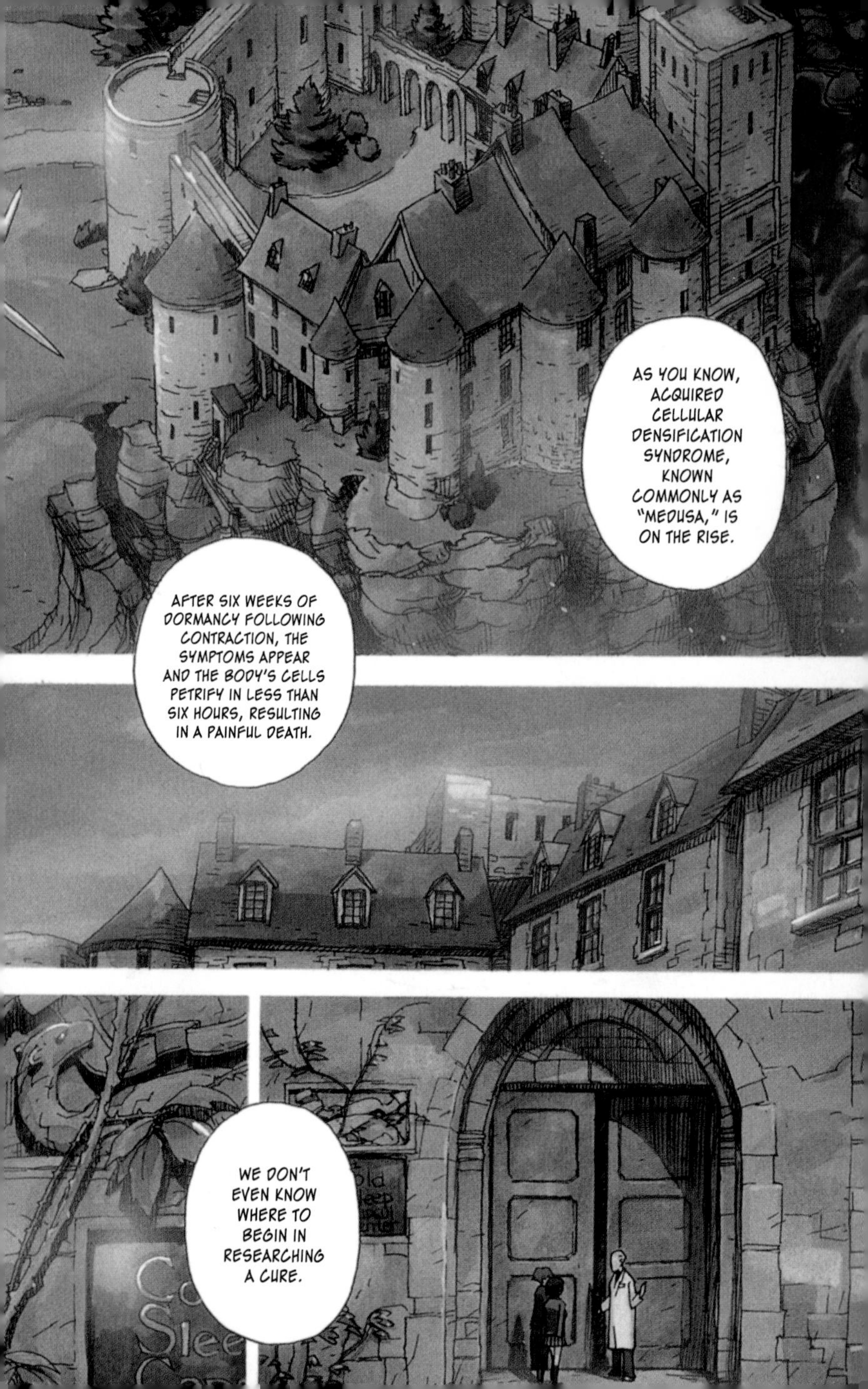
AS YOU KNOW, ACQUIRED CELLULAR DENSIFICATION SYNDROME, KNOWN COMMONLY AS "MEDUSA," IS ON THE RISE.
AFTER SIX WEEKS OF DORMANCY FOLLOWING CONTRACTION, THE SYMPTOMS APPEAR AND THE BODY'S CELLS PETRIFY IN LESS THAN SIX HOURS, RESULTING IN A PAINFUL DEATH.
WE DON'T EVEN KNOW WHERE TO BEGIN IN RESEARCHING A CURE.

いばらの王

King of Thorn.

①

岩原
裕二

Yuji Iwahara

King of Thorn Volume 1
Created by Yuji Iwahara

Translation - Alexis Kirsch
English Adaptation - Aaron Sparrow
Retouch and Lettering - Star Print Brokers
Production Artist - Michael Paolilli
Graphic Designer - James Lee

Editor - Tim Beedle
Digital Imaging Manager - Chris Buford
Pre-Production Supervisor - Erika Terriquez
Art Director - Anne Marie Horne
Production Manager - Elisabeth Brizzi
Managing Editor - Vy Nguyen
VP of Production - Ron Klamert
Editor-in-Chief - Rob Tokar
Publisher - Mike Kiley
President and C.O.O. - John Parker
C.E.O. and Chief Creative Officer - Stuart Levy

A  Manga

TOKYOPOP and 🐸 are trademarks or registered trademarks of TOKYOPOP Inc.

TOKYOPOP Inc.
5900 Wilshire Blvd. Suite 2000
Los Angeles, CA 90036

E-mail: info@TOKYOPOP.com
Come visit us online at www.TOKYOPOP.com

ISBN: 978-1-59816-235-6

First TOKYOPOP printing: June 2007
10 9 8 7 6 5 4 3 2 1
Printed in the USA

KING of THORN

Volume 1

Created by
Yuji Iwahara

HAMBURG // LONDON // LOS ANGELES // TOKYO

KING of THORN™

Contents

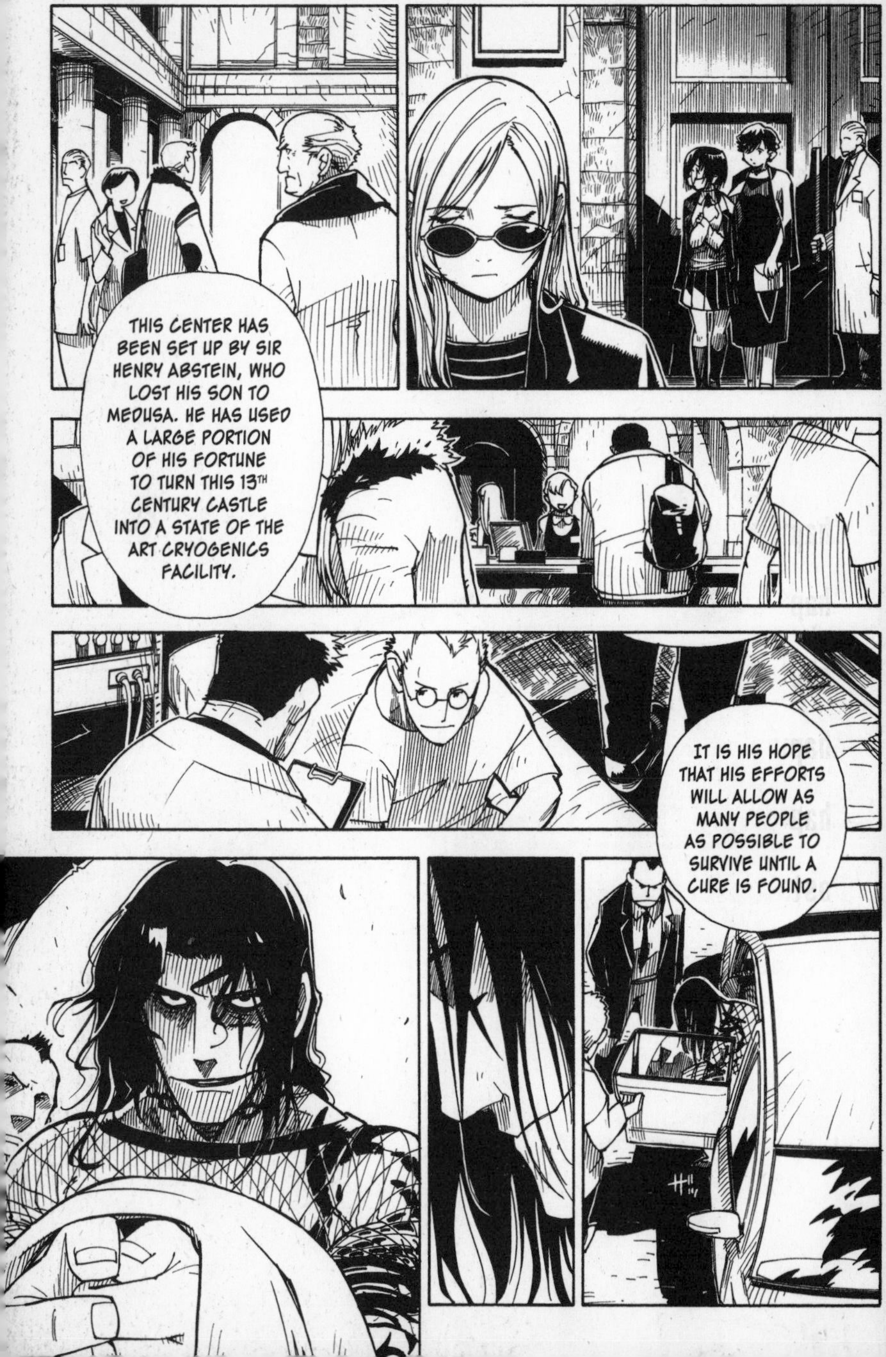
THIS CENTER HAS BEEN SET UP BY SIR HENRY ABSTEIN, WHO LOST HIS SON TO MEDUSA. HE HAS USED A LARGE PORTION OF HIS FORTUNE TO TURN THIS 13TH CENTURY CASTLE INTO A STATE OF THE ART CRYOGENICS FACILITY.
IT IS HIS HOPE THAT HIS EFFORTS WILL ALLOW AS MANY PEOPLE AS POSSIBLE TO SURVIVE UNTIL A CURE IS FOUND.

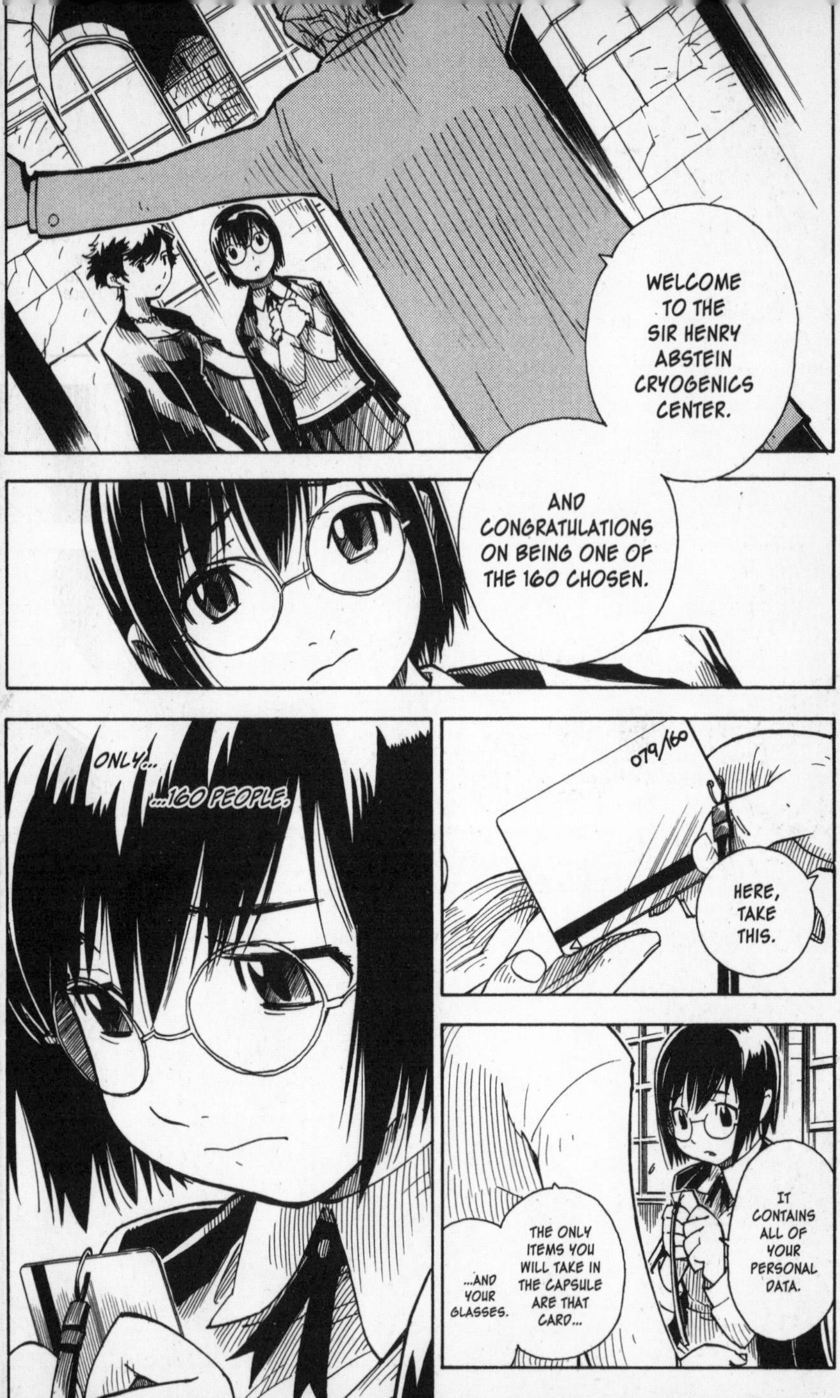
WELCOME TO THE SIR HENRY ABSTEIN CRYOGENICS CENTER.
AND CONGRATULATIONS ON BEING ONE OF THE 160 CHOSEN.
079/160
HERE, TAKE THIS.
IT CONTAINS ALL OF YOUR PERSONAL DATA.
THE ONLY ITEMS YOU WILL TAKE IN THE CAPSULE ARE THAT CARD...
...AND YOUR GLASSES.
ONLY...
...160 PEOPLE.

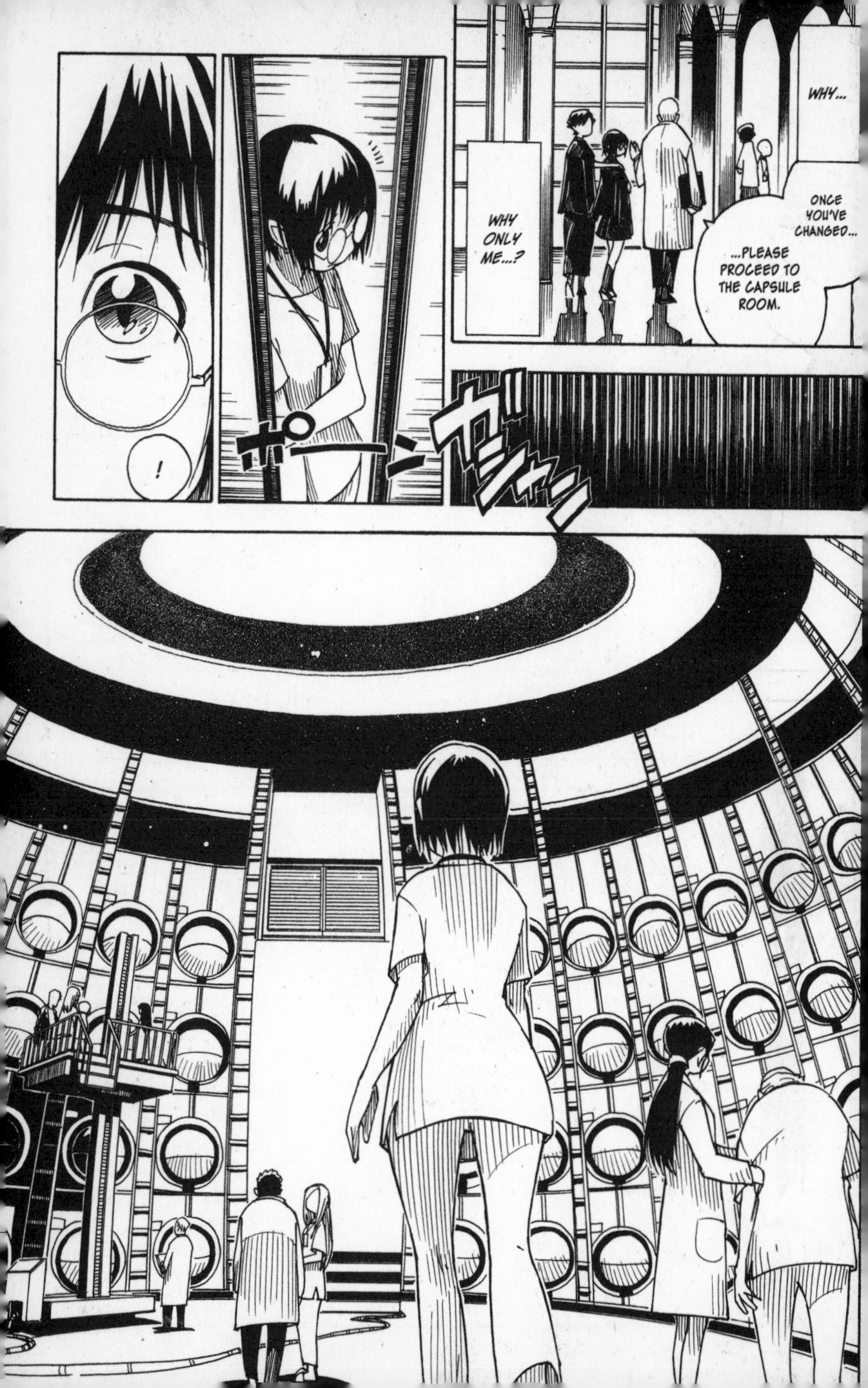
WHY...
ONCE YOU'VE CHANGED...
...PLEASE PROCEED TO THE CAPSULE ROOM.
WHY ONLY ME...?
ガシャン
ポーン
!

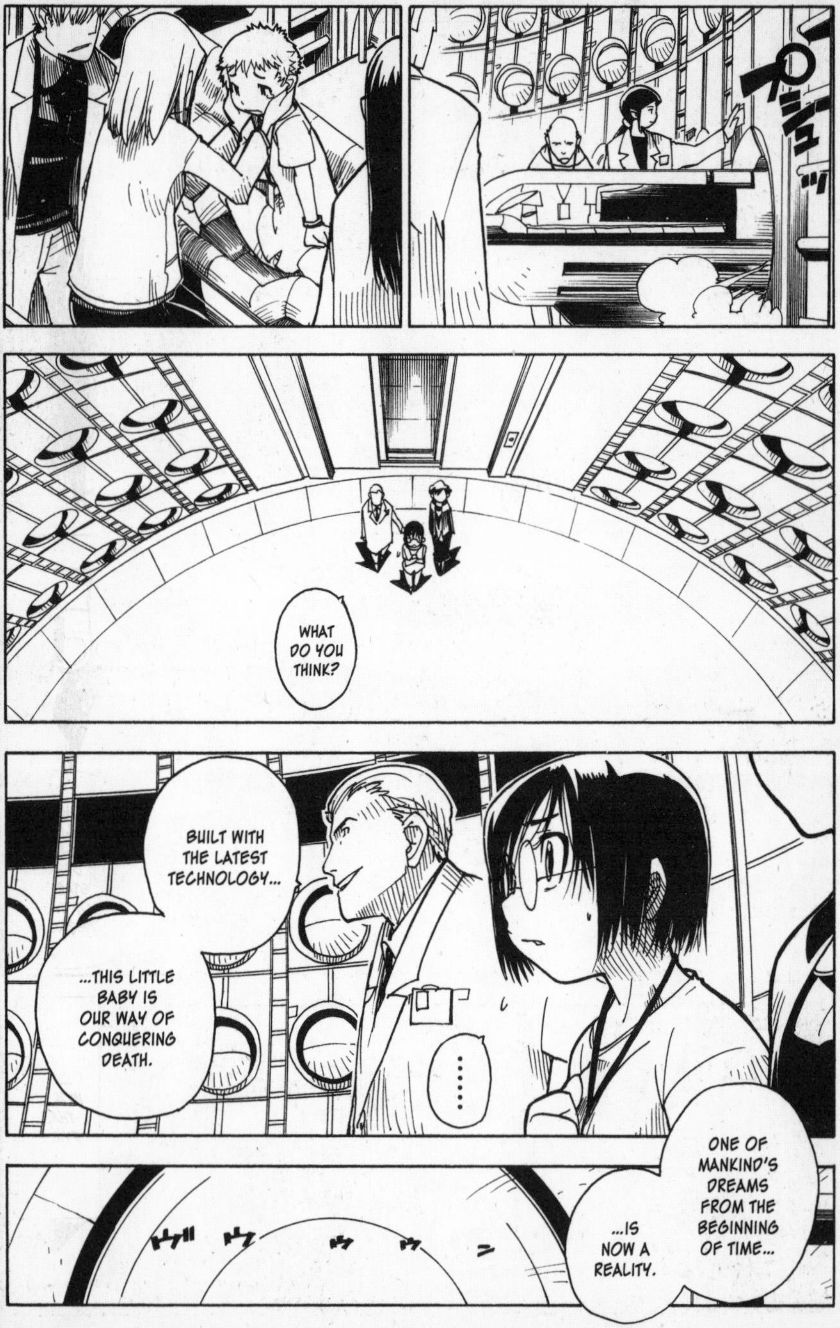
プシュッ
WHAT DO YOU THINK?
BUILT WITH THE LATEST TECHNOLOGY...
...THIS LITTLE BABY IS OUR WAY OF CONQUERING DEATH.
......
ONE OF MANKIND'S DREAMS FROM THE BEGINNING OF TIME...
...IS NOW A REALITY.

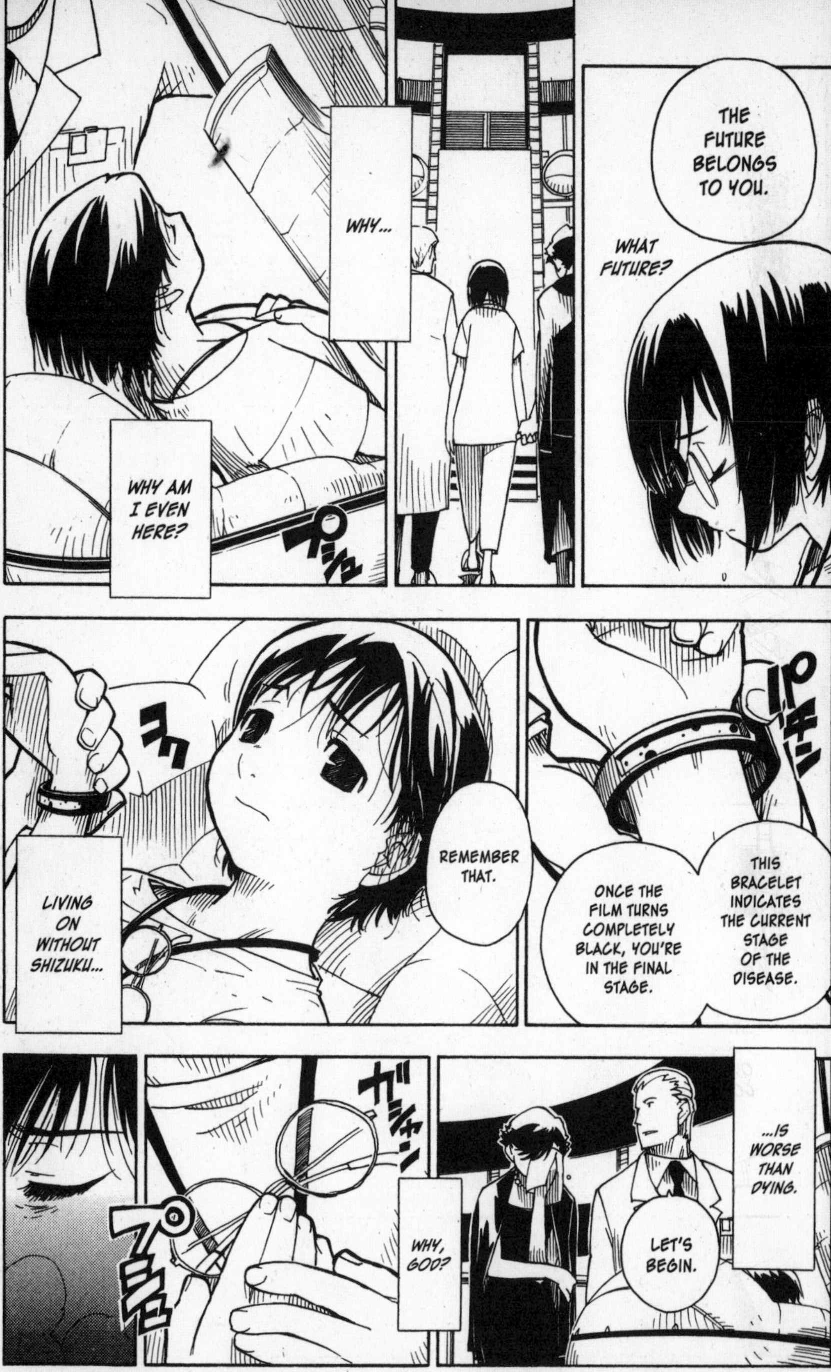
THE FUTURE BELONGS TO YOU.
WHAT FUTURE?
WHY...
WHY AM I EVEN HERE?
THIS BRACELET INDICATES THE CURRENT STAGE OF THE DISEASE.
ONCE THE FILM TURNS COMPLETELY BLACK, YOU'RE IN THE FINAL STAGE.
REMEMBER THAT.
LIVING ON WITHOUT SHIZUKU...
...IS WORSE THAN DYING.
LET'S BEGIN.
WHY, GOD?

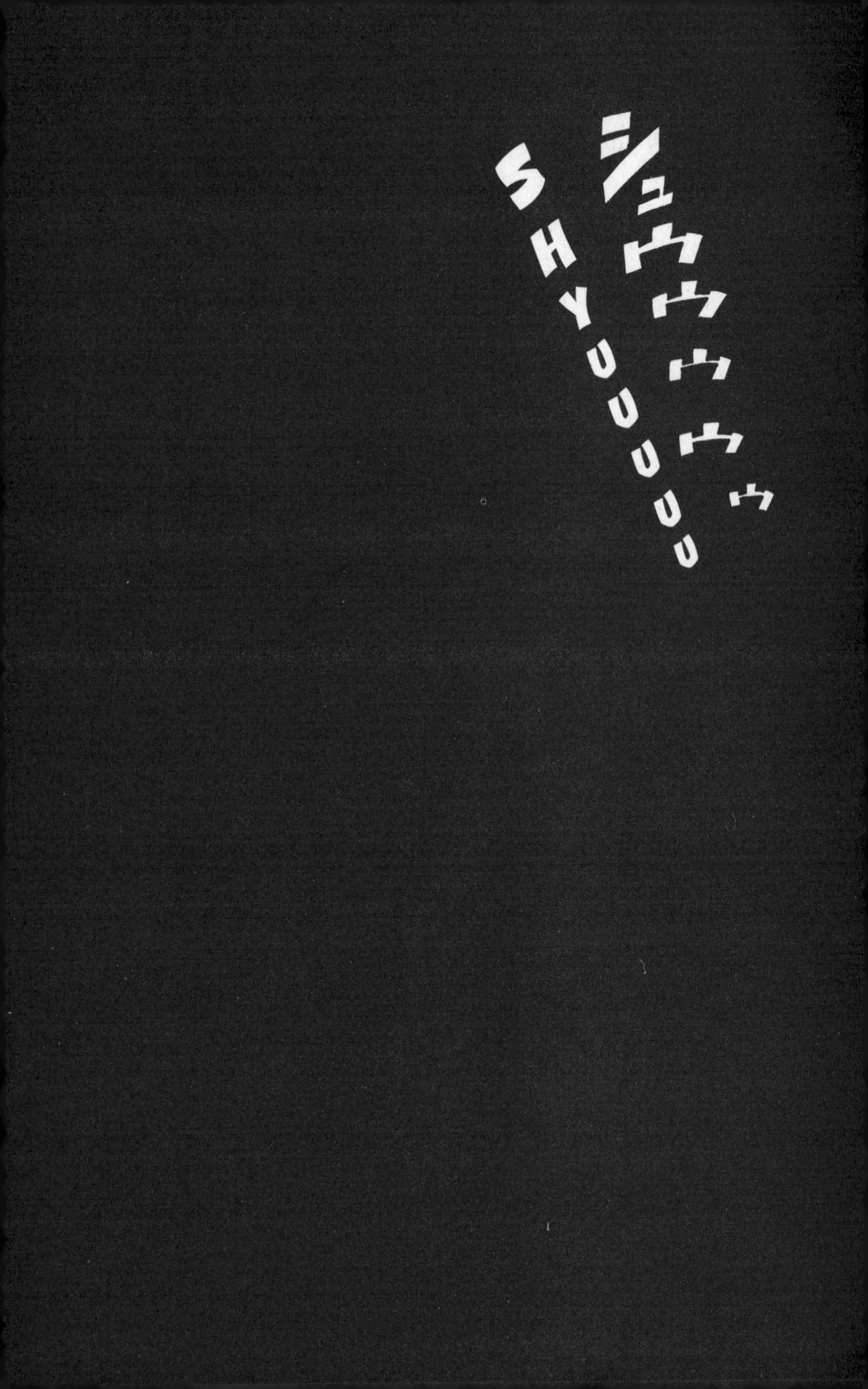
SHYUUUUU
シュウウウウゥ

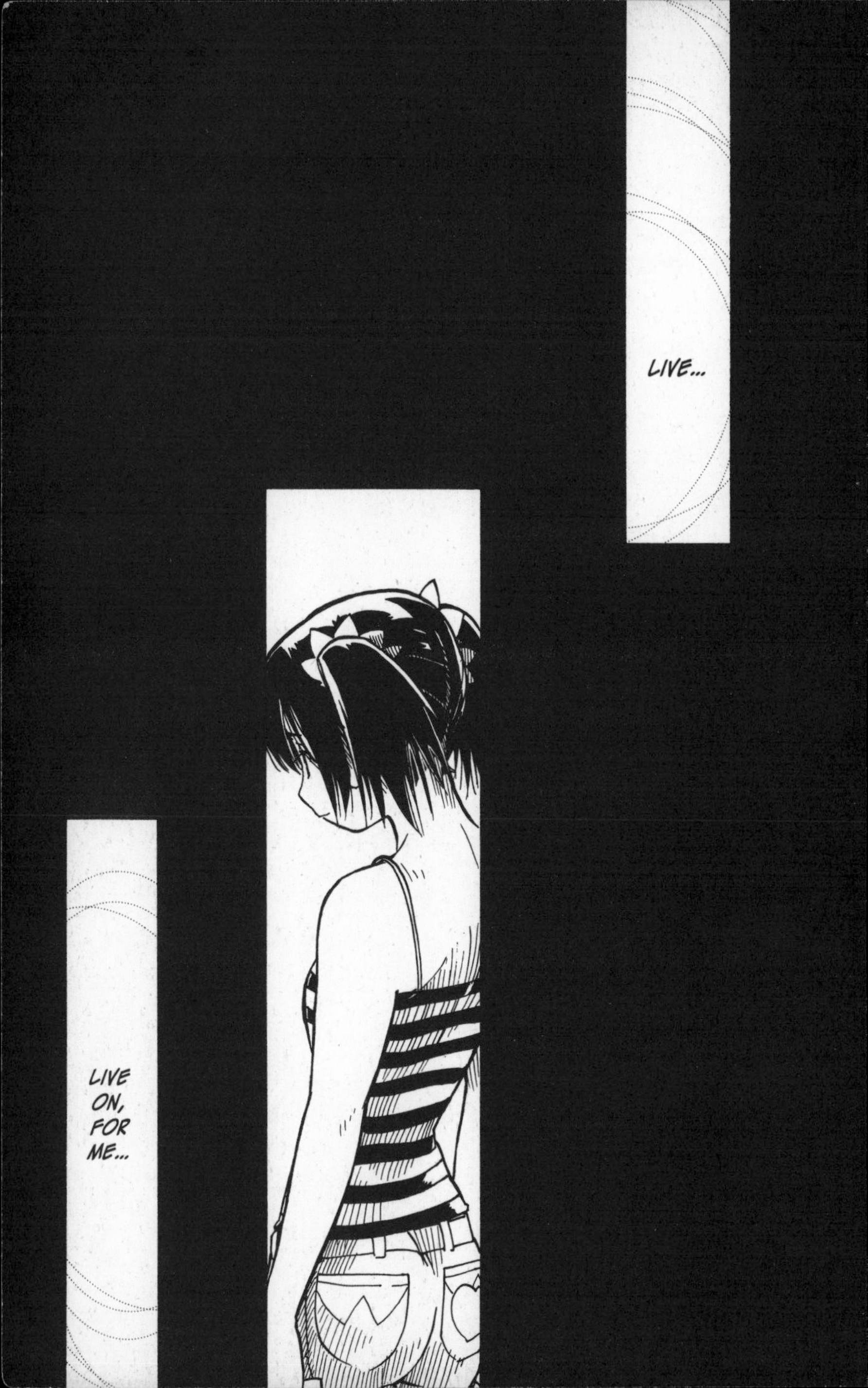
LIVE...
LIVE ON, FOR ME...

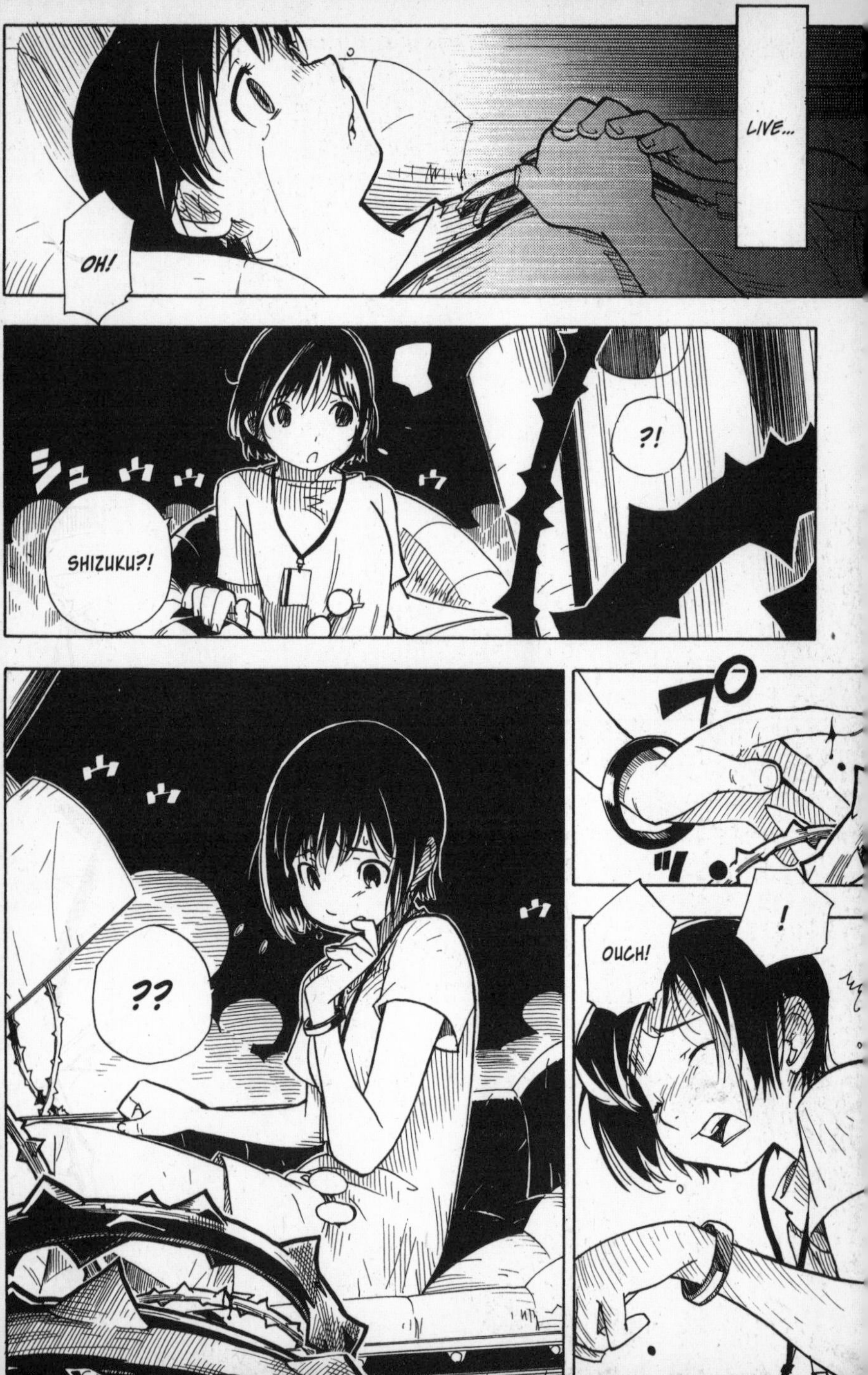
LIVE...
OH!
?!
SHIZUKU?!
!
OUCH!
??

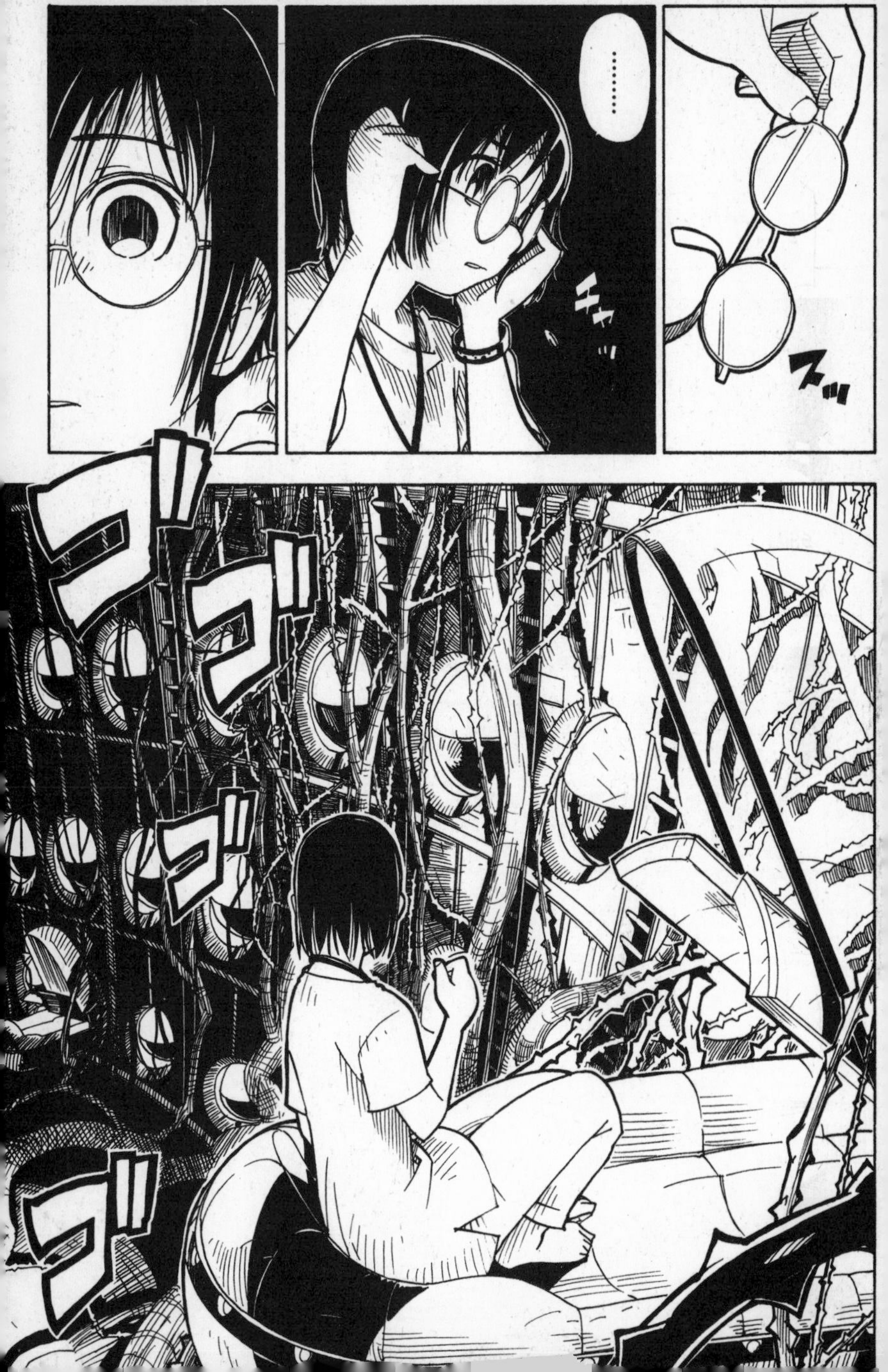
……
ゴ
ゴ
ゴ
ゴ

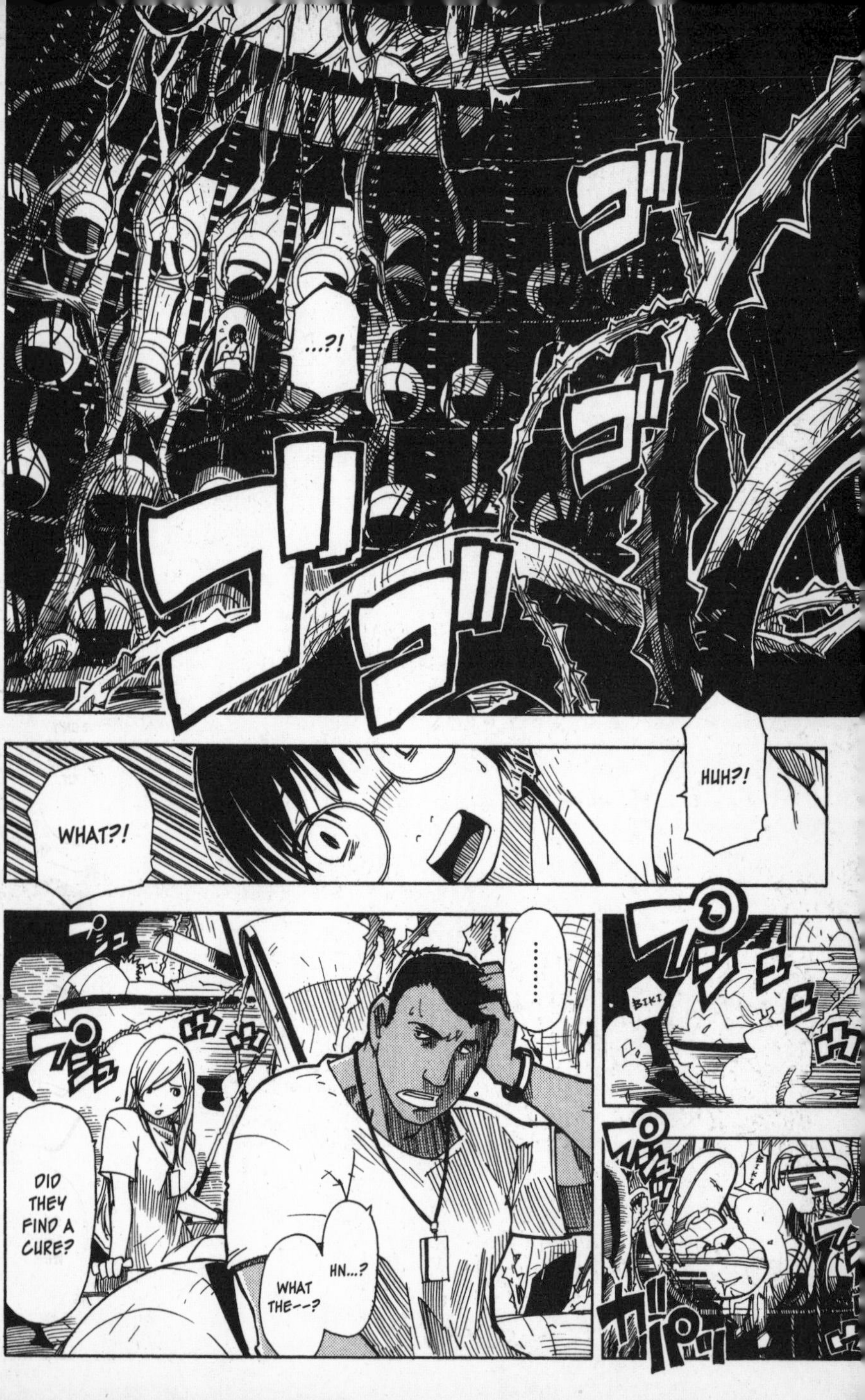

...?!
HUH?!
WHAT?!
BIKI
......
HN...?
WHAT THE--?
DID THEY FIND A CURE?

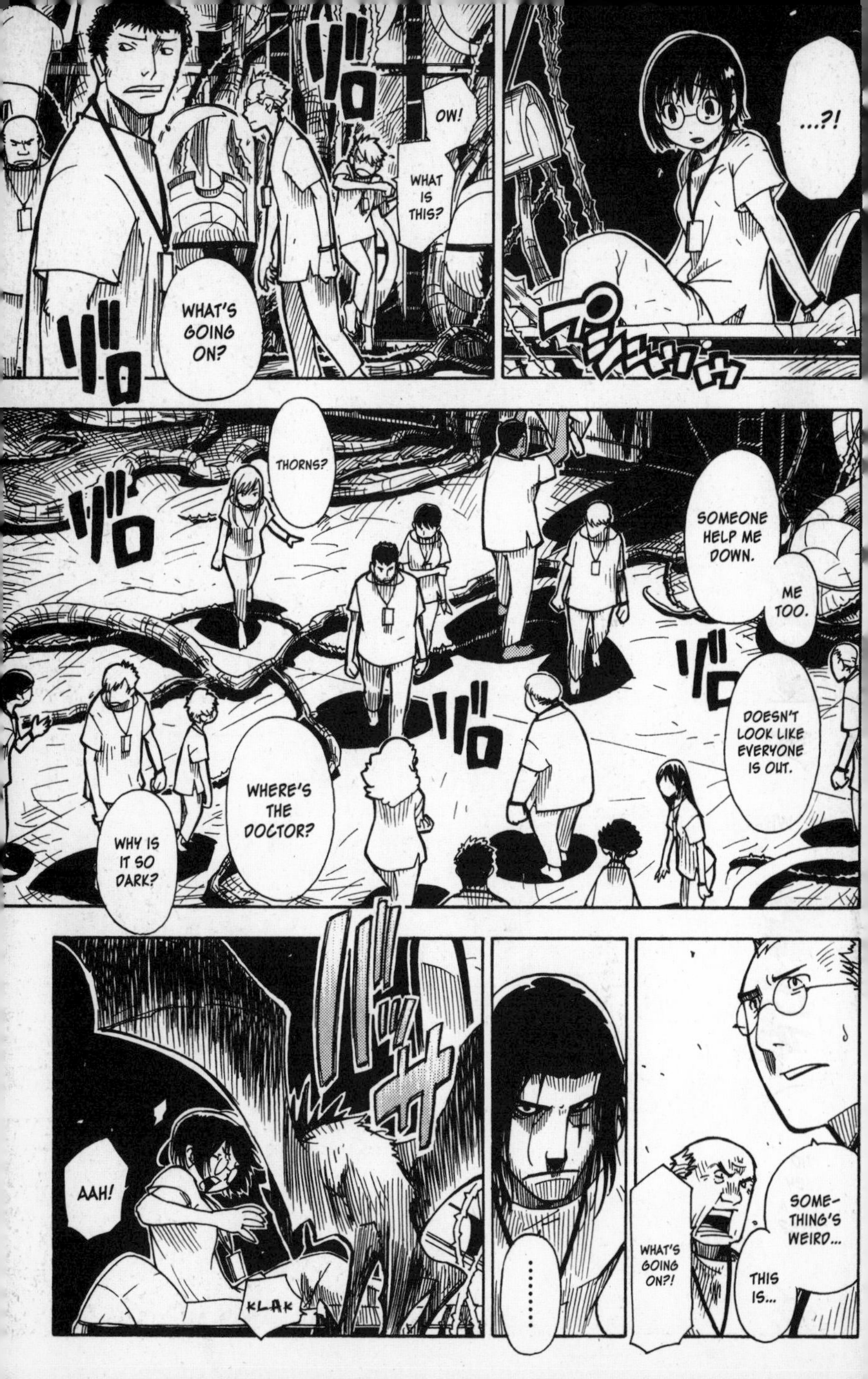
...?!
OW!
WHAT IS THIS?
ゾロ
WHAT'S GOING ON?
ゾロ
SOMEONE HELP ME DOWN.
ME TOO.
THORNS?
ゾロ
DOESN'T LOOK LIKE EVERYONE IS OUT.
ゾロ
WHERE'S THE DOCTOR?
WHY IS IT SO DARK?
SOME-THING'S WEIRD...
THIS IS...
WHAT'S GOING ON?!
......
AAH!
KLAK

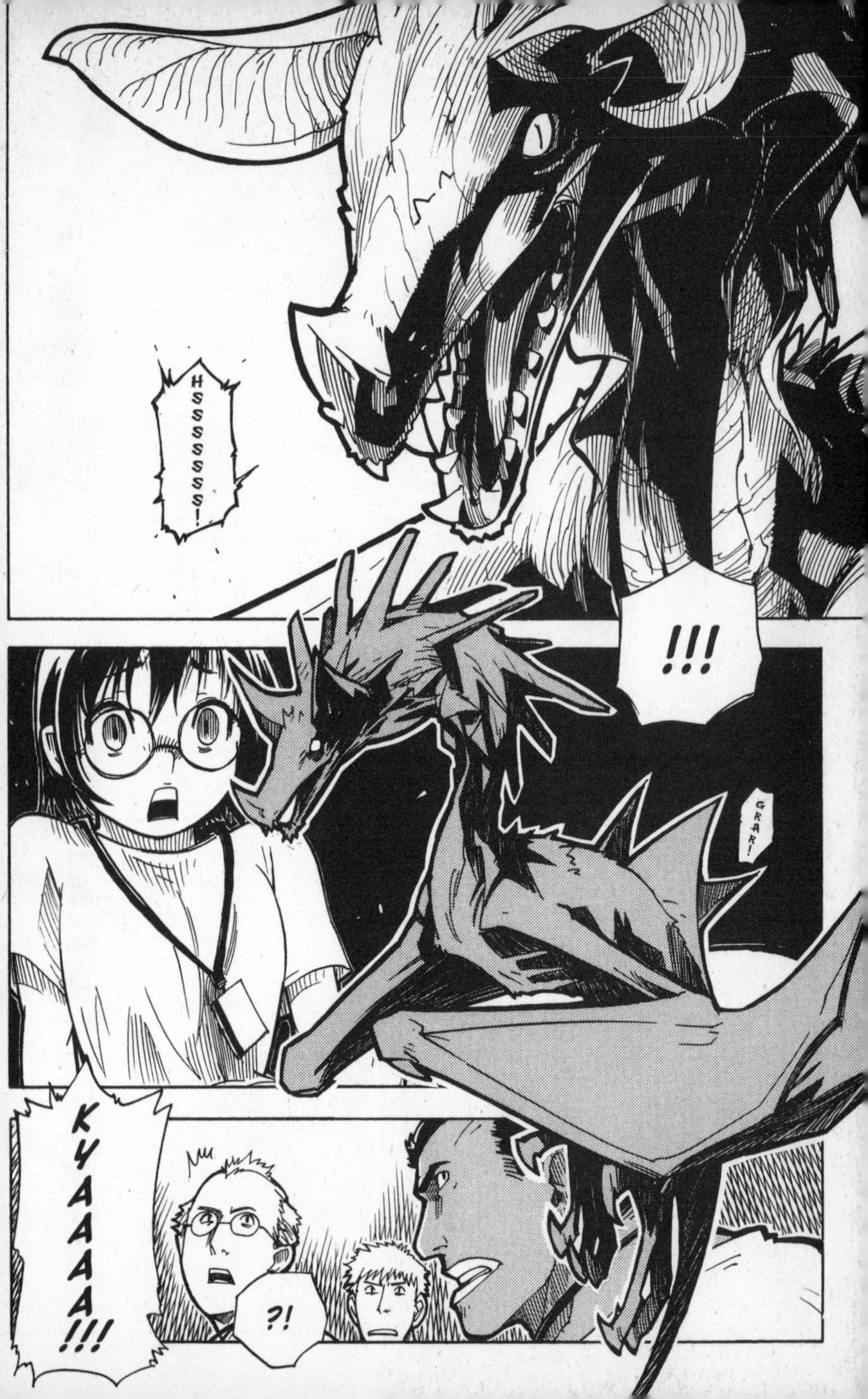
HSSSSSSS!
!!!
GRAR!
?!
KYAAAAA!!!

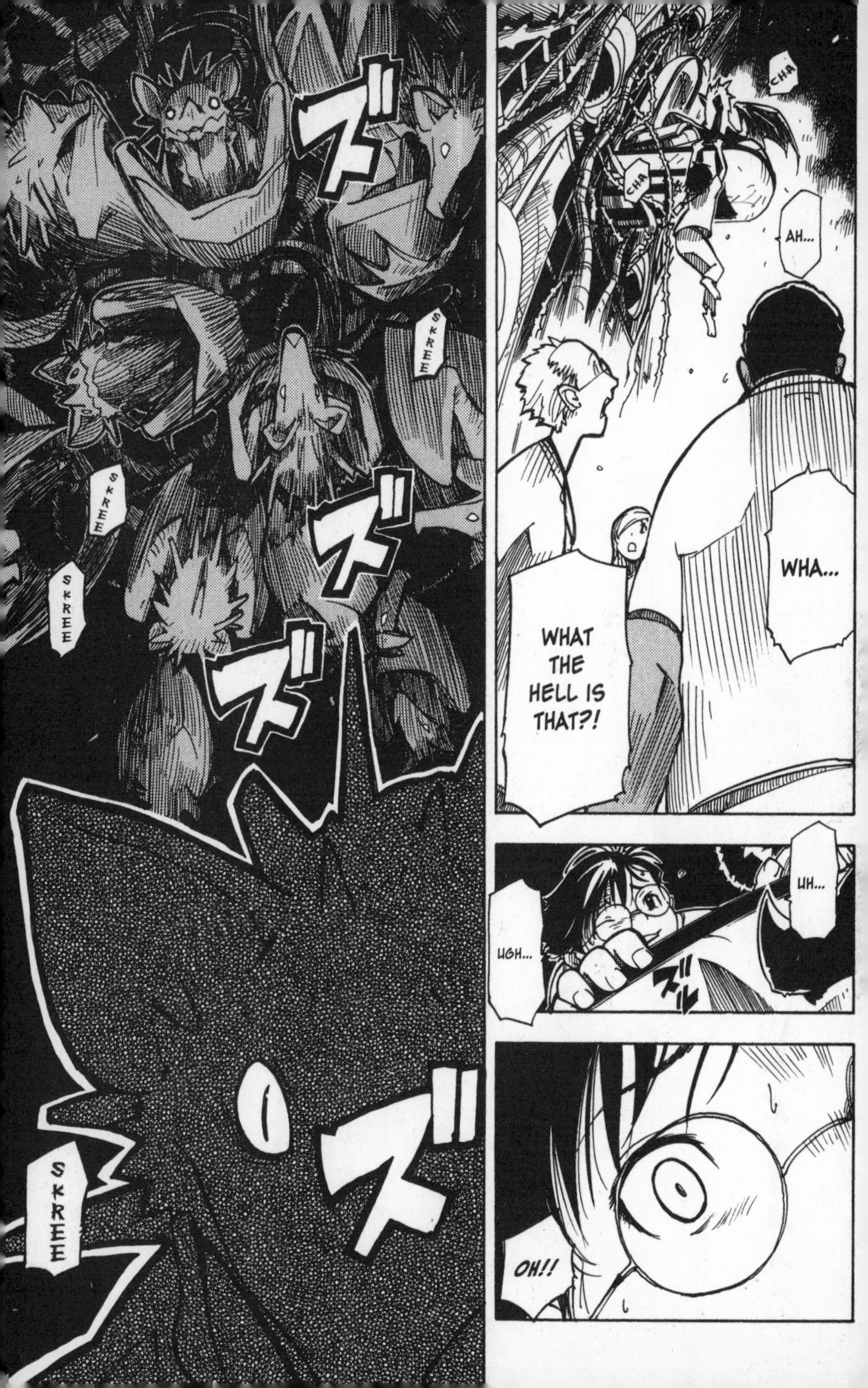
CHA
CHA
AH...
WHA...
WHAT THE HELL IS THAT?!
UH...
ズル
UGH...
OH!!
ズ
SKREE
ズ
SKREE
SKREE
ズ
ズ
SKREE

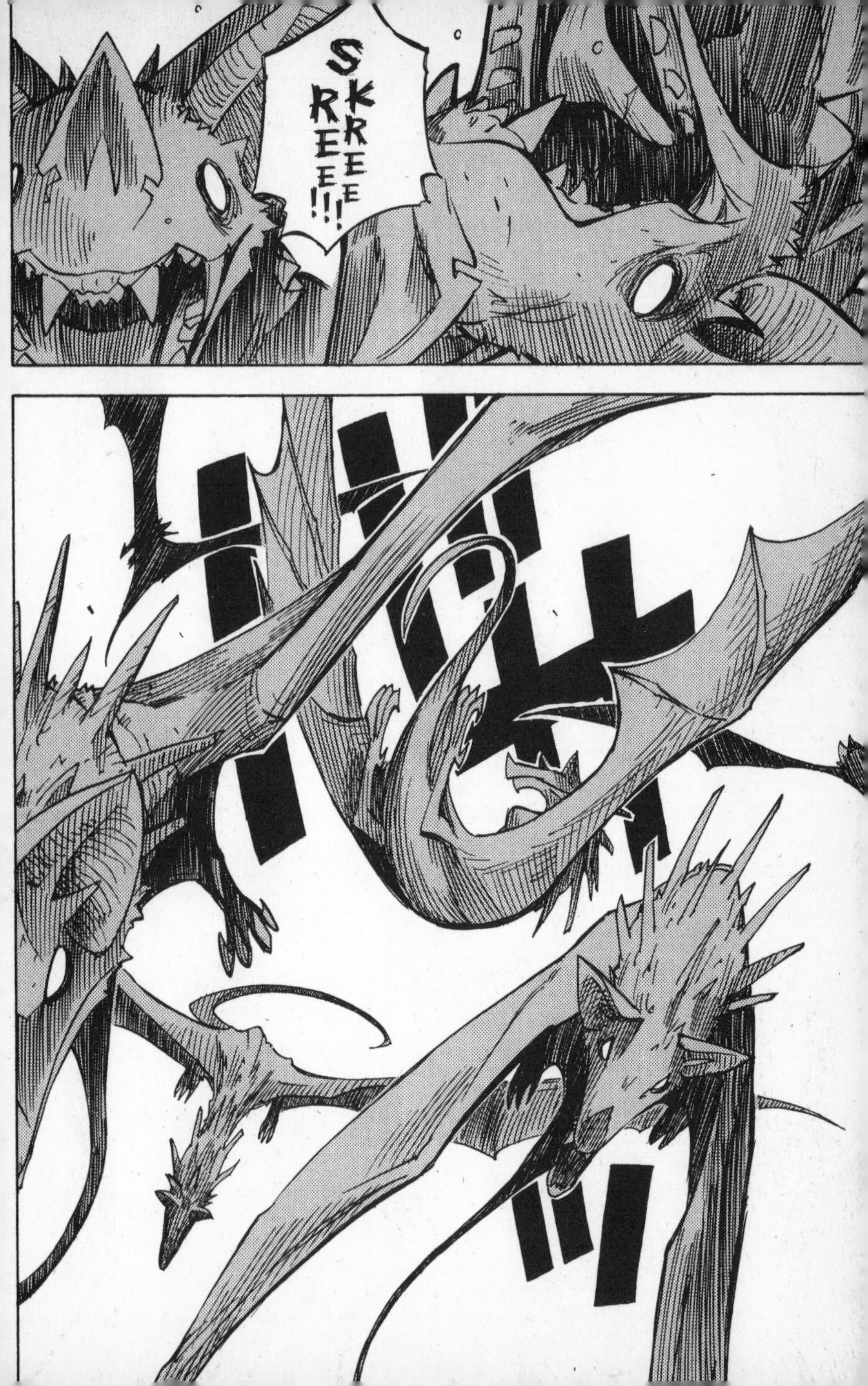
SKREEE
REEE!!!

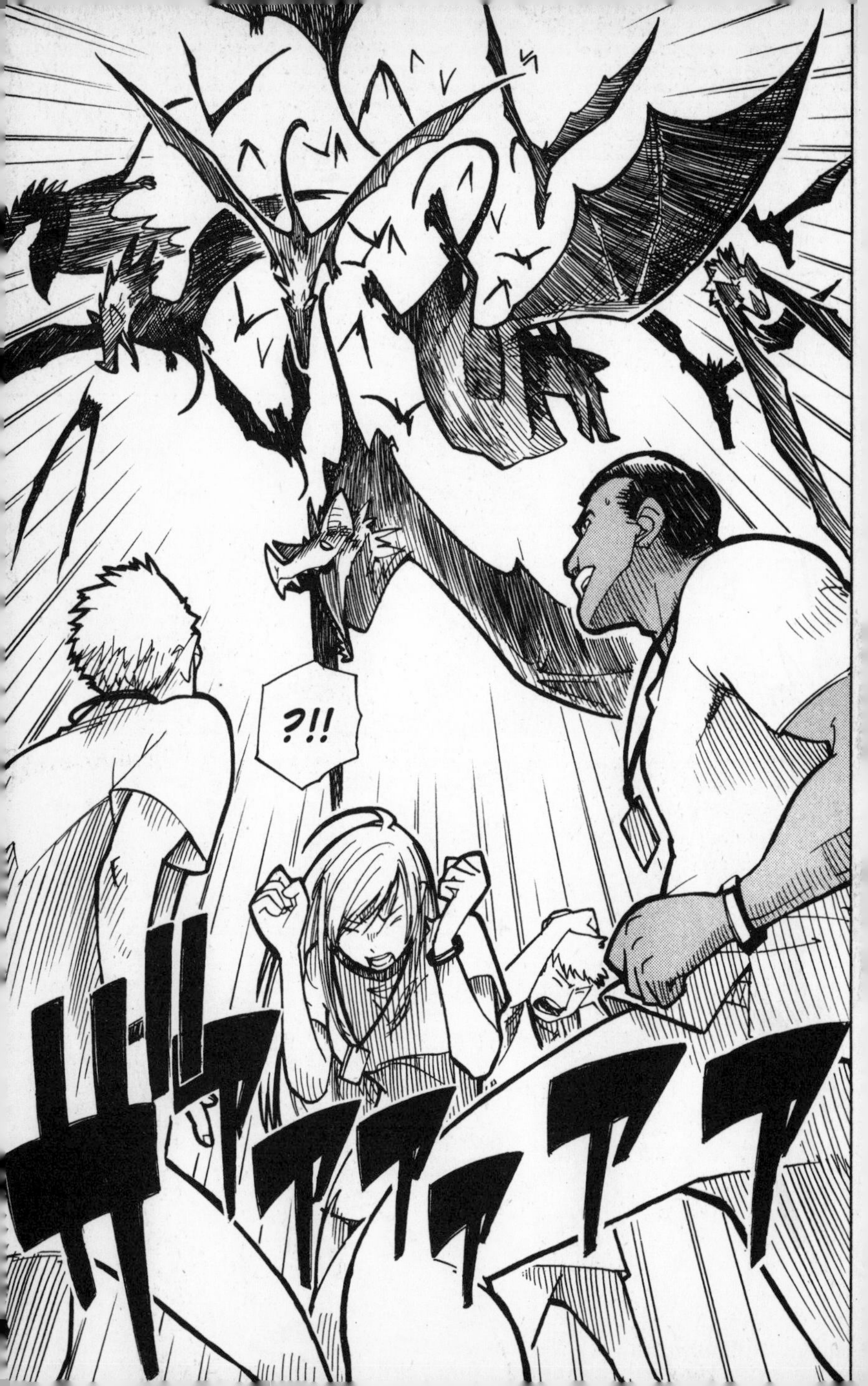
?!!

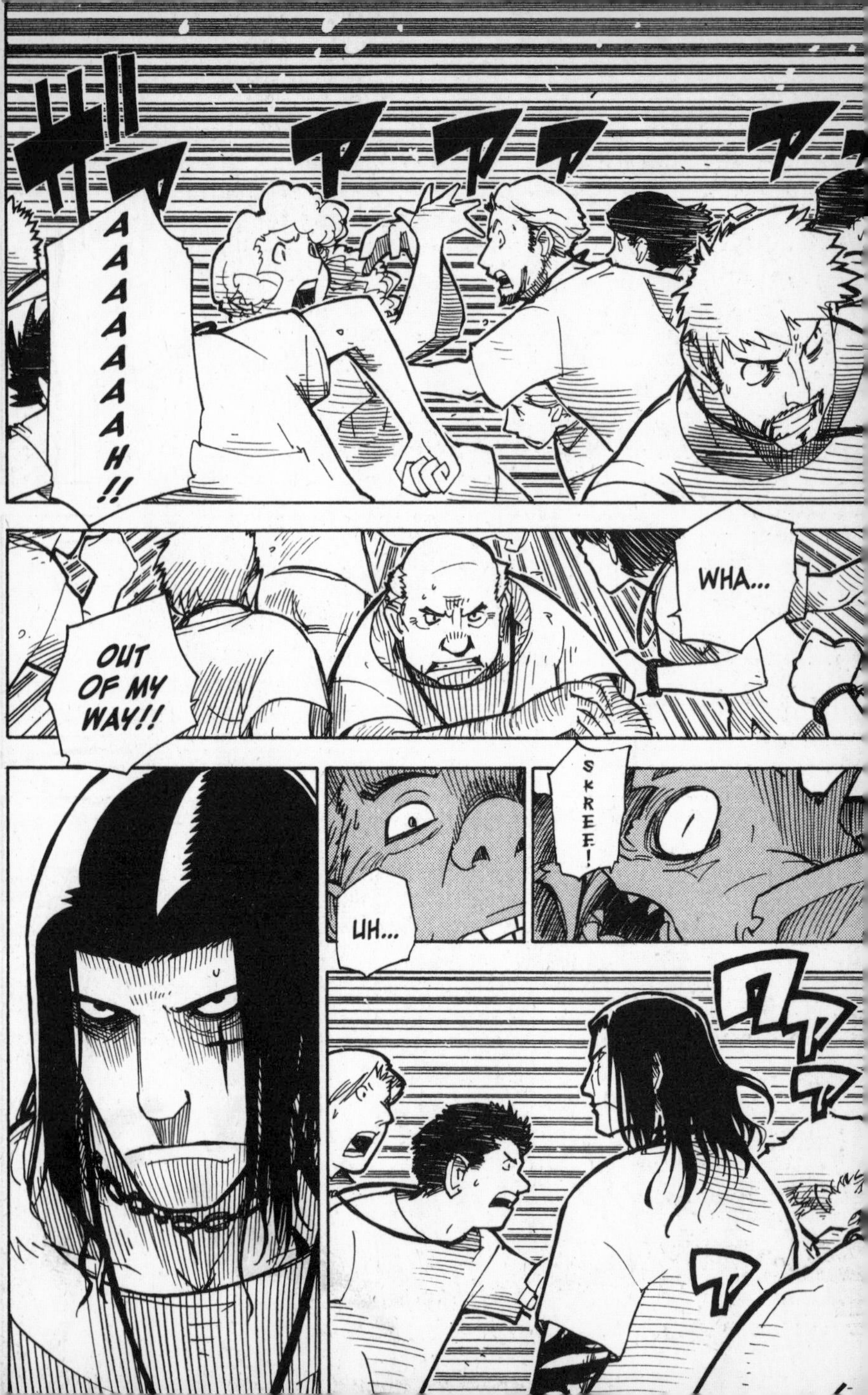

ザアアアア
AAAAAAAAAAH!!
WHA...
OUT OF MY WAY!!
SKREE!
UH...
ワァァァ

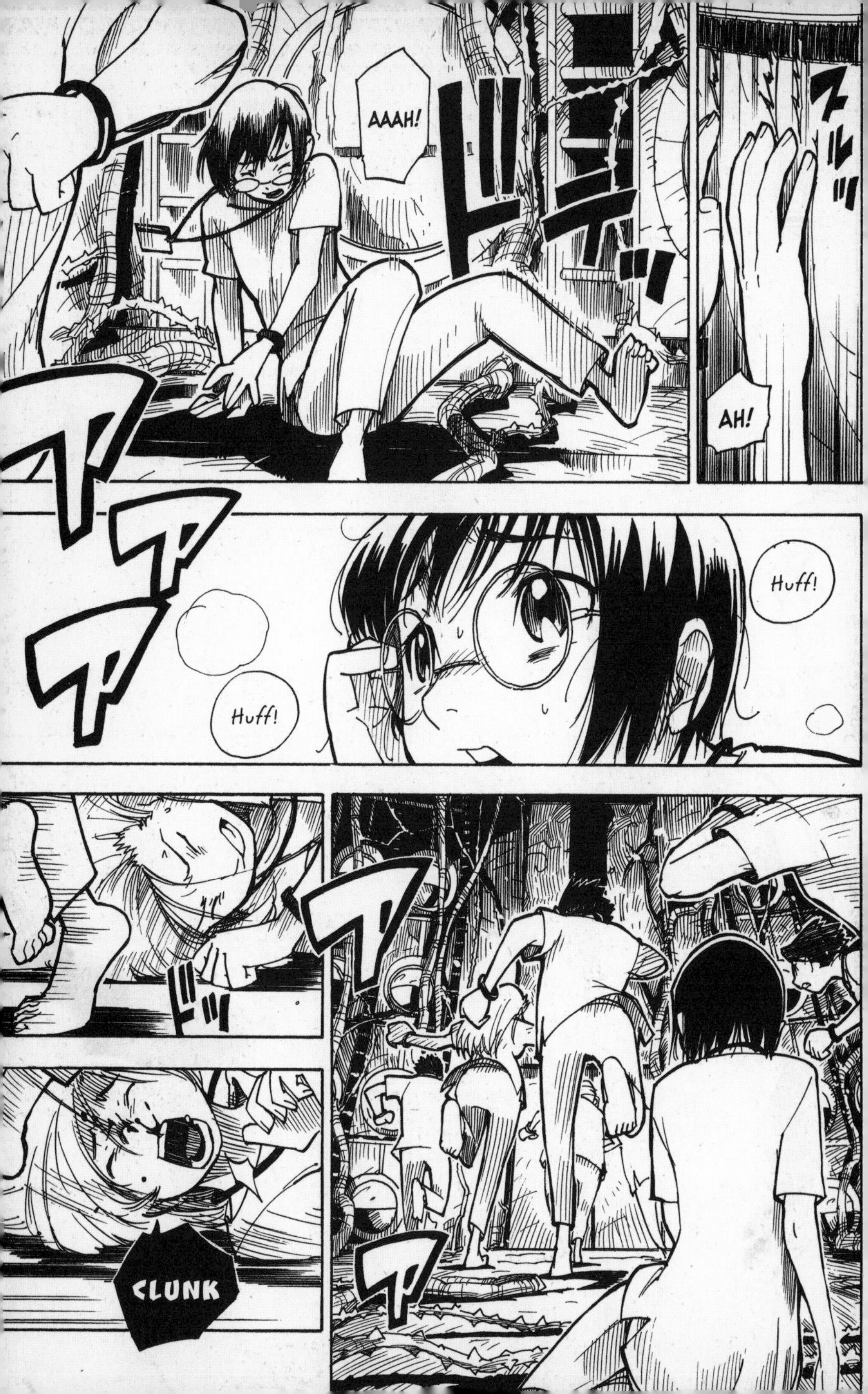
AH!
AAAH!
Huff!
Huff!
CLUNK

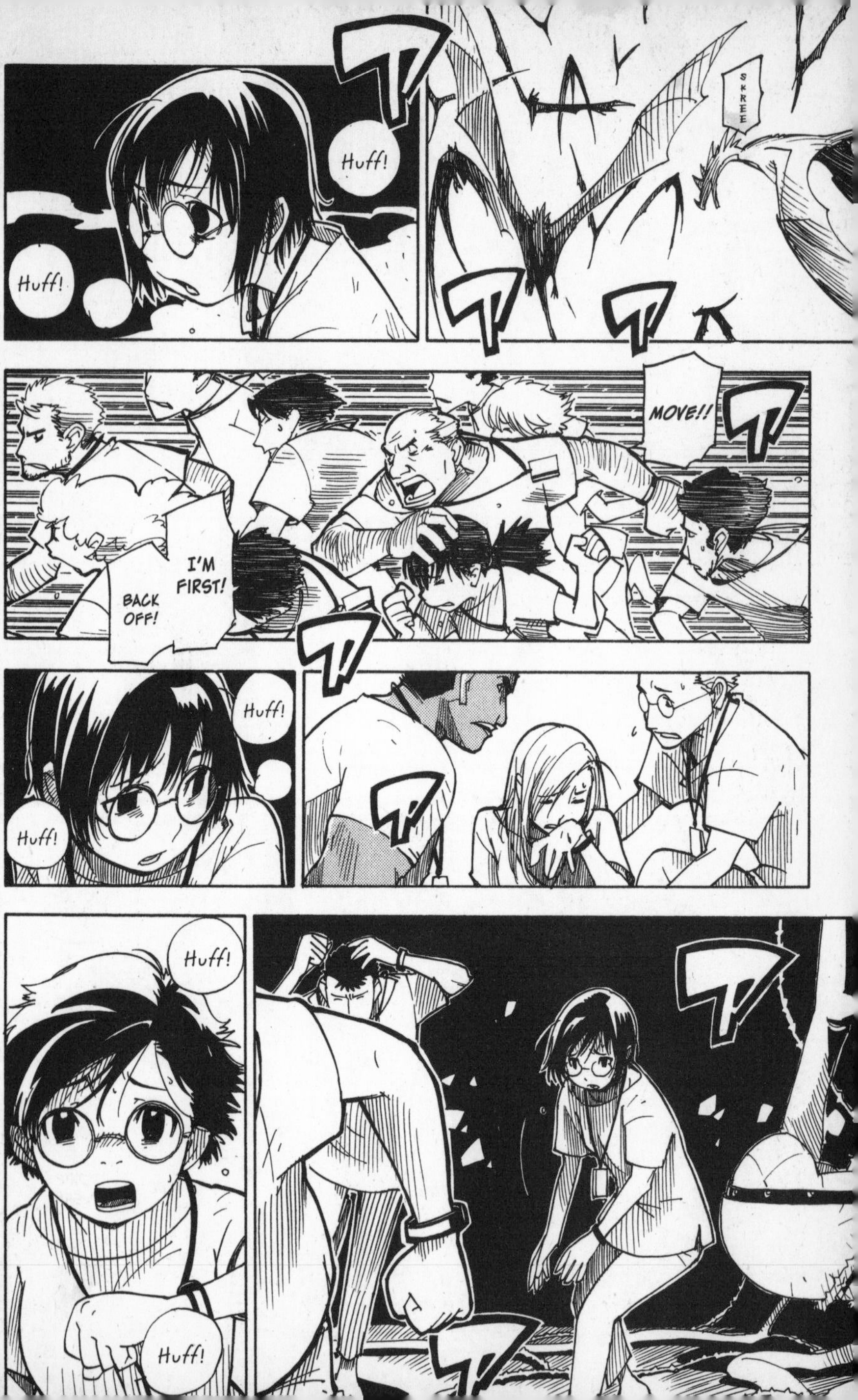
SKREE
Huff!
Huff!
MOVE!!
I'M FIRST!
BACK OFF!
Huff!
Huff!
Huff!
Huff!

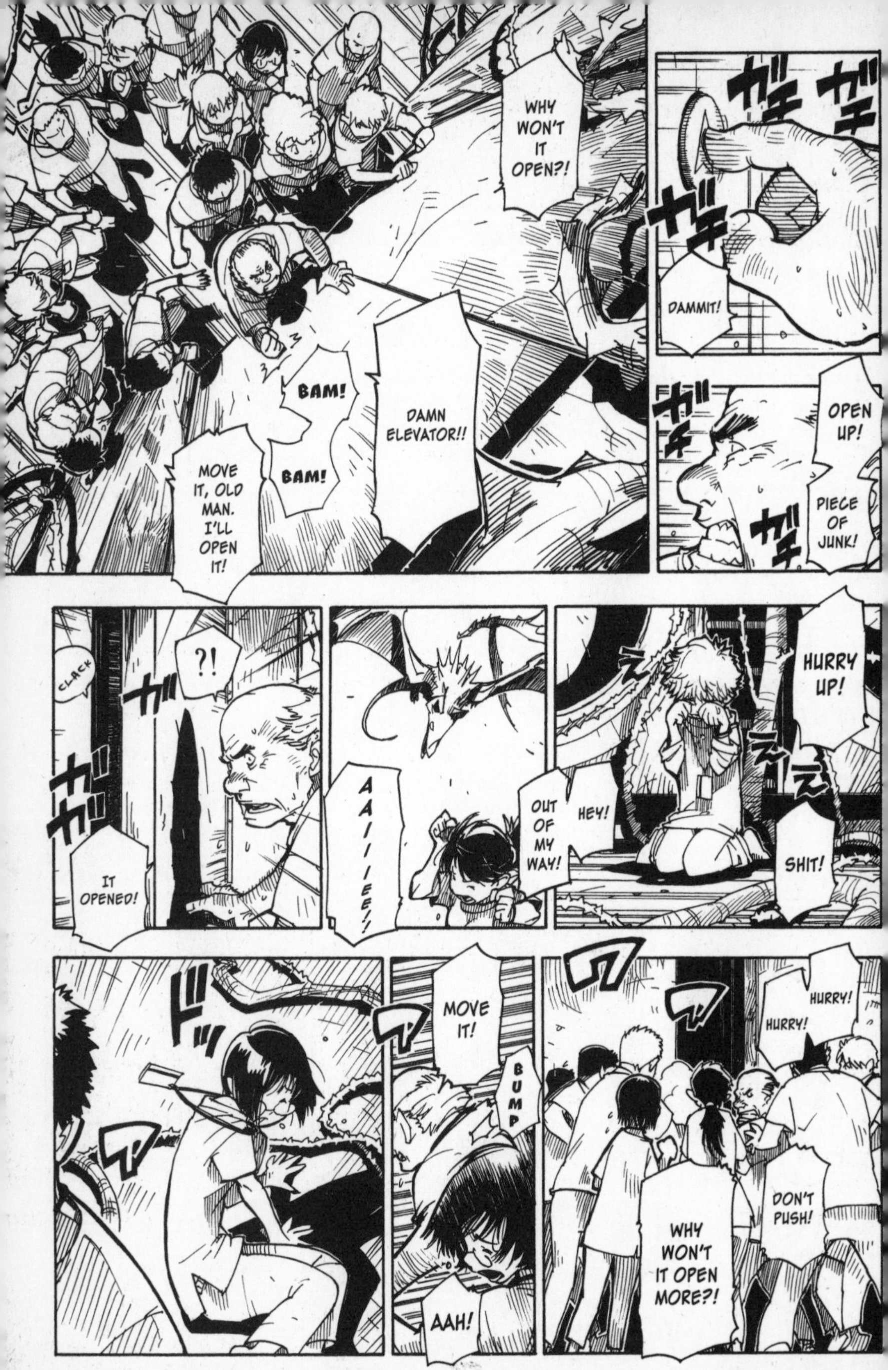
DAMMIT!
OPEN UP!
PIECE OF JUNK!
WHY WON'T IT OPEN?!
DAMN ELEVATOR!!
BAM!
BAM!
MOVE IT, OLD MAN. I'LL OPEN IT!
HURRY UP!
SHIT!
HEY!
OUT OF MY WAY!
AAIIIIEE!!
?!
CLACK
IT OPENED!
HURRY!
HURRY!
DON'T PUSH!
WHY WON'T IT OPEN MORE?!
MOVE IT!
BUMP
AAH!

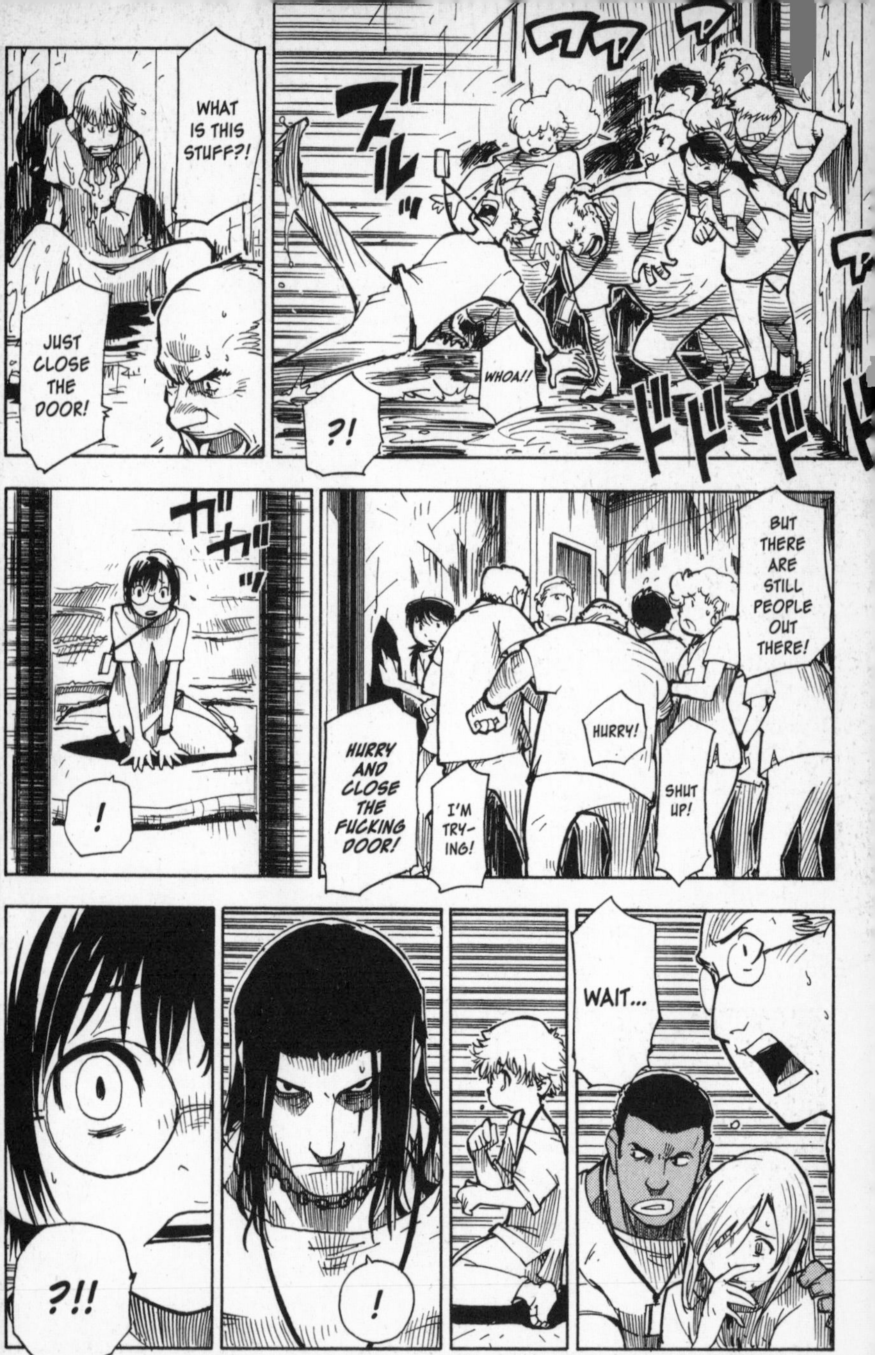
WHOA!!
?!
WHAT IS THIS STUFF?!
JUST CLOSE THE DOOR!
BUT THERE ARE STILL PEOPLE OUT THERE!
HURRY!
SHUT UP!
I'M TRY-ING!
HURRY AND CLOSE THE FUCKING DOOR!
!
WAIT...
!
?!!

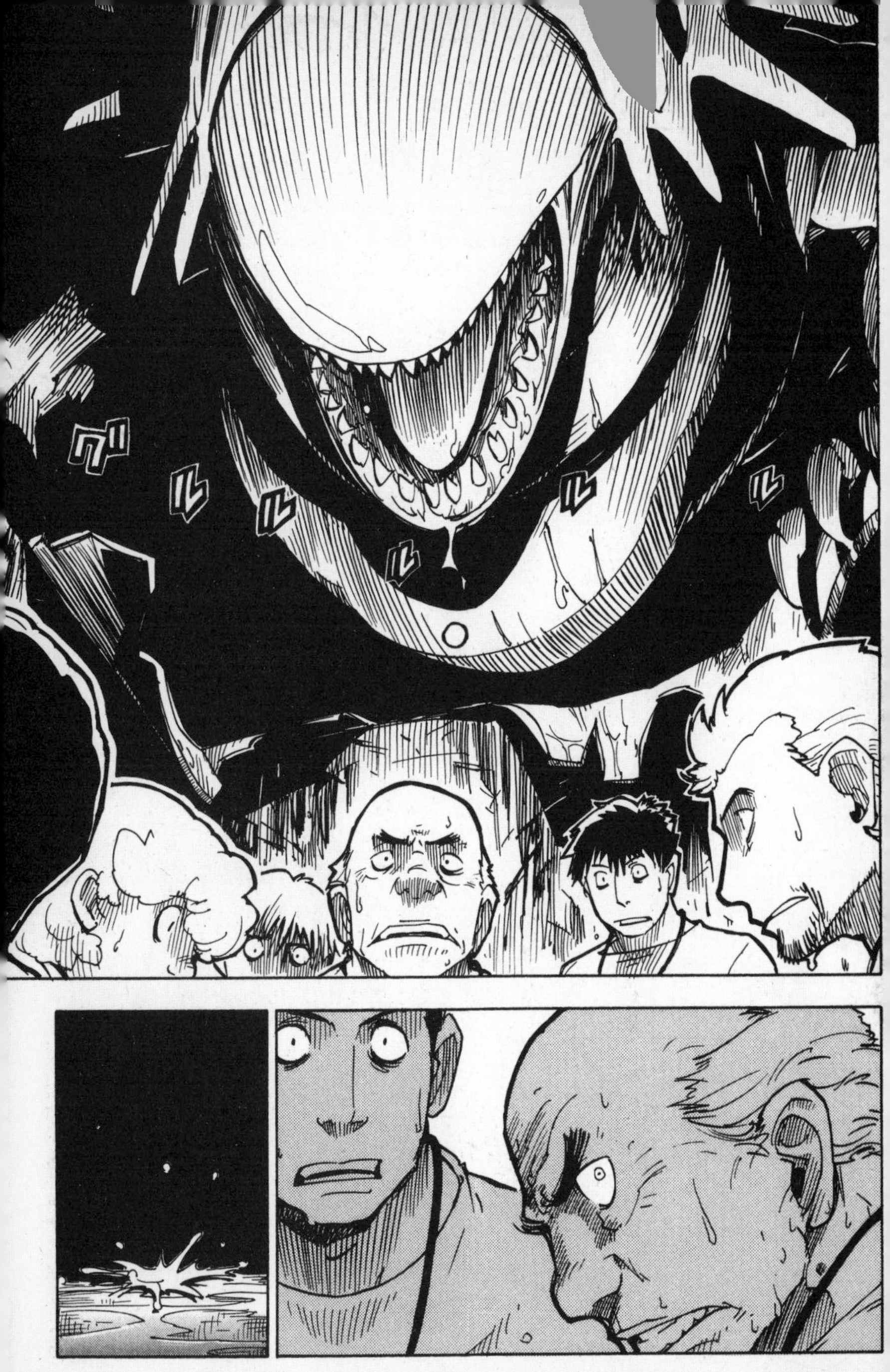
グルルルルル

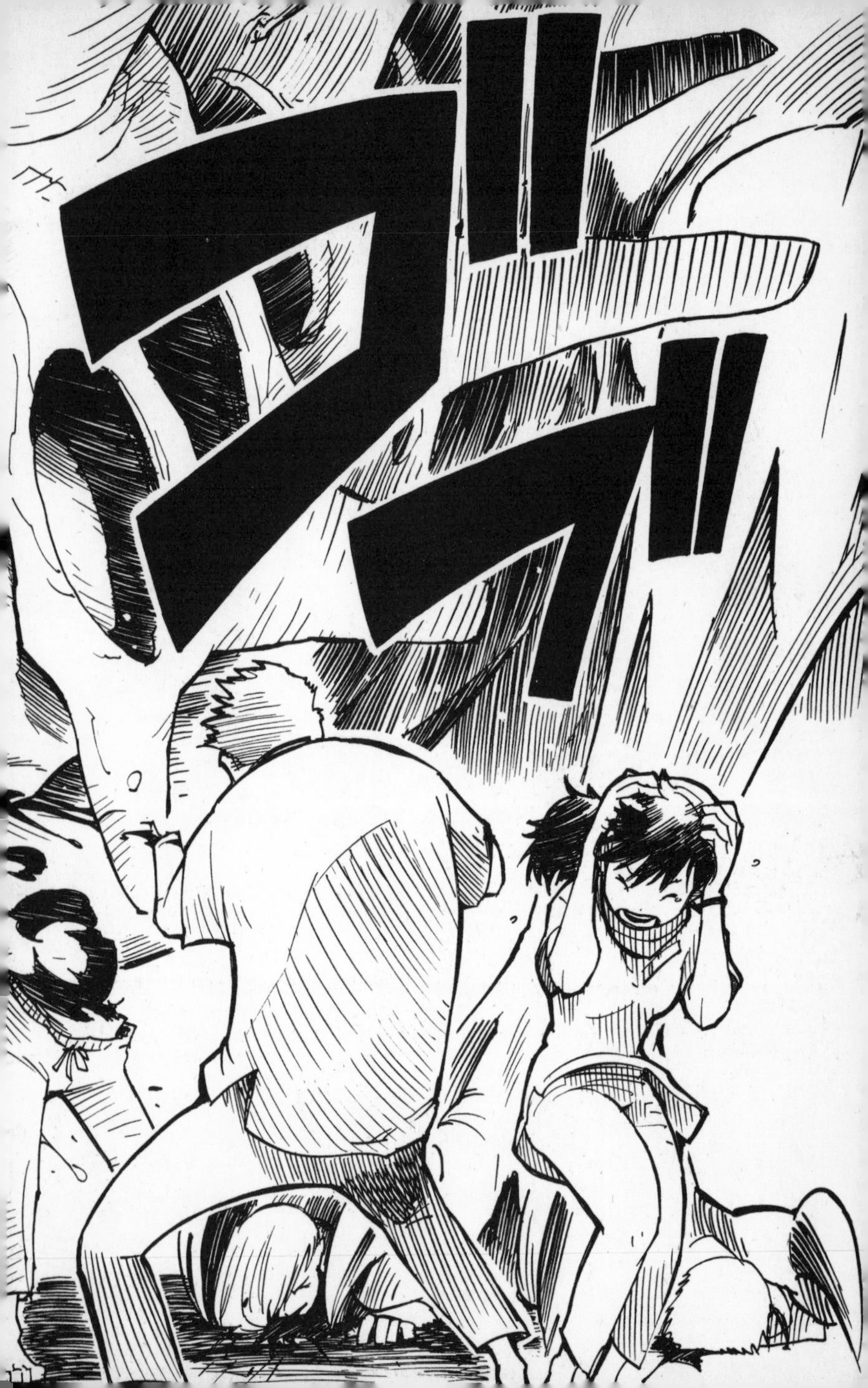
ゴゴ

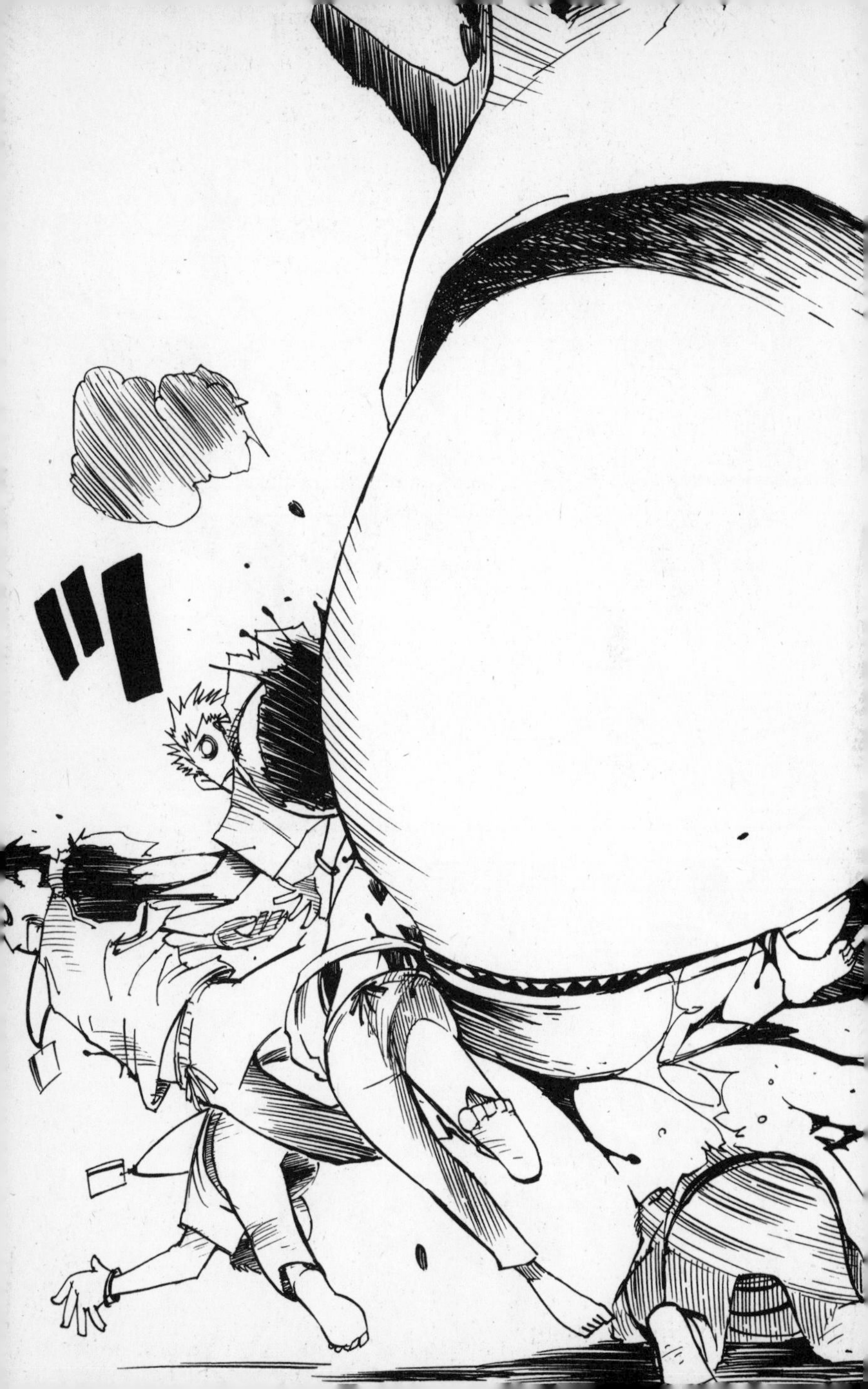

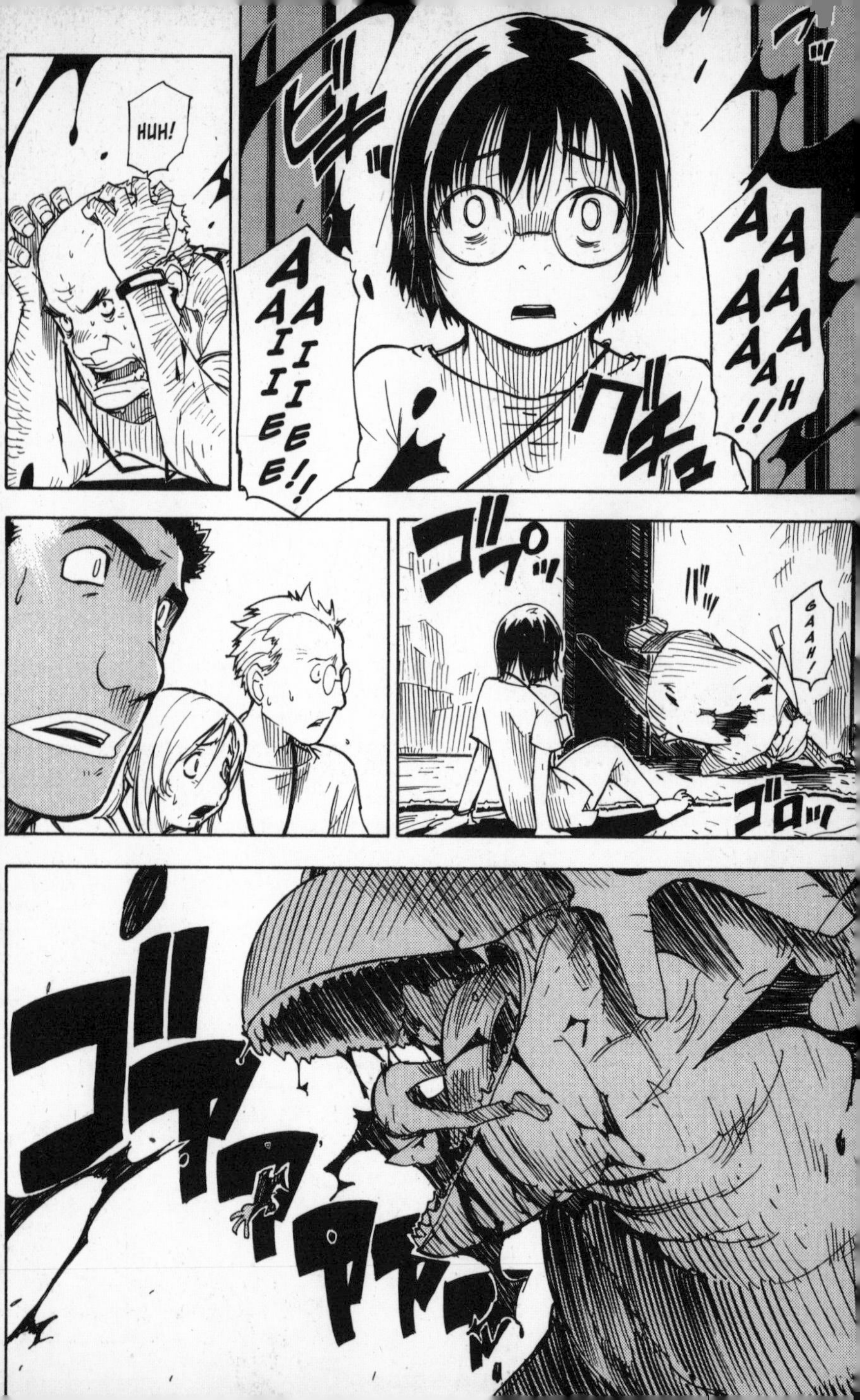
AAAAAAAH!!
AAAIIIIEEE!!
グチュ
HUH!
ゴプッ
GAAAH!
ゴロッ

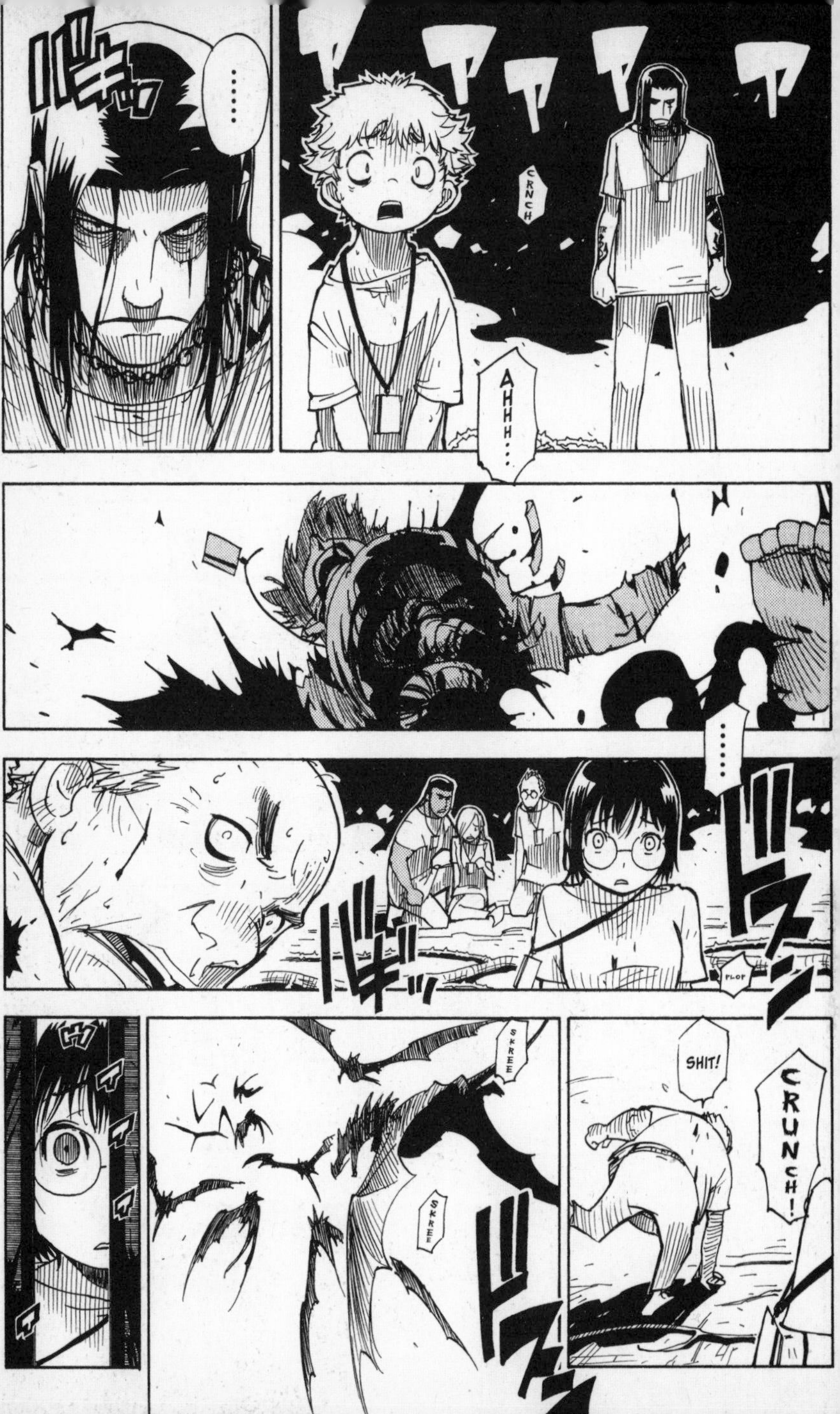
CRNCH
AHHH...
......
......
PLOP
CRUNCH!
SHIT!
SKREE
SKREE

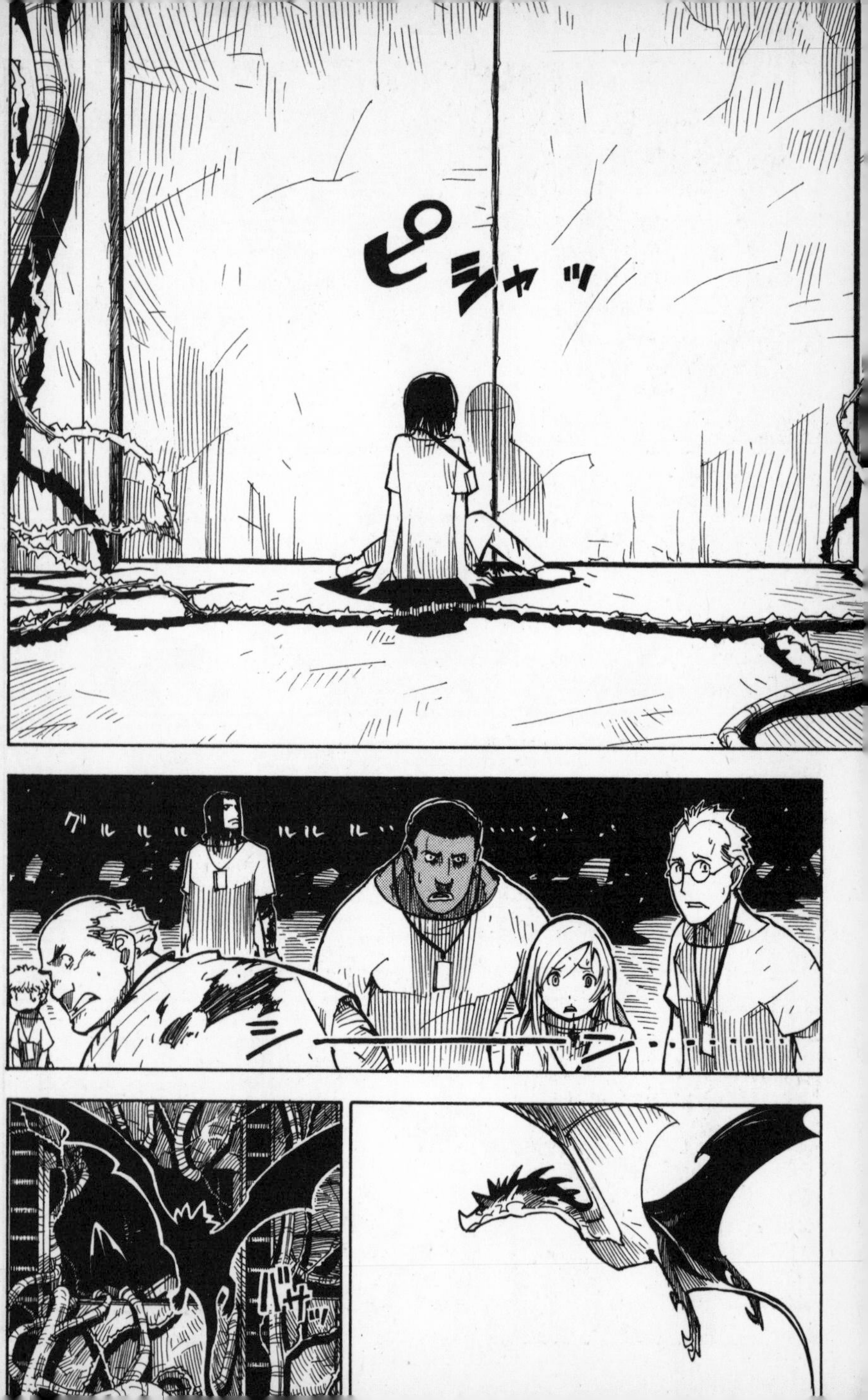
ピシャッ
グルルルルルルル…
バサッ

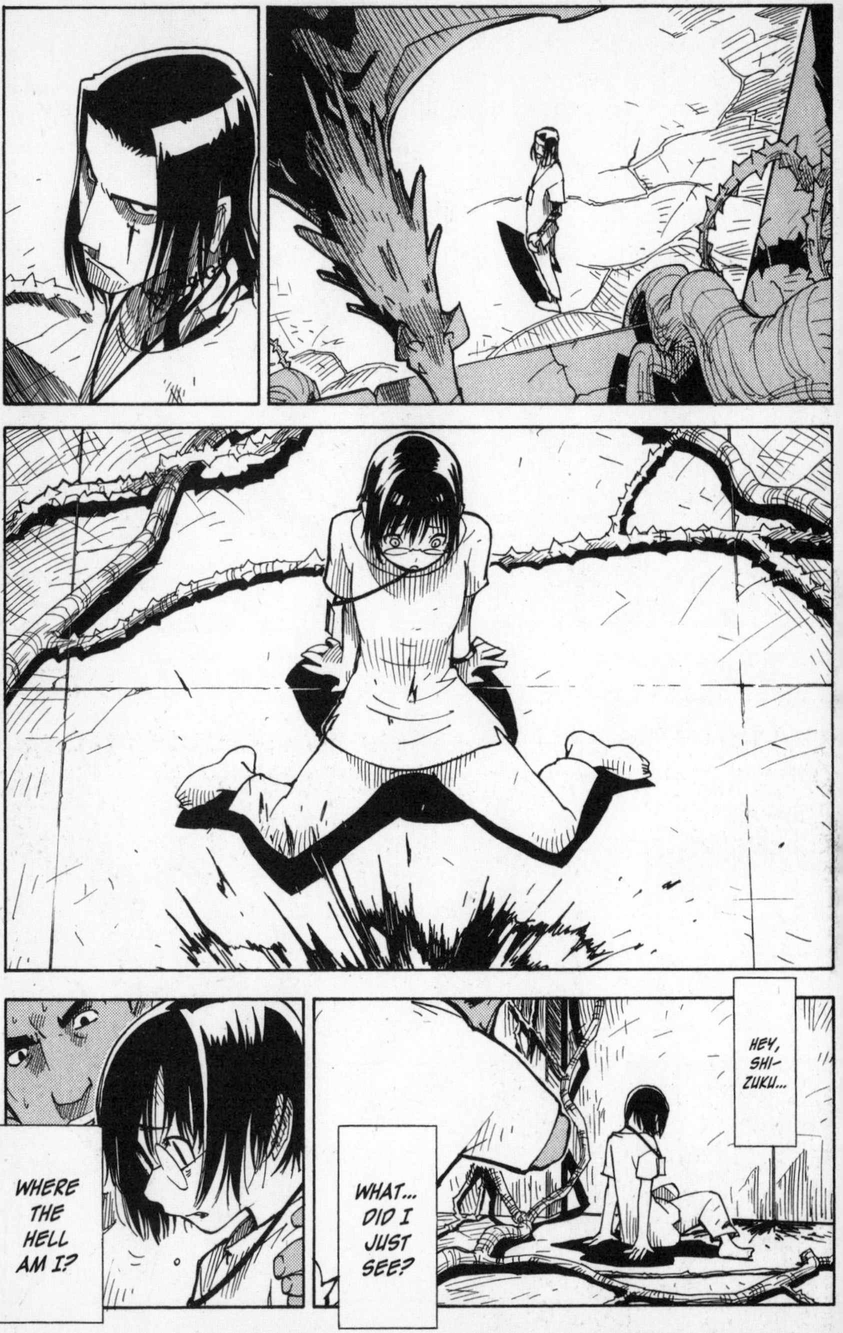
HEY, SHI-ZUKU...
WHAT... DID I JUST SEE?
WHERE THE HELL AM I?

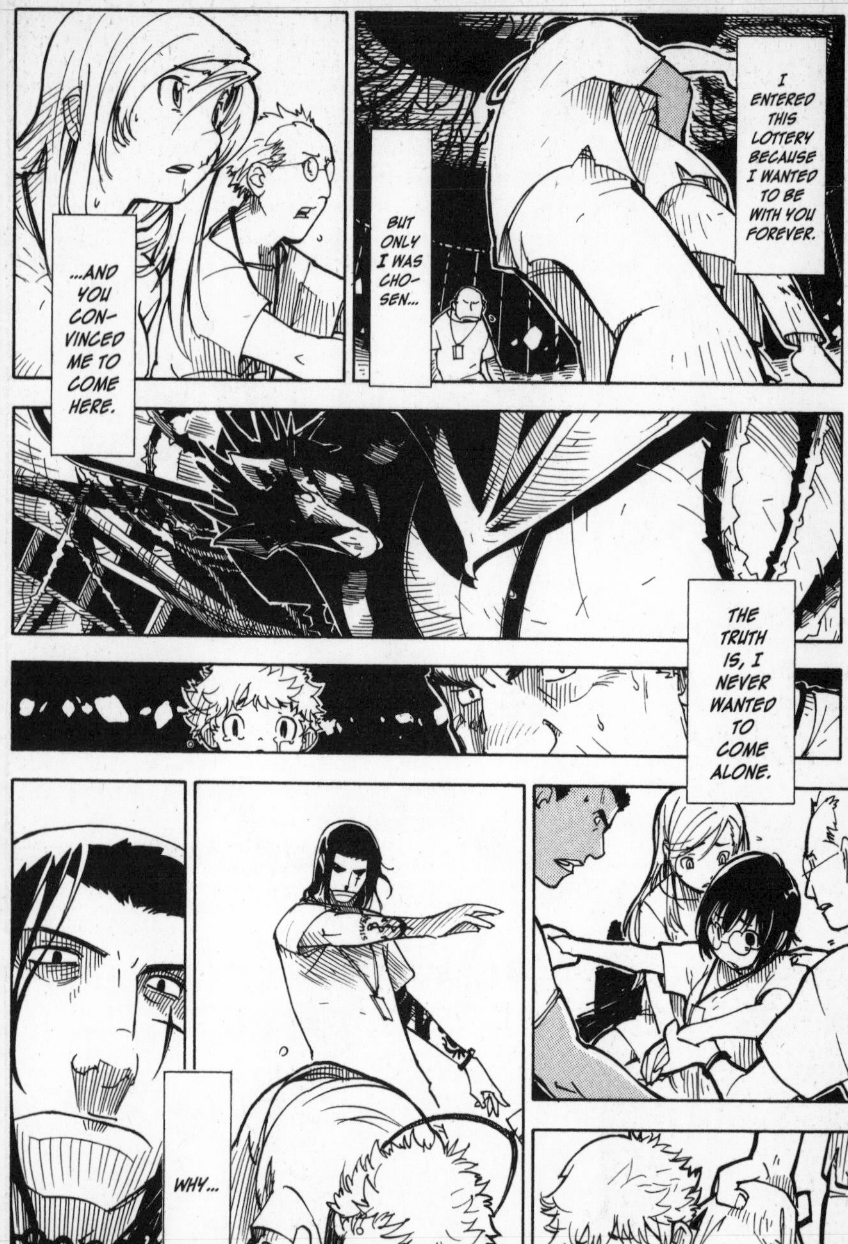
I ENTERED THIS LOTTERY BECAUSE I WANTED TO BE WITH YOU FOREVER.
BUT ONLY I WAS CHO-SEN...
...AND YOU CON-VINCED ME TO COME HERE.
THE TRUTH IS, I NEVER WANTED TO COME ALONE.
WHY...

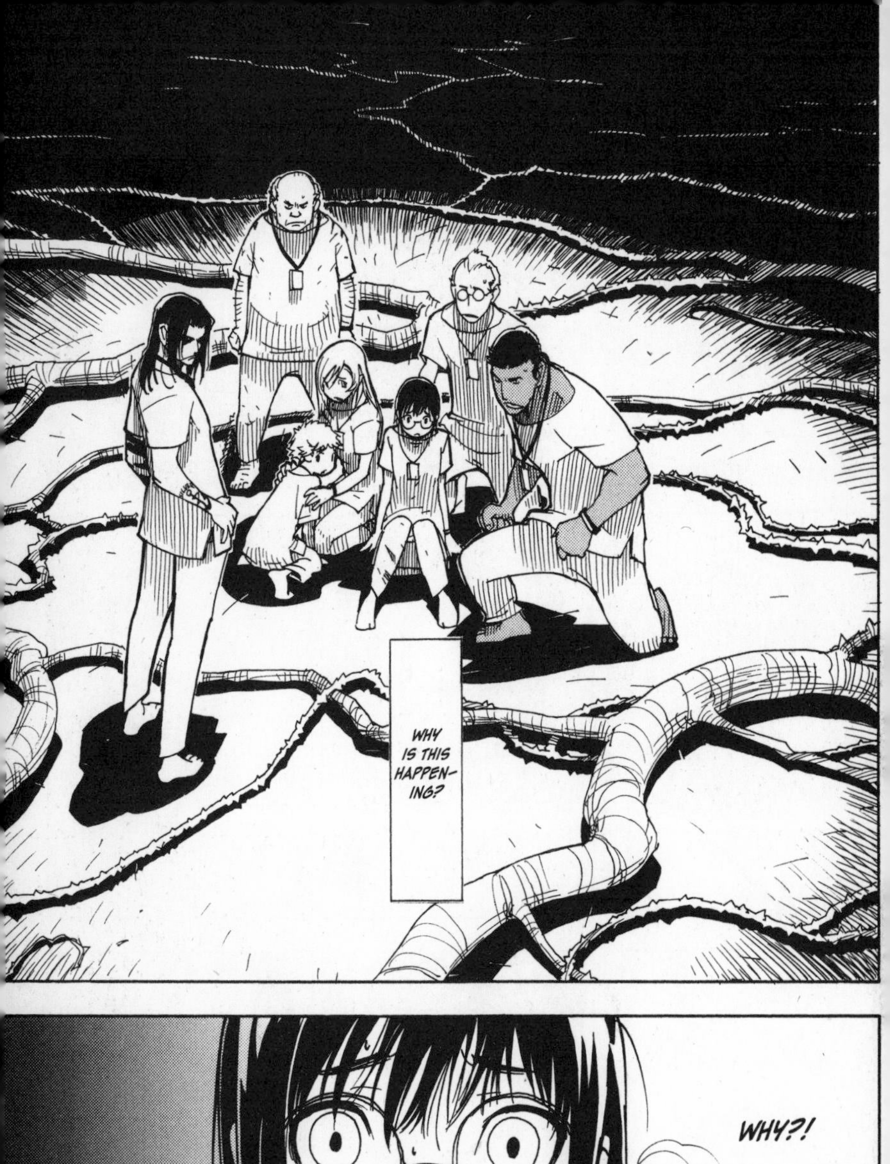
WHY IS THIS HAPPEN-ING?
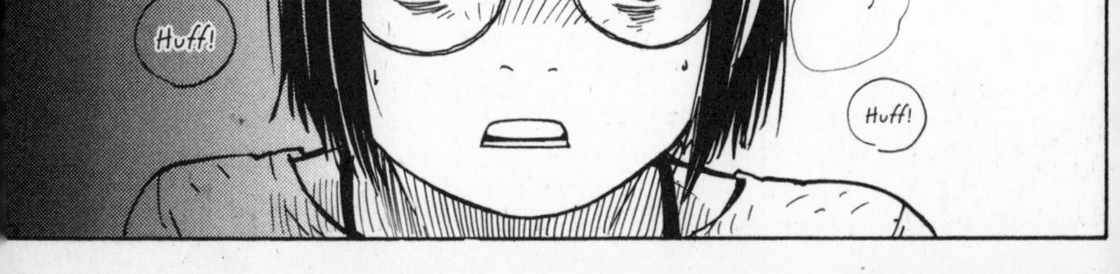
WHY?!
Huff!
Huff!

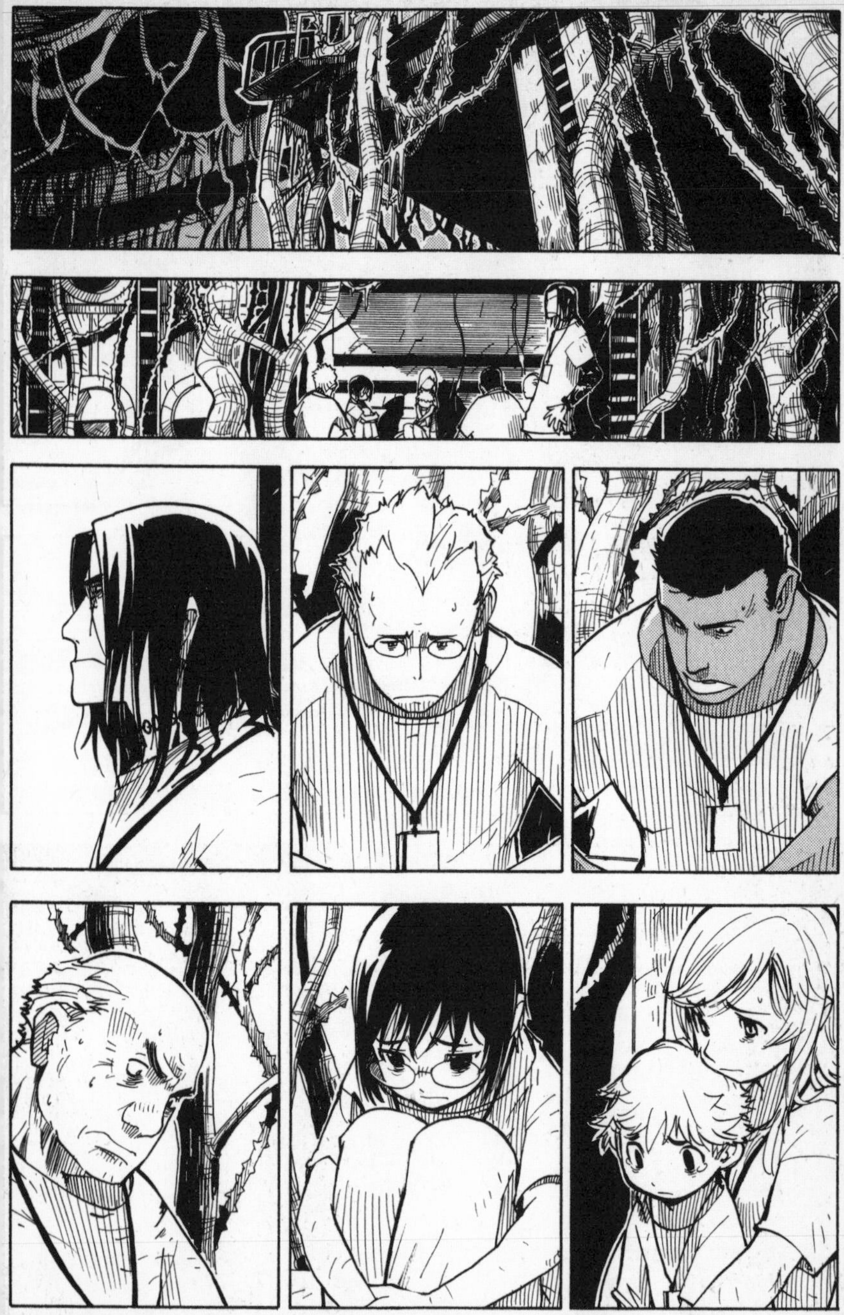

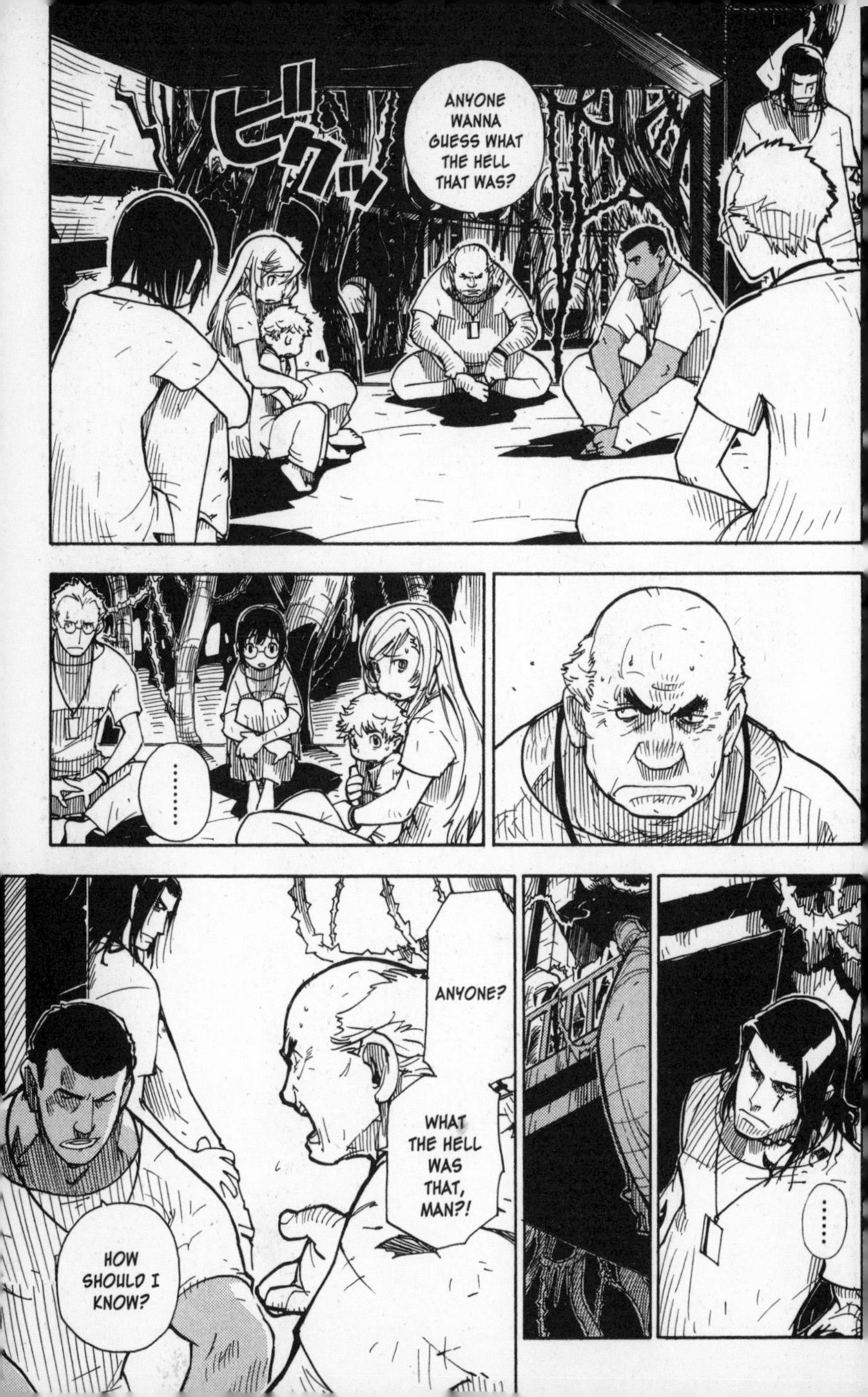
ビクッ
ANYONE WANNA GUESS WHAT THE HELL THAT WAS?
......
......
ANYONE?
WHAT THE HELL WAS THAT, MAN?!
HOW SHOULD I KNOW?

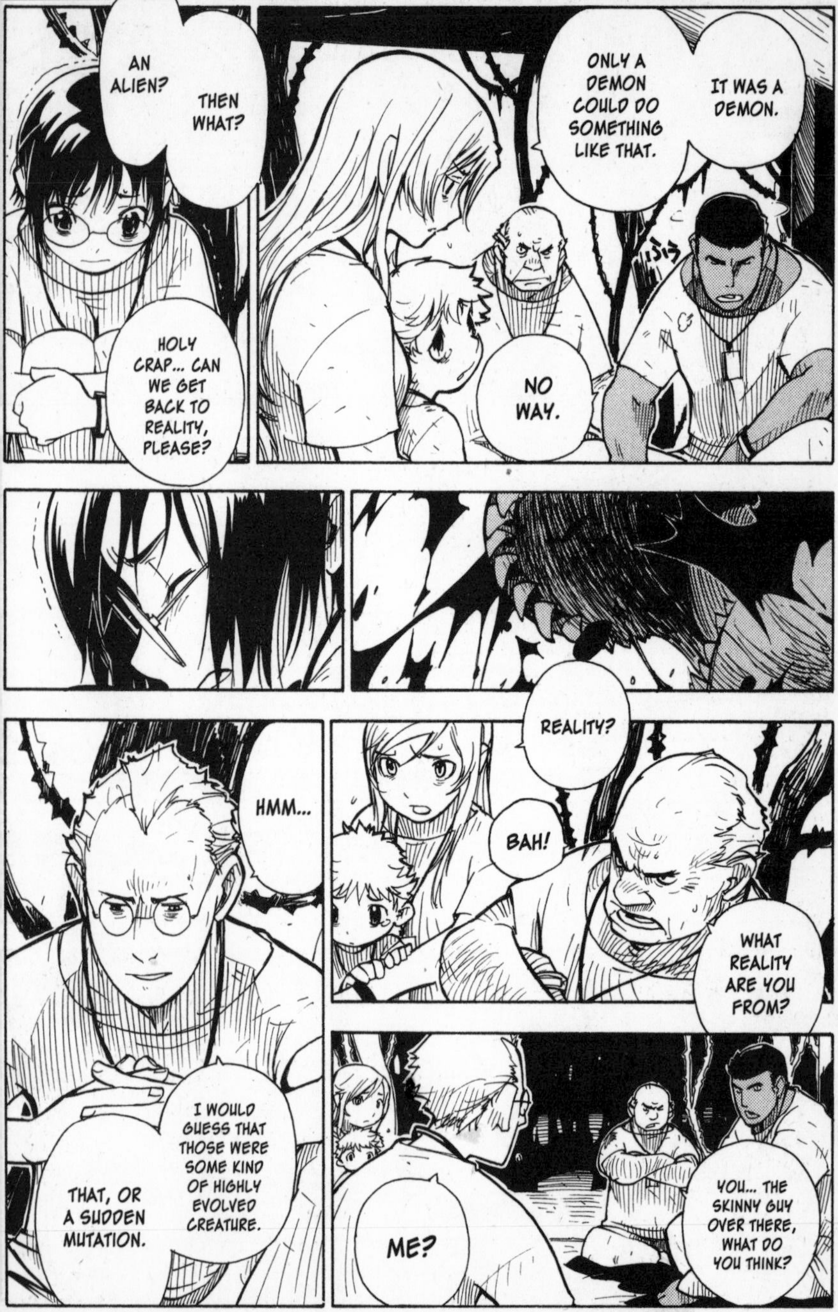
IT WAS A DEMON.
ONLY A DEMON COULD DO SOMETHING LIKE THAT.
NO WAY.
AN ALIEN?
THEN WHAT?
HOLY CRAP... CAN WE GET BACK TO REALITY, PLEASE?
REALITY?
BAH!
WHAT REALITY ARE YOU FROM?
YOU... THE SKINNY GUY OVER THERE, WHAT DO YOU THINK?
ME?
HMM...
I WOULD GUESS THAT THOSE WERE SOME KIND OF HIGHLY EVOLVED CREATURE.
THAT, OR A SUDDEN MUTATION.

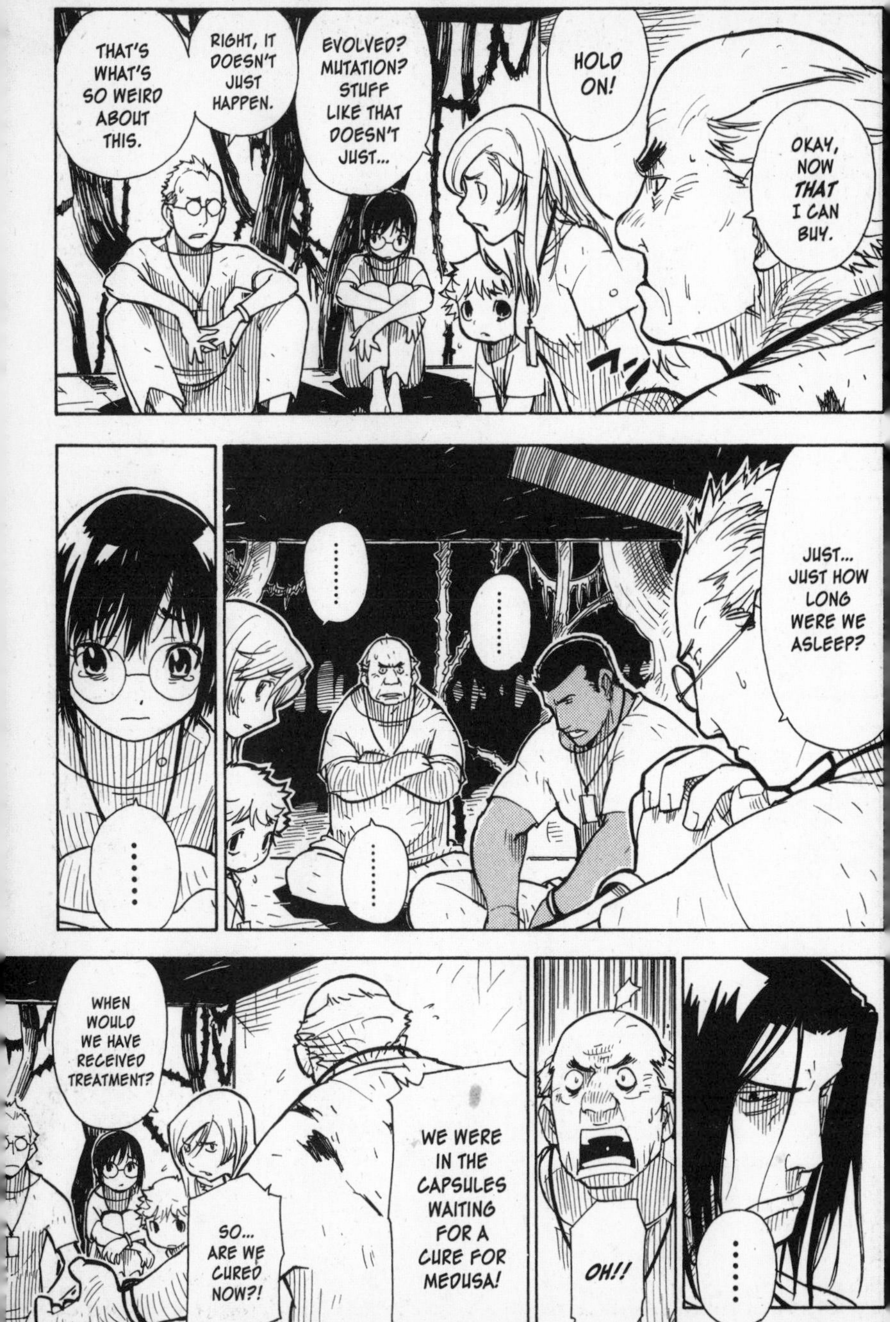
OKAY, NOW THAT I CAN BUY.
HOLD ON!
EVOLVED? MUTATION? STUFF LIKE THAT DOESN'T JUST...
RIGHT, IT DOESN'T JUST HAPPEN.
THAT'S WHAT'S SO WEIRD ABOUT THIS.
フン
JUST... JUST HOW LONG WERE WE ASLEEP?
......
......
......
......
......
OH!!
WE WERE IN THE CAPSULES WAITING FOR A CURE FOR MEDUSA!
WHEN WOULD WE HAVE RECEIVED TREATMENT?
SO... ARE WE CURED NOW?!

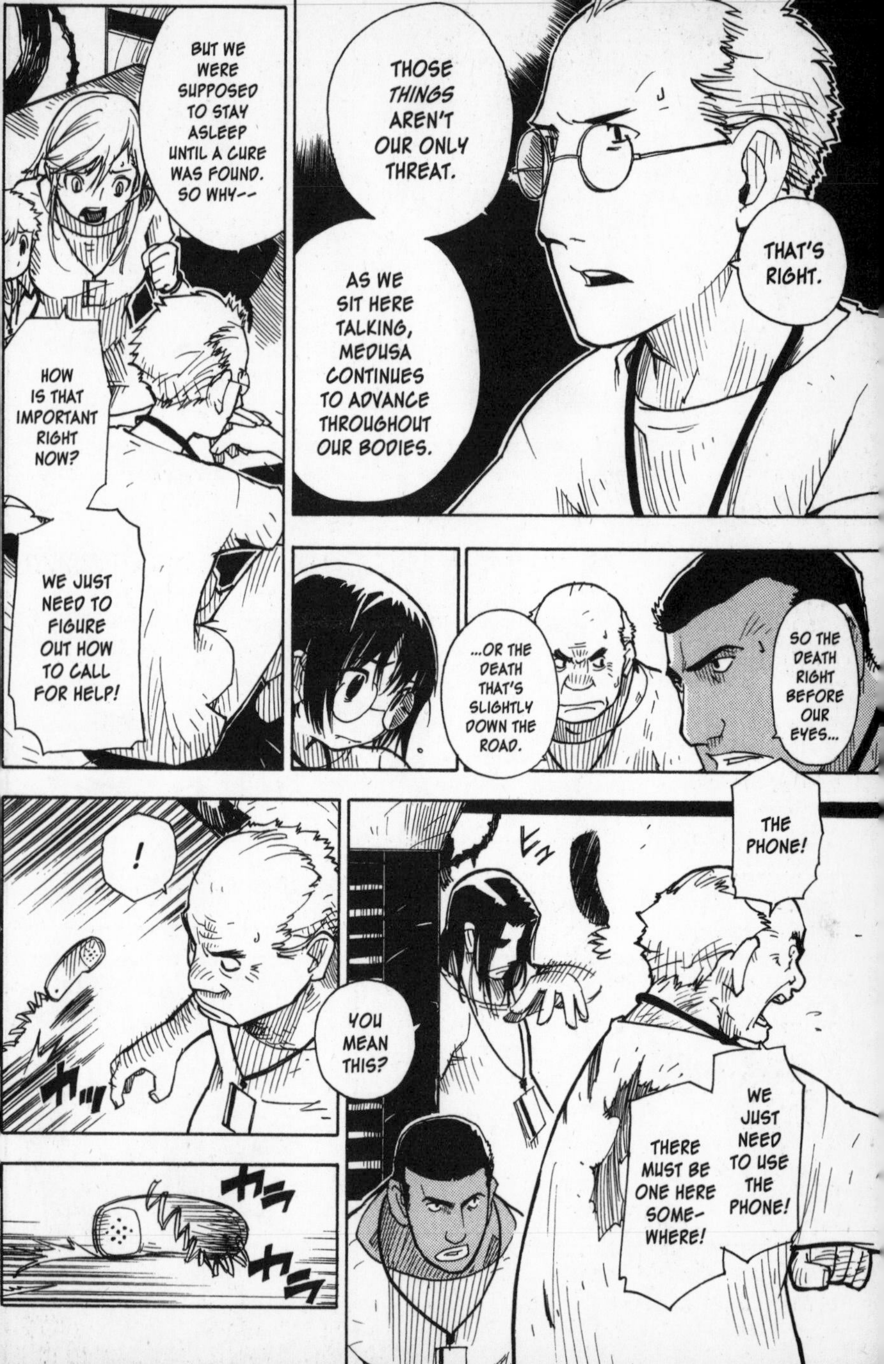
THAT'S RIGHT.
THOSE THINGS AREN'T OUR ONLY THREAT.
AS WE SIT HERE TALKING, MEDUSA CONTINUES TO ADVANCE THROUGHOUT OUR BODIES.
SO THE DEATH RIGHT BEFORE OUR EYES...
...OR THE DEATH THAT'S SLIGHTLY DOWN THE ROAD.
BUT WE WERE SUPPOSED TO STAY ASLEEP UNTIL A CURE WAS FOUND. SO WHY--
HOW IS THAT IMPORTANT RIGHT NOW?
WE JUST NEED TO FIGURE OUT HOW TO CALL FOR HELP!
THE PHONE!
WE JUST NEED TO USE THE PHONE!
THERE MUST BE ONE HERE SOMEWHERE!
YOU MEAN THIS?
!
ガッ
カラ
カラ

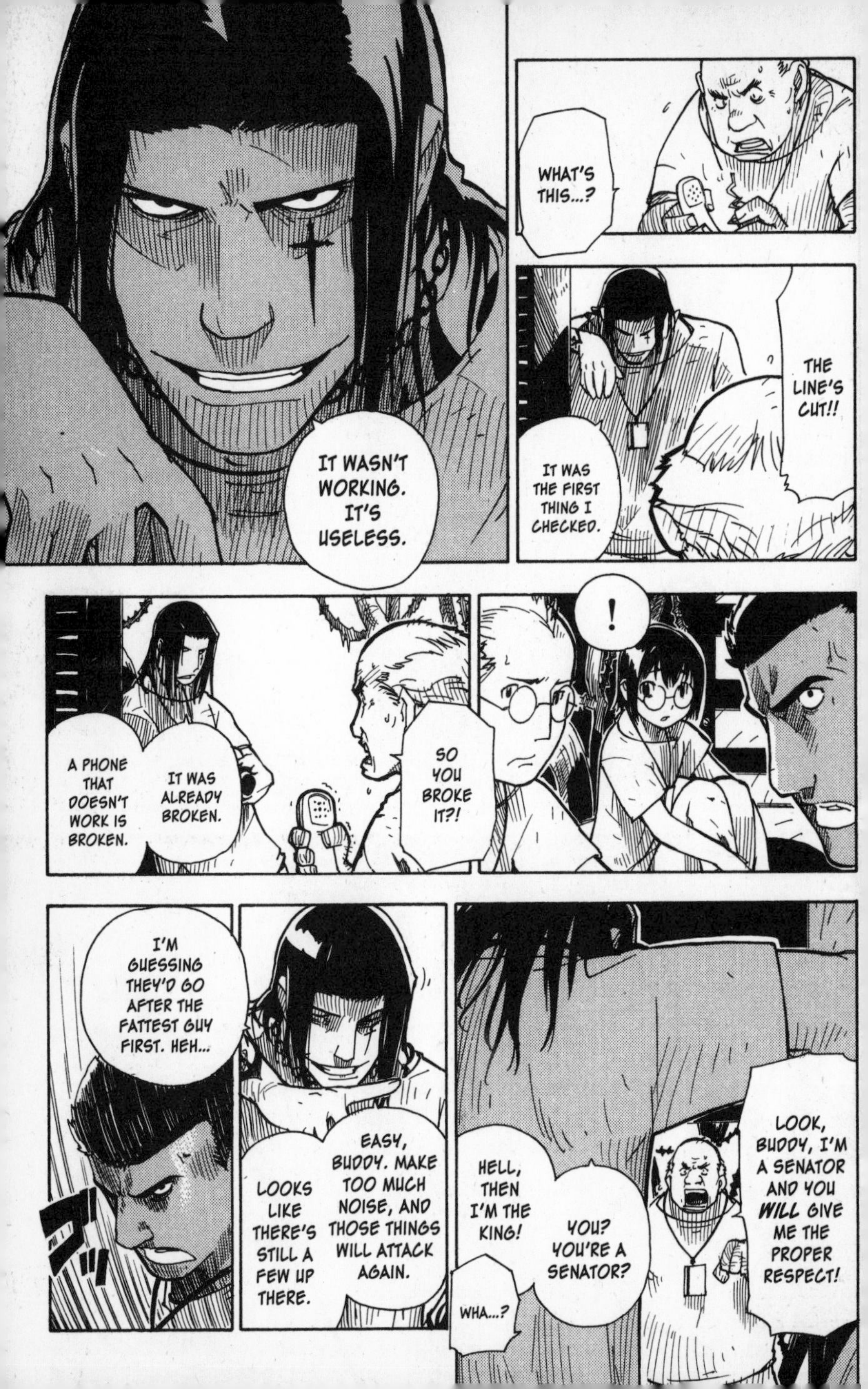
WHAT'S THIS...?
THE LINE'S CUT!!
IT WAS THE FIRST THING I CHECKED.
IT WASN'T WORKING. IT'S USELESS.
!
SO YOU BROKE IT?!
IT WAS ALREADY BROKEN.
A PHONE THAT DOESN'T WORK IS BROKEN.
LOOK, BUDDY, I'M A SENATOR AND YOU WILL GIVE ME THE PROPER RESPECT!
YOU? YOU'RE A SENATOR?
HELL, THEN I'M THE KING!
WHA...?
EASY, BUDDY. MAKE TOO MUCH NOISE, AND THOSE THINGS WILL ATTACK AGAIN.
LOOKS LIKE THERE'S STILL A FEW UP THERE.
I'M GUESSING THEY'D GO AFTER THE FATTEST GUY FIRST. HEH...

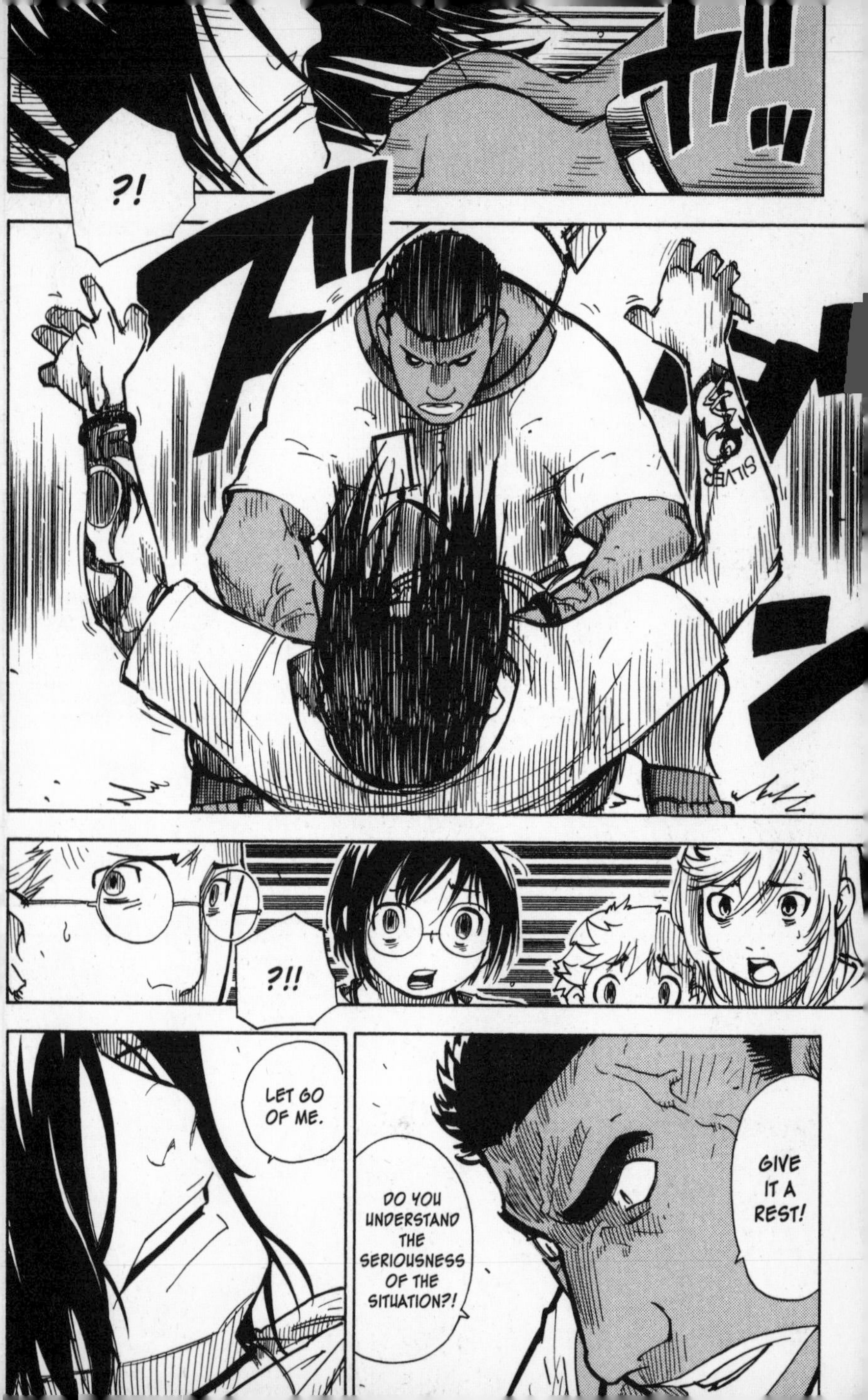
?!
SILVER
?!!
GIVE IT A REST!
DO YOU UNDERSTAND THE SERIOUSNESS OF THE SITUATION?!
LET GO OF ME.

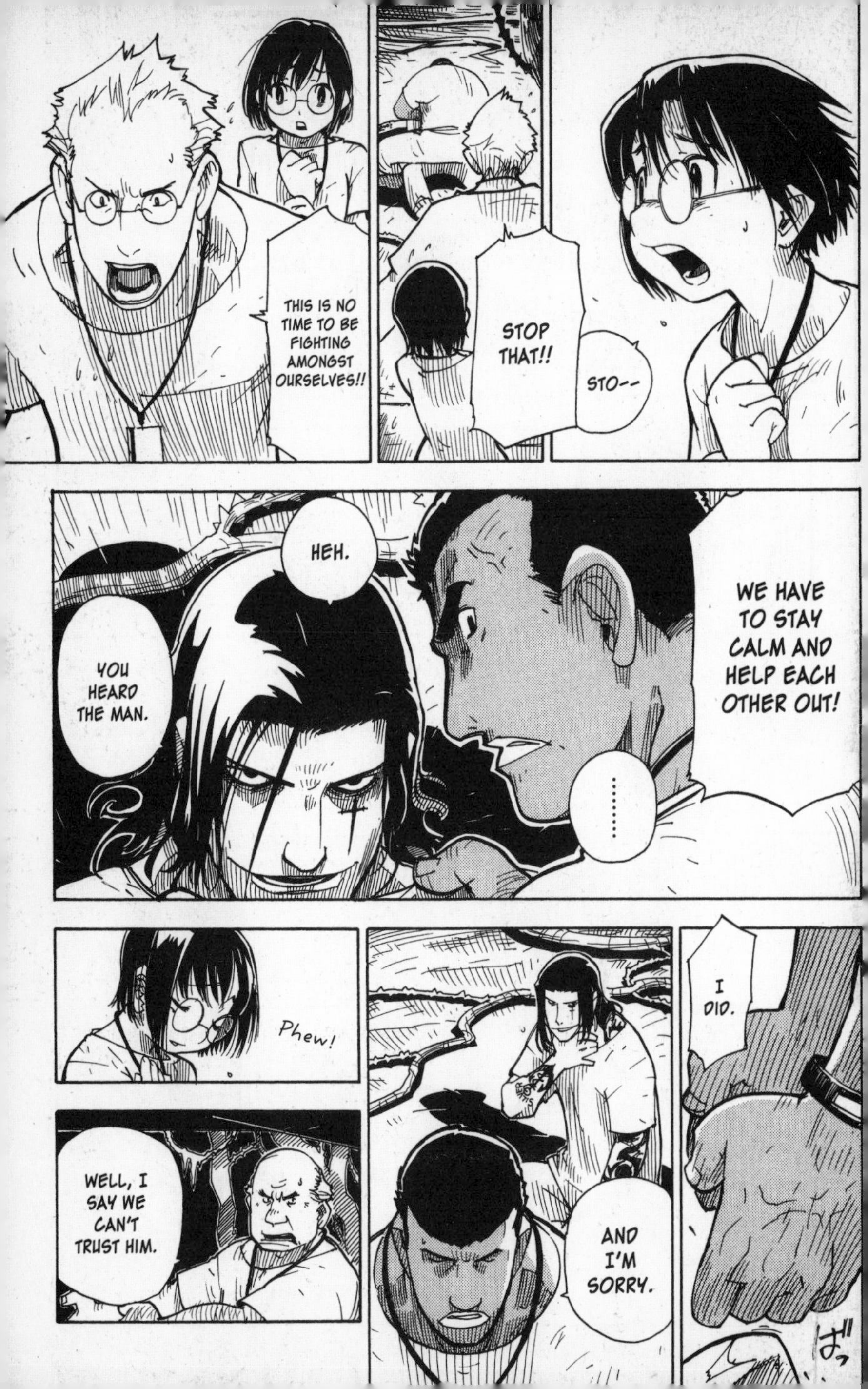
STO--
STOP THAT!!
THIS IS NO TIME TO BE FIGHTING AMONGST OURSELVES!!
WE HAVE TO STAY CALM AND HELP EACH OTHER OUT!
HEH.
......
YOU HEARD THE MAN.
I DID.
ばっ
AND I'M SORRY.
Phew!
WELL, I SAY WE CAN'T TRUST HIM.

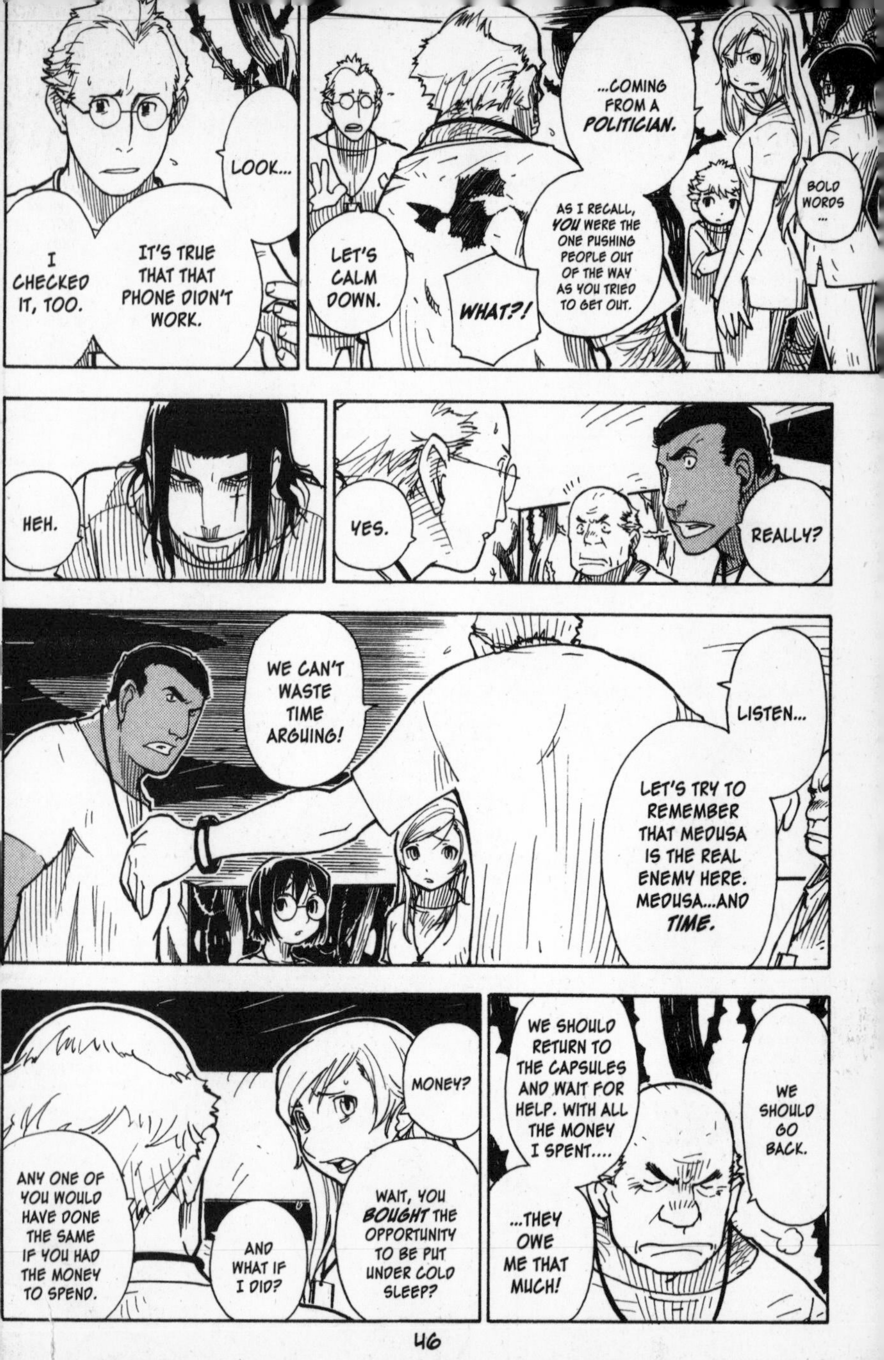
BOLD WORDS ...
...COMING FROM A POLITICIAN.
WHAT?!
AS I RECALL, YOU WERE THE ONE PUSHING PEOPLE OUT OF THE WAY AS YOU TRIED TO GET OUT.
LET'S CALM DOWN.
LOOK...
IT'S TRUE THAT THAT PHONE DIDN'T WORK.
I CHECKED IT, TOO.
REALLY?
YES.
HEH.
LISTEN...
LET'S TRY TO REMEMBER THAT MEDUSA IS THE REAL ENEMY HERE. MEDUSA...AND TIME.
WE CAN'T WASTE TIME ARGUING!
WE SHOULD GO BACK.
WE SHOULD RETURN TO THE CAPSULES AND WAIT FOR HELP. WITH ALL THE MONEY I SPENT....
...THEY OWE ME THAT MUCH!
MONEY?
WAIT, YOU BOUGHT THE OPPORTUNITY TO BE PUT UNDER COLD SLEEP?
AND WHAT IF I DID?
ANY ONE OF YOU WOULD HAVE DONE THE SAME IF YOU HAD THE MONEY TO SPEND.

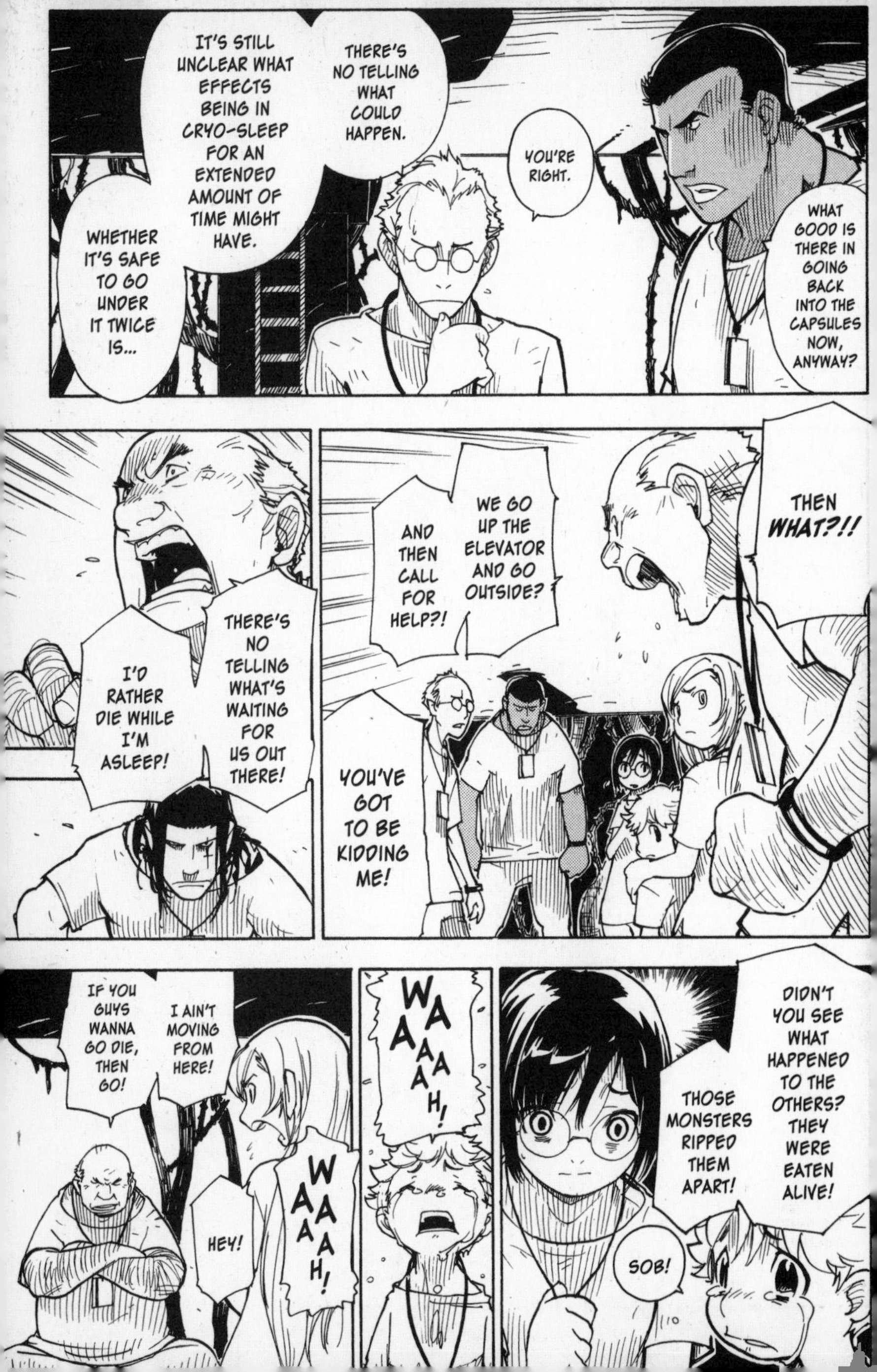
WHAT GOOD IS THERE IN GOING BACK INTO THE CAPSULES NOW, ANYWAY?
YOU'RE RIGHT.
THERE'S NO TELLING WHAT COULD HAPPEN.
IT'S STILL UNCLEAR WHAT EFFECTS BEING IN CRYO-SLEEP FOR AN EXTENDED AMOUNT OF TIME MIGHT HAVE.
WHETHER IT'S SAFE TO GO UNDER IT TWICE IS...
THEN *WHAT?!!*
WE GO UP THE ELEVATOR AND GO OUTSIDE?
AND THEN CALL FOR HELP?!
YOU'VE GOT TO BE KIDDING ME!
THERE'S NO TELLING WHAT'S WAITING FOR US OUT THERE!
I'D RATHER DIE WHILE I'M ASLEEP!
DIDN'T YOU SEE WHAT HAPPENED TO THE OTHERS? THEY WERE EATEN ALIVE!
THOSE MONSTERS RIPPED THEM APART!
SOB!
WAAAAAH!
WAAAAAH!
I AIN'T MOVING FROM HERE!
IF YOU GUYS WANNA GO DIE, THEN GO!
HEY!

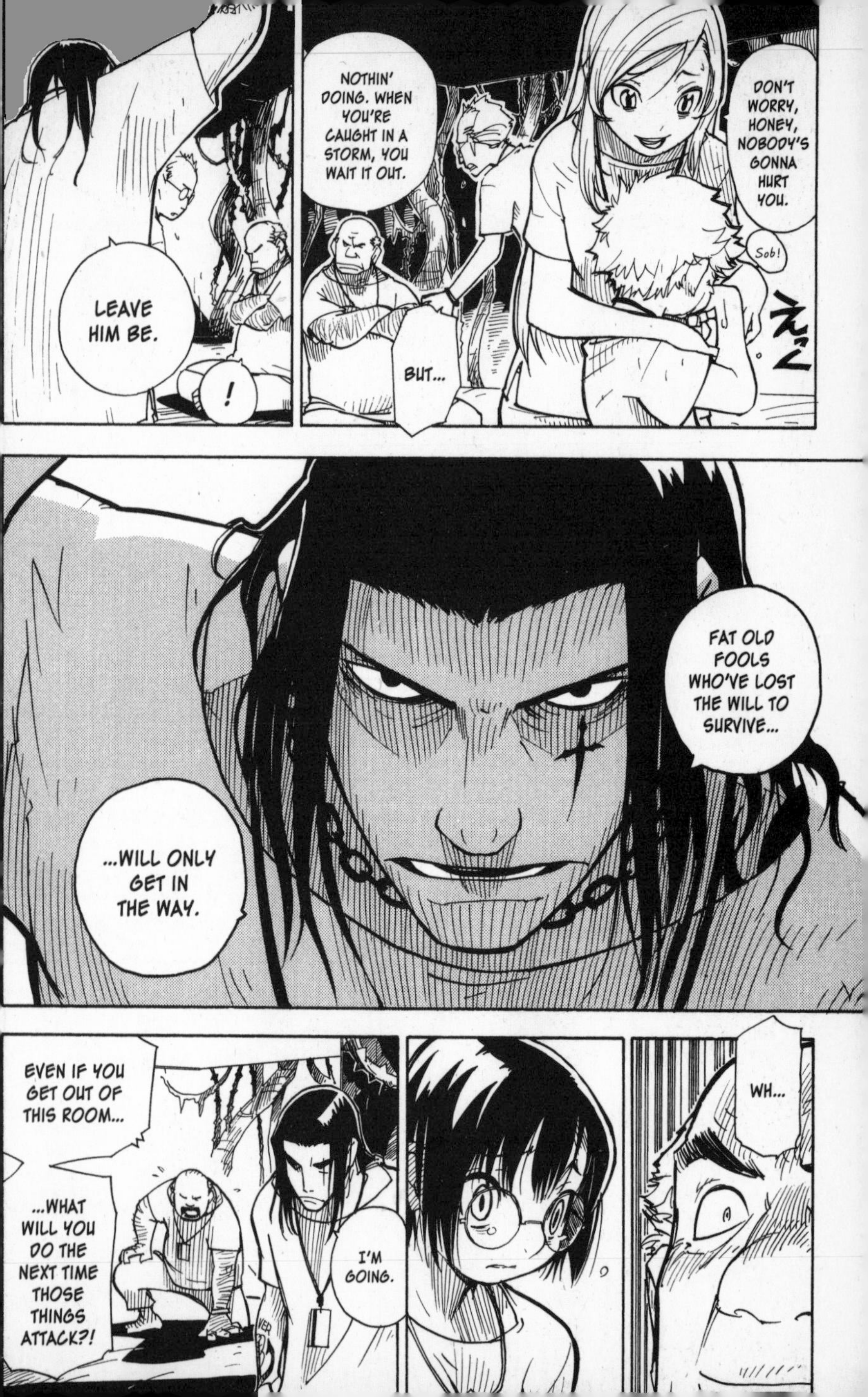
DON'T WORRY, HONEY, NOBODY'S GONNA HURT YOU.
Sob!
NOTHIN' DOING. WHEN YOU'RE CAUGHT IN A STORM, YOU WAIT IT OUT.
BUT...
LEAVE HIM BE.
!
FAT OLD FOOLS WHO'VE LOST THE WILL TO SURVIVE...
...WILL ONLY GET IN THE WAY.
WH...
I'M GOING.
EVEN IF YOU GET OUT OF THIS ROOM...
...WHAT WILL YOU DO THE NEXT TIME THOSE THINGS ATTACK?!

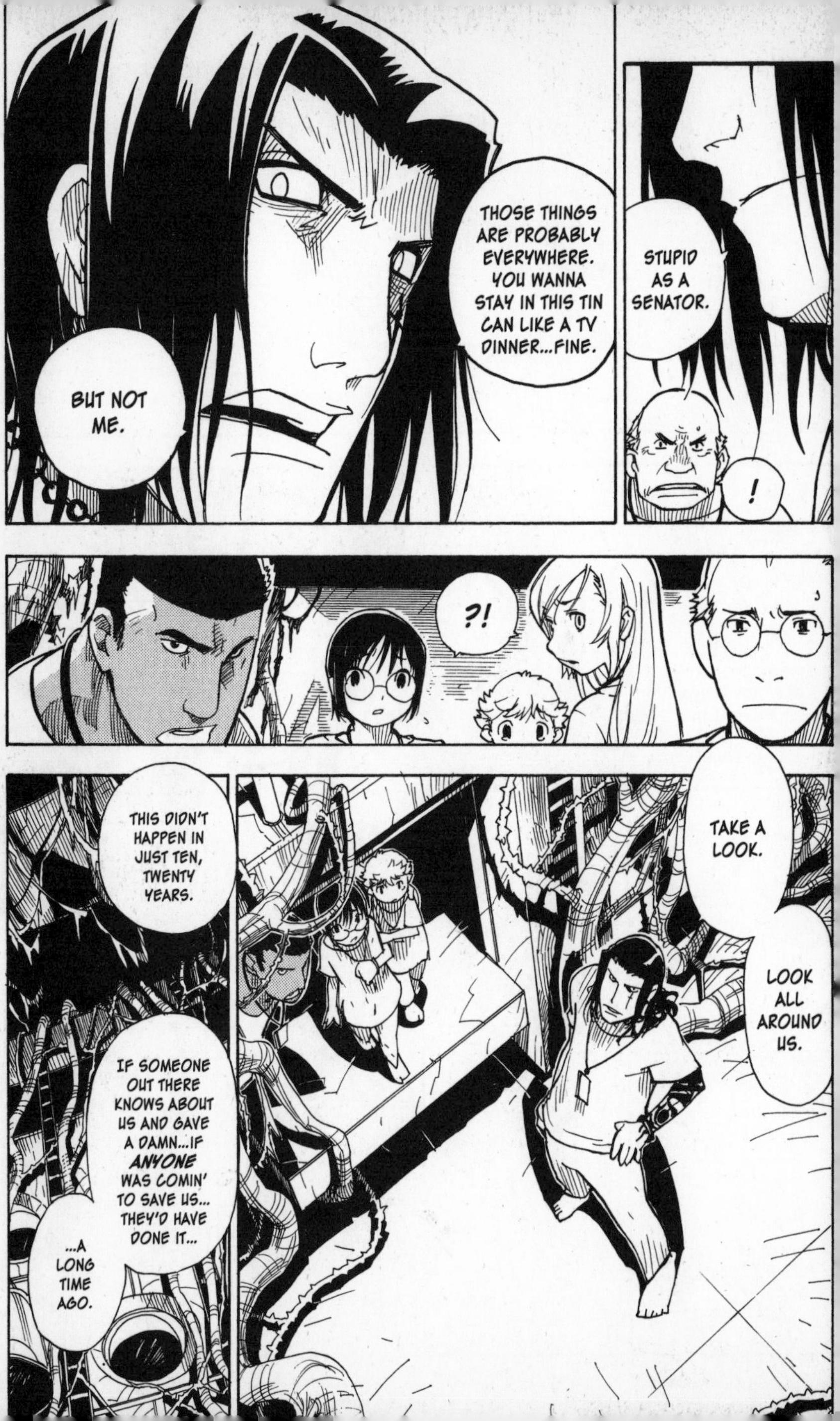
STUPID AS A SENATOR.
!
THOSE THINGS ARE PROBABLY EVERYWHERE. YOU WANNA STAY IN THIS TIN CAN LIKE A TV DINNER...FINE.
BUT NOT ME.
?!
TAKE A LOOK.
LOOK ALL AROUND US.
THIS DIDN'T HAPPEN IN JUST TEN, TWENTY YEARS.
IF SOMEONE OUT THERE KNOWS ABOUT US AND GAVE A DAMN...IF *ANYONE* WAS COMIN' TO SAVE US... THEY'D HAVE DONE IT...
...A LONG TIME AGO.

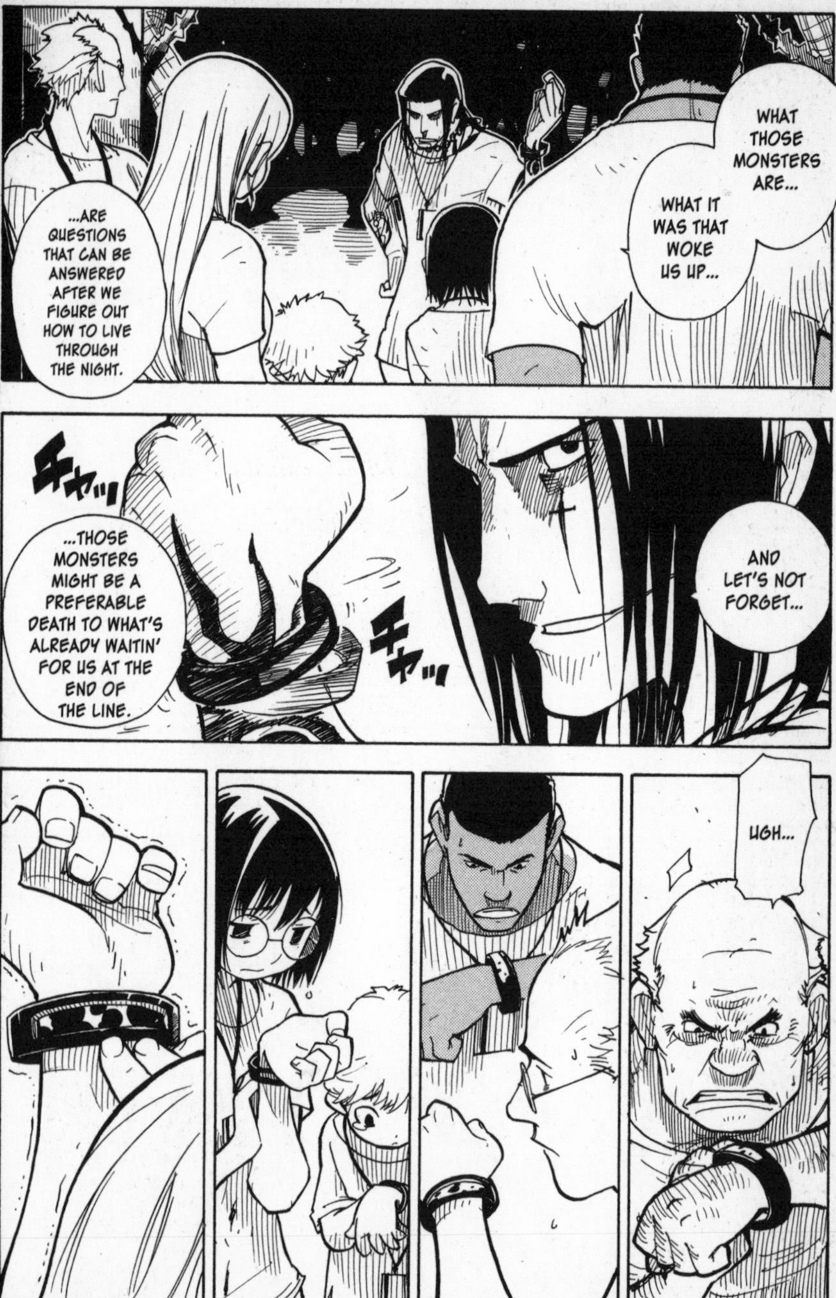

WHAT THOSE MONSTERS ARE...
WHAT IT WAS THAT WOKE US UP...
...ARE QUESTIONS THAT CAN BE ANSWERED AFTER WE FIGURE OUT HOW TO LIVE THROUGH THE NIGHT.
AND LET'S NOT FORGET...
チャッ
...THOSE MONSTERS MIGHT BE A PREFERABLE DEATH TO WHAT'S ALREADY WAITIN' FOR US AT THE END OF THE LINE.
チャッ
UGH...

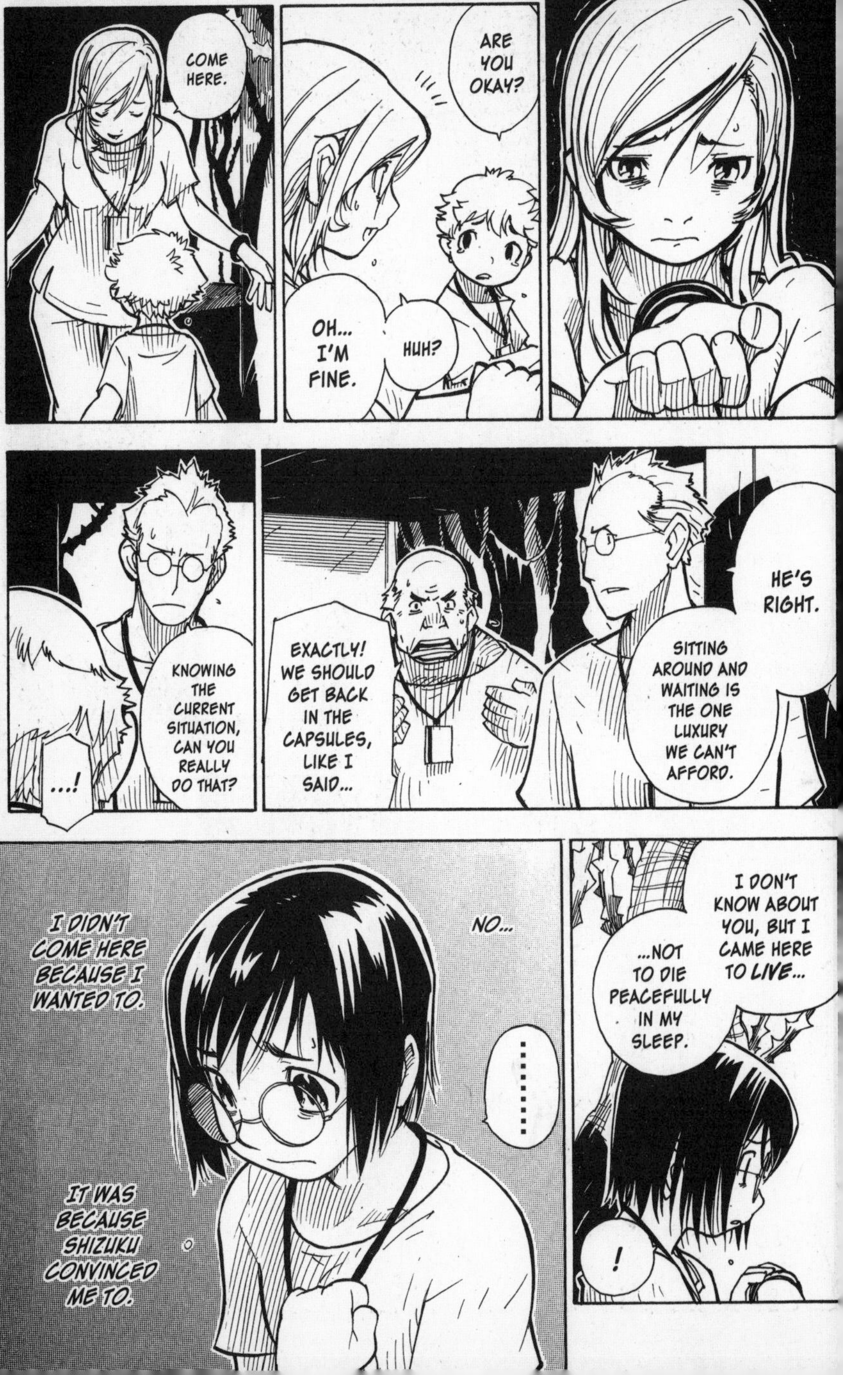
ARE YOU OKAY?
HUH?
OH... I'M FINE.
COME HERE.
HE'S RIGHT.
SITTING AROUND AND WAITING IS THE ONE LUXURY WE CAN'T AFFORD.
EXACTLY! WE SHOULD GET BACK IN THE CAPSULES, LIKE I SAID...
KNOWING THE CURRENT SITUATION, CAN YOU REALLY DO THAT?
...!
I DON'T KNOW ABOUT YOU, BUT I CAME HERE TO *LIVE*...
...NOT TO DIE PEACEFULLY IN MY SLEEP.
!
NO...
I DIDN'T COME HERE BECAUSE I WANTED TO.
......
IT WAS BECAUSE SHIZUKU CONVINCED ME TO.

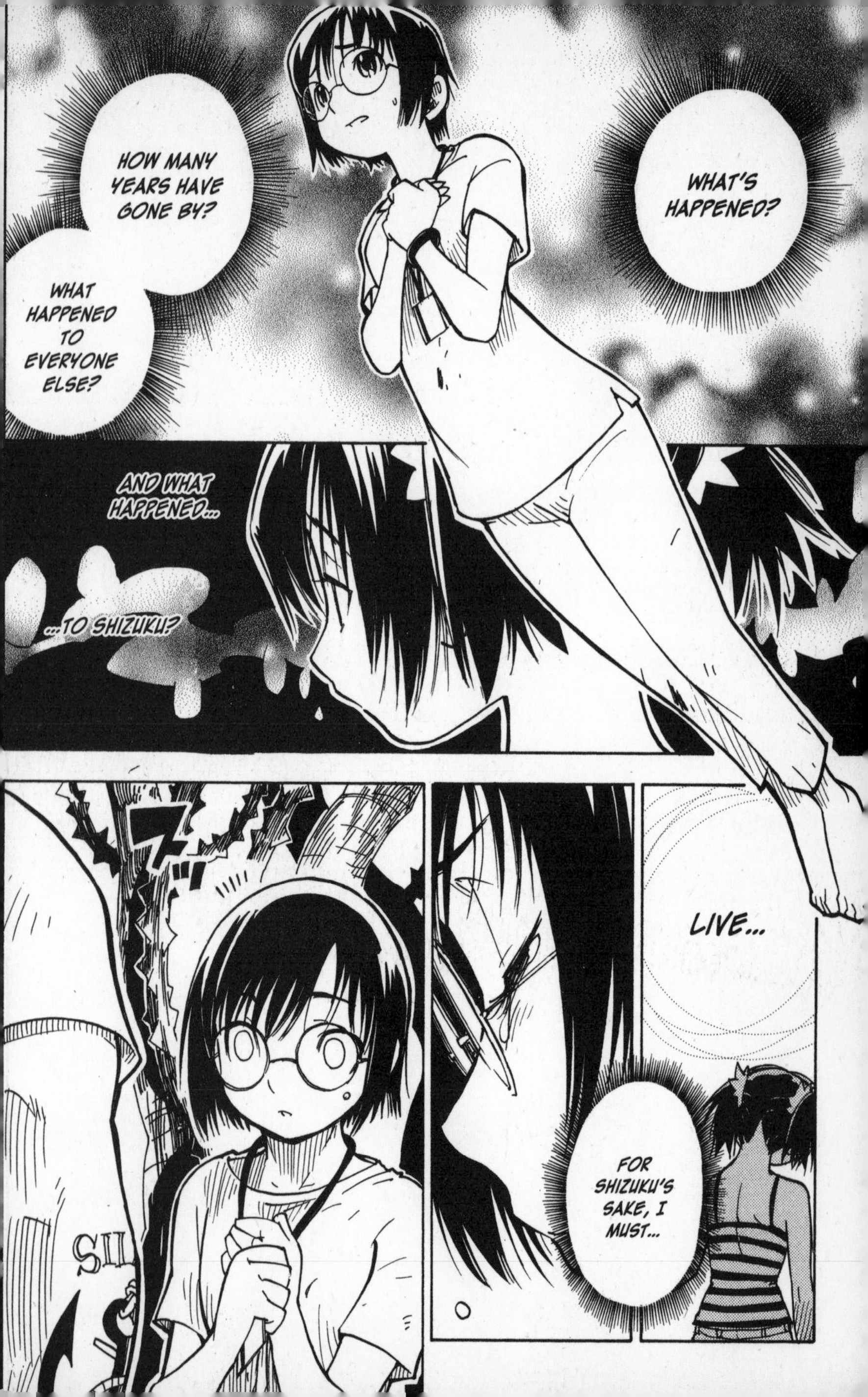
WHAT'S HAPPENED?
HOW MANY YEARS HAVE GONE BY?
WHAT HAPPENED TO EVERYONE ELSE?
AND WHAT HAPPENED...
...TO SHIZUKU?
LIVE...
FOR SHIZUKU'S SAKE, I MUST...

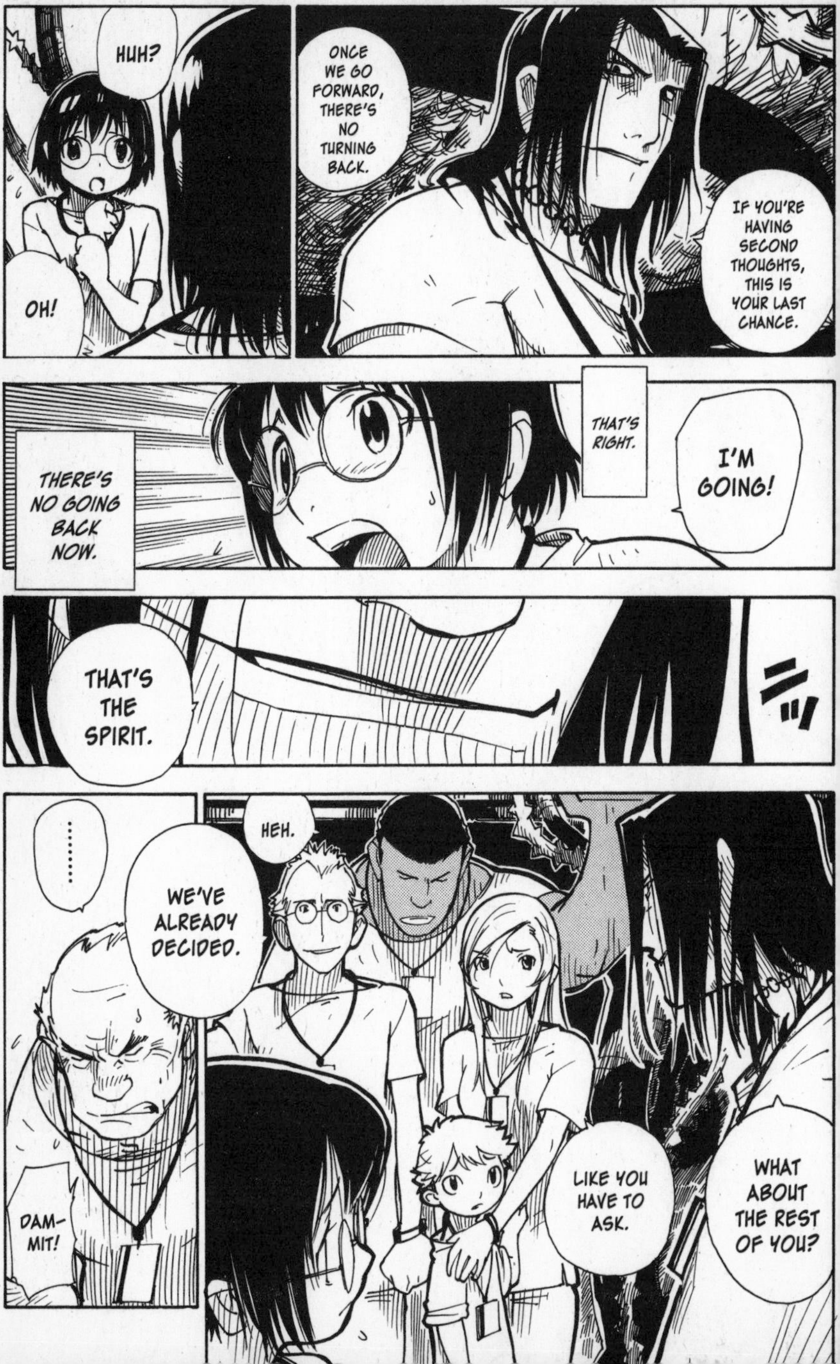

ONCE WE GO FORWARD, THERE'S NO TURNING BACK.
IF YOU'RE HAVING SECOND THOUGHTS, THIS IS YOUR LAST CHANCE.
HUH?
OH!
I'M GOING!
THAT'S RIGHT.
THERE'S NO GOING BACK NOW.
THAT'S THE SPIRIT.
WHAT ABOUT THE REST OF YOU?
HEH.
LIKE YOU HAVE TO ASK.
WE'VE ALREADY DECIDED.
......
DAM-MIT!

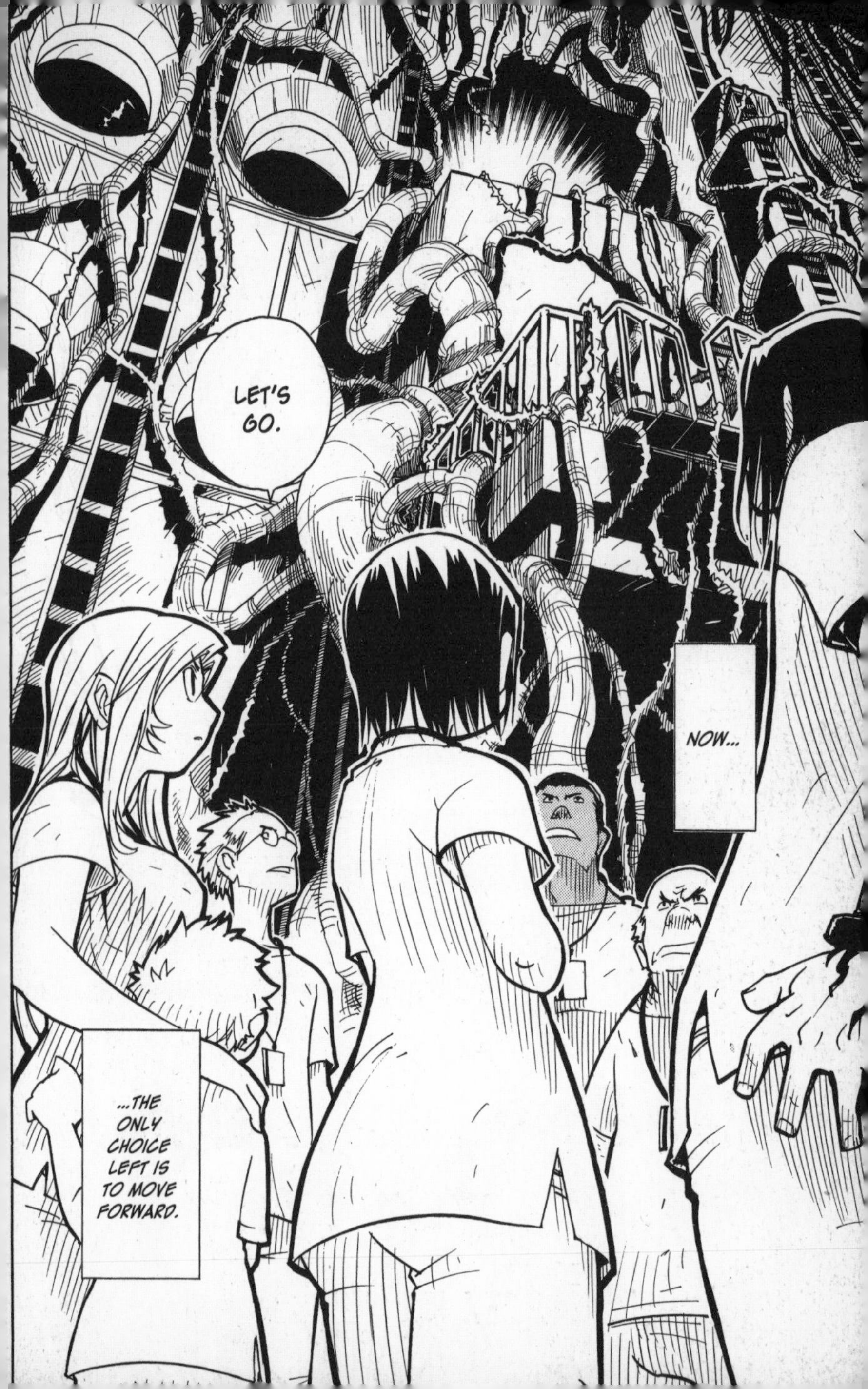
LET'S GO.
NOW...
...THE ONLY CHOICE LEFT IS TO MOVE FORWARD.

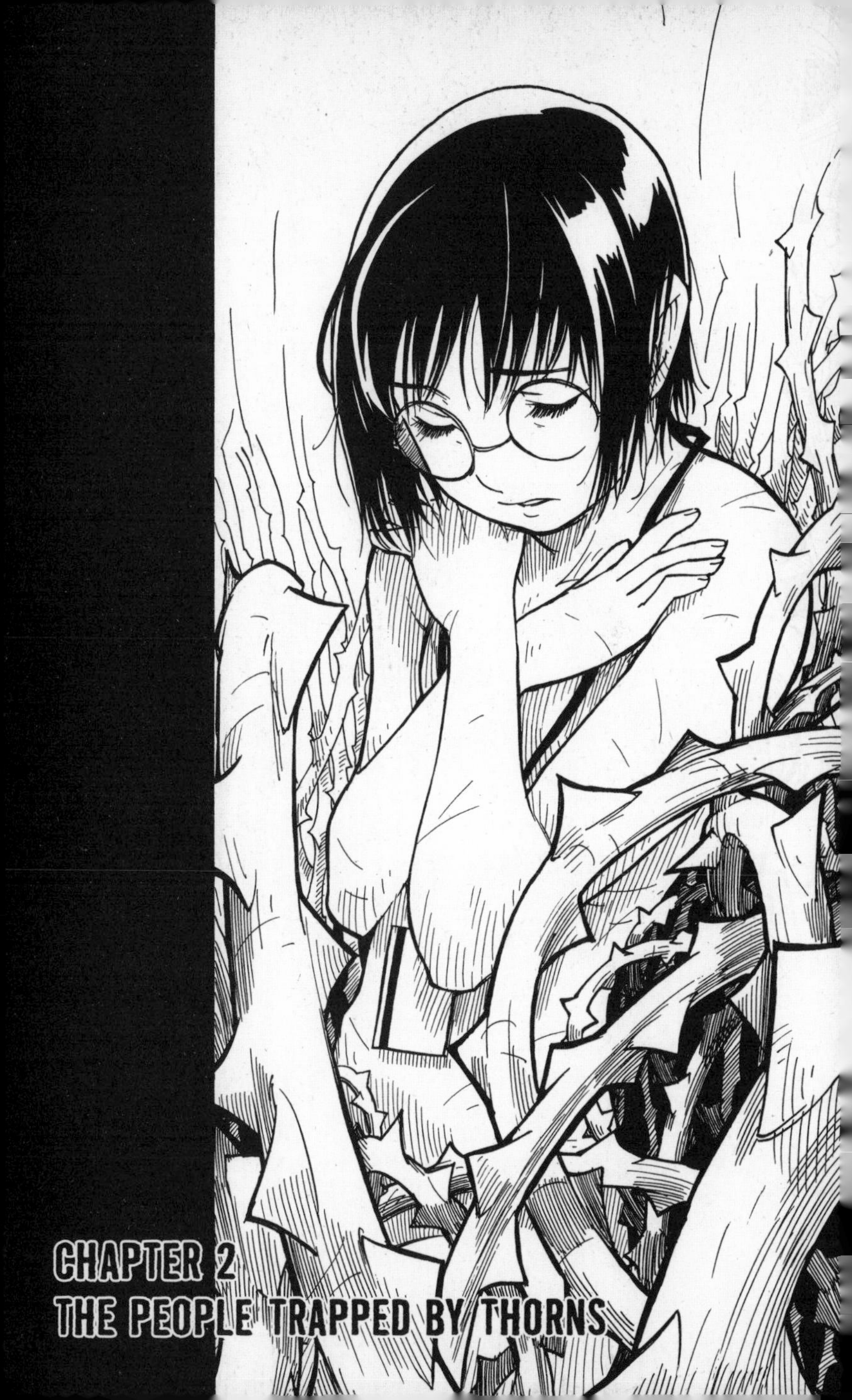

CHAPTER 2
THE PEOPLE TRAPPED BY THORNS

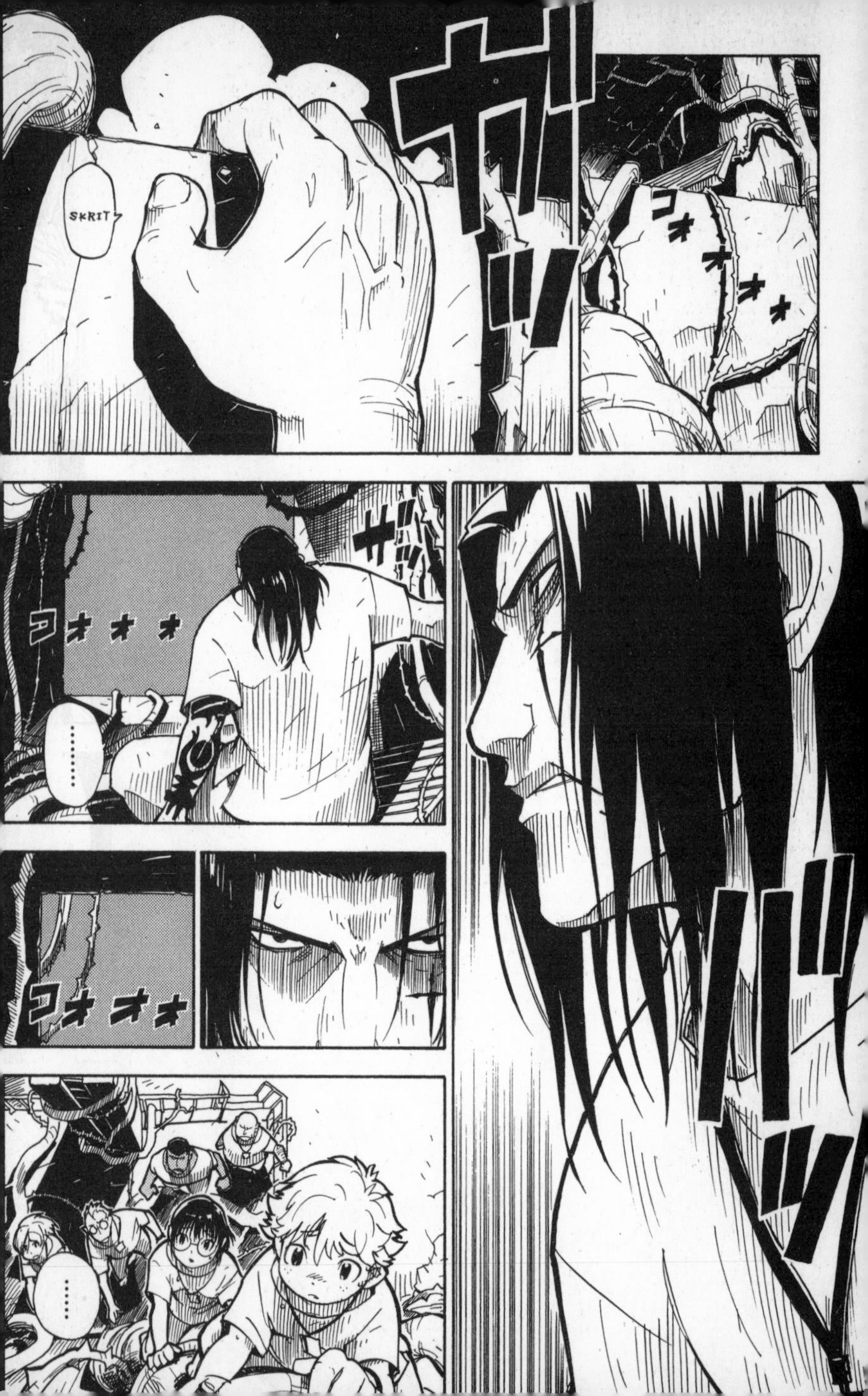
コオオオオ
SKRIT
ガッ
ザッ
コオオオ
……
コオオオ
……

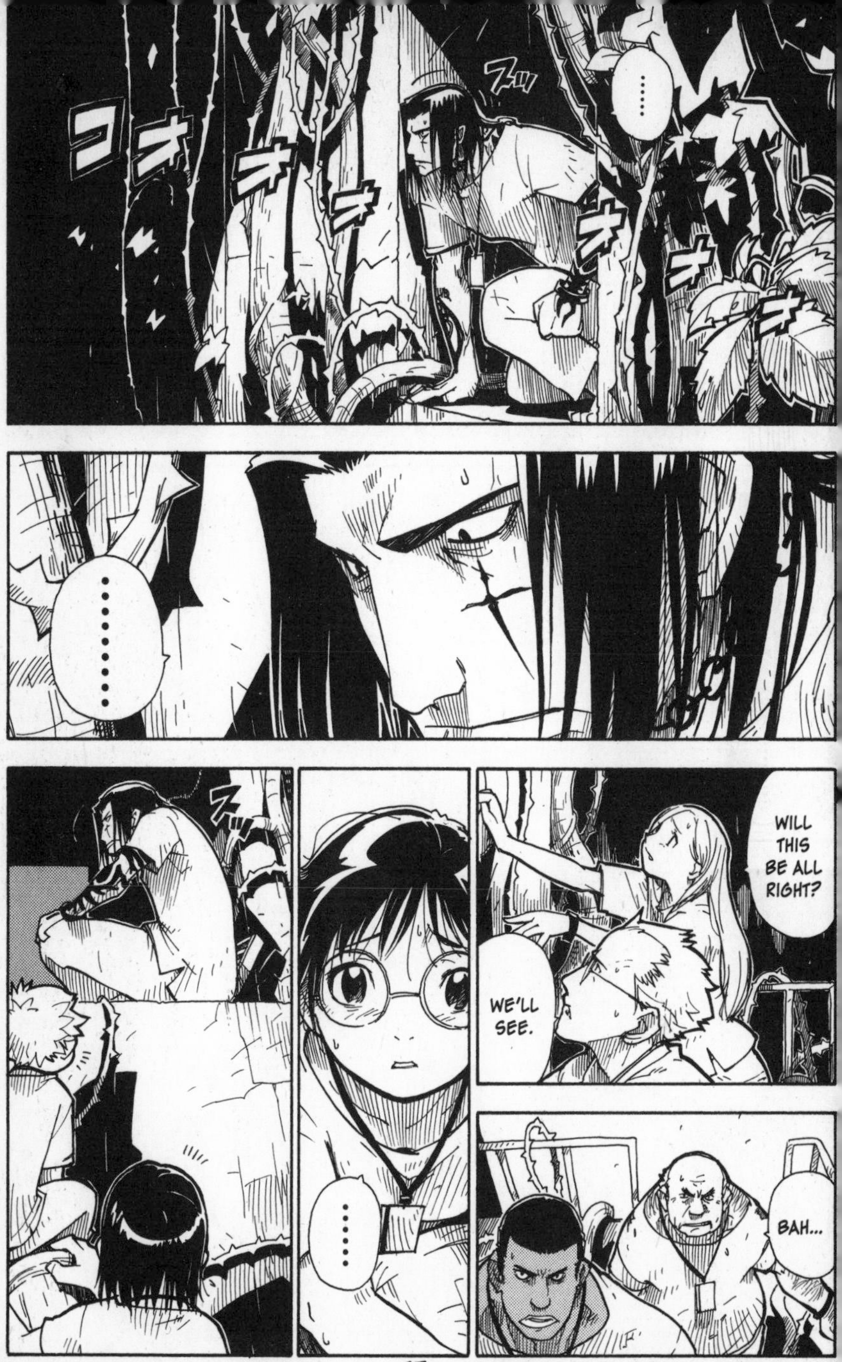
ズッ
……
コオオオオオオ
……
WILL THIS BE ALL RIGHT?
WE'LL SEE.
BAH...
……
ズッ

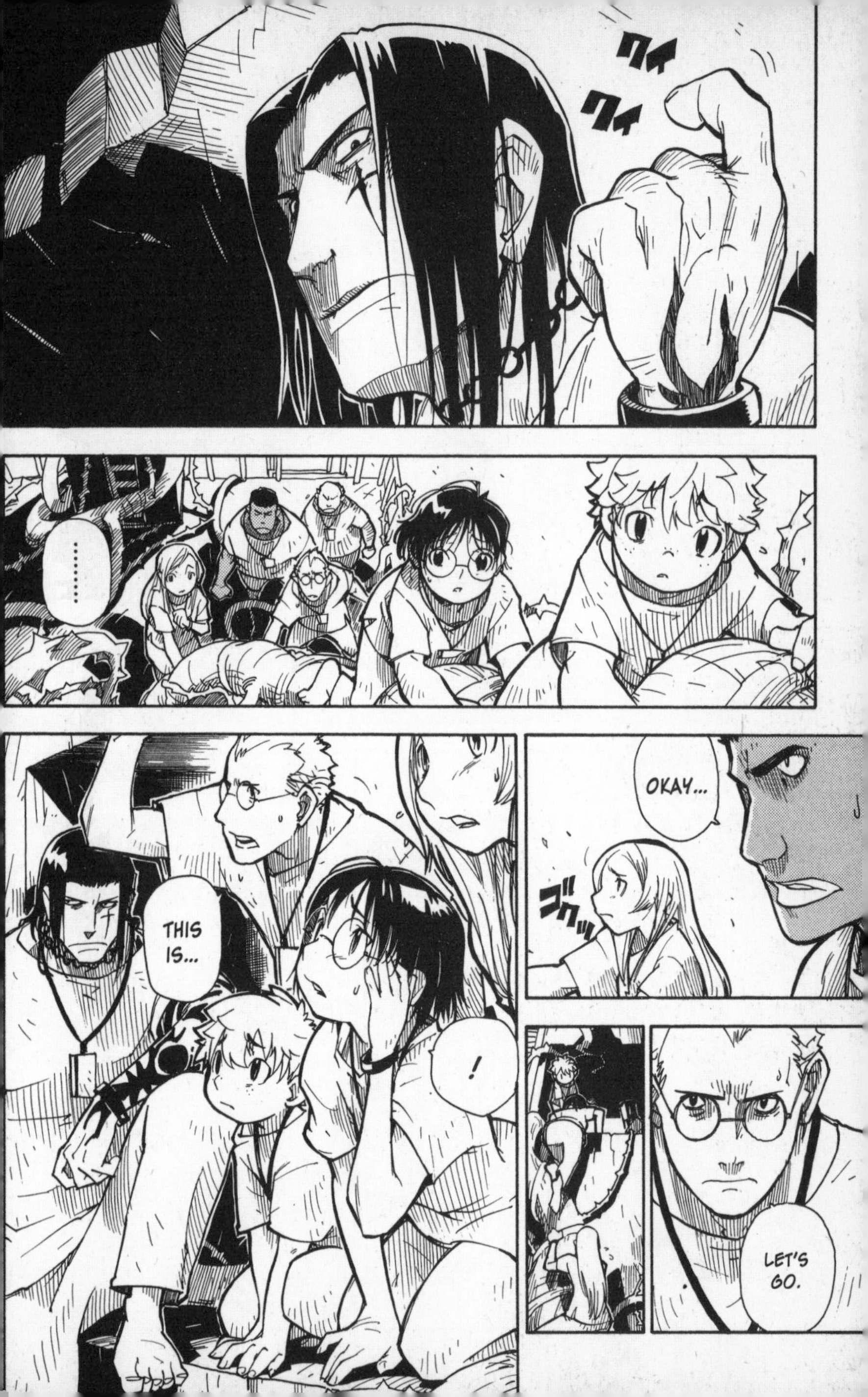
......
OKAY...
LET'S GO.
THIS IS...
!

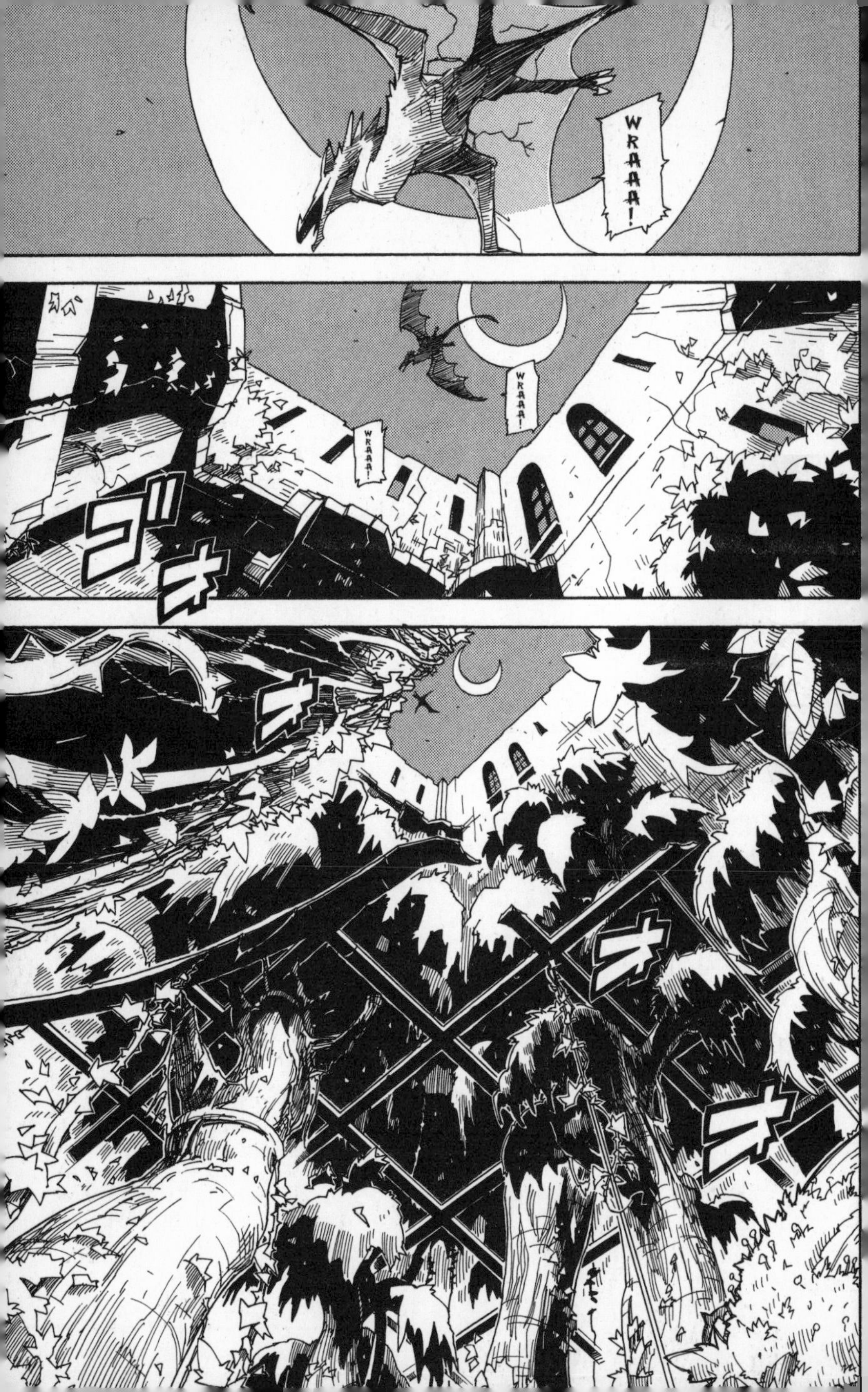
WRAAAA!
WRAAAA!
WRAAAA!
ゴオ
オオオ

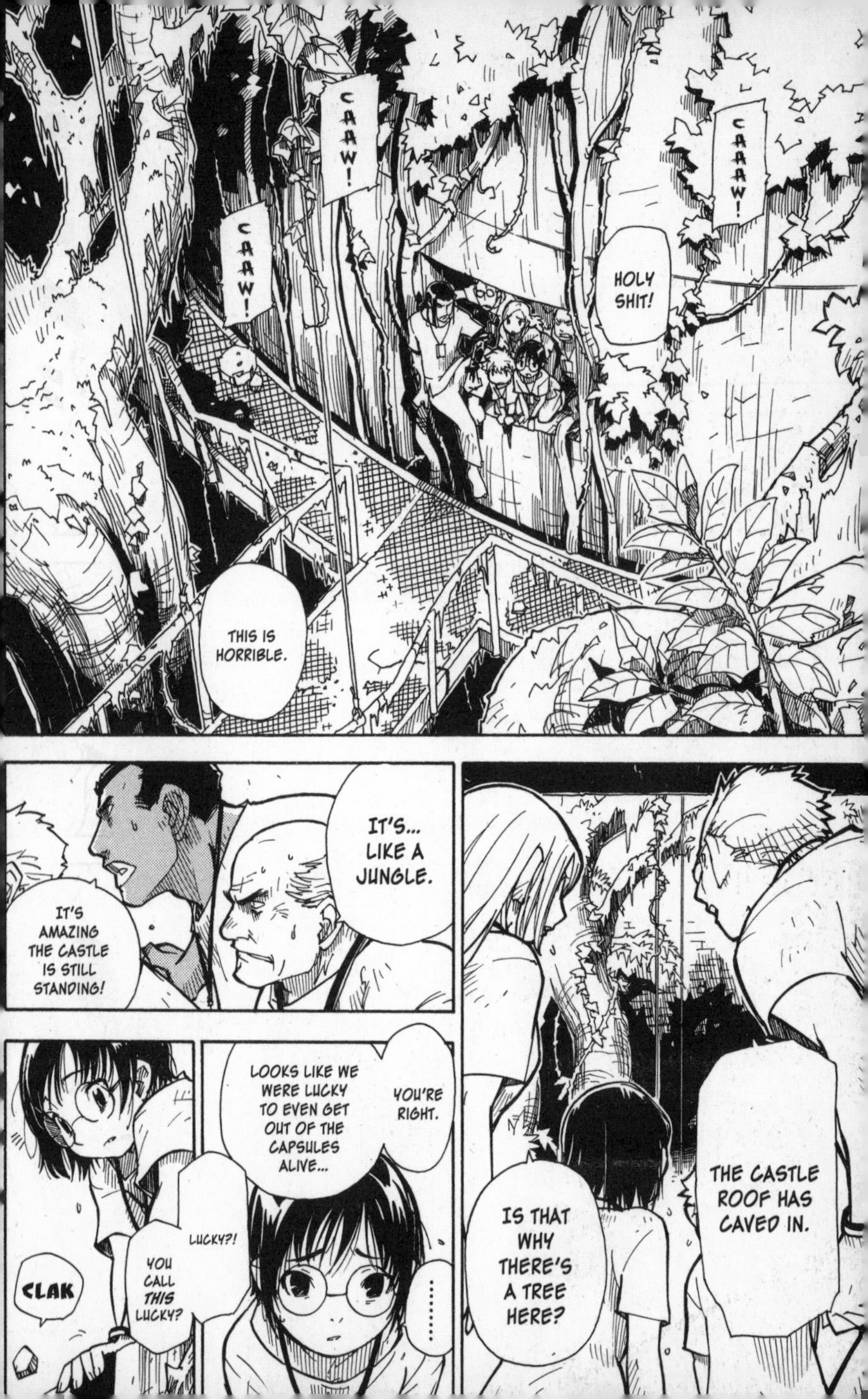
CAAAAW!
HOLY SHIT!
CAAAW!
CAAAW!
THIS IS HORRIBLE.
THE CASTLE ROOF HAS CAVED IN.
IS THAT WHY THERE'S A TREE HERE?
IT'S... LIKE A JUNGLE.
IT'S AMAZING THE CASTLE IS STILL STANDING!
LOOKS LIKE WE WERE LUCKY TO EVEN GET OUT OF THE CAPSULES ALIVE...
YOU'RE RIGHT.
......
LUCKY?!
YOU CALL *THIS* LUCKY?
CLAK

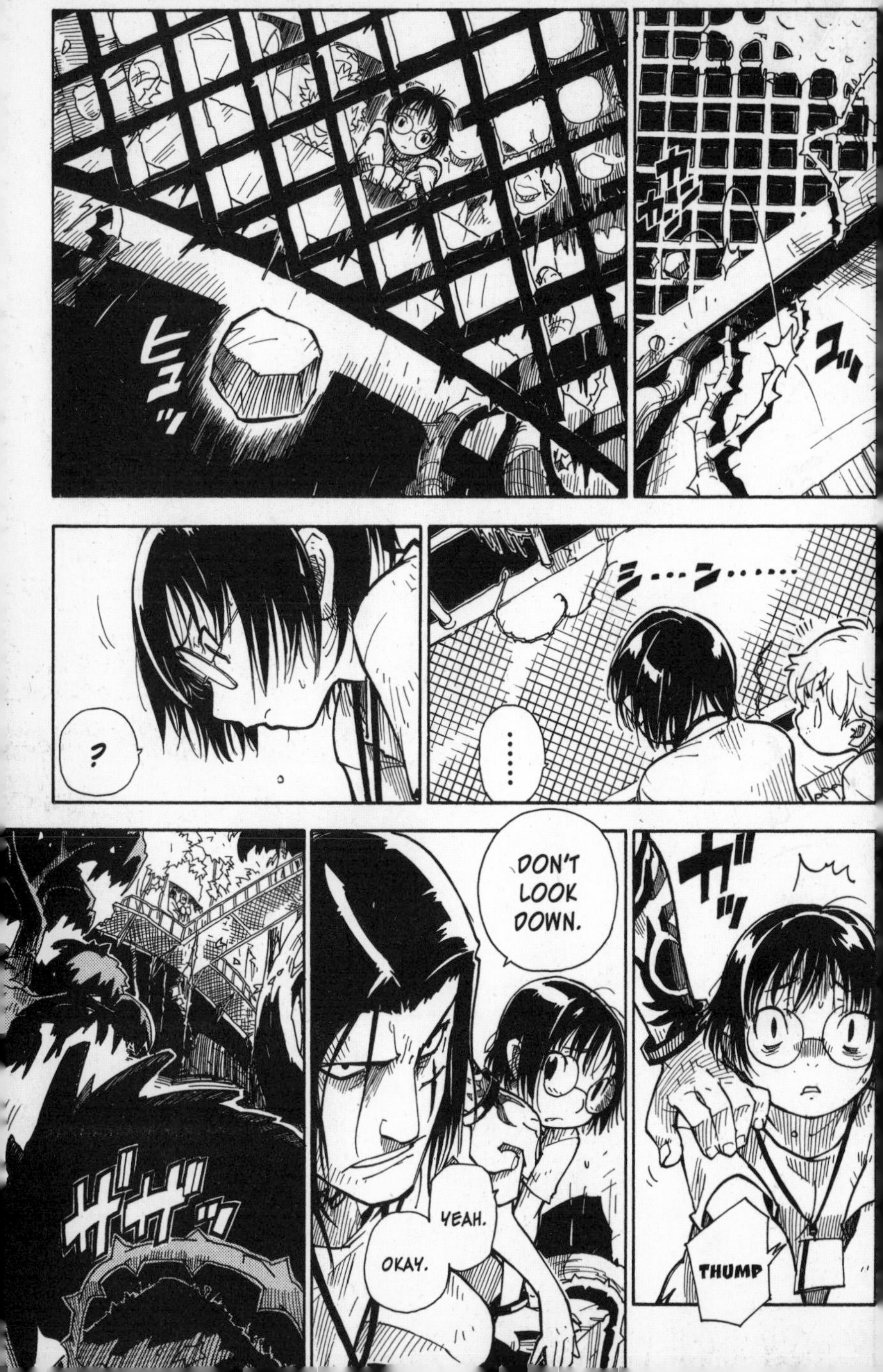
ゴッ
ヒュッ
シ…ン……
……
?
ガッ
THUMP
DON'T LOOK DOWN.
YEAH.
OKAY.
ザザッ

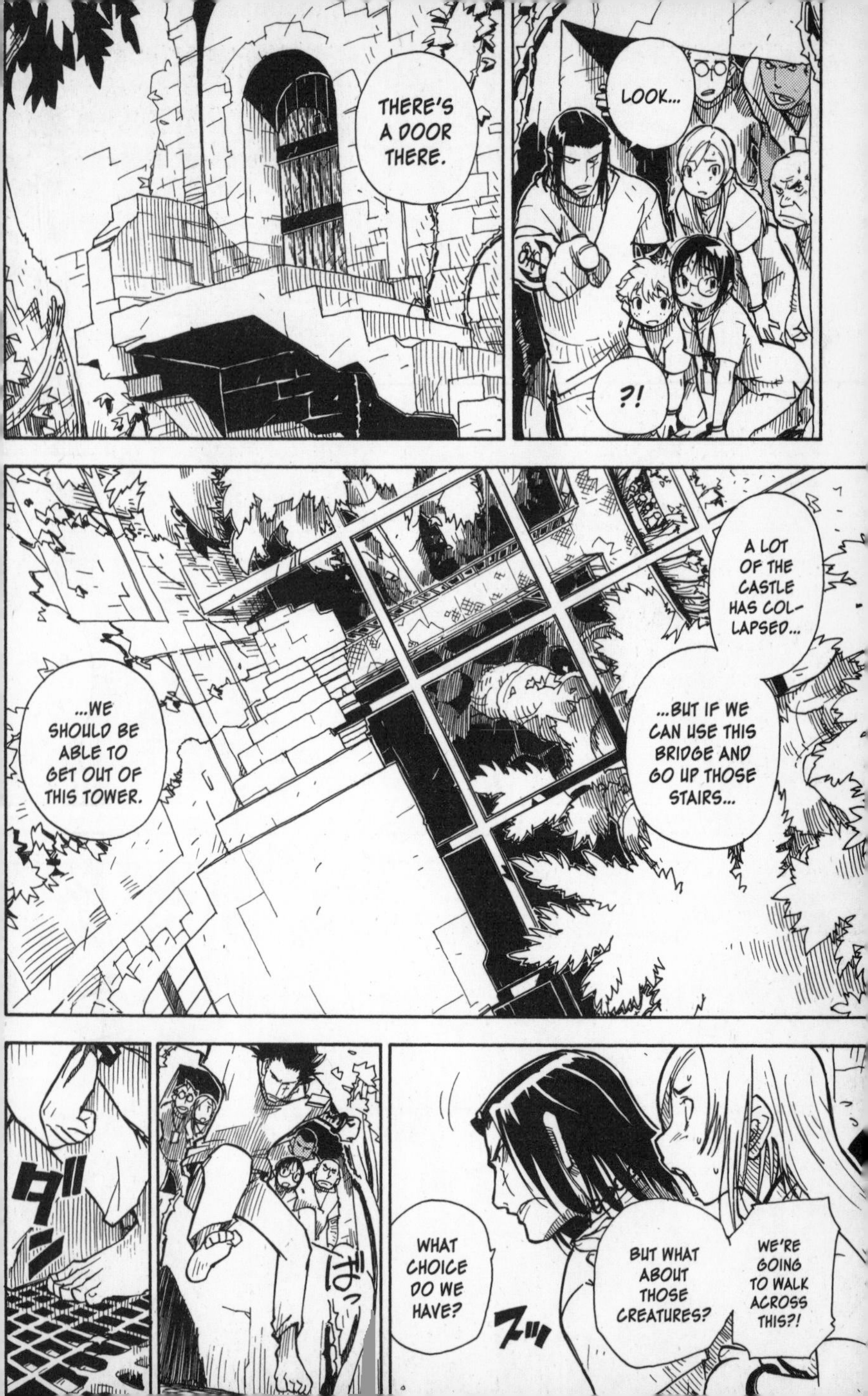
LOOK...
?!
THERE'S A DOOR THERE.
A LOT OF THE CASTLE HAS COL-LAPSED...
...BUT IF WE CAN USE THIS BRIDGE AND GO UP THOSE STAIRS...
...WE SHOULD BE ABLE TO GET OUT OF THIS TOWER.
WE'RE GOING TO WALK ACROSS THIS?!
BUT WHAT ABOUT THOSE CREATURES?
WHAT CHOICE DO WE HAVE?
ズッ
ばっ
ダン

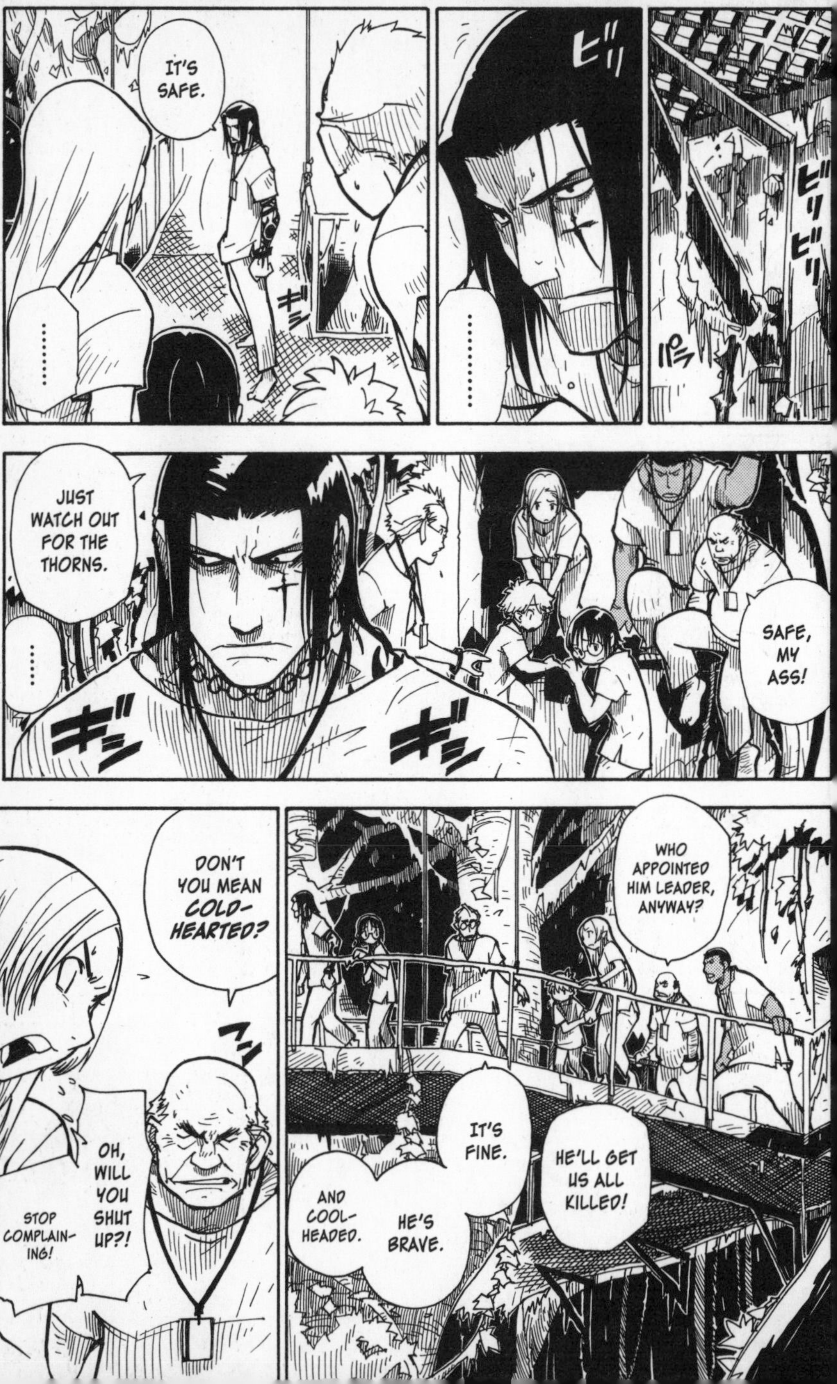
ビリ
ビリ
ビリ
パラ
ビリ
......
IT'S SAFE.
......
ギシ
SAFE, MY ASS!
JUST WATCH OUT FOR THE THORNS.
......
ギシ
ギシ
WHO APPOINTED HIM LEADER, ANYWAY?
HE'LL GET US ALL KILLED!
IT'S FINE.
HE'S BRAVE.
AND COOL-HEADED.
DON'T YOU MEAN COLD-HEARTED?
フン
OH, WILL YOU SHUT UP?!
STOP COMPLAIN-ING!

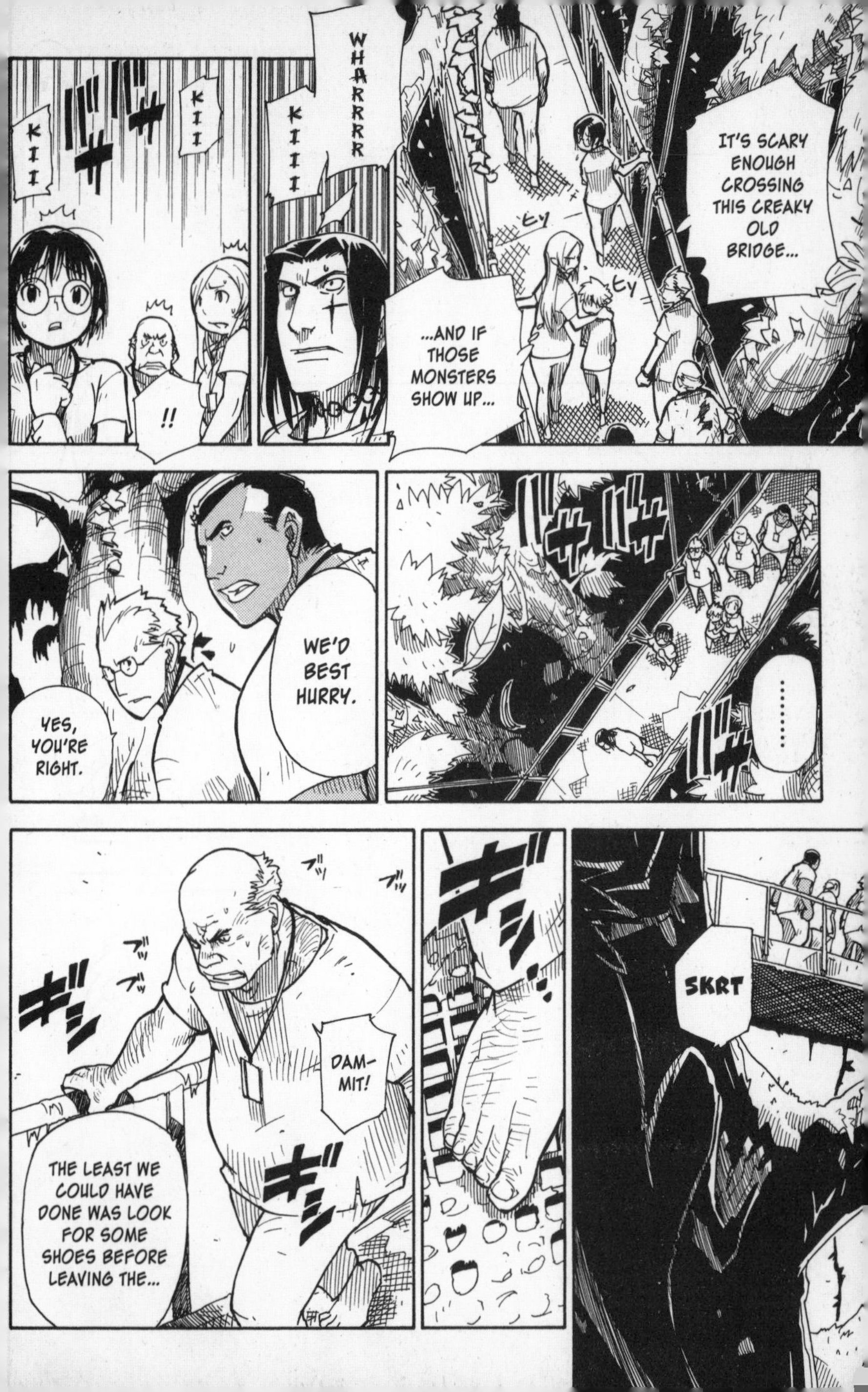
IT'S SCARY ENOUGH CROSSING THIS CREAKY OLD BRIDGE...
...AND IF THOSE MONSTERS SHOW UP...
WHARRRR
KIII
KIII
KIII
!!
......
WE'D BEST HURRY.
YES, YOU'RE RIGHT.
SKRT
DAM-MIT!
THE LEAST WE COULD HAVE DONE WAS LOOK FOR SOME SHOES BEFORE LEAVING THE...

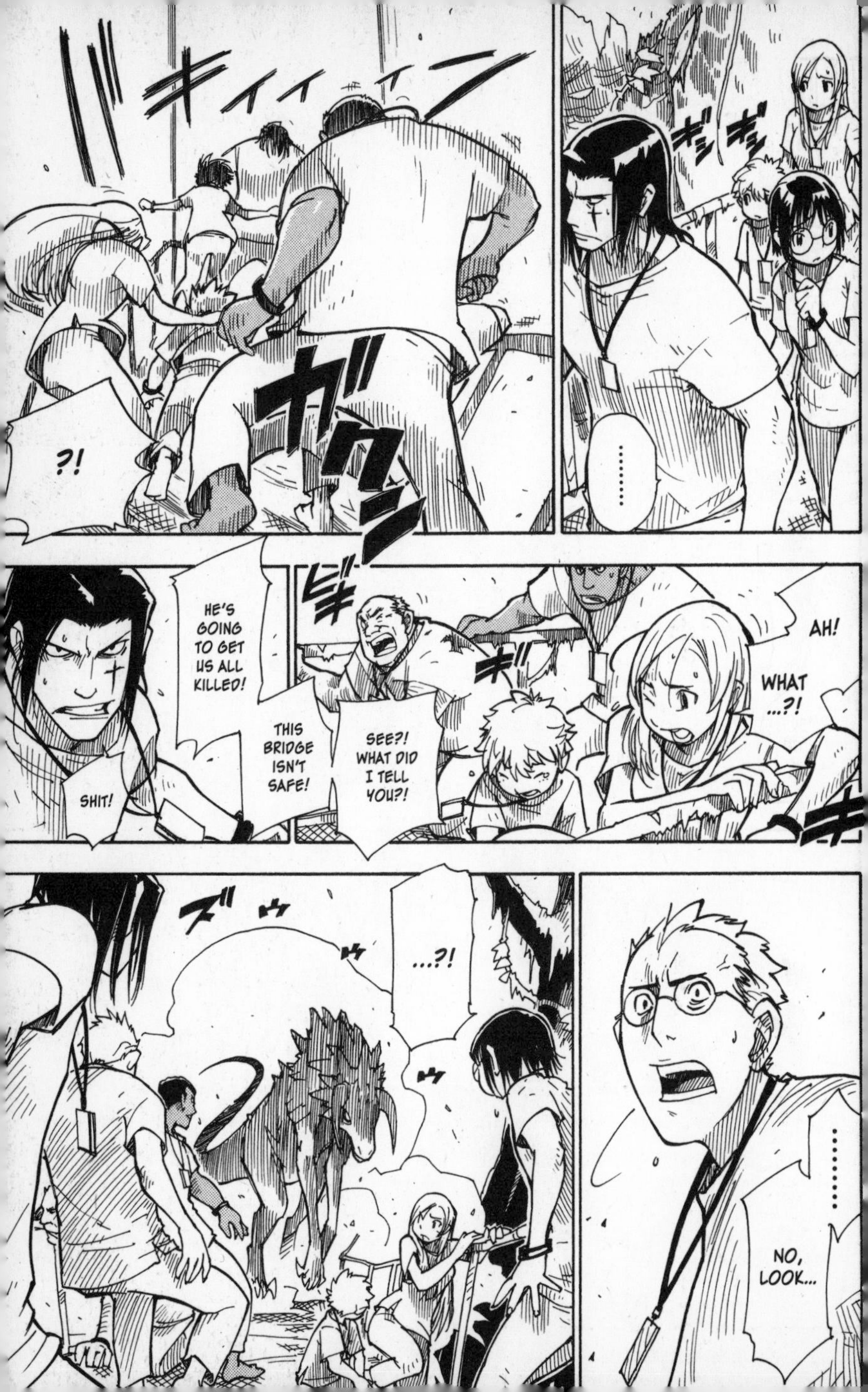
......
?!
AH!
WHAT ...?!
SEE?! WHAT DID I TELL YOU?!
THIS BRIDGE ISN'T SAFE!
HE'S GOING TO GET US ALL KILLED!
SHIT!
......
NO, LOOK...
...?!

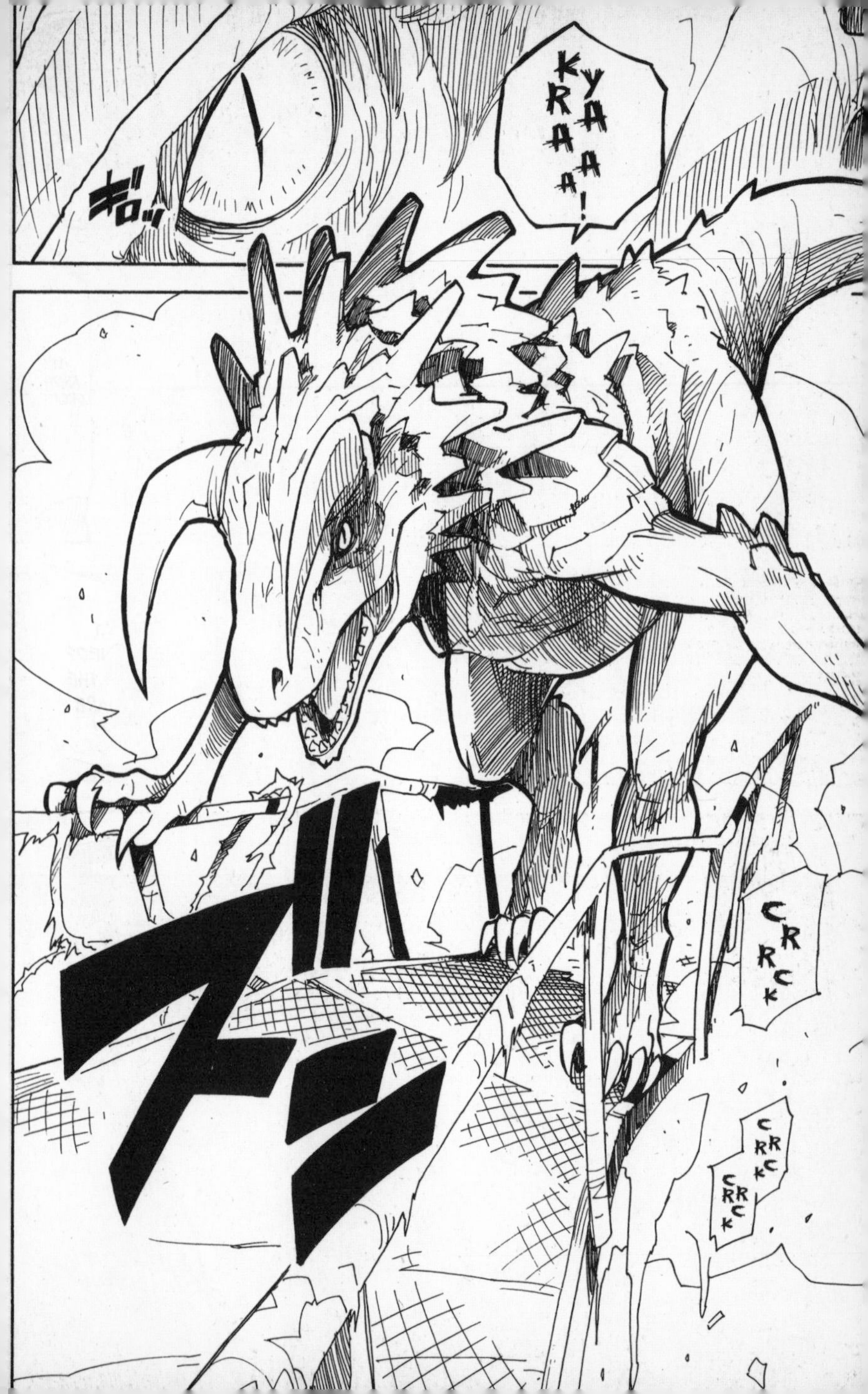
ギロッ
KYRAAAA!
CRCK
CRCK
CRCK

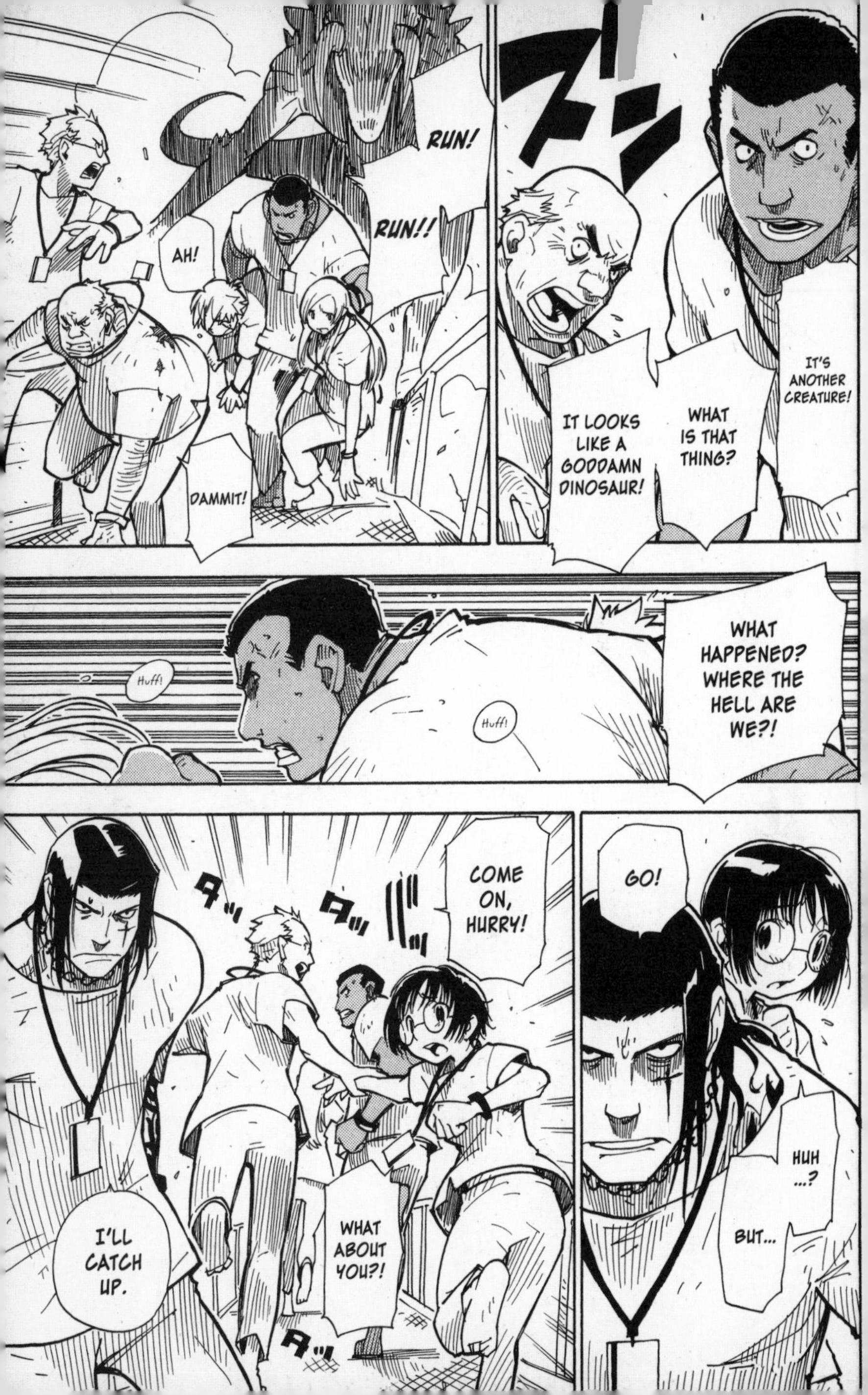
IT'S ANOTHER CREATURE!
WHAT IS THAT THING?
IT LOOKS LIKE A GODDAMN DINOSAUR!
RUN!
RUN!!
AH!
DAMMIT!
WHAT HAPPENED? WHERE THE HELL ARE WE?!
Huff!
Huff!
GO!
HUH ...?
BUT...
COME ON, HURRY!
WHAT ABOUT YOU?!
I'LL CATCH UP.

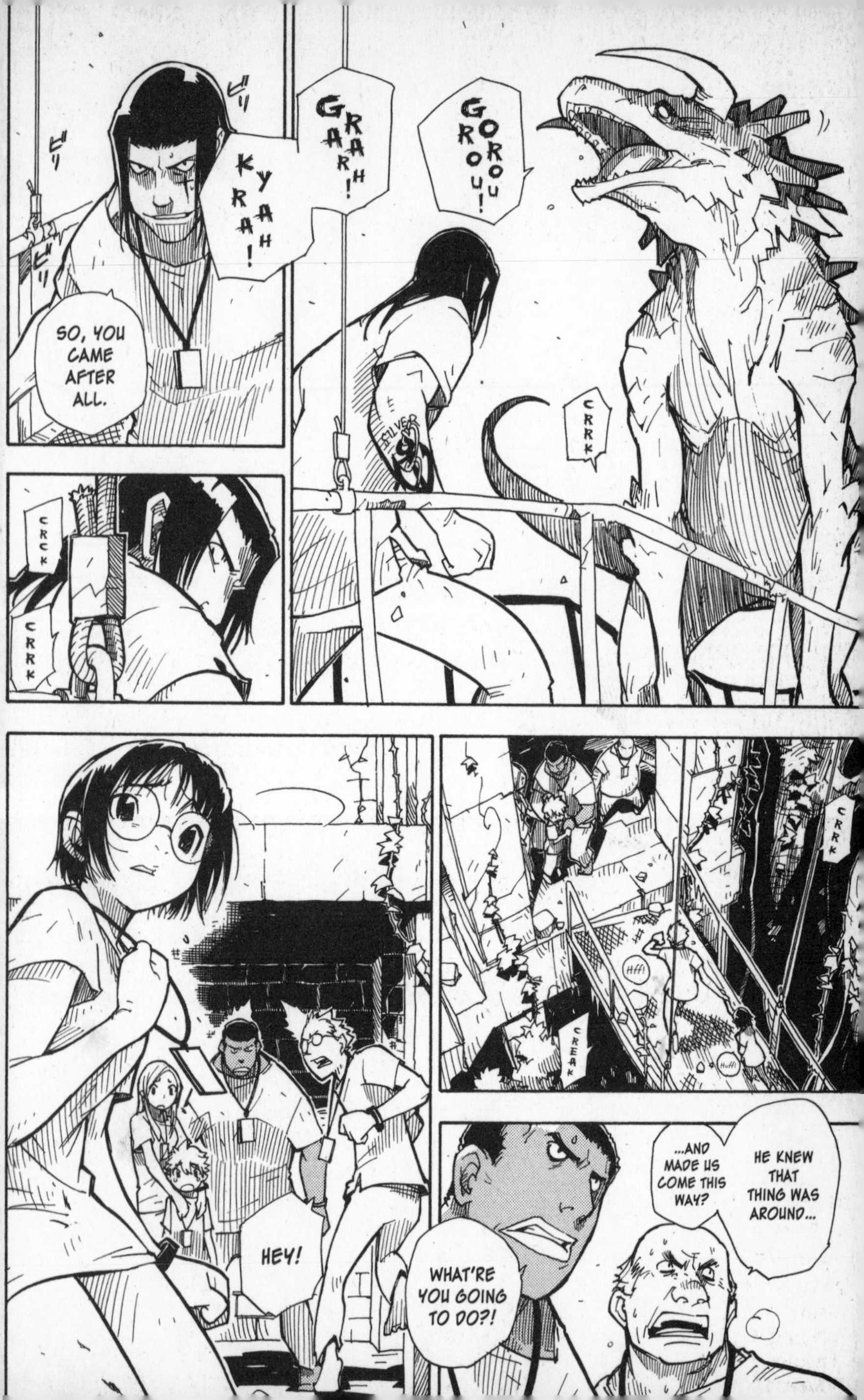
GORROOUU!
GRAARH!
CRRK
KYRAAH!
SO, YOU CAME AFTER ALL.
CRCK
CRRK
CRRK
HFF!
CREAK
HUFF!
HEY!
HE KNEW THAT THING WAS AROUND...
...AND MADE US COME THIS WAY?
WHAT'RE YOU GOING TO DO?!

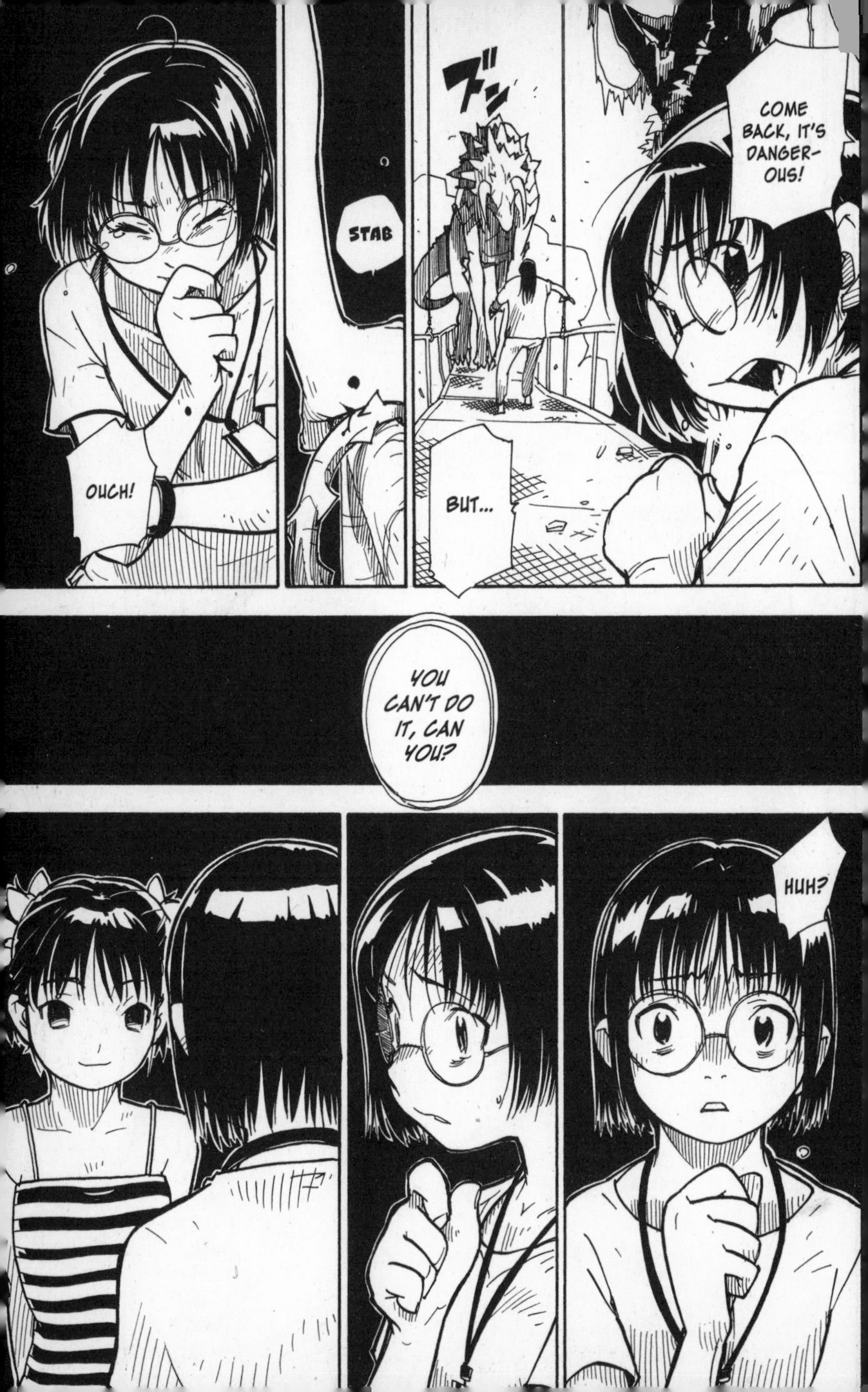
COME BACK, IT'S DANGER-OUS!
ブン
BUT...
STAB
OUCH!
YOU CAN'T DO IT, CAN YOU?
HUH?

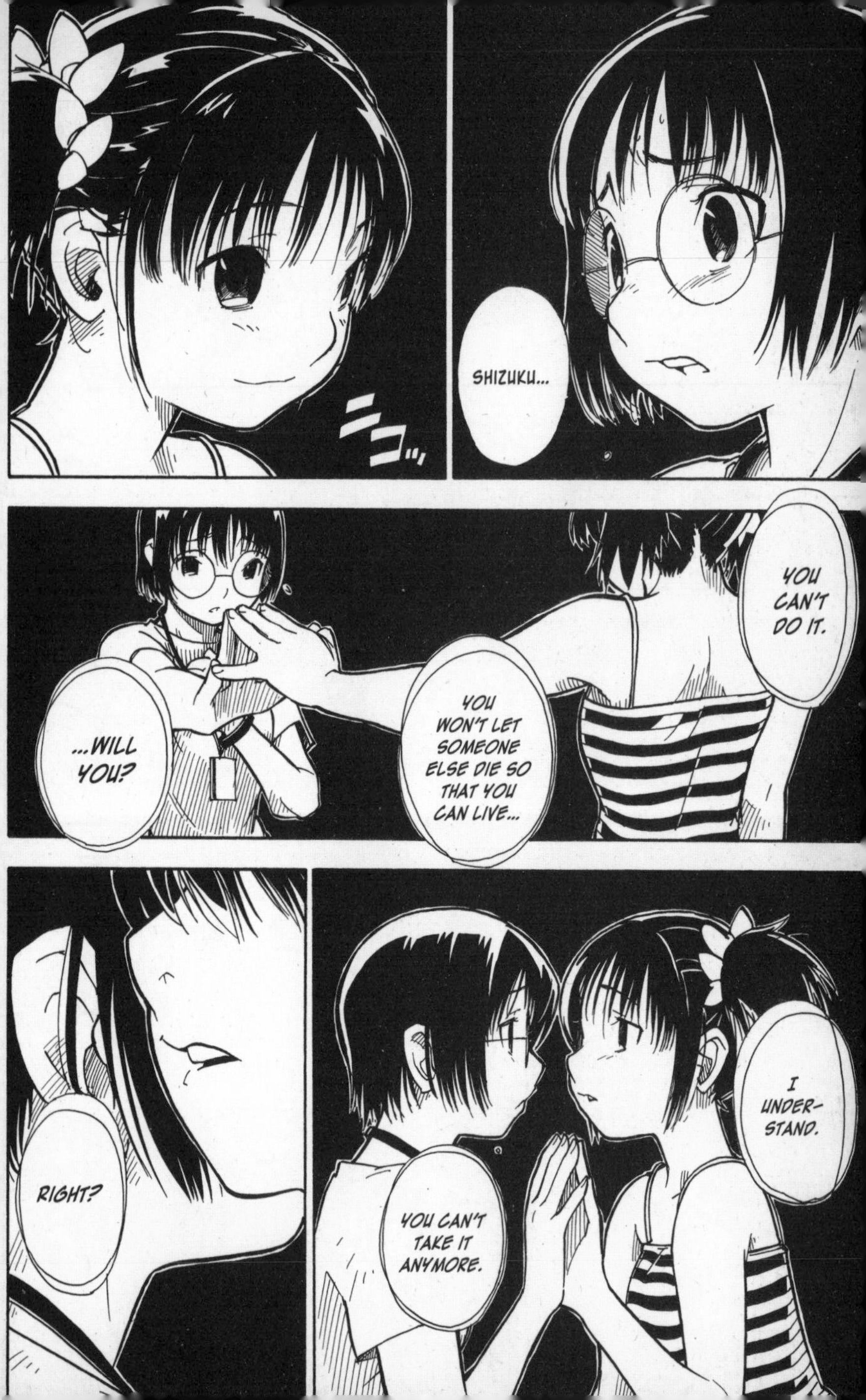
SHIZUKU...
ニコッ
YOU CAN'T DO IT.
YOU WON'T LET SOMEONE ELSE DIE SO THAT YOU CAN LIVE...
...WILL YOU?
I UNDER-STAND.
YOU CAN'T TAKE IT ANYMORE.
RIGHT?

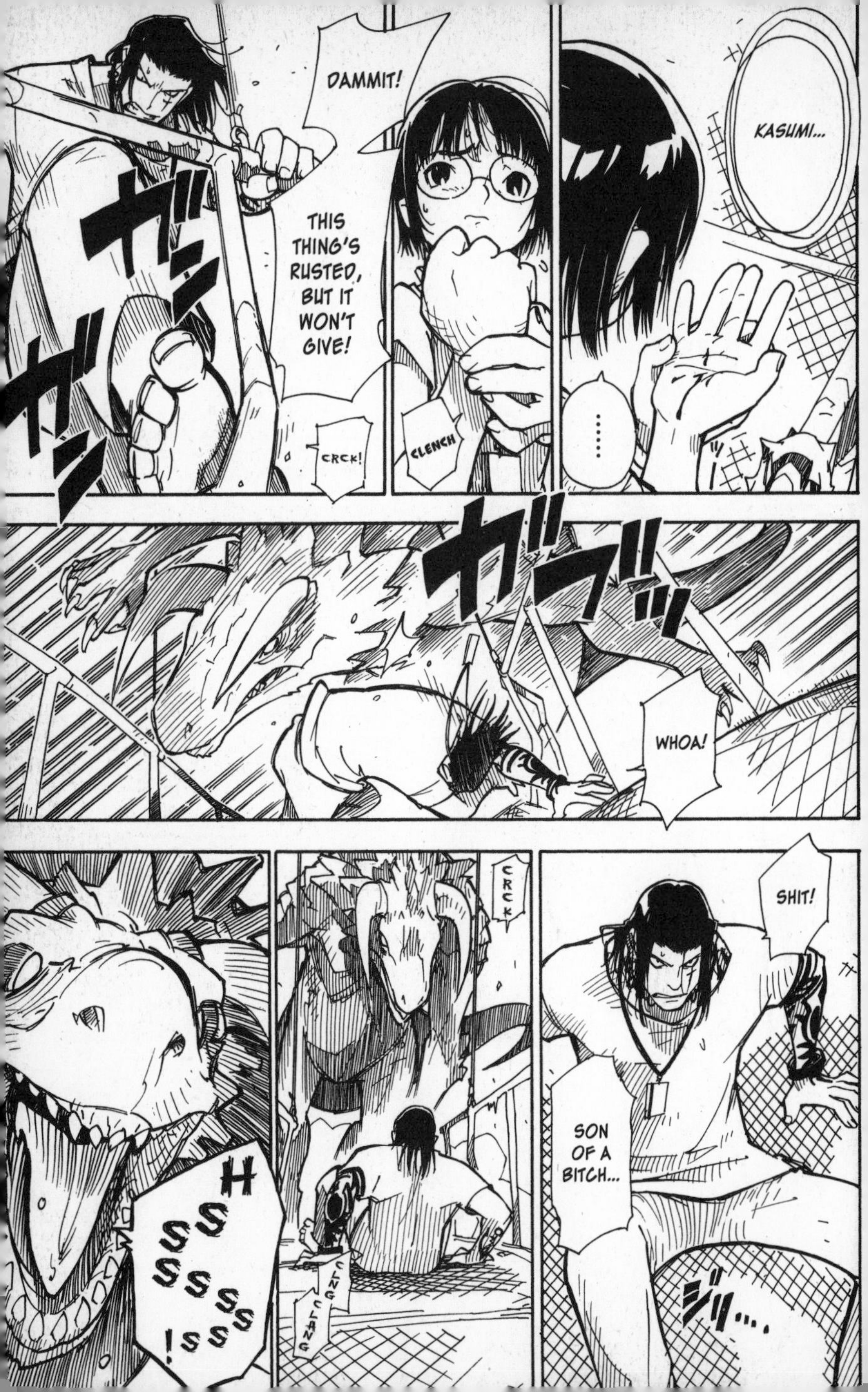
KASUMI...
......
CLENCH
DAMMIT!
THIS THING'S RUSTED, BUT IT WON'T GIVE!
CRCK!
WHOA!
SHIT!
SON OF A BITCH...
CRCK
CLNG
CLANG
CLANG
HSSSSSSSSSSS!

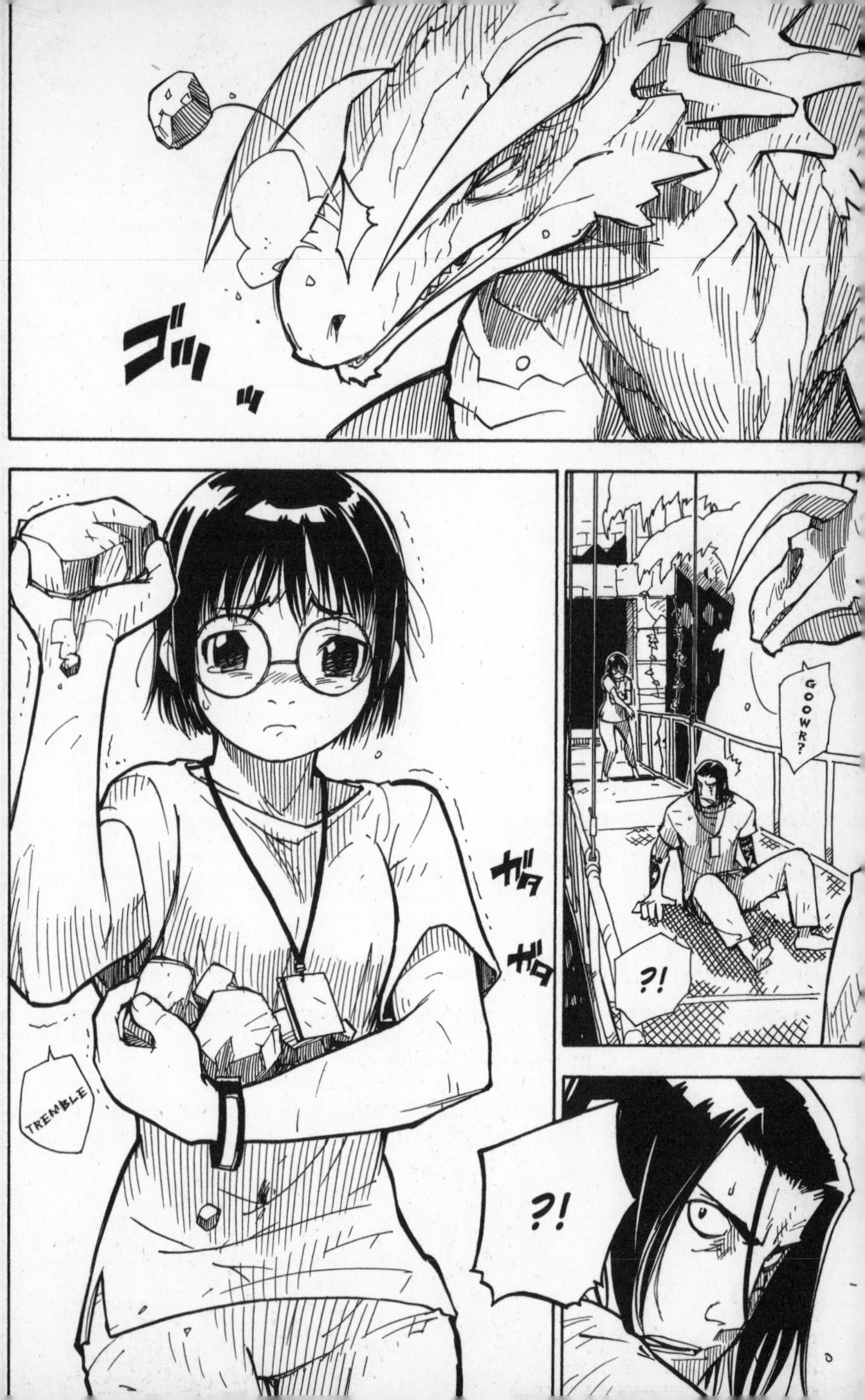
ゴッッ
GOOOWR?
?!
?!
ガタ
ガタ
TREMBLE

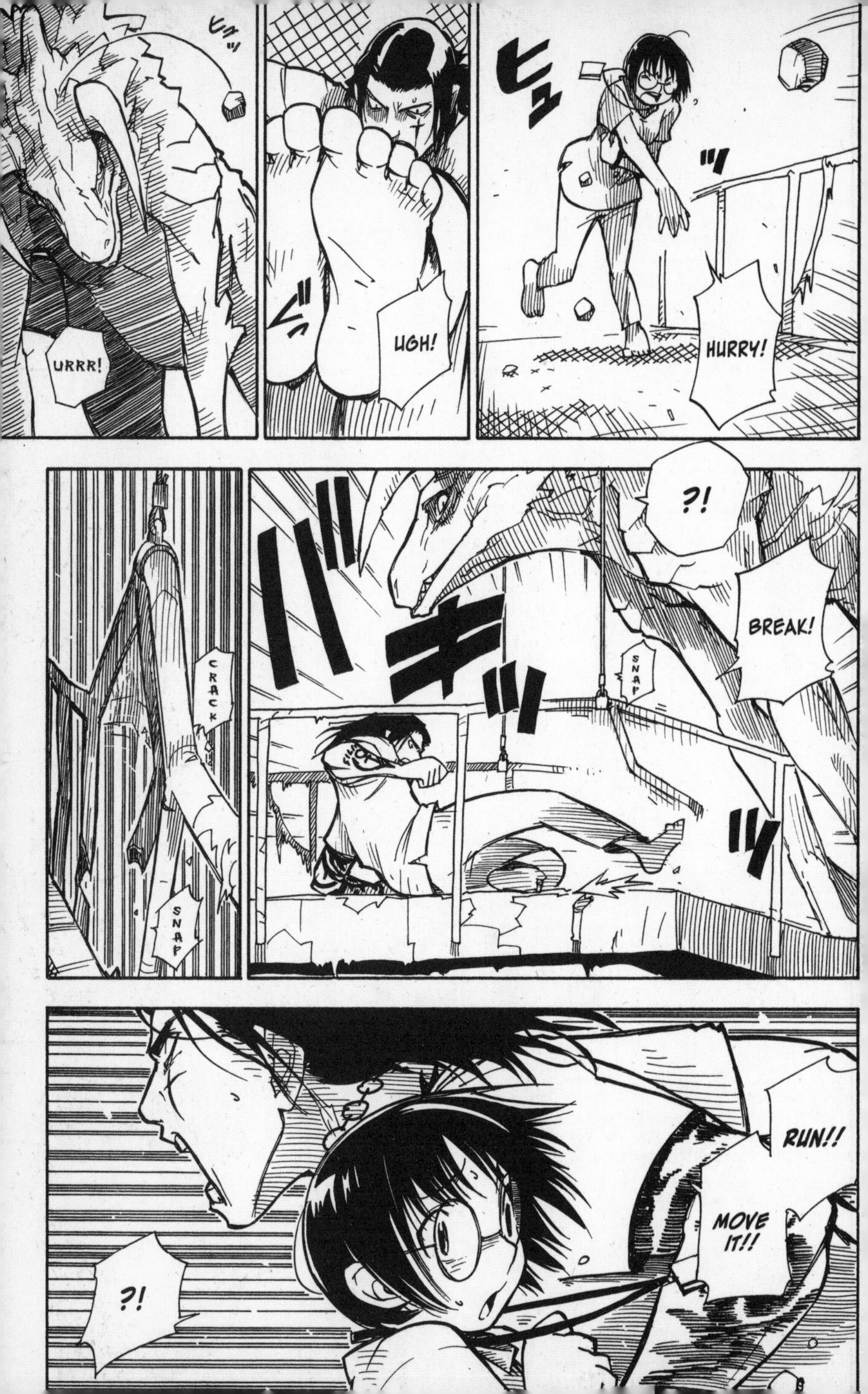
ヒュ
HURRY!
UGH!
URRR!
?!
BREAK!
バキッ
SNAP
CRACK
SNAP
RUN!!
MOVE IT!!
?!

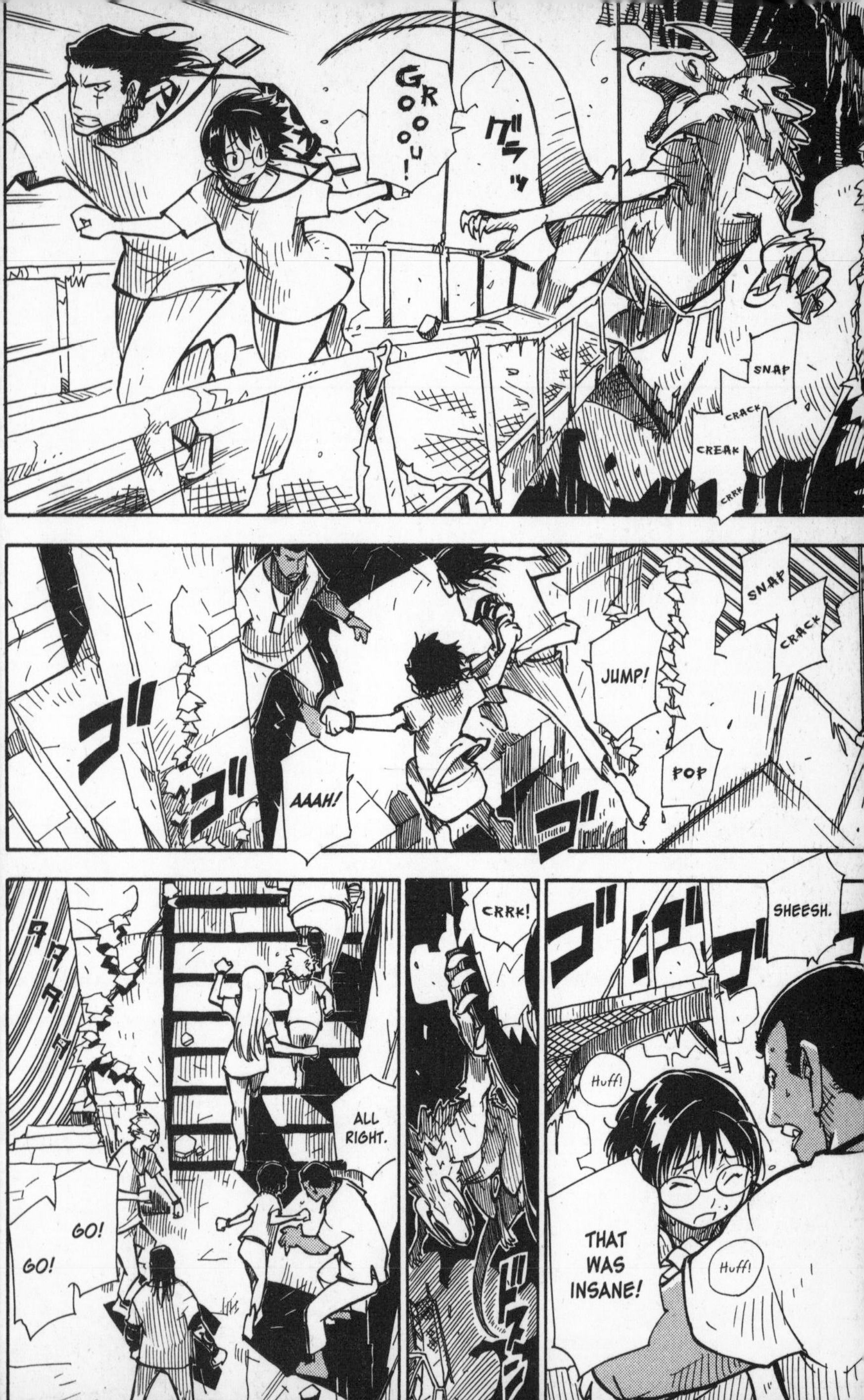
GROOOU!
グラッ
SNAP
CRACK
CREAK
CRRK
SNAP
CRACK
JUMP!
POP
AAAH!
SHEESH.
Huff!
THAT WAS INSANE!
Huff!
CRRK!
ALL RIGHT.
GO!
GO!

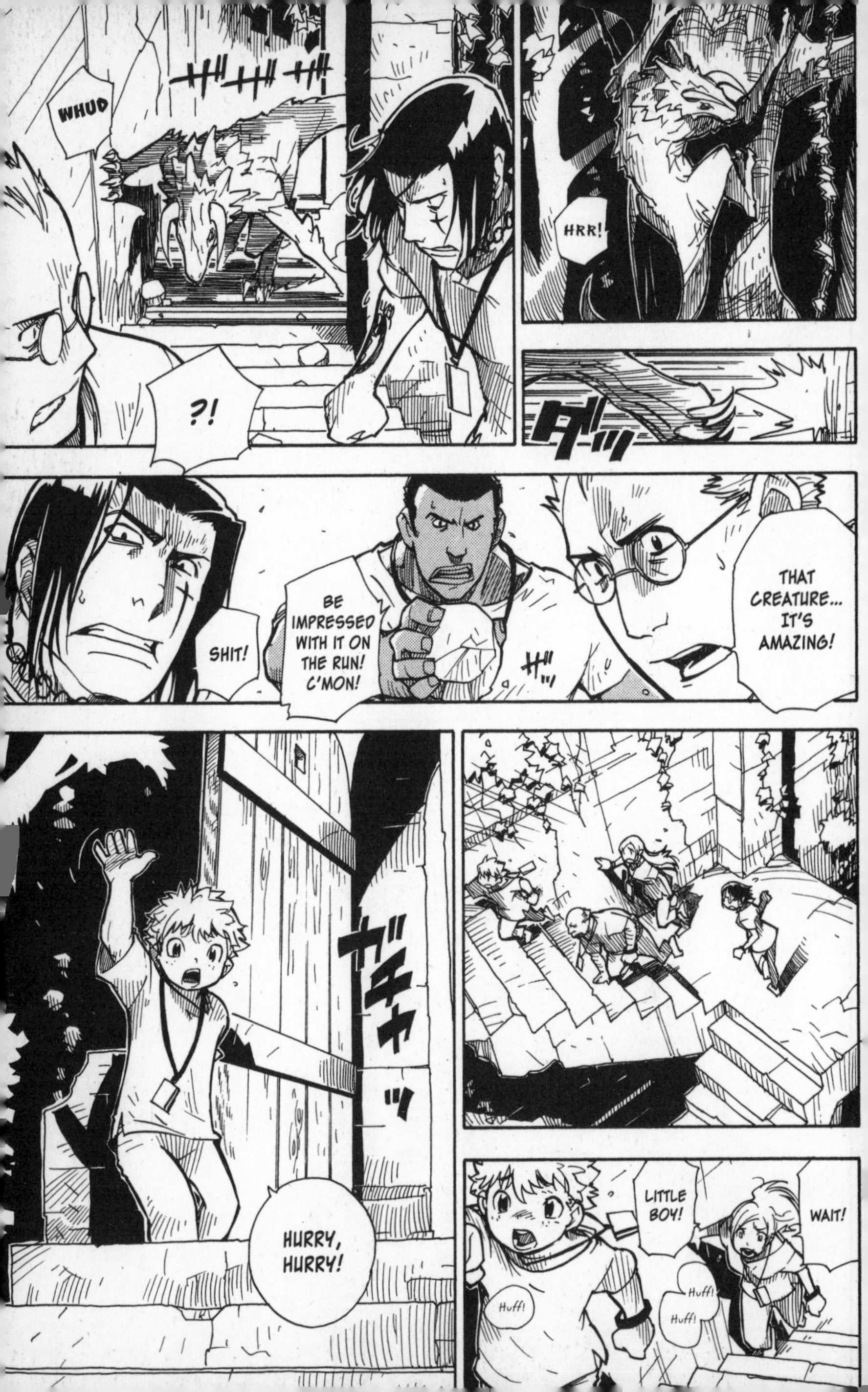
HRR!
ダッ
WHUD
?!
THAT CREATURE... IT'S AMAZING!
BE IMPRESSED WITH IT ON THE RUN! C'MON!
SHIT!
WAIT!
LITTLE BOY!
Huff!
Huff!
Huff!
ガチャッ
HURRY, HURRY!

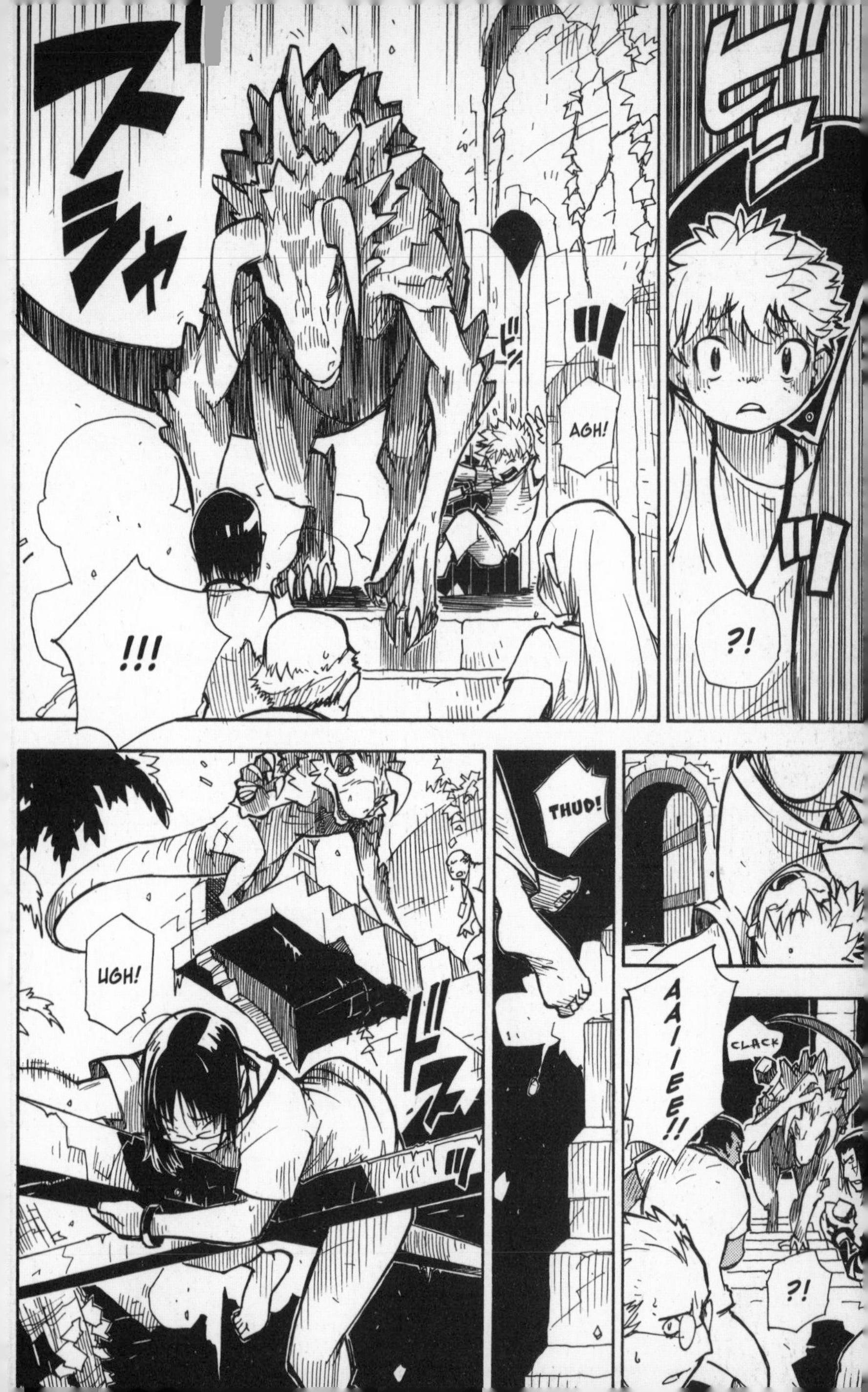
?!
AGH!
!!!
AAIIEEE!!
CLACK
?!
THUD!
UGH!

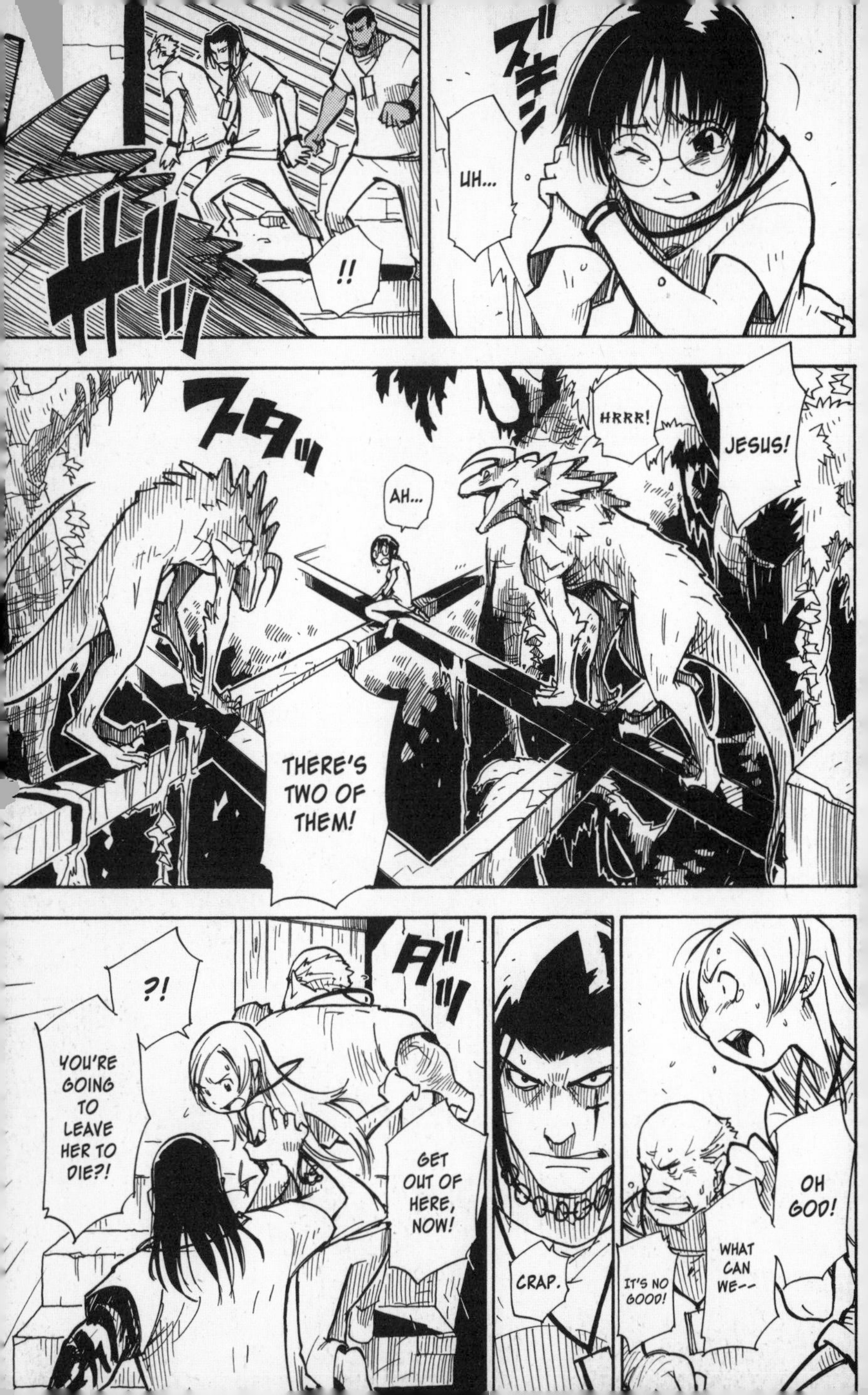
UH...
!!
JESUS!
HRRR!
AH...
THERE'S TWO OF THEM!
OH GOD!
WHAT CAN WE--
IT'S NO GOOD!
CRAP.
?!
GET OUT OF HERE, NOW!
YOU'RE GOING TO LEAVE HER TO DIE?!

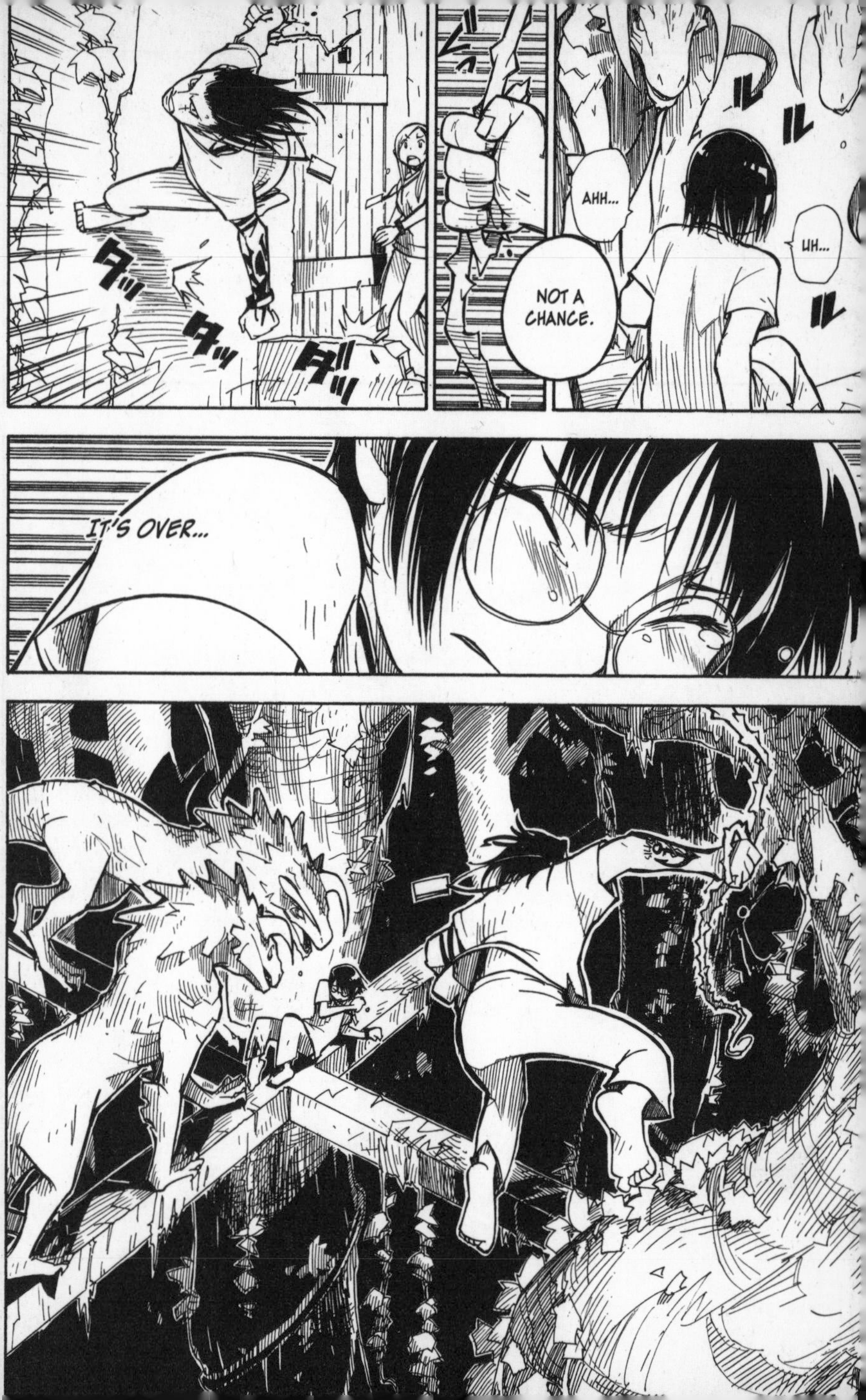
AHH...
UH...
NOT A CHANCE.
タッ
タッ
ダッ
IT'S OVER...

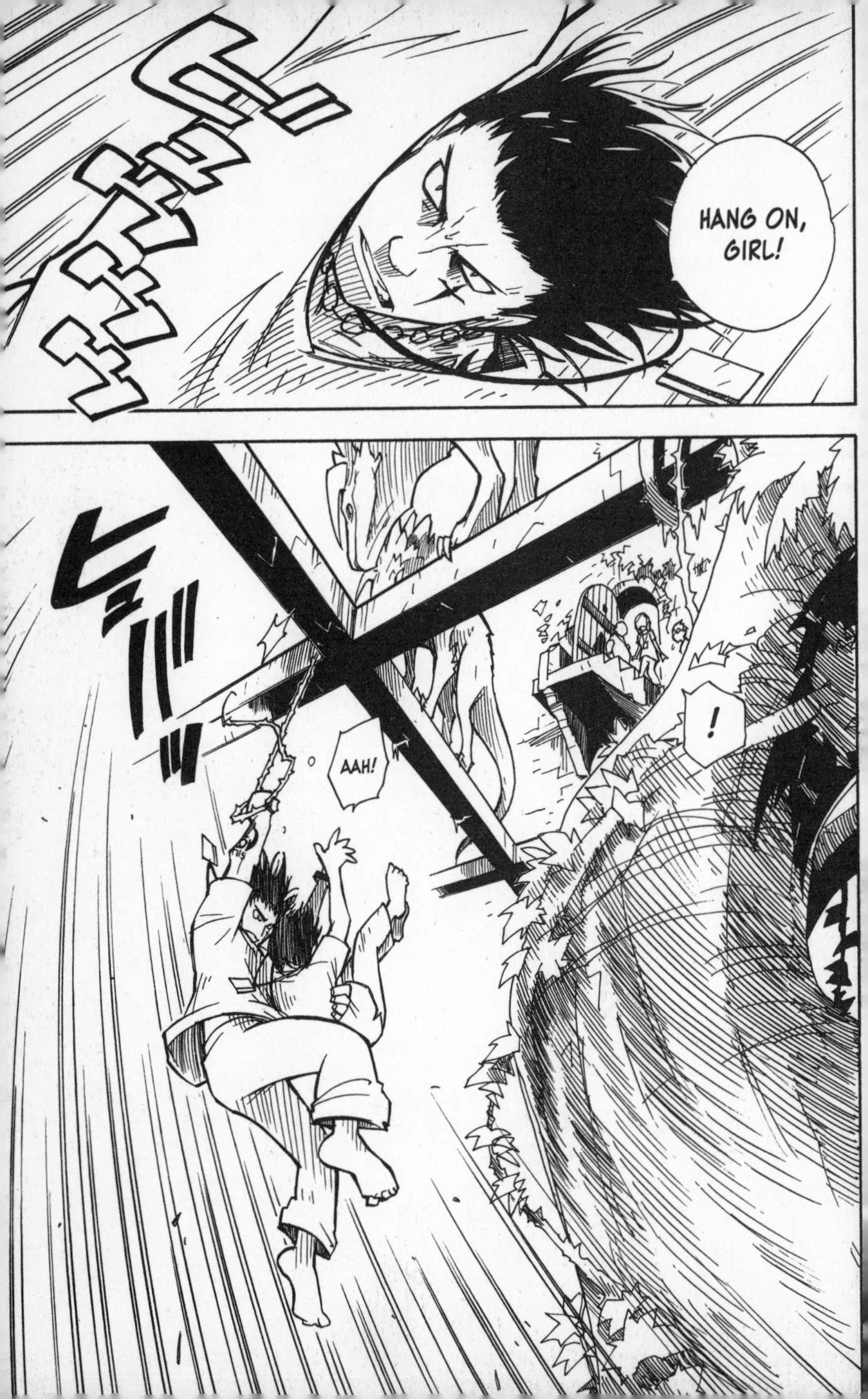
HANG ON, GIRL!
!
AAH!

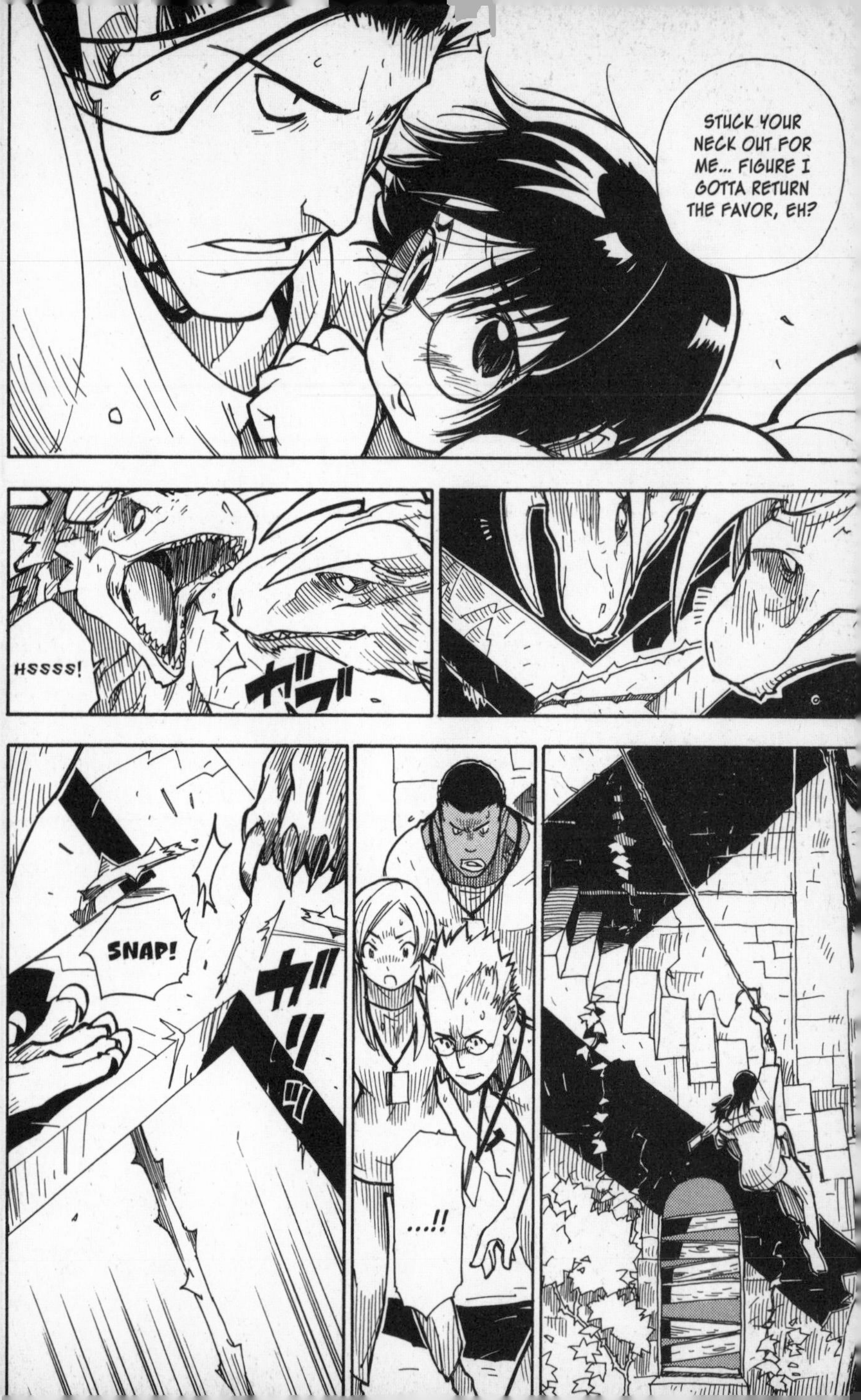
STUCK YOUR NECK OUT FOR ME... FIGURE I GOTTA RETURN THE FAVOR, EH?
HSSSS!
...!!
SNAP!

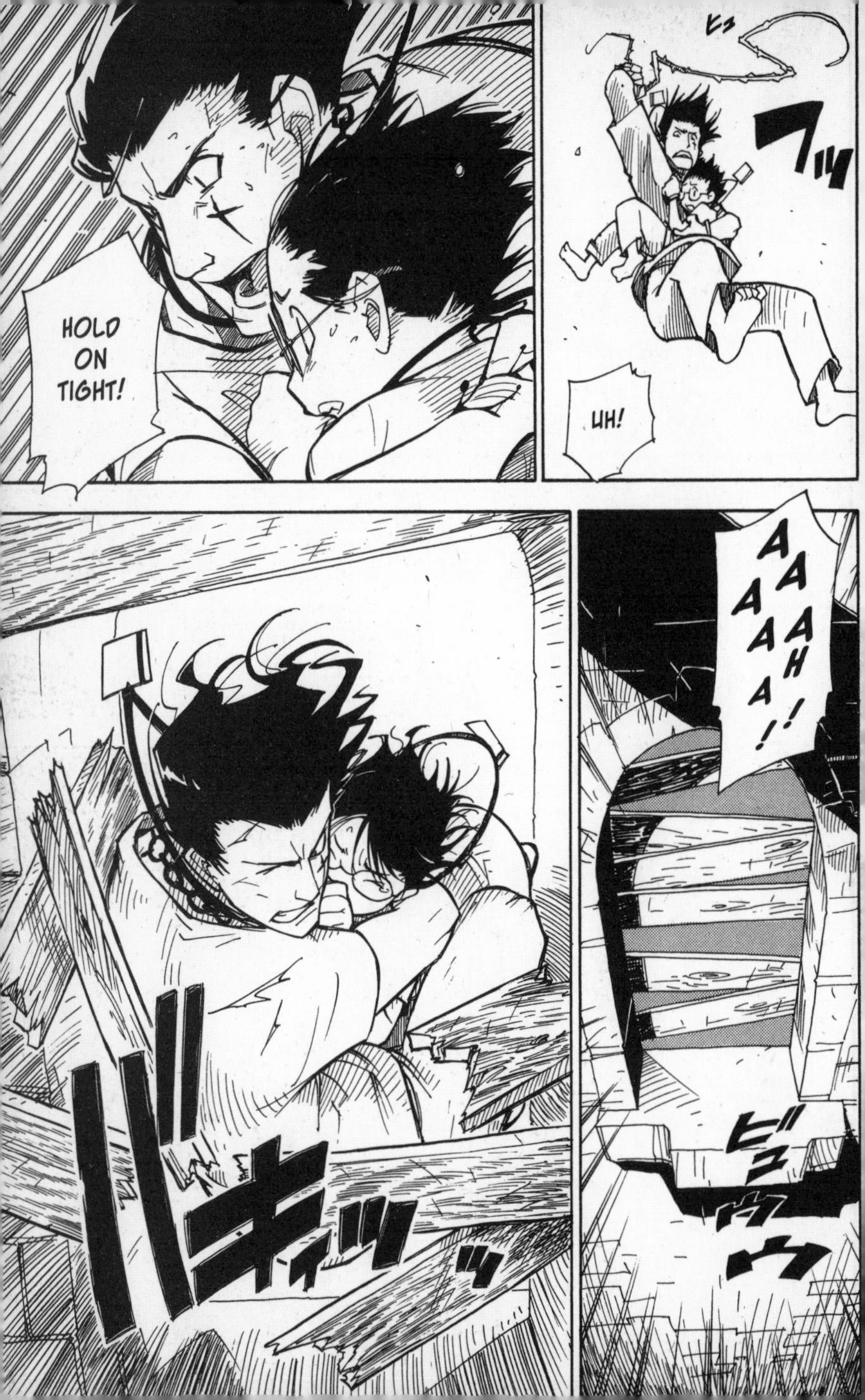
UH!
HOLD ON TIGHT!
AAAAAAHA!!

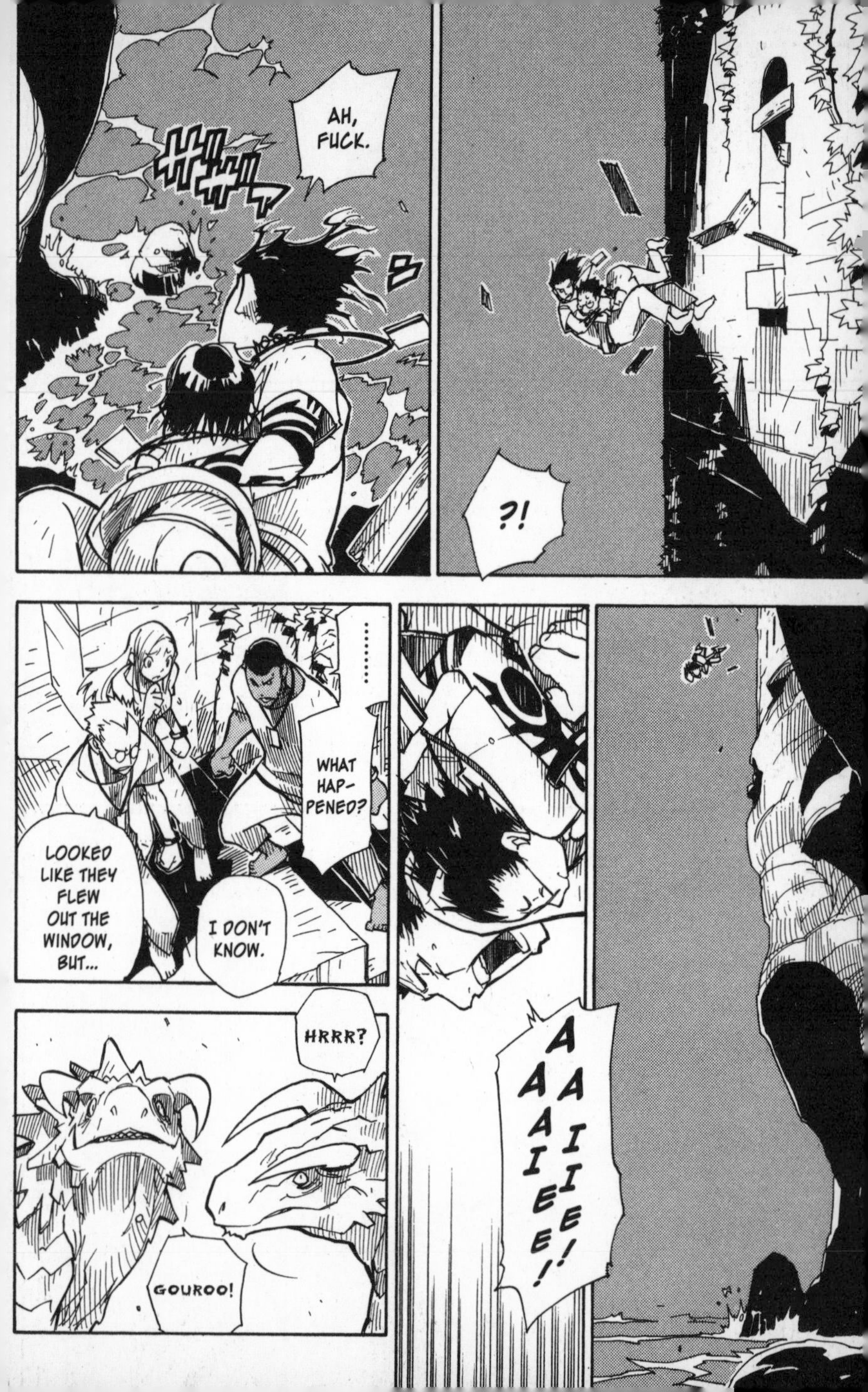
?!
AH, FUCK.
AAIIE!
AAIEE!
......
WHAT HAP-PENED?
LOOKED LIKE THEY FLEW OUT THE WINDOW, BUT...
I DON'T KNOW.
HRRR?
GOUROO!

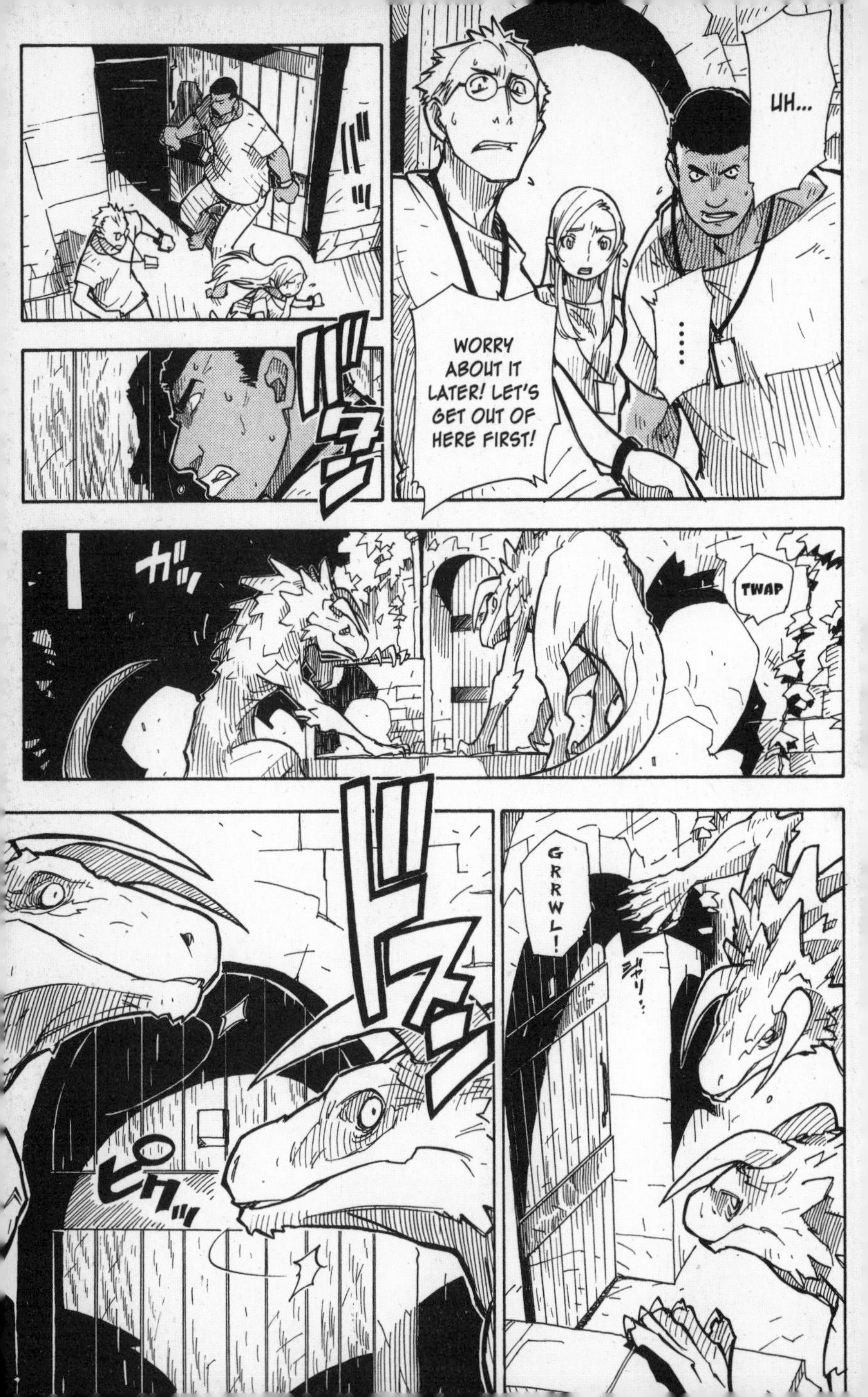
UH...
......
WORRY ABOUT IT LATER! LET'S GET OUT OF HERE FIRST!
TWAP
GRRWL!

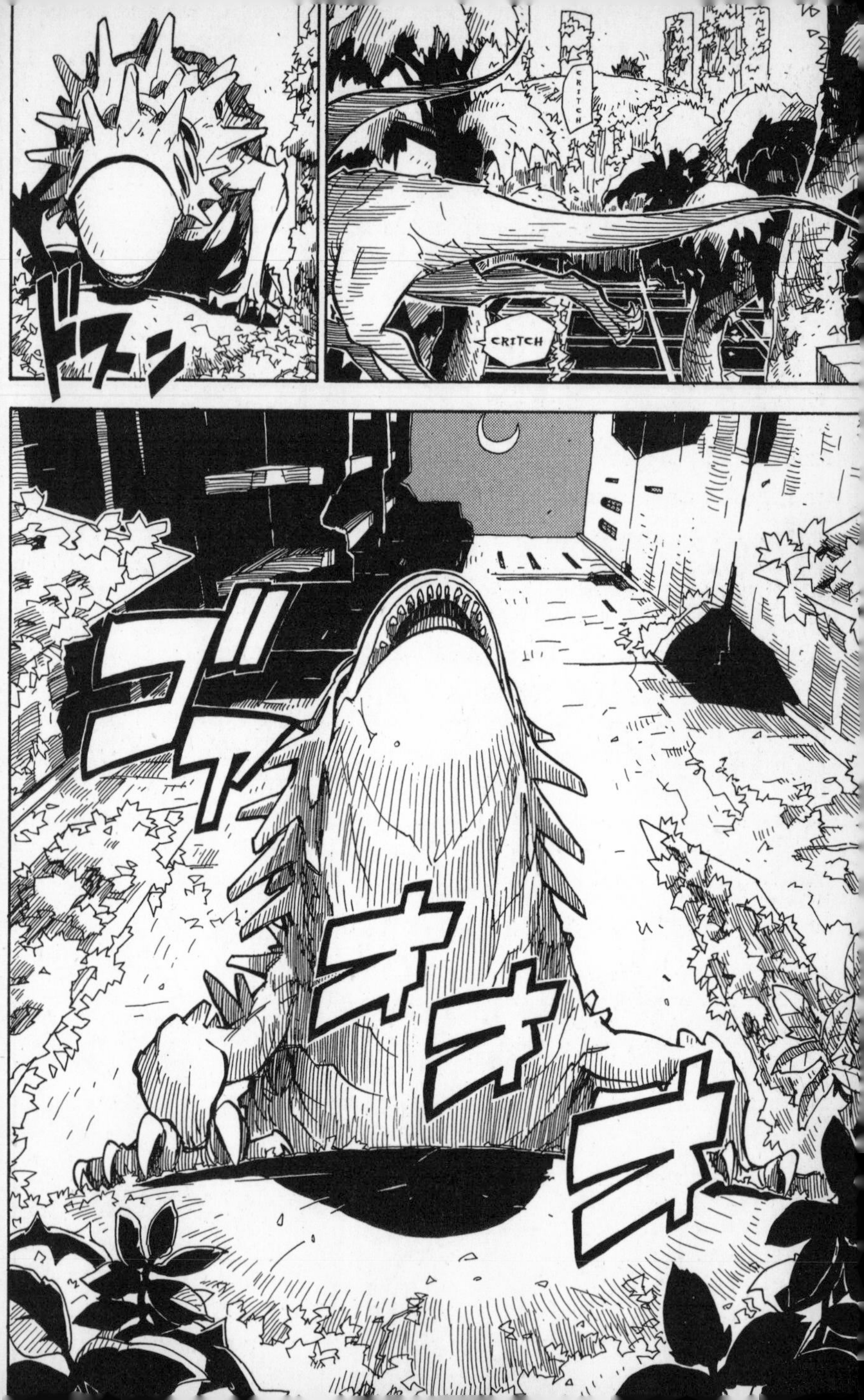
CRITCH
CRITCH
ドスン
ゴァオオオ

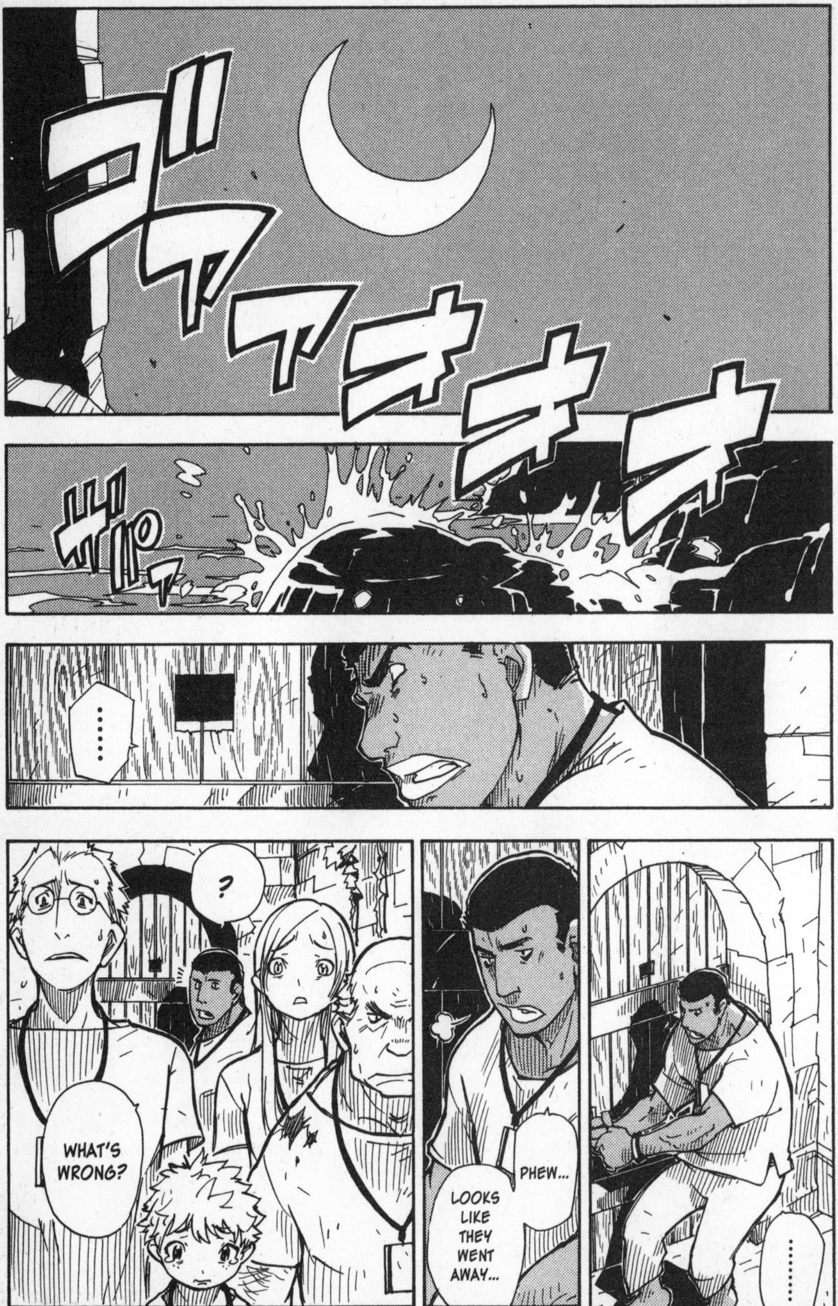

ゴファァオオオ
ザパァ
……
……
PHEW...
LOOKS LIKE THEY WENT AWAY...
?
WHAT'S WRONG?

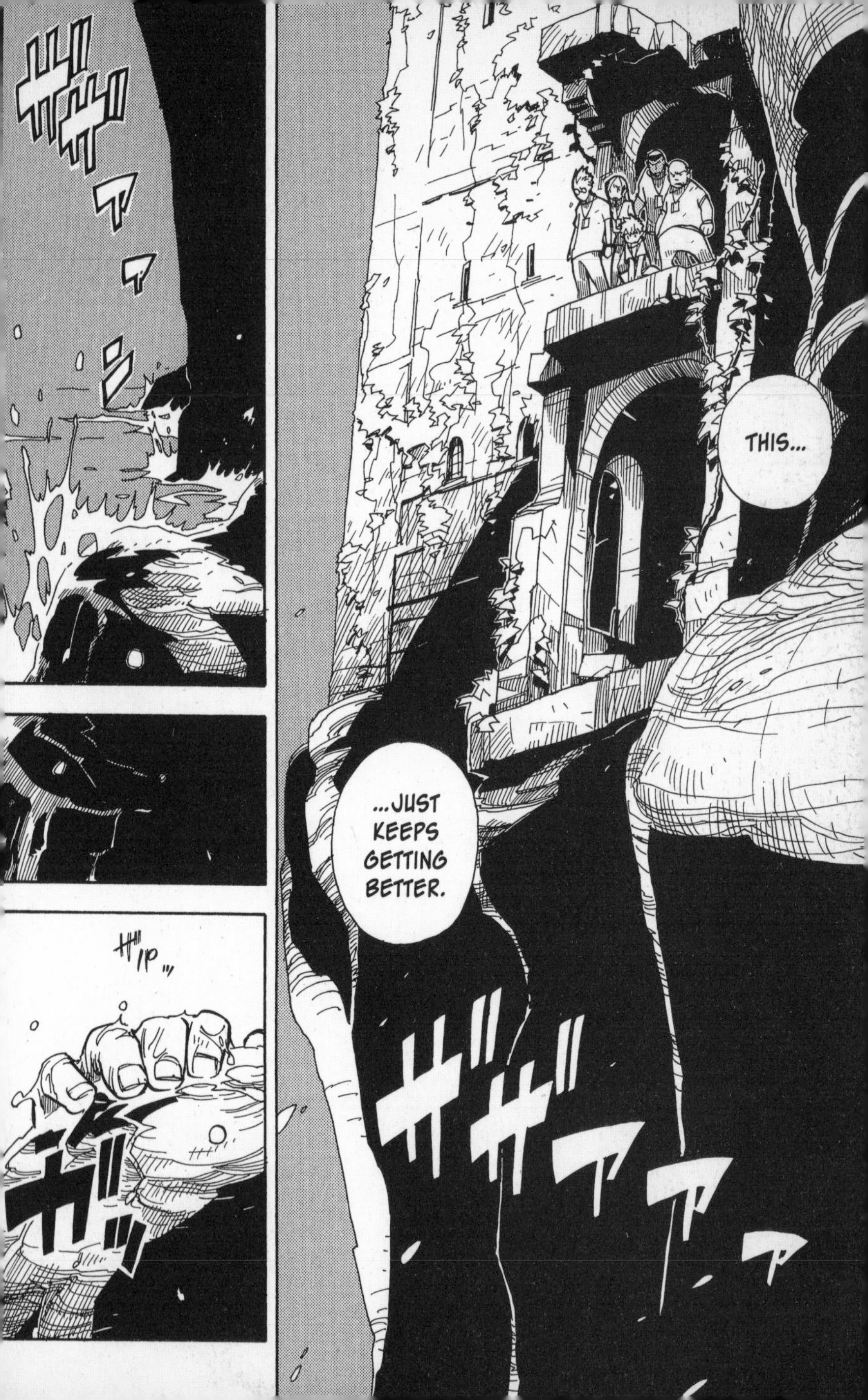
THIS...
...JUST KEEPS GETTING BETTER.

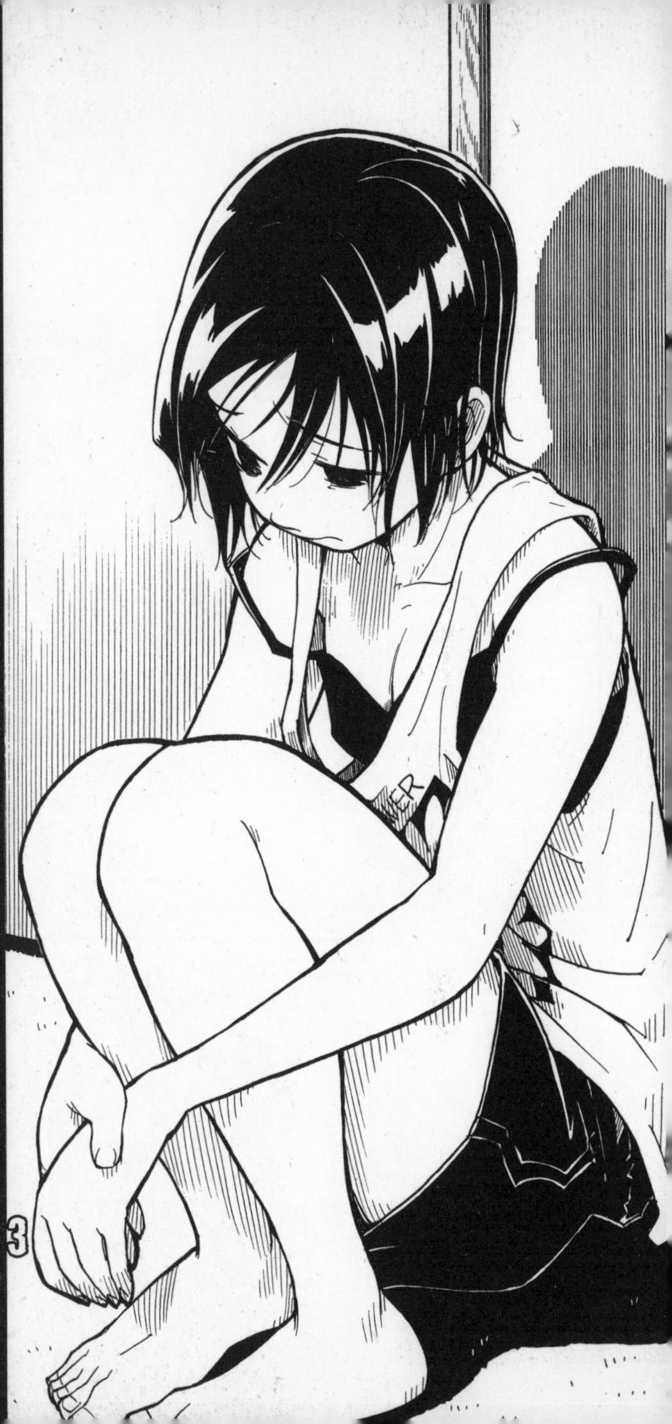

CHAPTER 3
THAT DAY

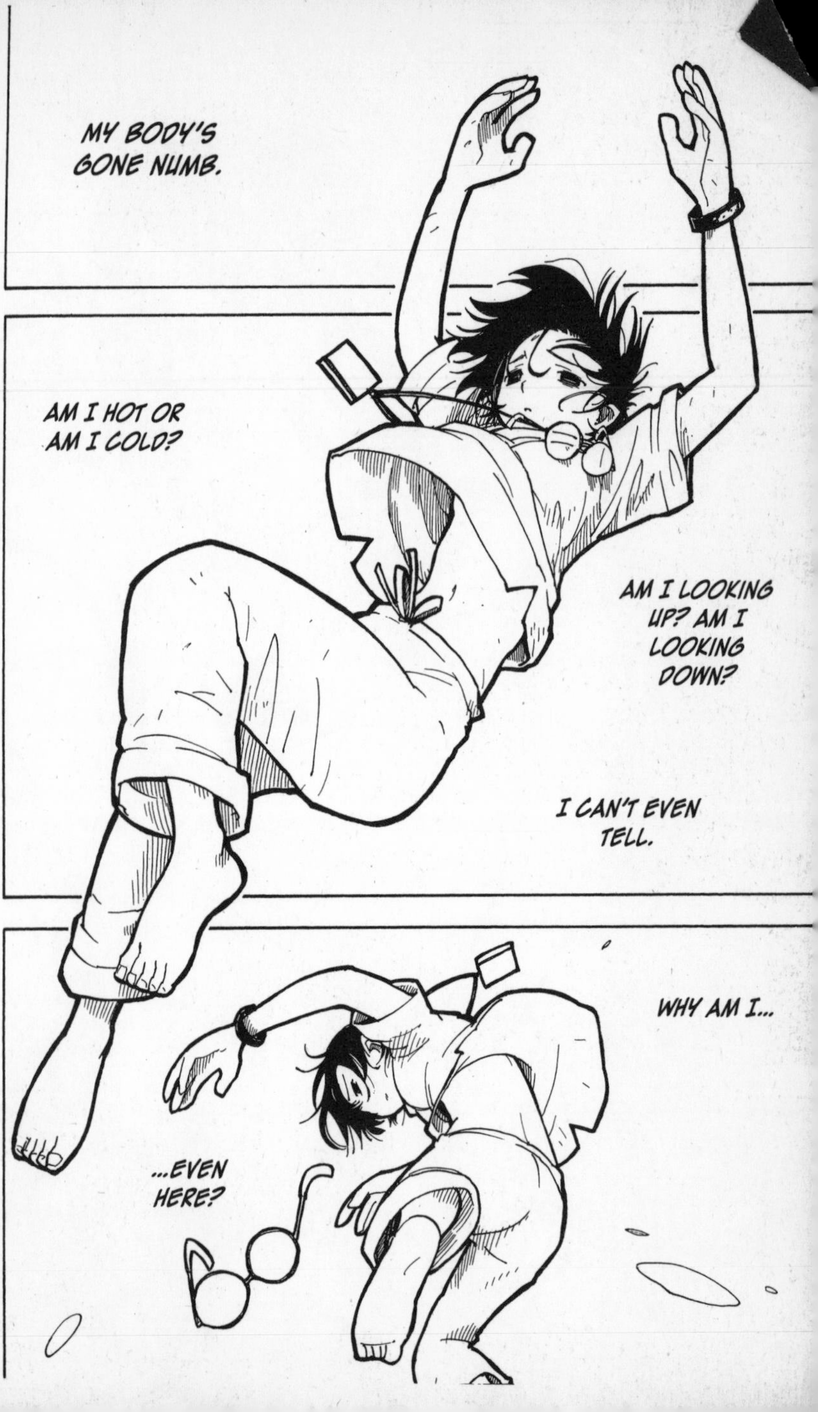
MY BODY'S GONE NUMB.
AM I HOT OR AM I COLD?
AM I LOOKING UP? AM I LOOKING DOWN?
I CAN'T EVEN TELL.
WHY AM I...
...EVEN HERE?

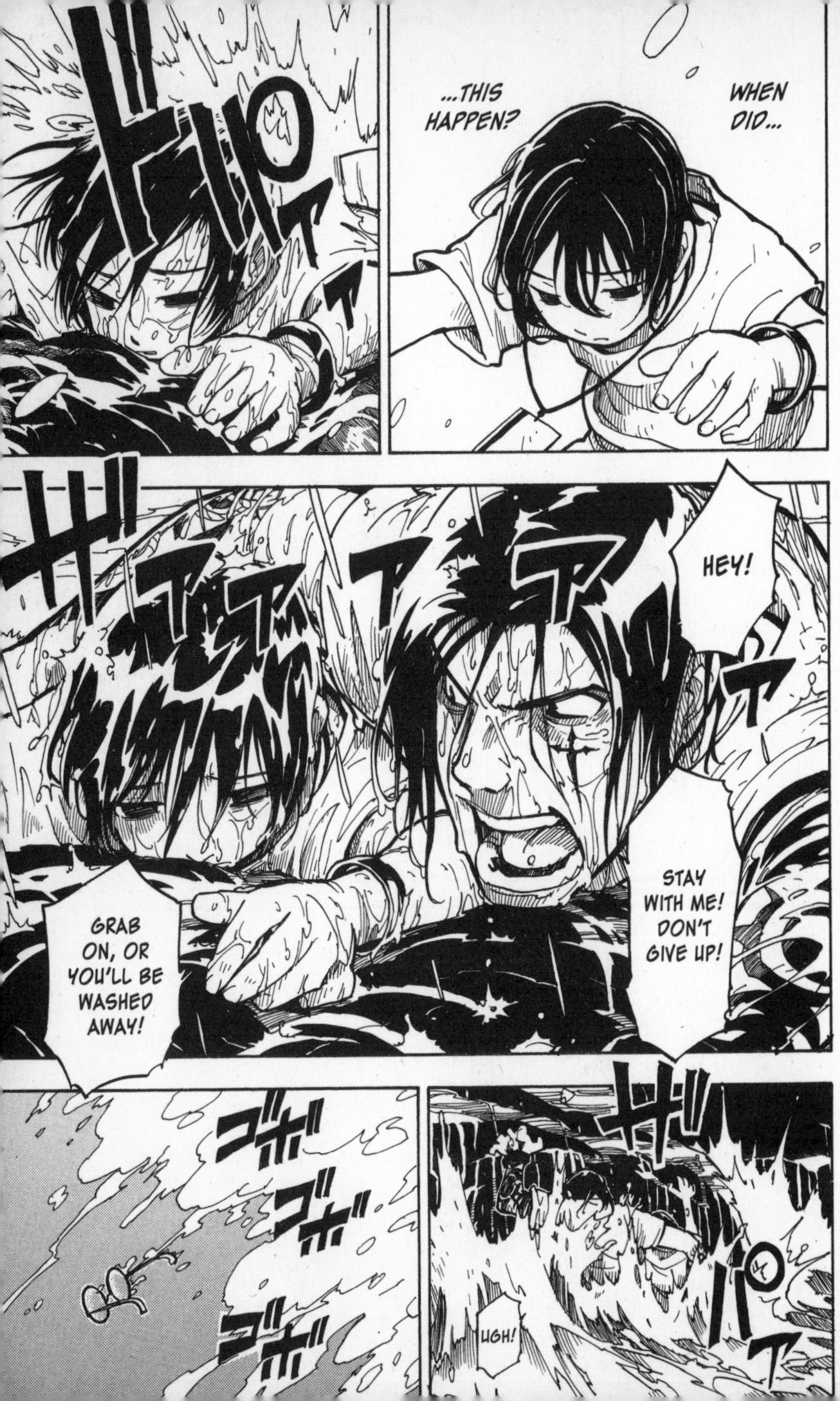
WHEN DID...
...THIS HAPPEN?
HEY!
STAY WITH ME! DON'T GIVE UP!
GRAB ON, OR YOU'LL BE WASHED AWAY!
UGH!

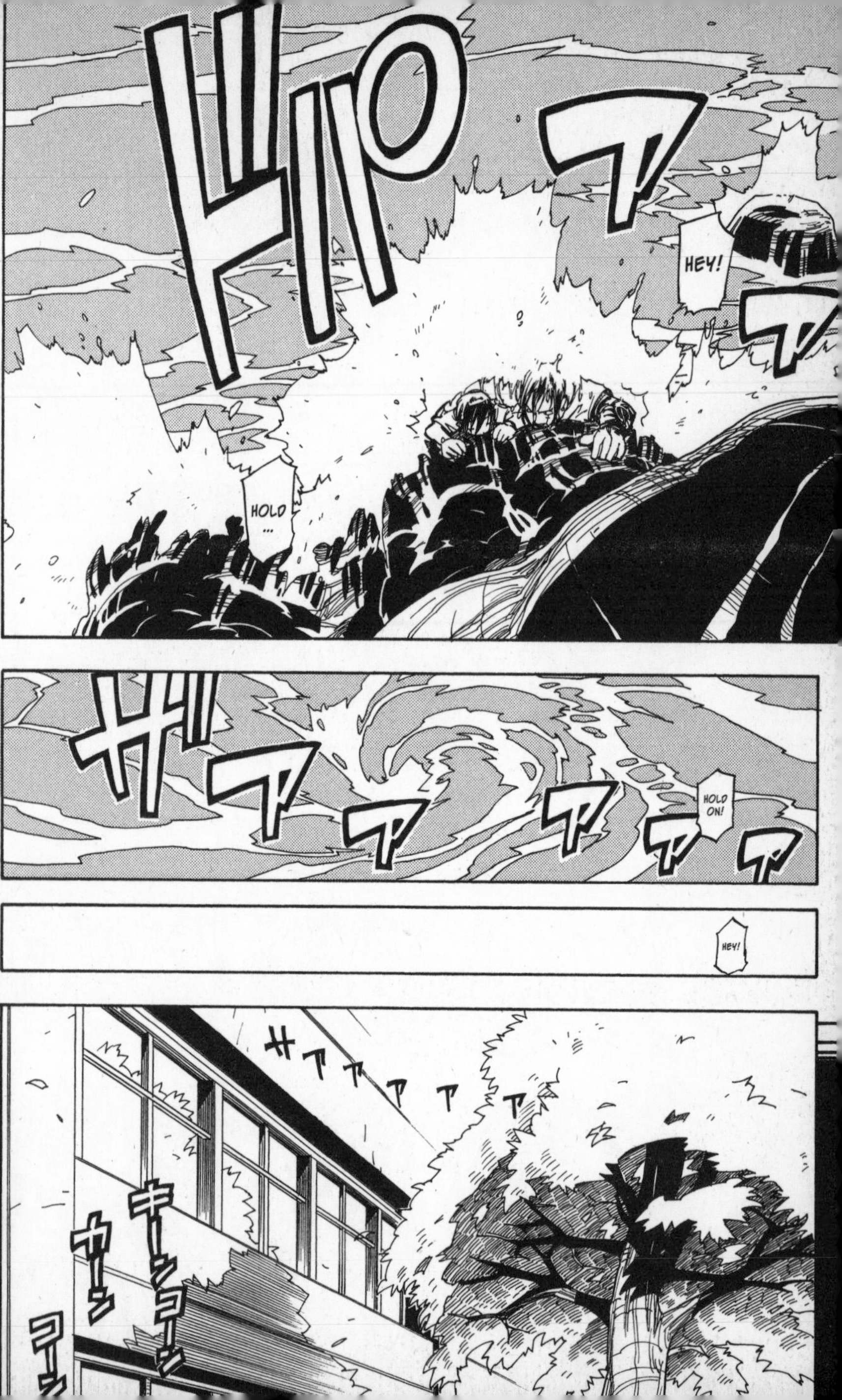
ドッパァァ
HEY!
HOLD ...
ザァァァァァァ
HOLD ON!
HEY!
サァァァァァ
キーンコーン
カーン

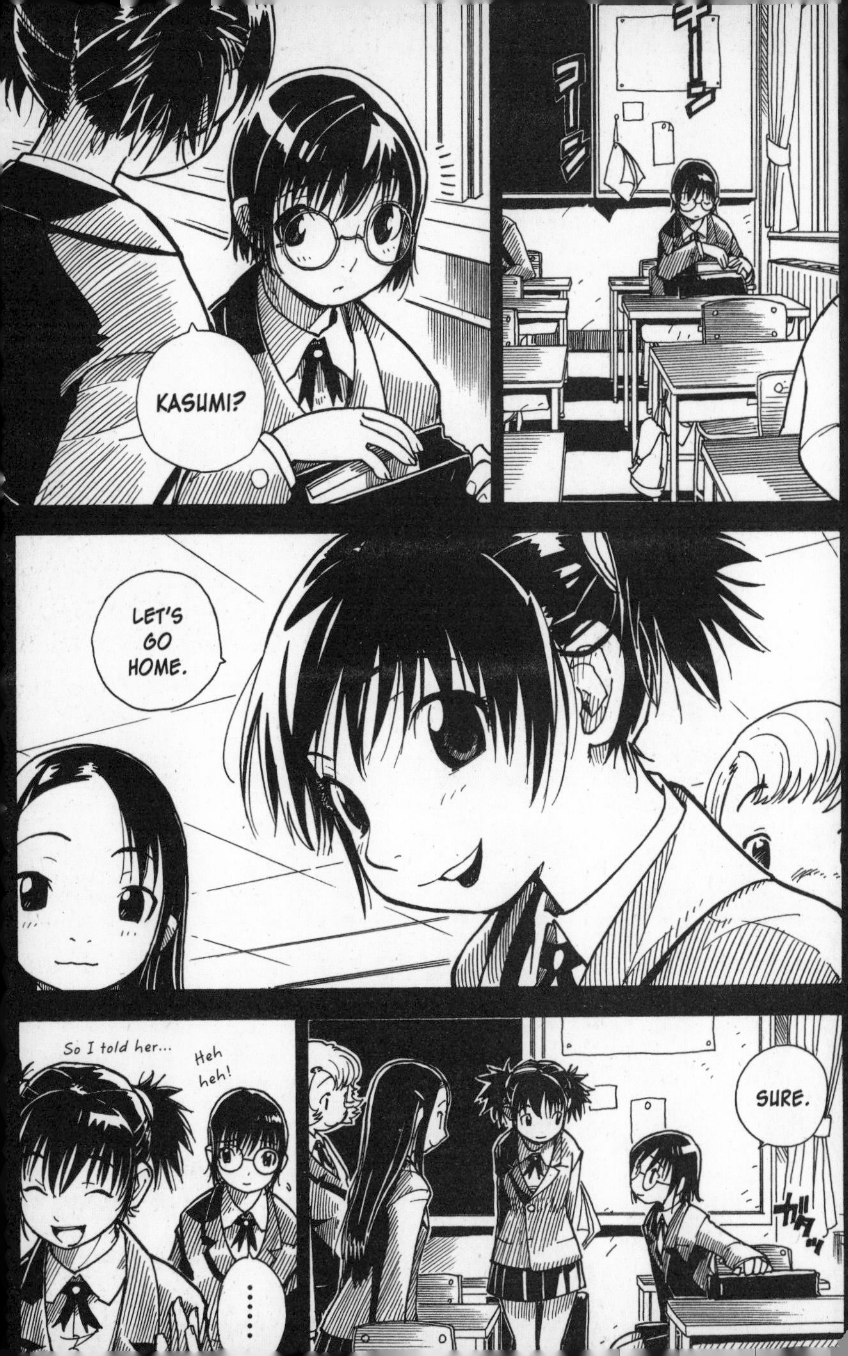
KASUMI?
LET'S GO HOME.
SURE.
So I told her...
Heh heh!
......

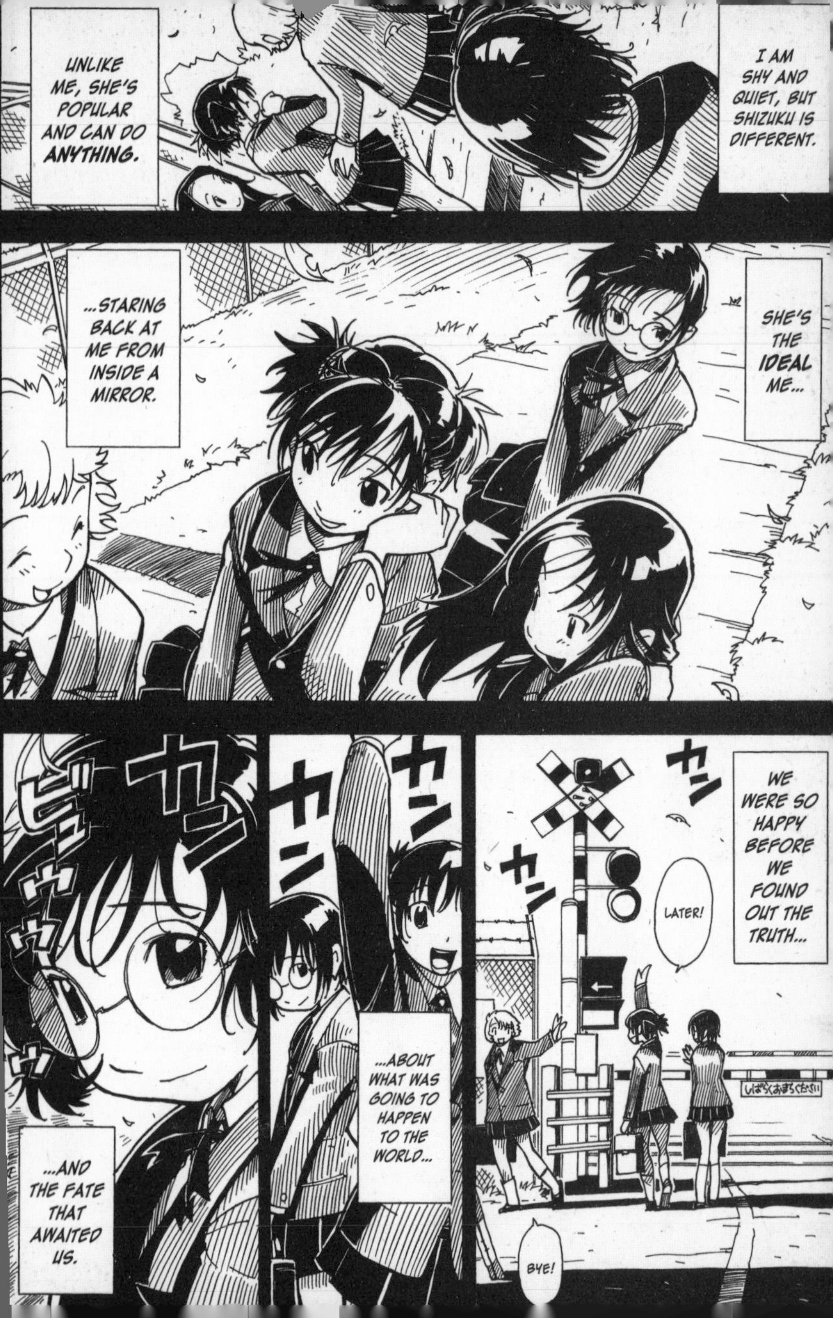
I AM SHY AND QUIET, BUT SHIZUKU IS DIFFERENT.
UNLIKE ME, SHE'S POPULAR AND CAN DO **ANYTHING.**
SHE'S THE **IDEAL** ME...
...STARING BACK AT ME FROM INSIDE A MIRROR.
WE WERE SO HAPPY BEFORE WE FOUND OUT THE TRUTH...
カン
カン
LATER!
しばらくおまちください
BYE!
カン
カン
...ABOUT WHAT WAS GOING TO HAPPEN TO THE WORLD...
カン
ビュウウウ
...AND THE FATE THAT AWAITED US.

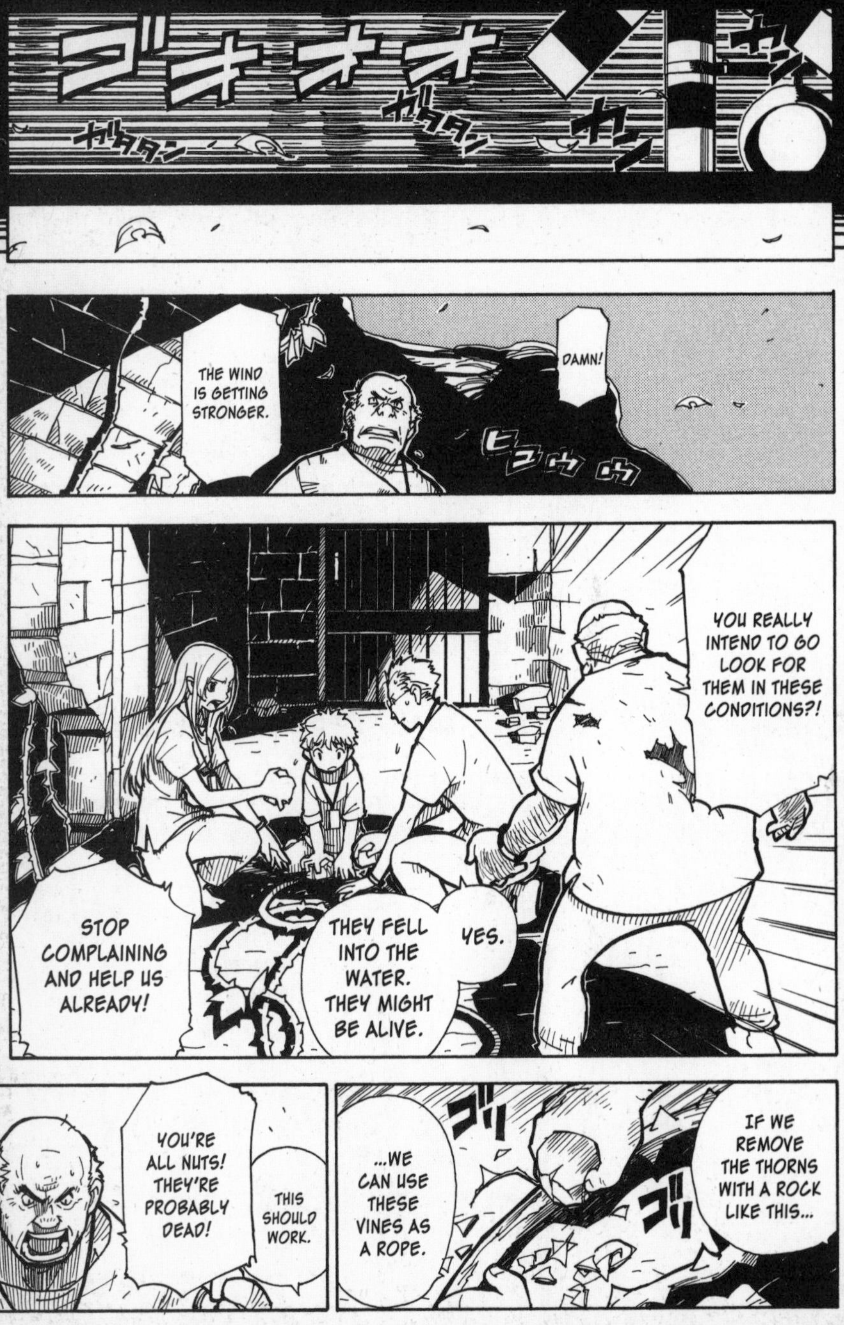
ゴオオオ
ガタタン
ガタタン
DAMN!
THE WIND IS GETTING STRONGER.
ヒュウウ
YOU REALLY INTEND TO GO LOOK FOR THEM IN THESE CONDITIONS?!
YES.
THEY FELL INTO THE WATER. THEY MIGHT BE ALIVE.
STOP COMPLAINING AND HELP US ALREADY!
IF WE REMOVE THE THORNS WITH A ROCK LIKE THIS...
ゴリ
ゴリ
...WE CAN USE THESE VINES AS A ROPE.
THIS SHOULD WORK.
YOU'RE ALL NUTS! THEY'RE PROBABLY DEAD!

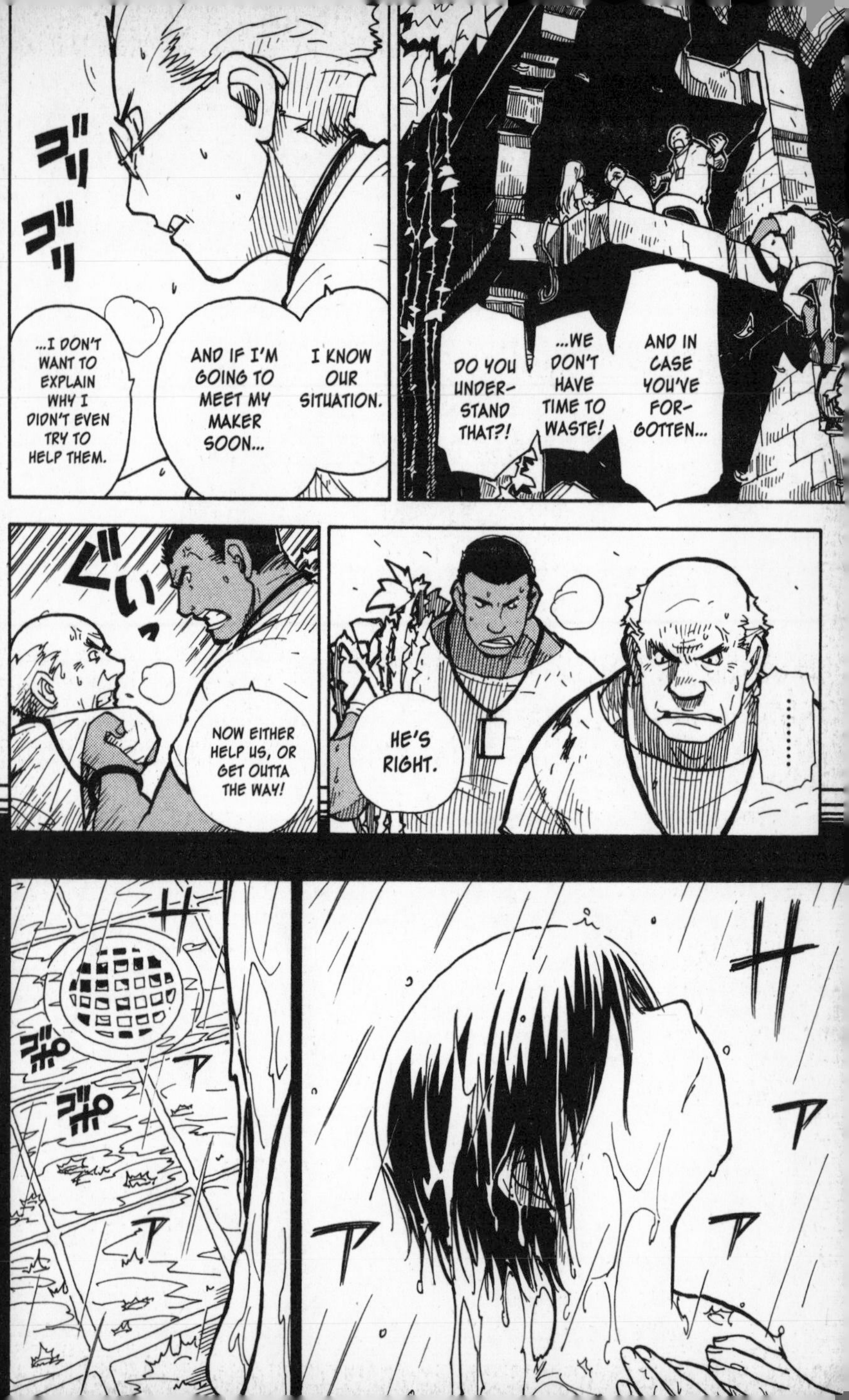
AND IN CASE YOU'VE FOR-GOTTEN...
...WE DON'T HAVE TIME TO WASTE!
DO YOU UNDER-STAND THAT?!
ゴリ ゴリ
I KNOW OUR SITUATION.
AND IF I'M GOING TO MEET MY MAKER SOON...
...I DON'T WANT TO EXPLAIN WHY I DIDN'T EVEN TRY TO HELP THEM.
......
HE'S RIGHT.
ぐいっ
NOW EITHER HELP US, OR GET OUTTA THE WAY!
ゴポ ゴポ

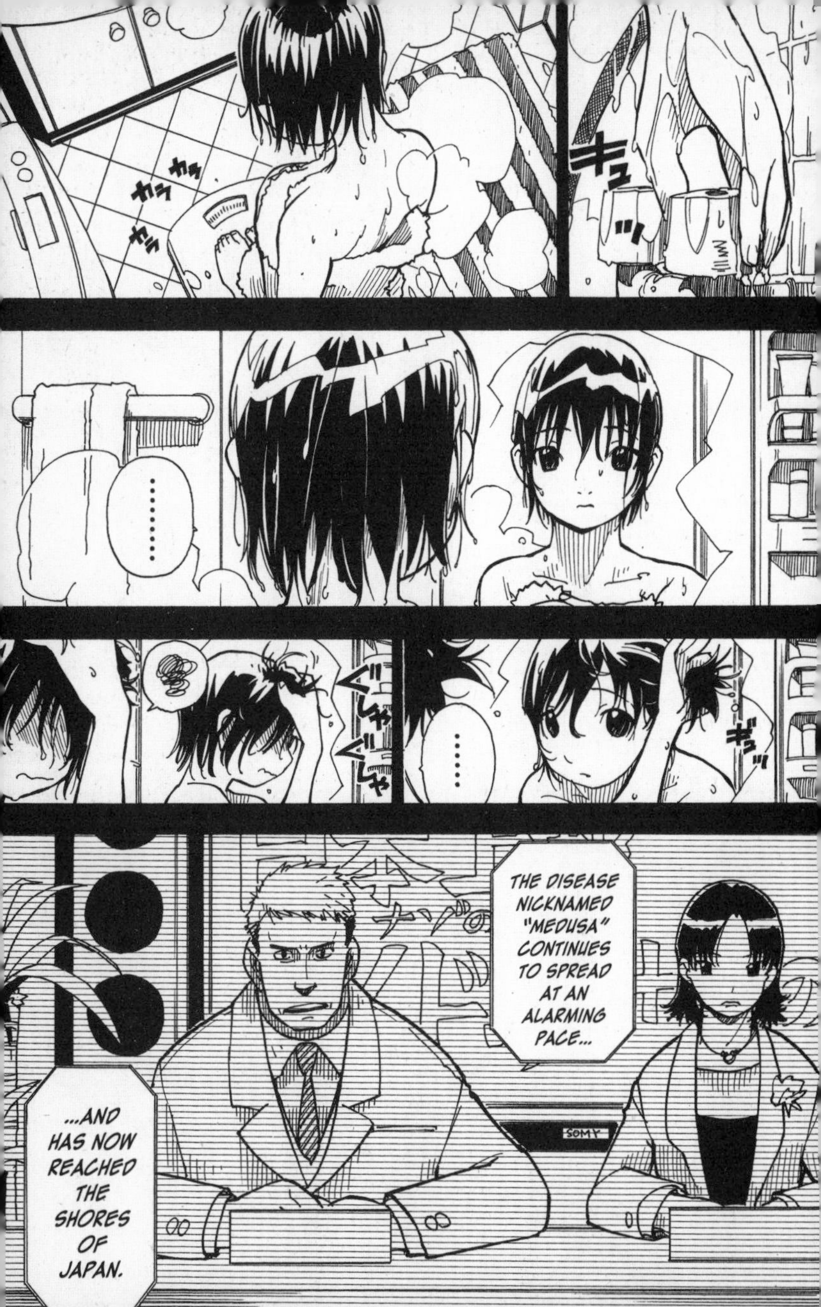

....
......
THE DISEASE NICKNAMED "MEDUSA" CONTINUES TO SPREAD AT AN ALARMING PACE...
...AND HAS NOW REACHED THE SHORES OF JAPAN.

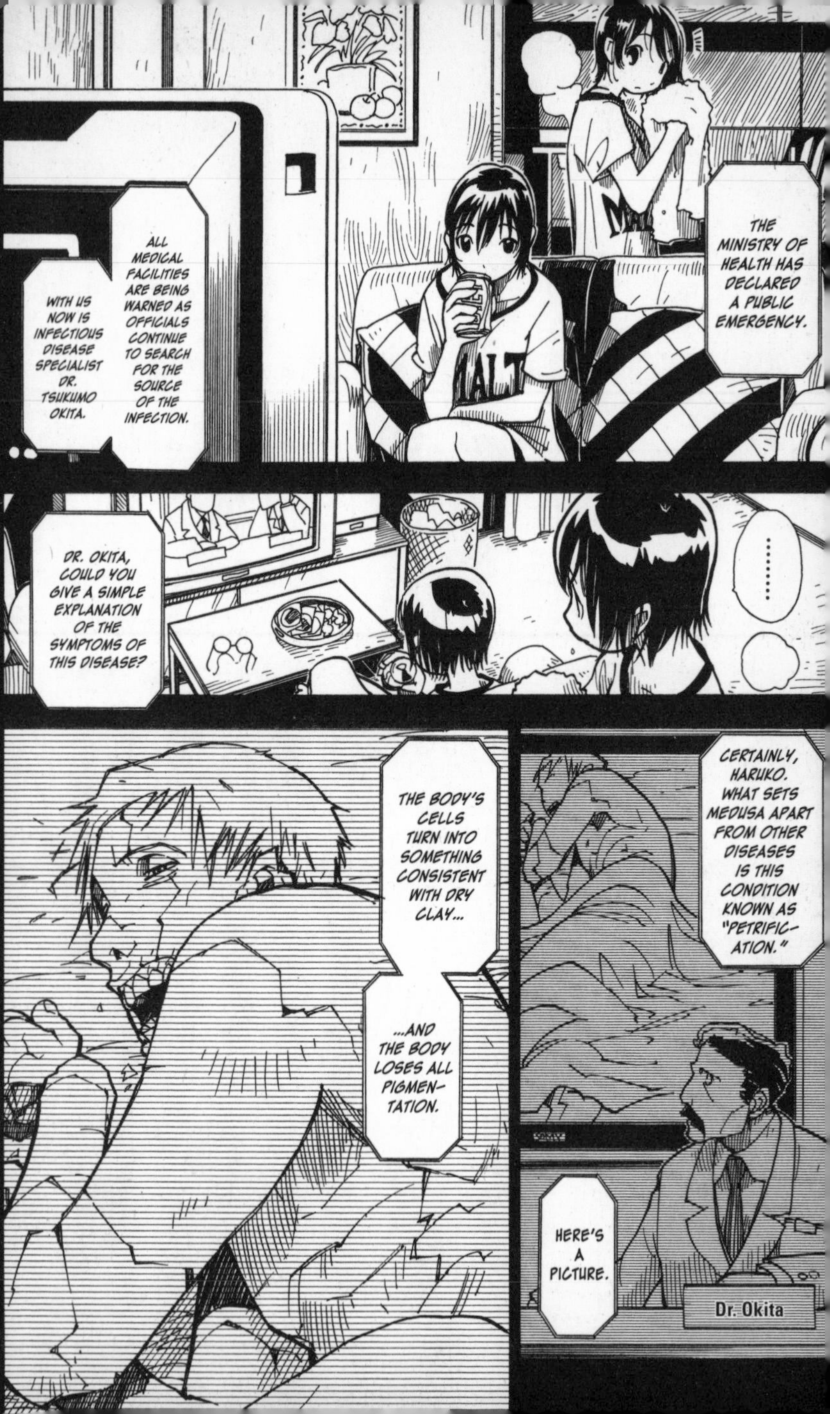
THE MINISTRY OF HEALTH HAS DECLARED A PUBLIC EMERGENCY.
ALL MEDICAL FACILITIES ARE BEING WARNED AS OFFICIALS CONTINUE TO SEARCH FOR THE SOURCE OF THE INFECTION.
WITH US NOW IS INFECTIOUS DISEASE SPECIALIST DR. TSUKUMO OKITA.
......
DR. OKITA, COULD YOU GIVE A SIMPLE EXPLANATION OF THE SYMPTOMS OF THIS DISEASE?
CERTAINLY, HARUKO. WHAT SETS MEDUSA APART FROM OTHER DISEASES IS THIS CONDITION KNOWN AS "PETRIFIC-ATION."
Dr. Okita
HERE'S A PICTURE.
THE BODY'S CELLS TURN INTO SOMETHING CONSISTENT WITH DRY CLAY...
...AND THE BODY LOSES ALL PIGMEN-TATION.

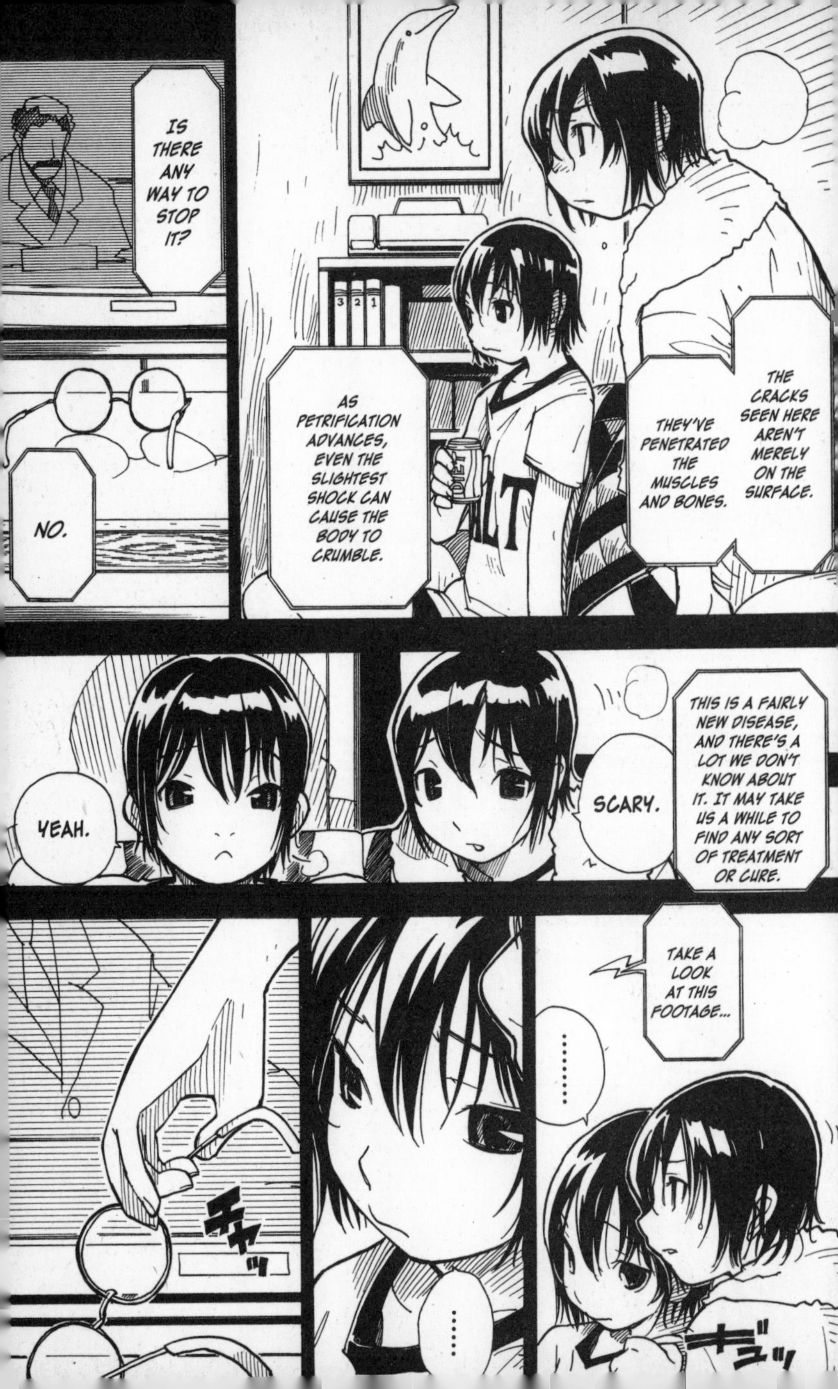
THE CRACKS SEEN HERE AREN'T MERELY ON THE SURFACE.
THEY'VE PENETRATED THE MUSCLES AND BONES.
AS PETRIFICATION ADVANCES, EVEN THE SLIGHTEST SHOCK CAN CAUSE THE BODY TO CRUMBLE.
IS THERE ANY WAY TO STOP IT?
NO.
THIS IS A FAIRLY NEW DISEASE, AND THERE'S A LOT WE DON'T KNOW ABOUT IT. IT MAY TAKE US A WHILE TO FIND ANY SORT OF TREATMENT OR CURE.
SCARY.
YEAH.
TAKE A LOOK AT THIS FOOTAGE...
......
ギュッ
......
チャッ

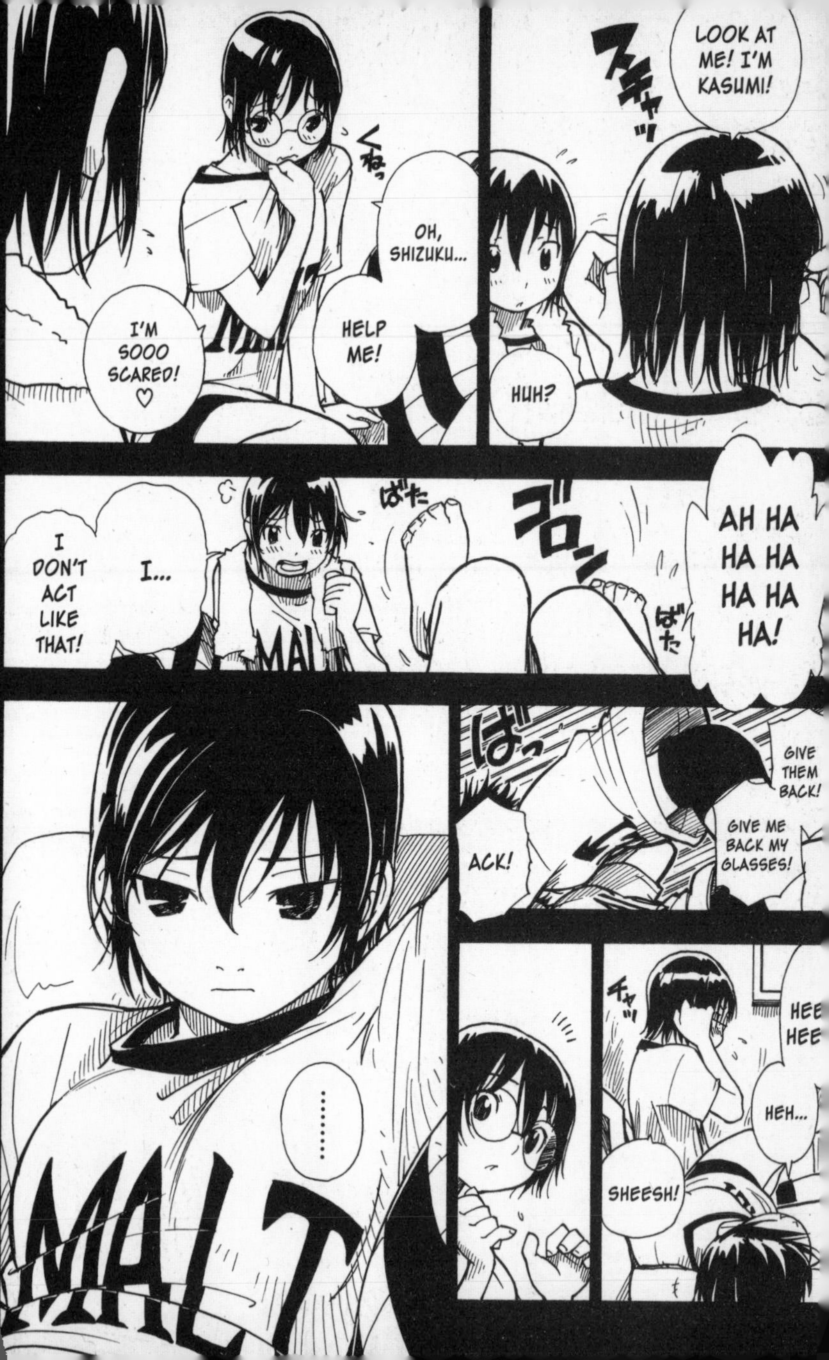
スチャッ
LOOK AT ME! I'M KASUMI!
HUH?
OH, SHIZUKU...
くねっ
HELP ME!
I'M SOOO SCARED! ♡
AH HA HA HA HA HA HA!
ゴロン
ばた
ばた
I...
I DON'T ACT LIKE THAT!
ばっ
GIVE THEM BACK!
GIVE ME BACK MY GLASSES!
ACK!
HEE HEE
チャッ
HEH...
SHEESH!
......

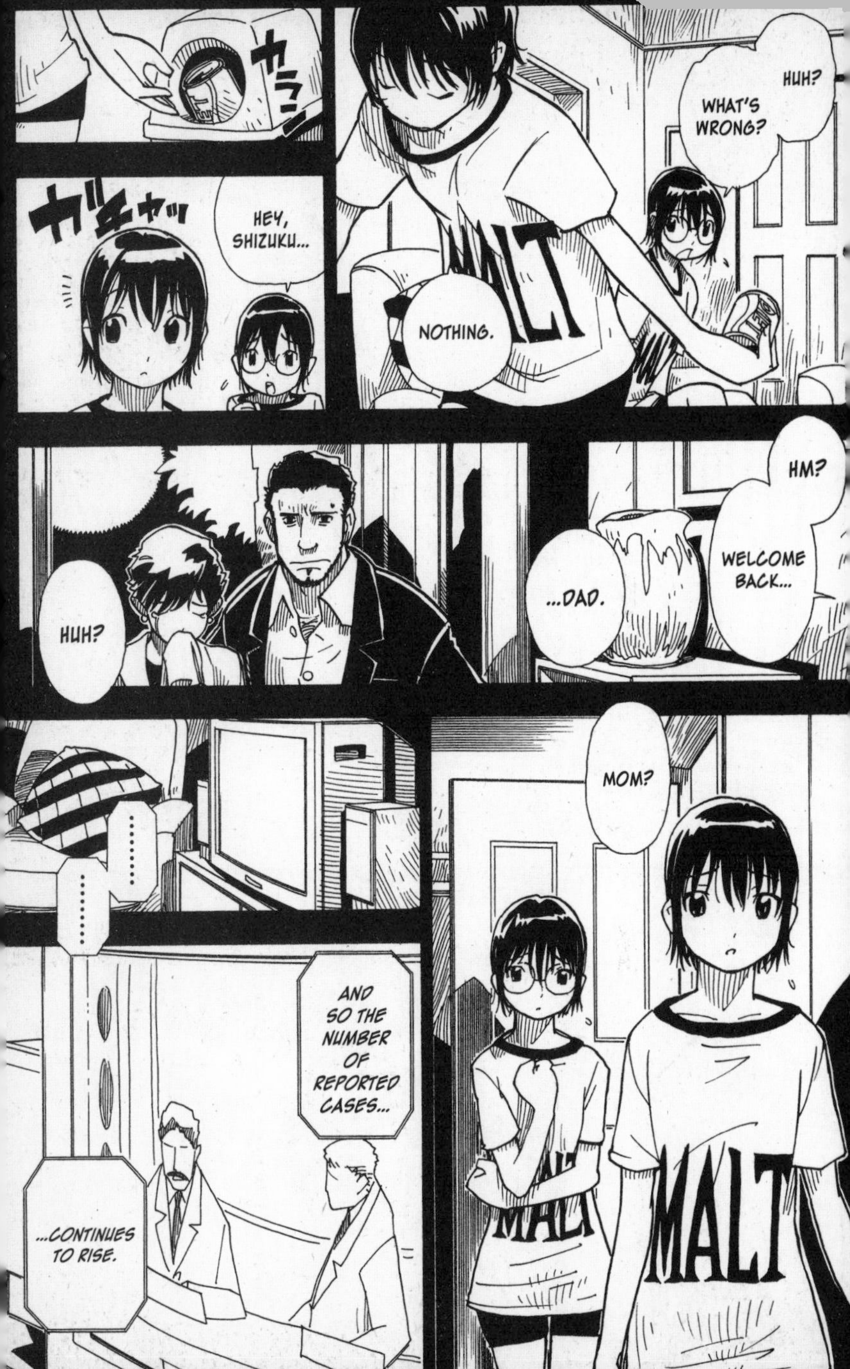

HUH? WHAT'S WRONG?
NOTHING.
カラン
ガチャッ
HEY, SHIZUKU...
HM?
WELCOME BACK...
...DAD.
HUH?
MOM?
......
......
AND SO THE NUMBER OF REPORTED CASES...
...CONTINUES TO RISE.

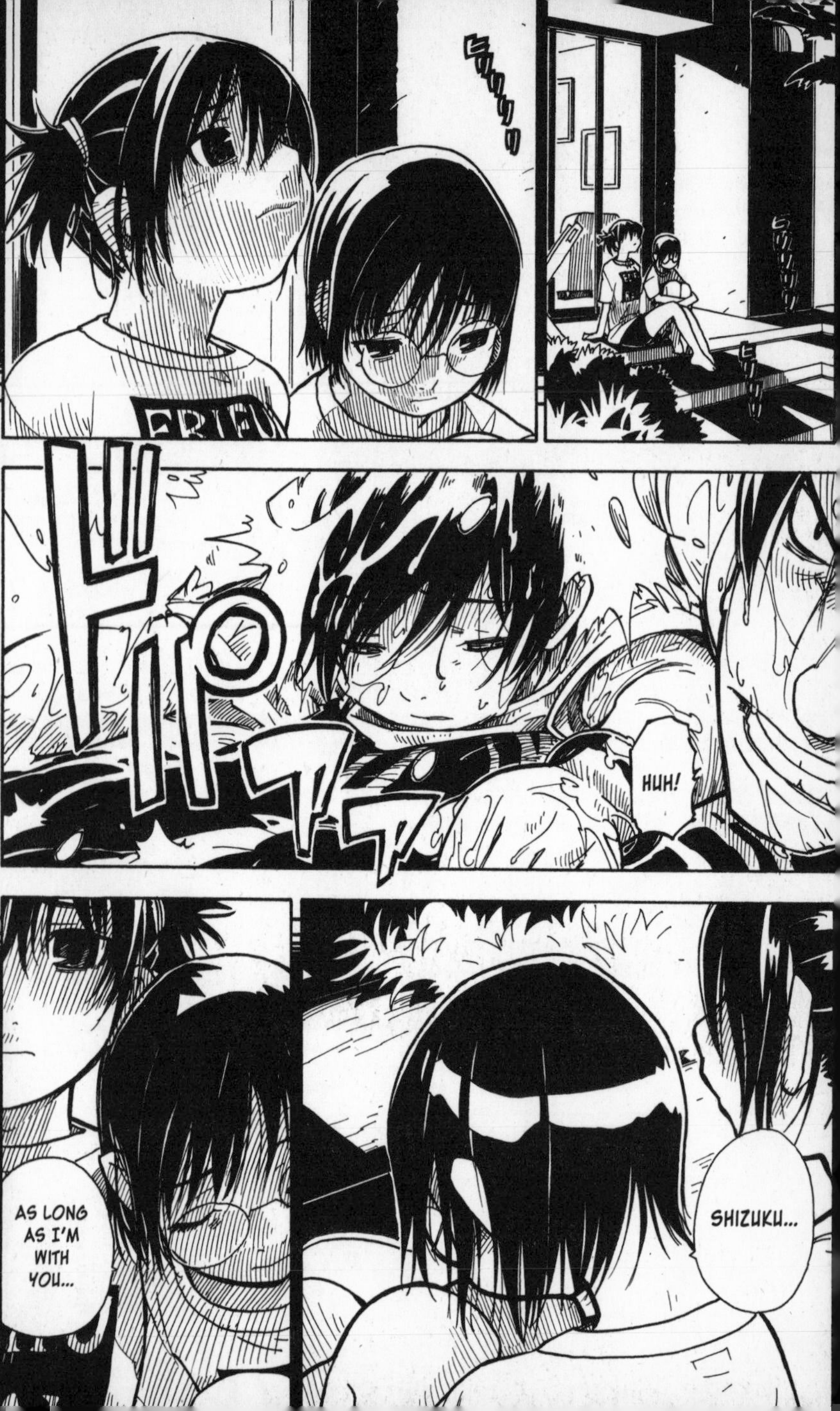
HUH!
SHIZUKU...
AS LONG AS I'M WITH YOU...

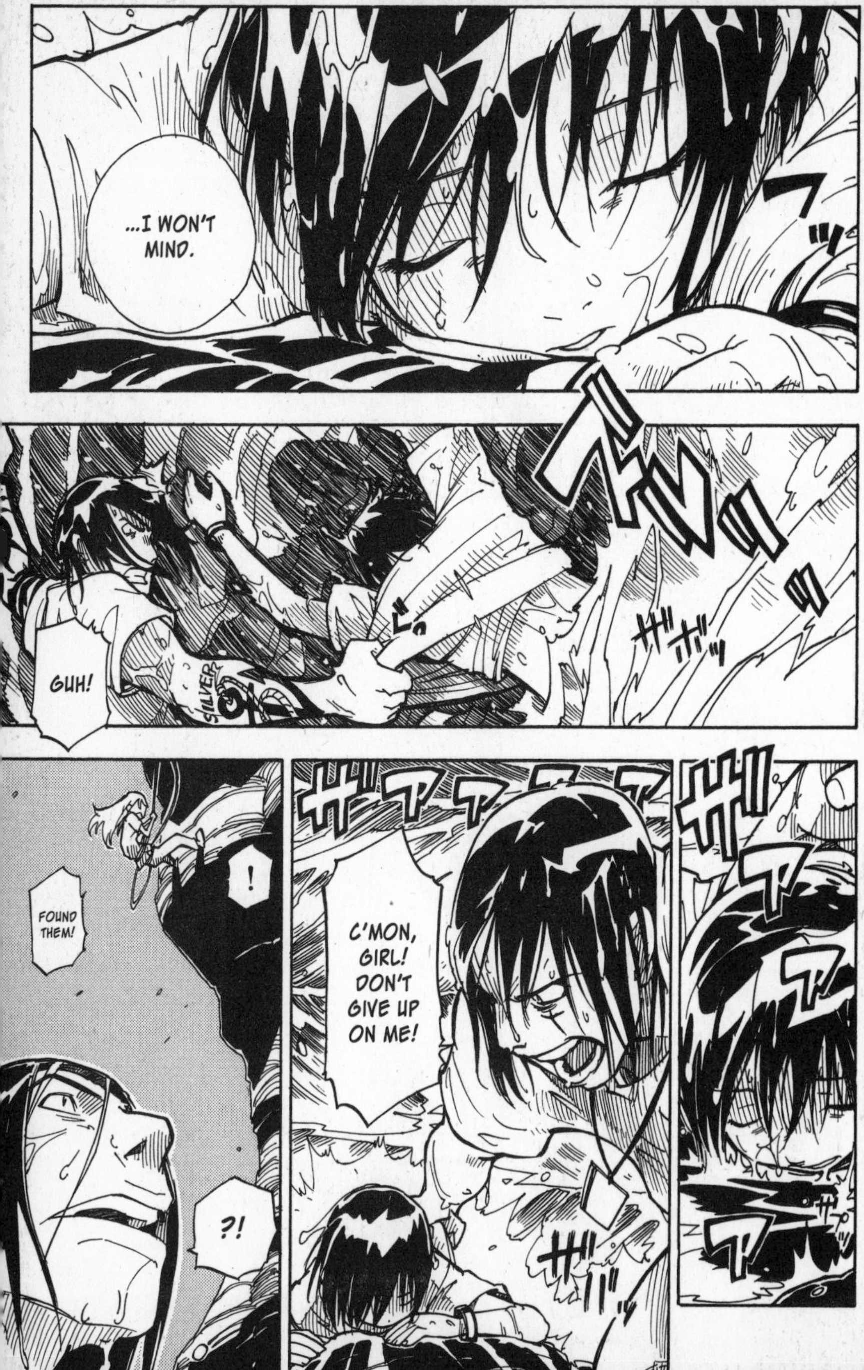
...I WON'T MIND.
GUH!
C'MON, GIRL! DON'T GIVE UP ON ME!
!
FOUND THEM!
?!

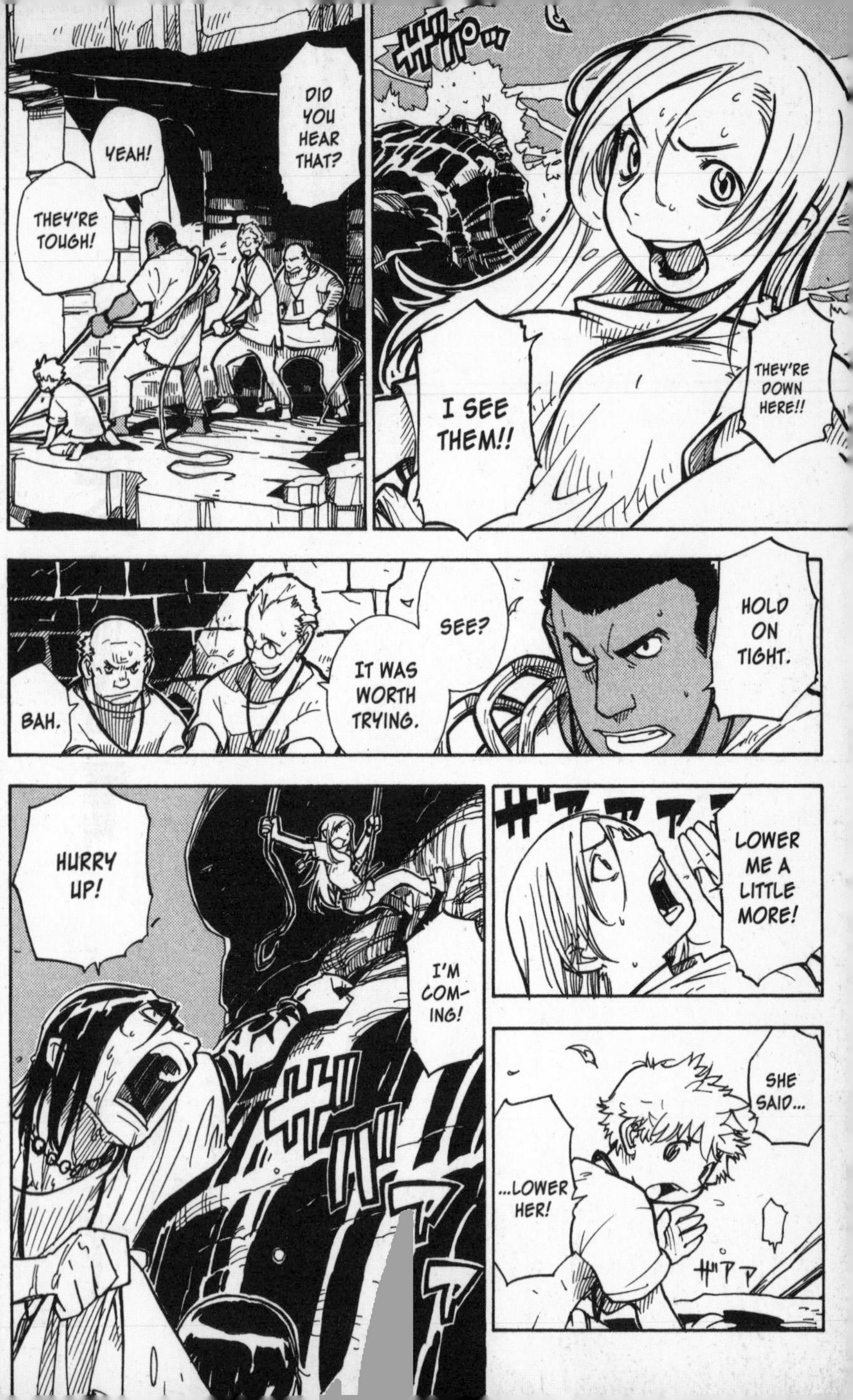
THEY'RE DOWN HERE!!
I SEE THEM!!
DID YOU HEAR THAT?
YEAH!
THEY'RE TOUGH!
HOLD ON TIGHT.
SEE?
IT WAS WORTH TRYING.
BAH.
LOWER ME A LITTLE MORE!
SHE SAID...
...LOWER HER!
HURRY UP!
I'M COM-ING!

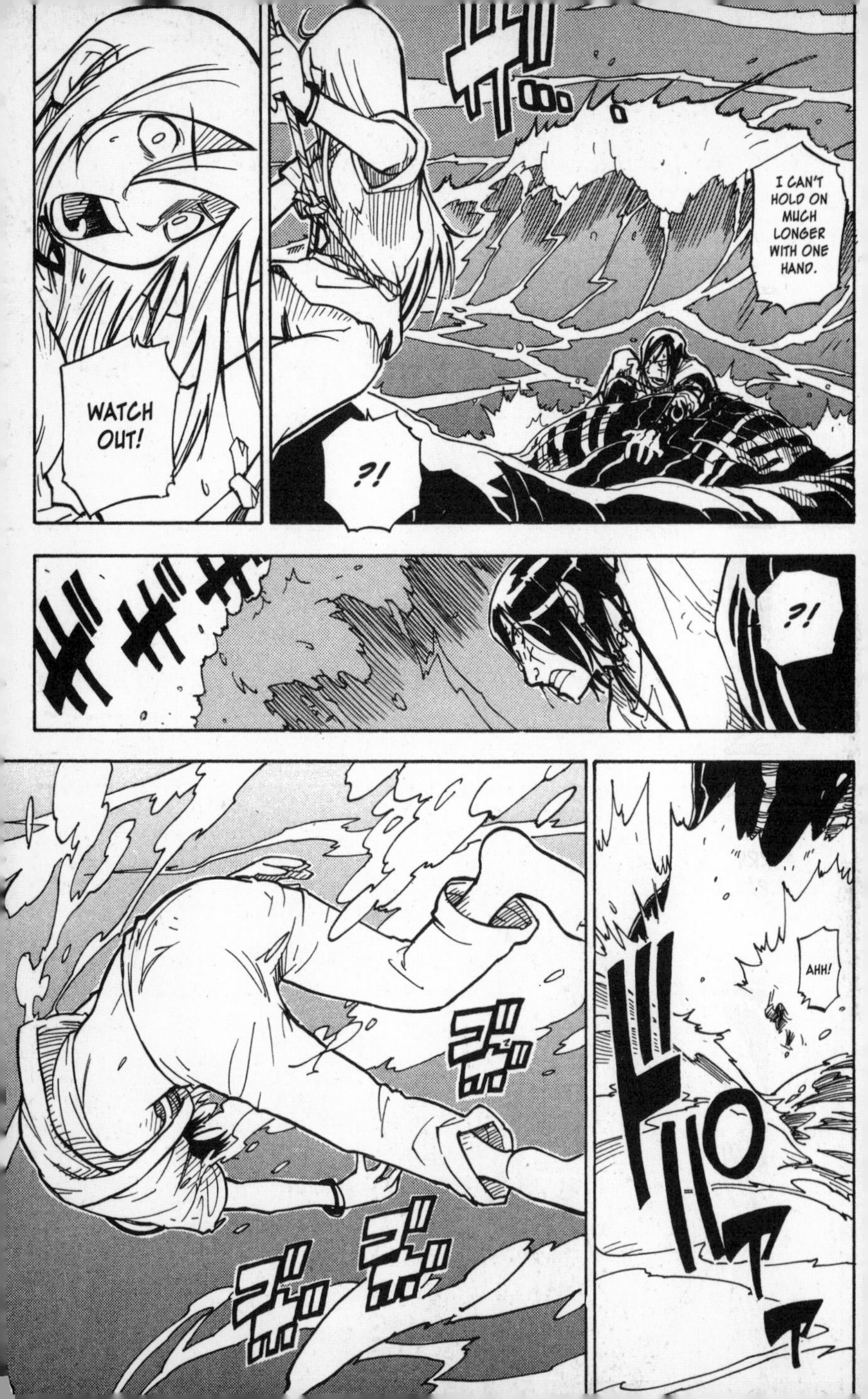
I CAN'T HOLD ON MUCH LONGER WITH ONE HAND.
?!
WATCH OUT!
?!
AHH!

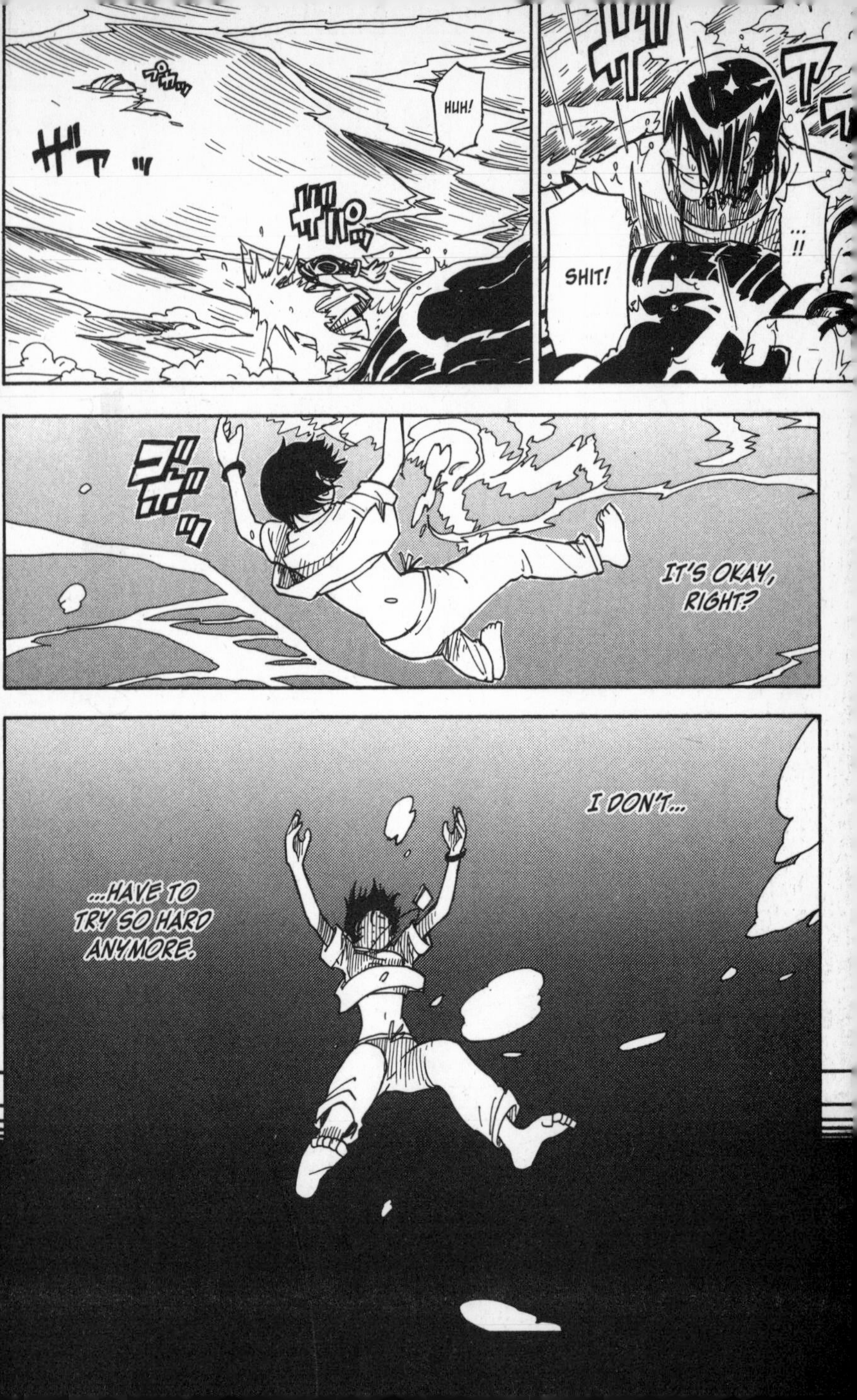
SHIT!
...!!
HUH!
IT'S OKAY, RIGHT?
I DON'T...
...HAVE TO TRY SO HARD ANYMORE.

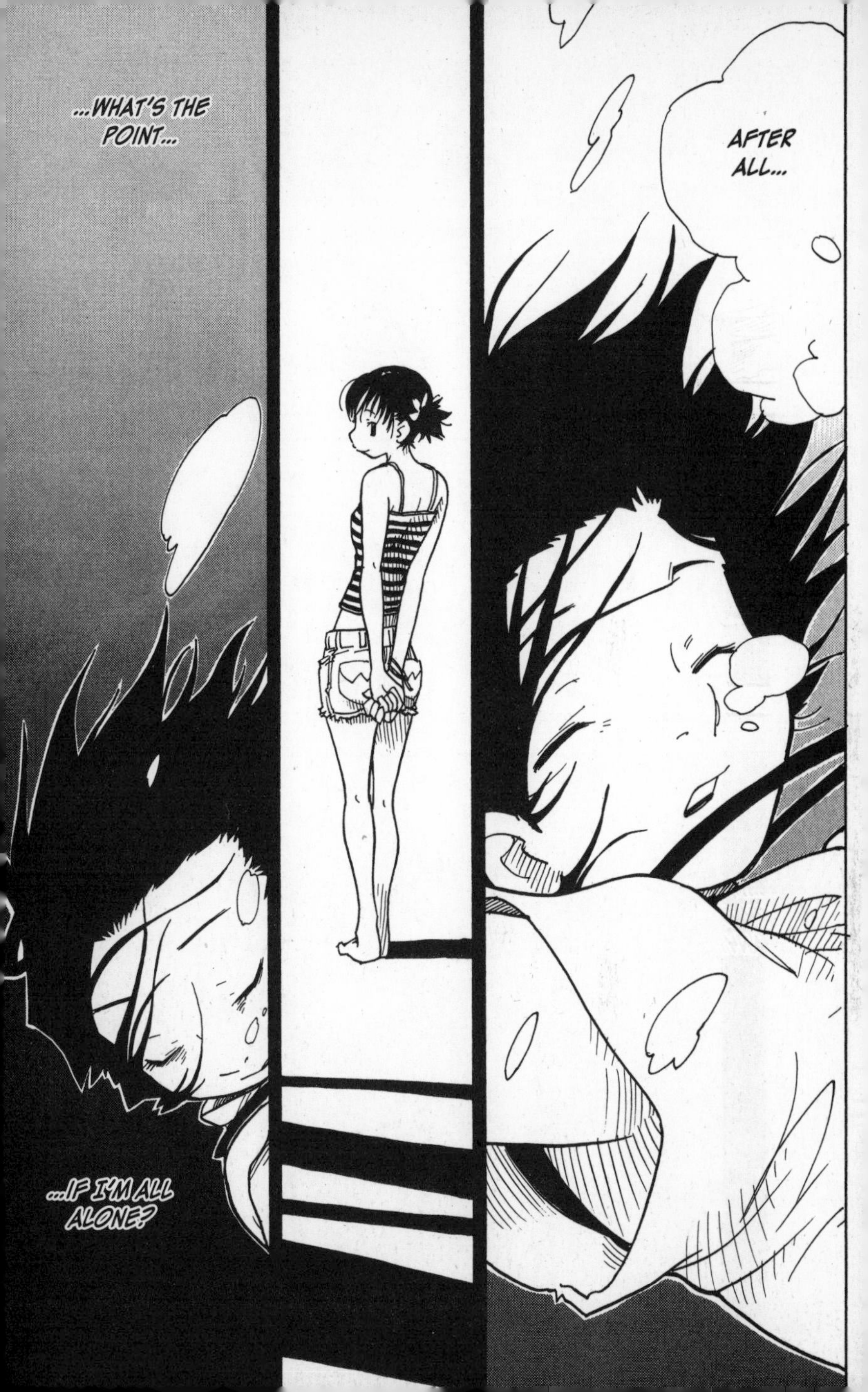
AFTER ALL...
...WHAT'S THE POINT...
...IF I'M ALL ALONE?

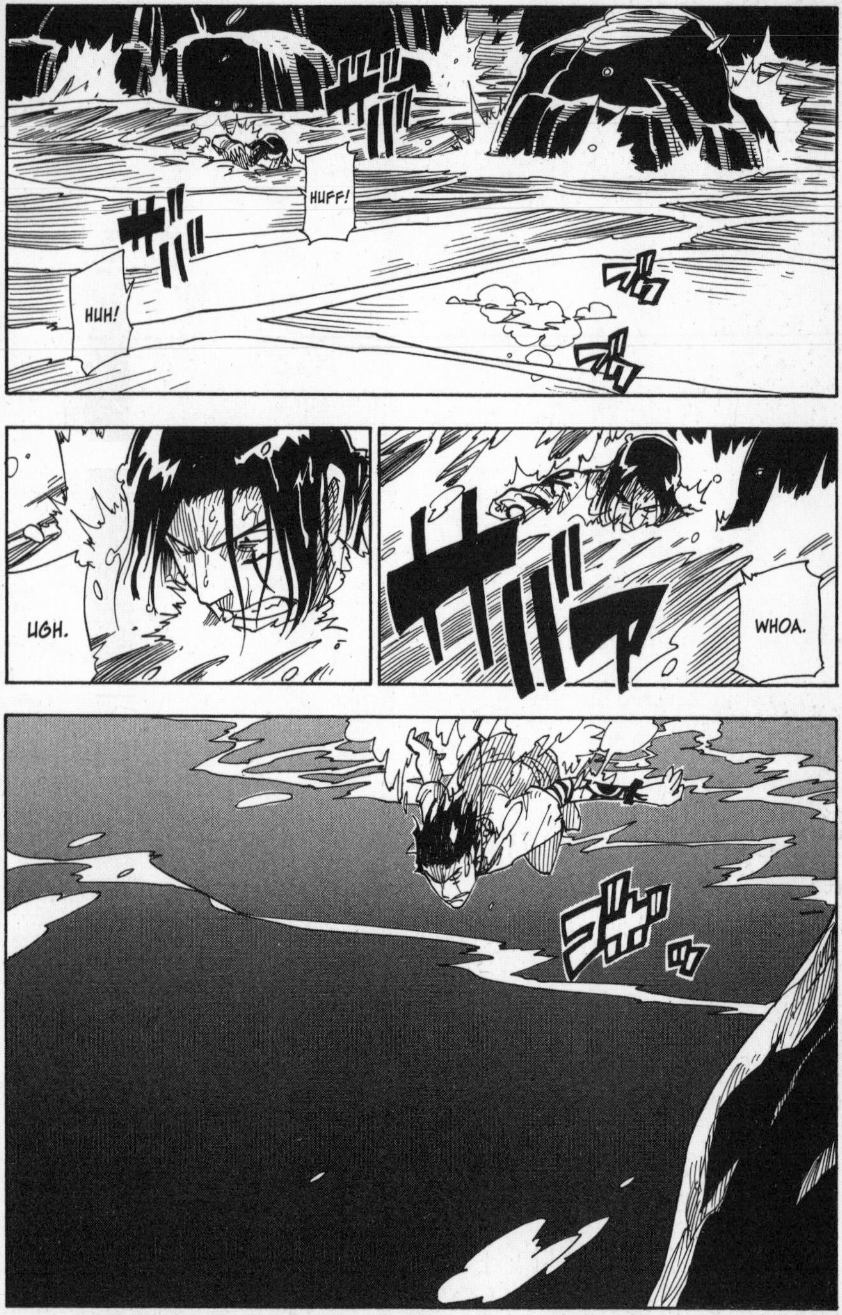
HUFF!
HUH!
WHOA.
UGH.

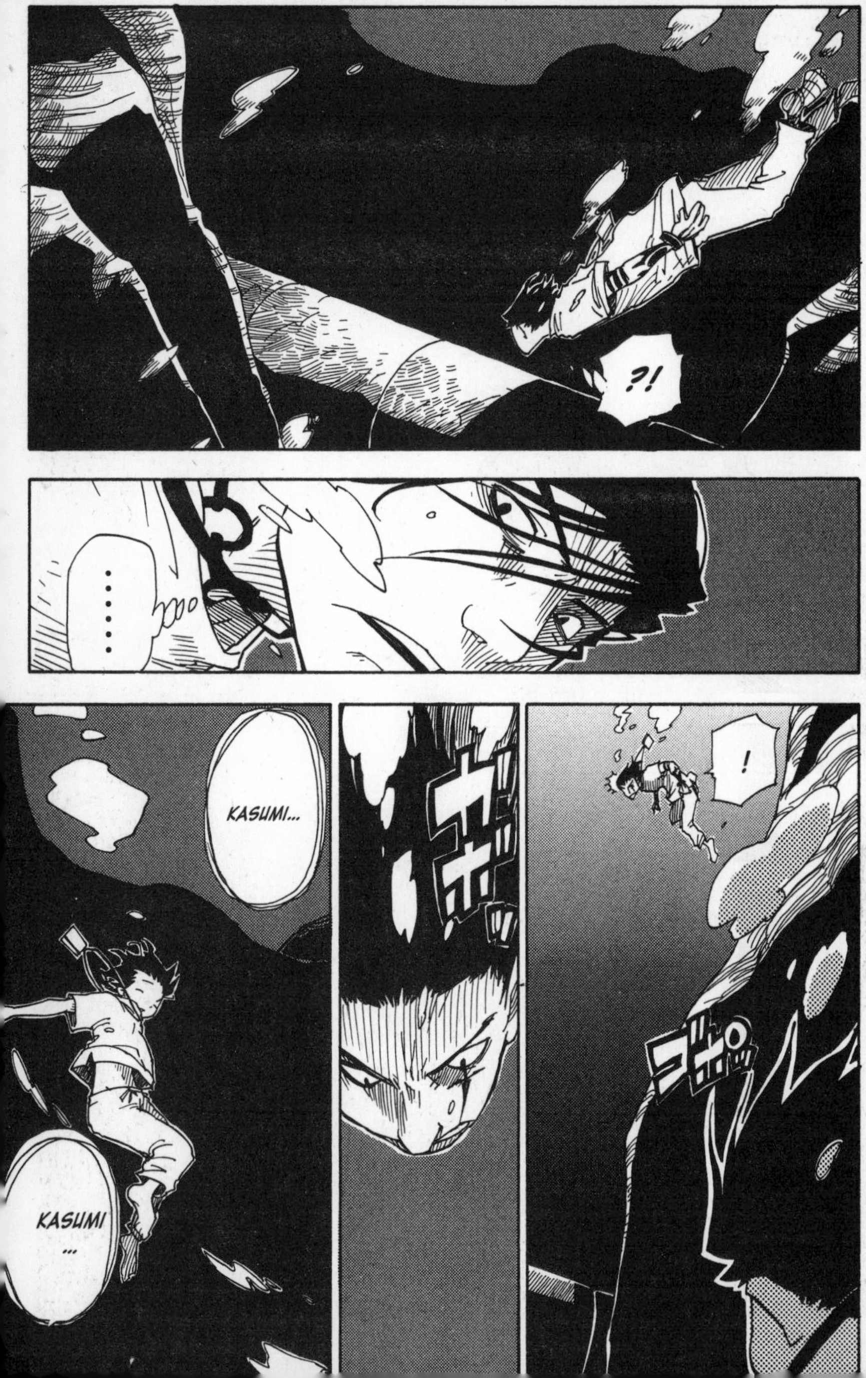
?!
......
!
KASUMI...
KASUMI
...

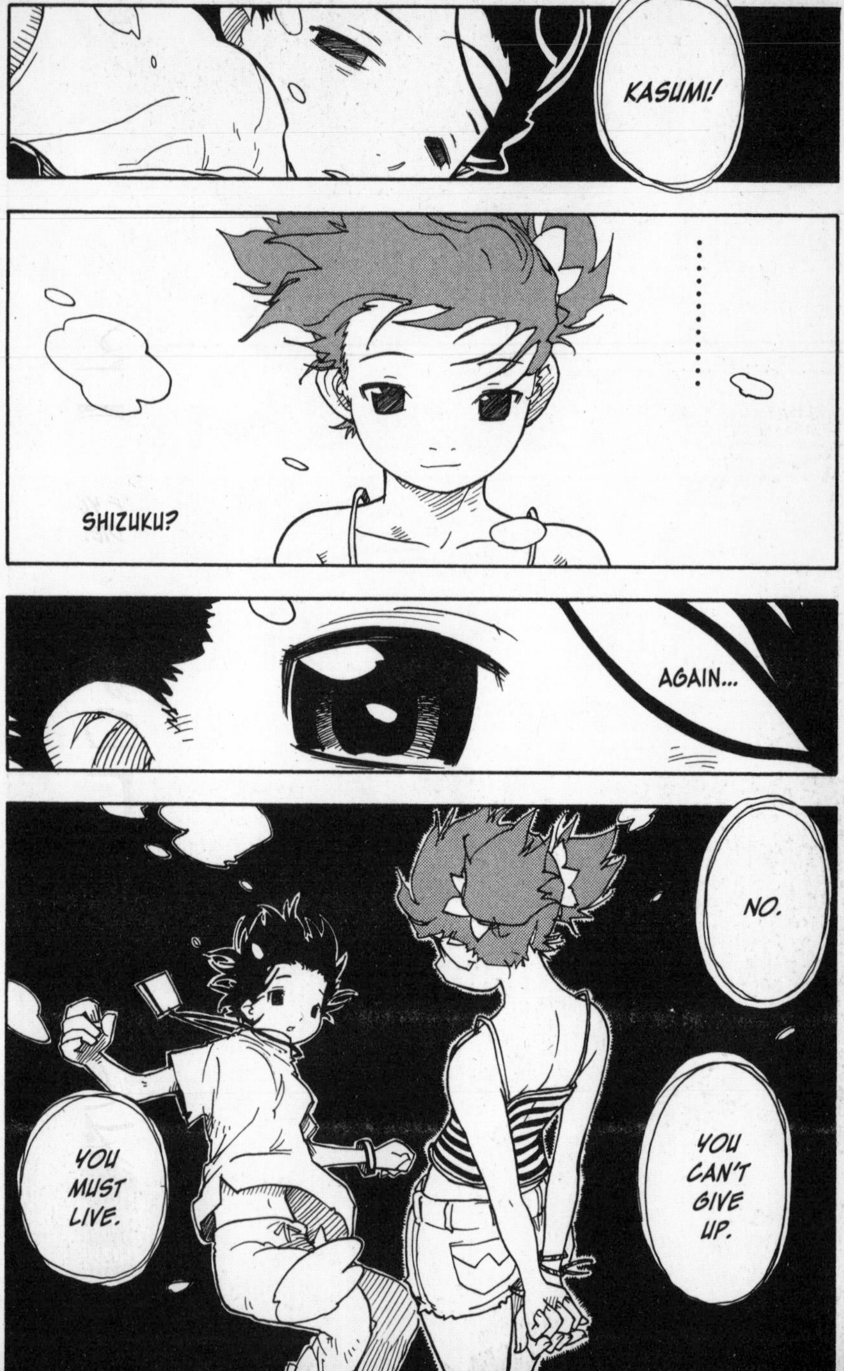
KASUMI!
......
SHIZUKU?
AGAIN...
NO.
YOU CAN'T GIVE UP.
YOU MUST LIVE.

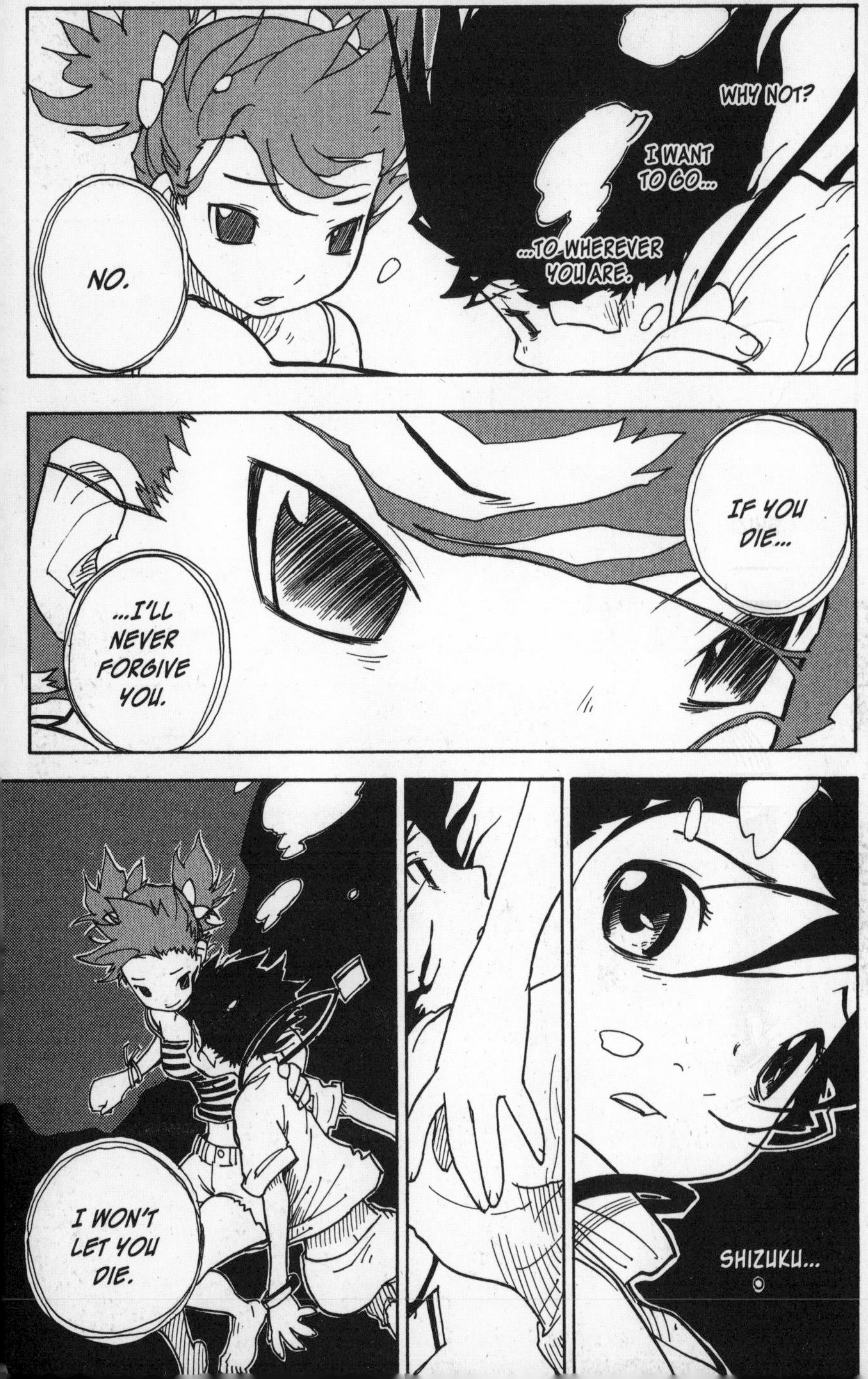
WHY NOT?
I WANT TO GO...
...TO WHEREVER YOU ARE.
NO.
IF YOU DIE...
...I'LL NEVER FORGIVE YOU.
SHIZUKU...
I WON'T LET YOU DIE.

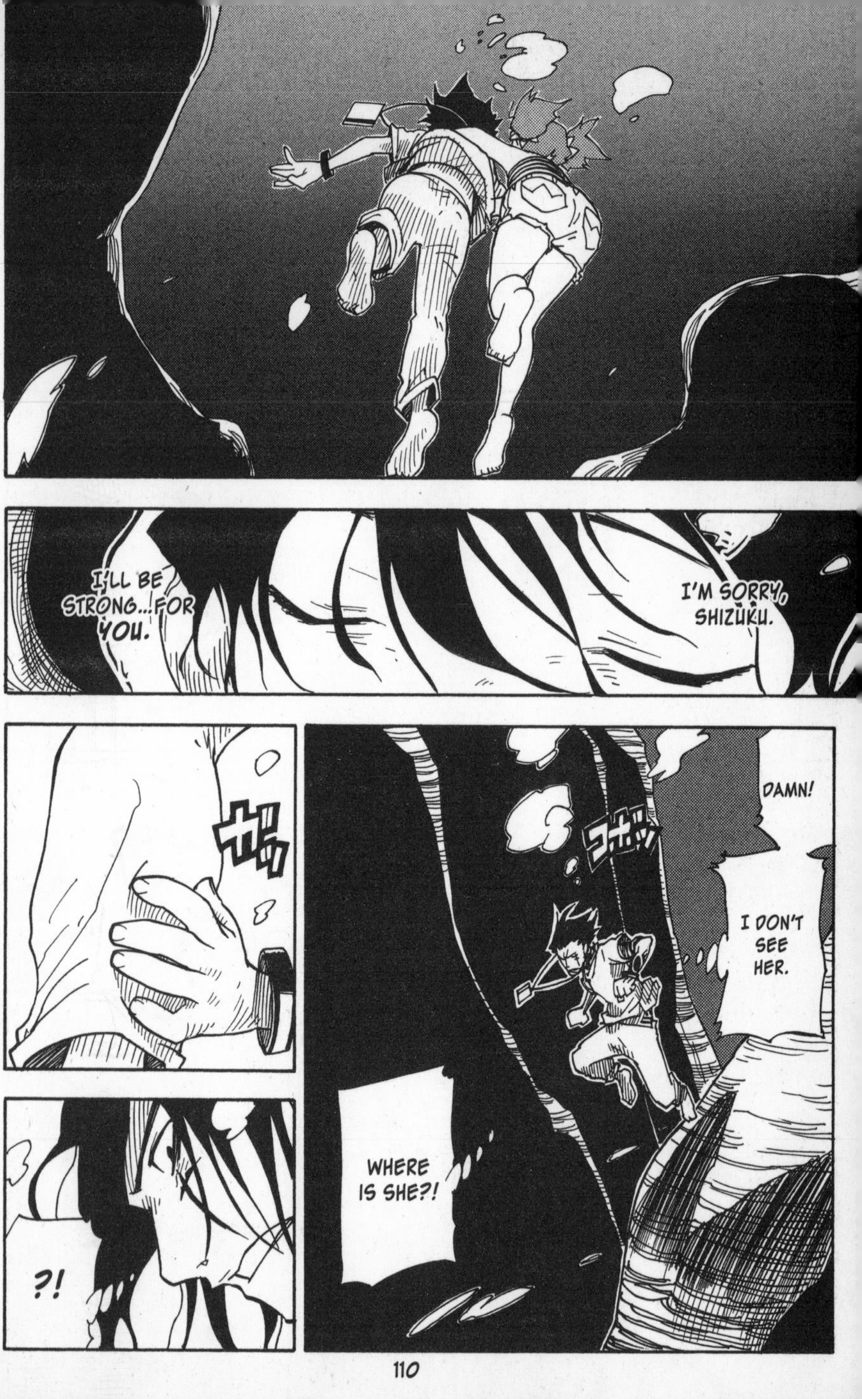
I'M SORRY, SHIZUKU.
I'LL BE STRONG... FOR YOU.
DAMN!
I DON'T SEE HER.
WHERE IS SHE?!
?!

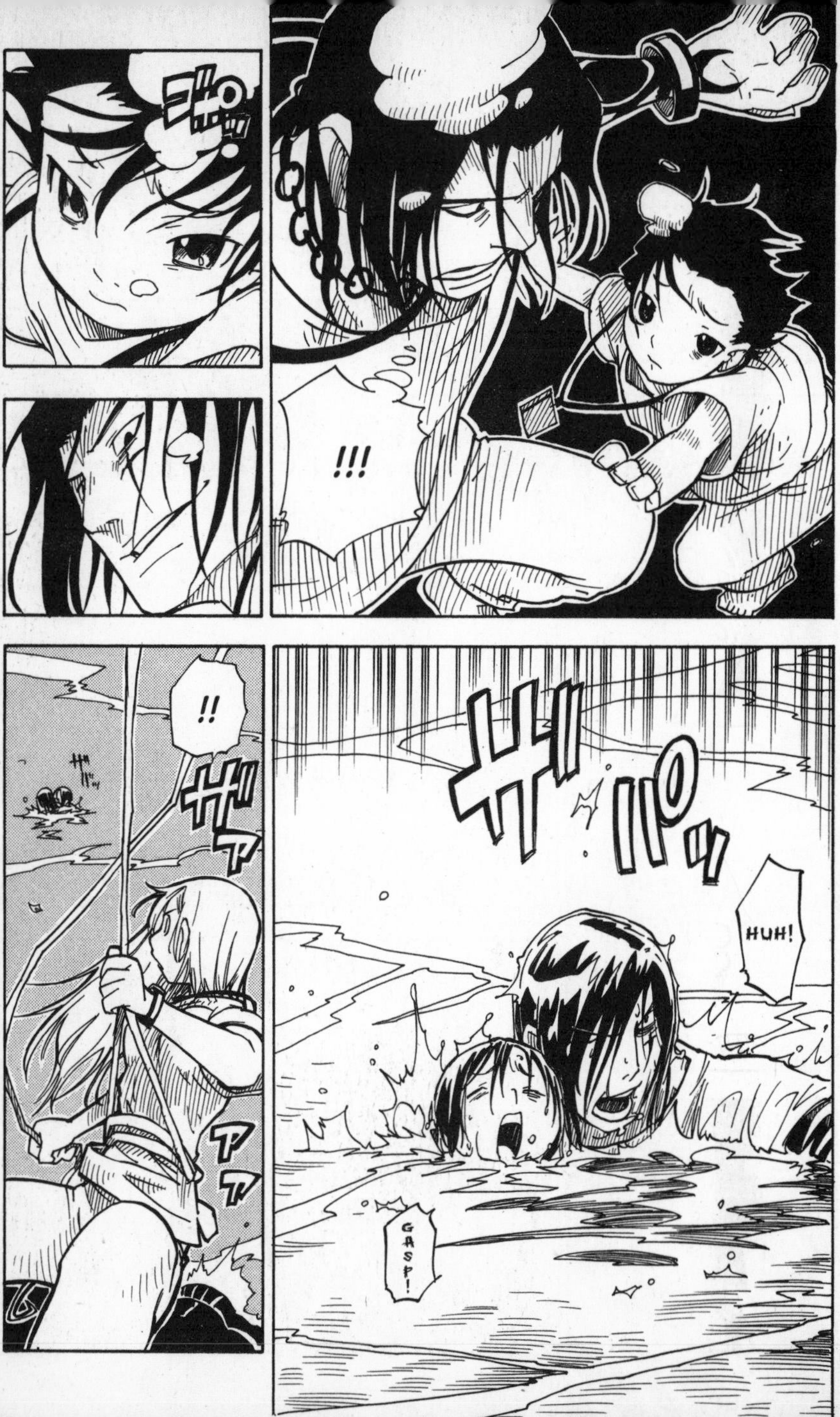

!!!
ザパッ
HUH!
GASP!
!!

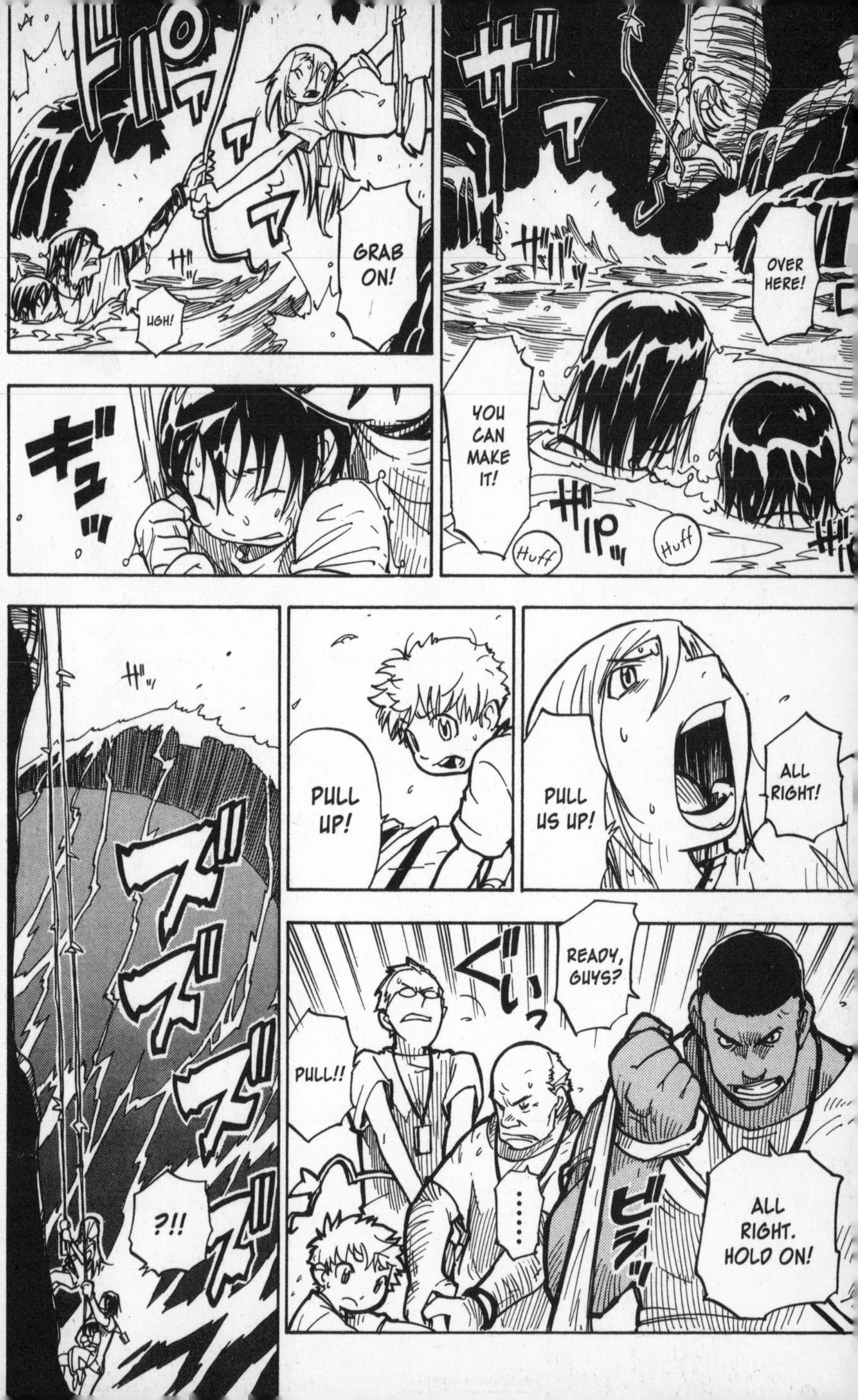
OVER HERE!
YOU CAN MAKE IT!
Huff
Huff
GRAB ON!
UGH!
ALL RIGHT!
PULL US UP!
PULL UP!
READY, GUYS?
ALL RIGHT. HOLD ON!
......
PULL!!
?!!

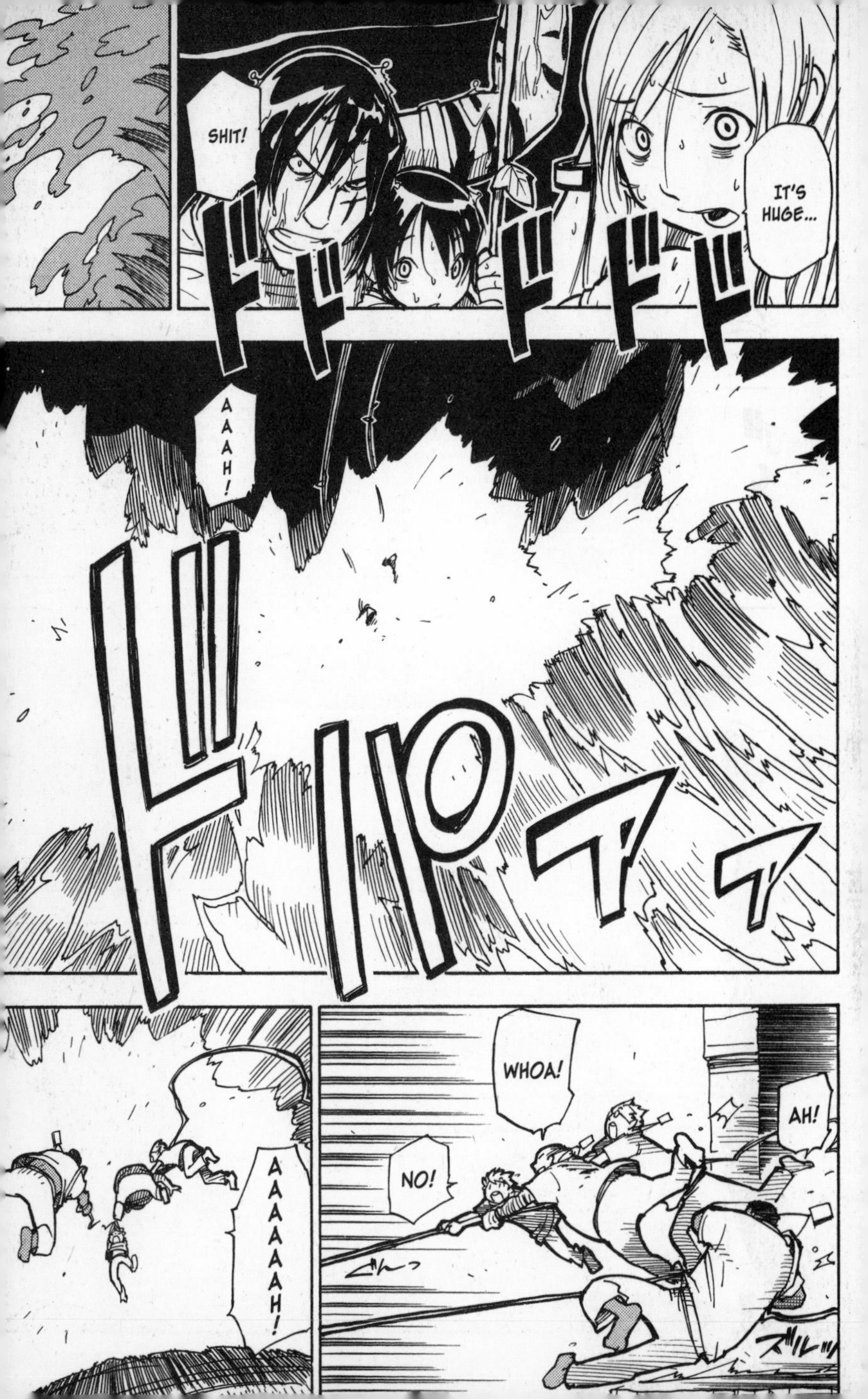
IT'S HUGE...
SHIT!
AAAH!
AH!
WHOA!
NO!
AAAAAAAAH!

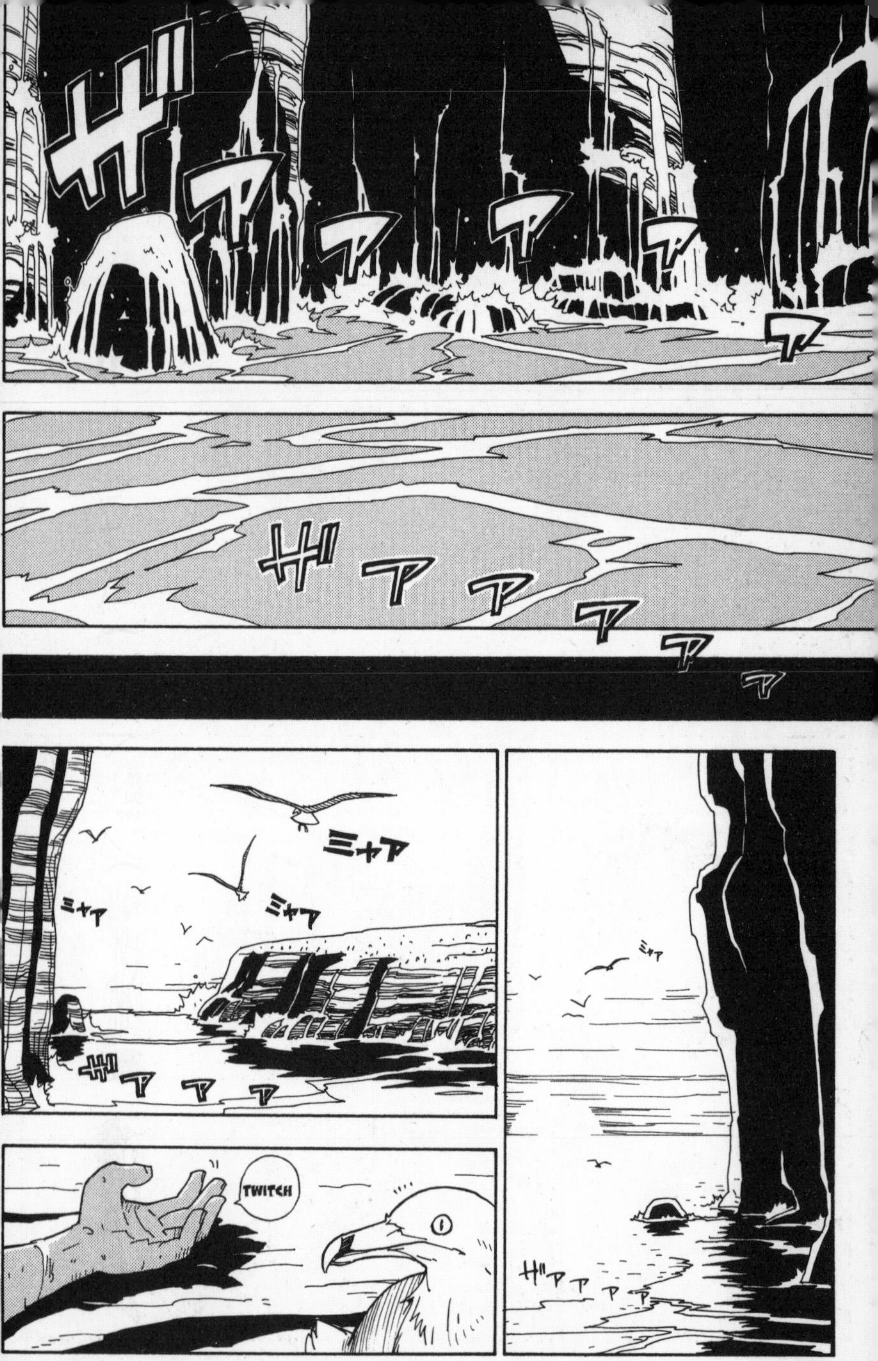

ザァァァァァ
ザァァァァァ
ミャア
ザァァァァ
ミャア
ミャア
ミャア
ザァァァ
TWITCH

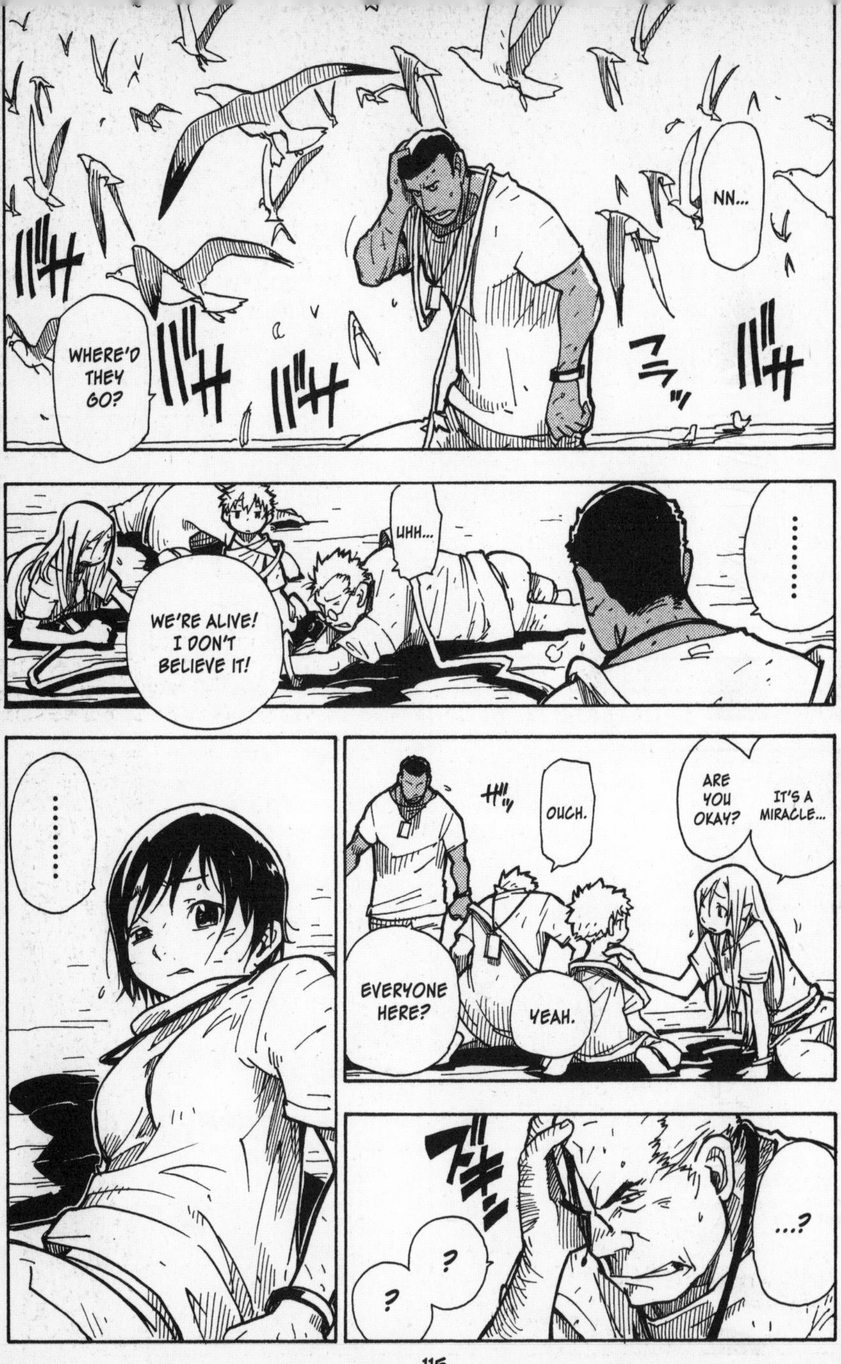
NN...
WHERE'D THEY GO?
......
UHH...
WE'RE ALIVE! I DON'T BELIEVE IT!
IT'S A MIRACLE...
ARE YOU OKAY?
OUCH.
YEAH.
EVERYONE HERE?
...?
?
?
......

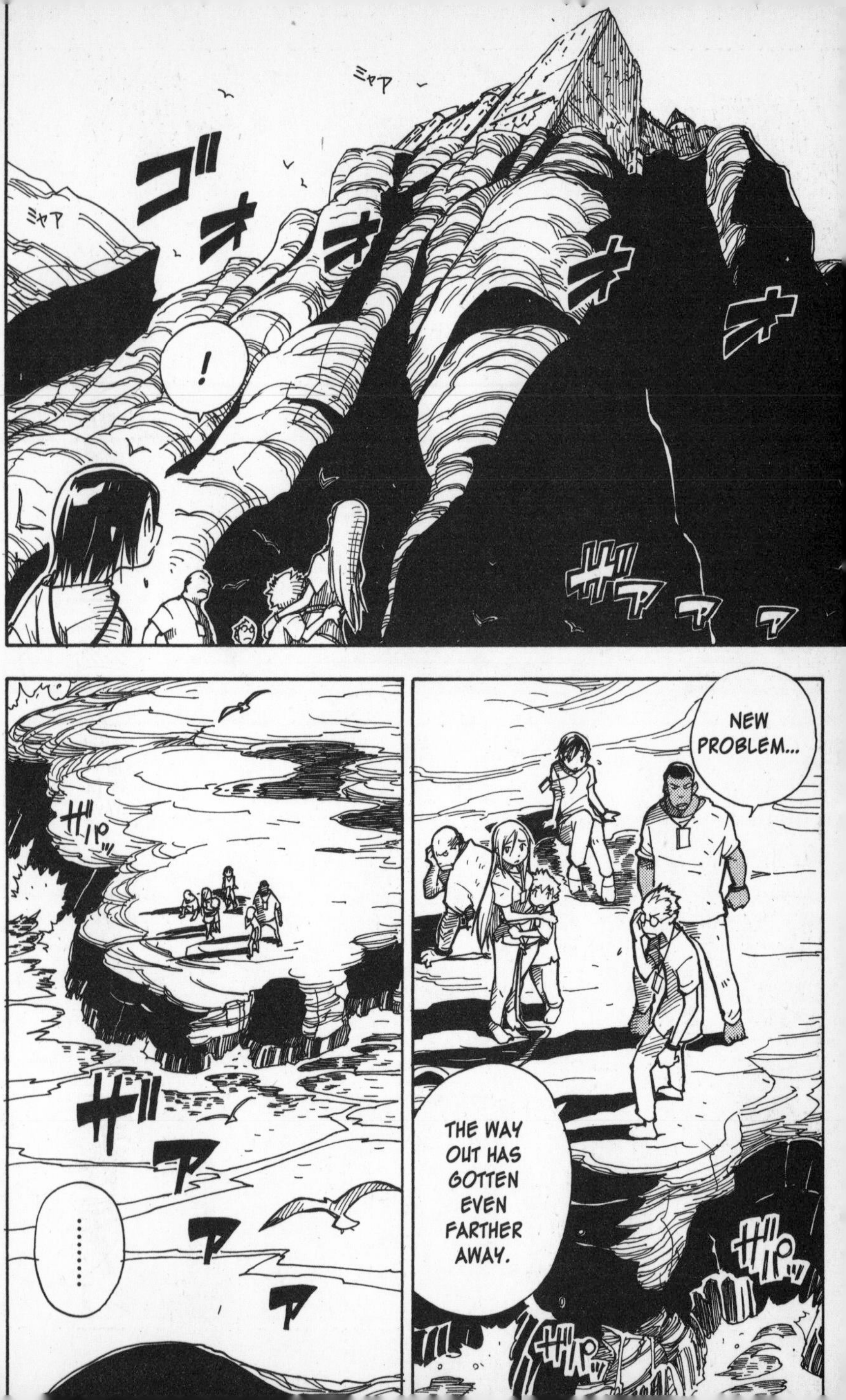
ミャア
ミャア
ゴオオオオ
!
ザァァァ
NEW PROBLEM...
THE WAY OUT HAS GOTTEN EVEN FARTHER AWAY.
ザパッ
ザパッ
ザパッ
ザァァァ
......

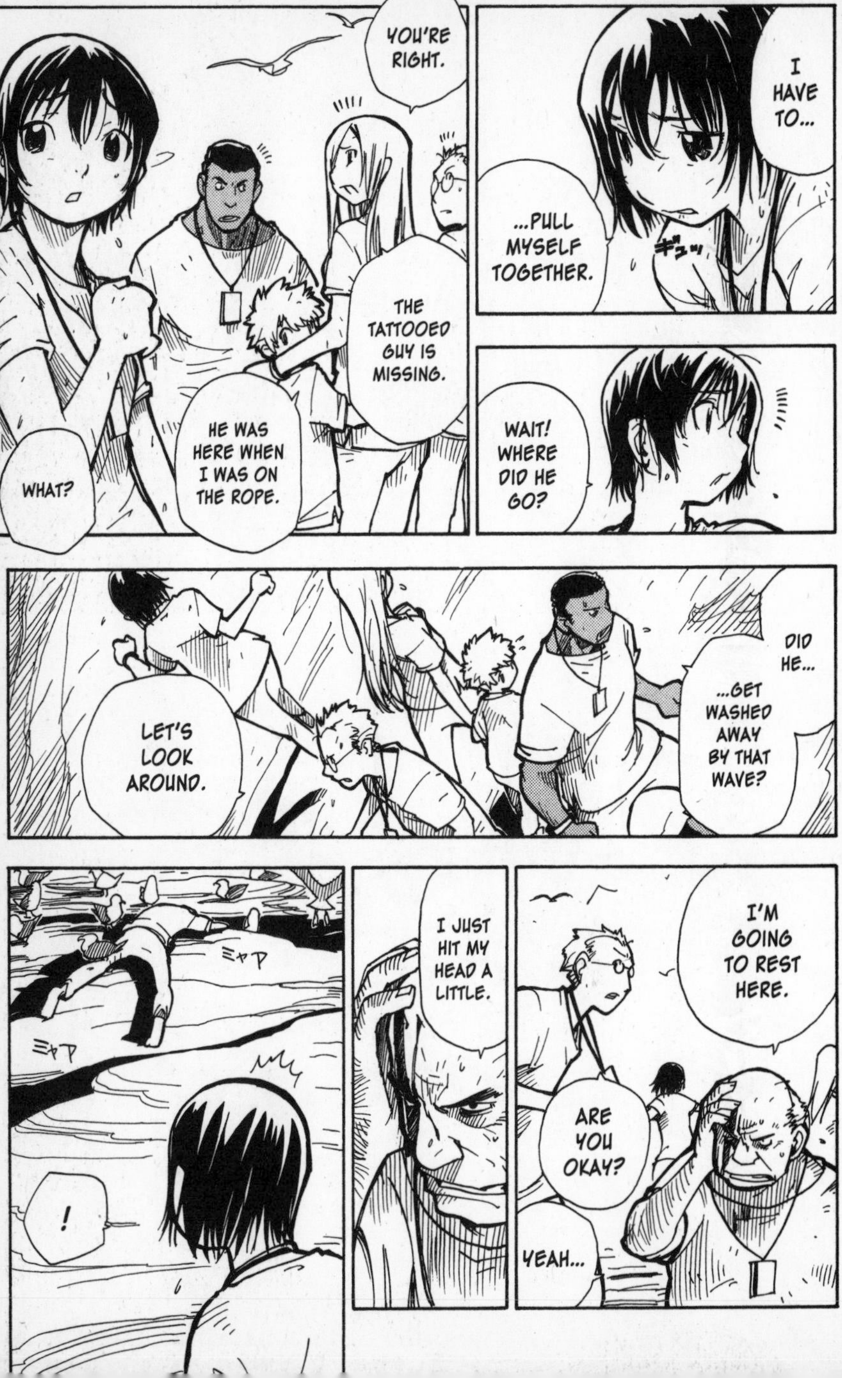
I HAVE TO...
...PULL MYSELF TOGETHER.
ギュッ
WAIT! WHERE DID HE GO?
YOU'RE RIGHT.
THE TATTOOED GUY IS MISSING.
HE WAS HERE WHEN I WAS ON THE ROPE.
WHAT?
DID HE...
...GET WASHED AWAY BY THAT WAVE?
LET'S LOOK AROUND.
I'M GOING TO REST HERE.
ARE YOU OKAY?
YEAH...
I JUST HIT MY HEAD A LITTLE.
ミャア
ミャア
!

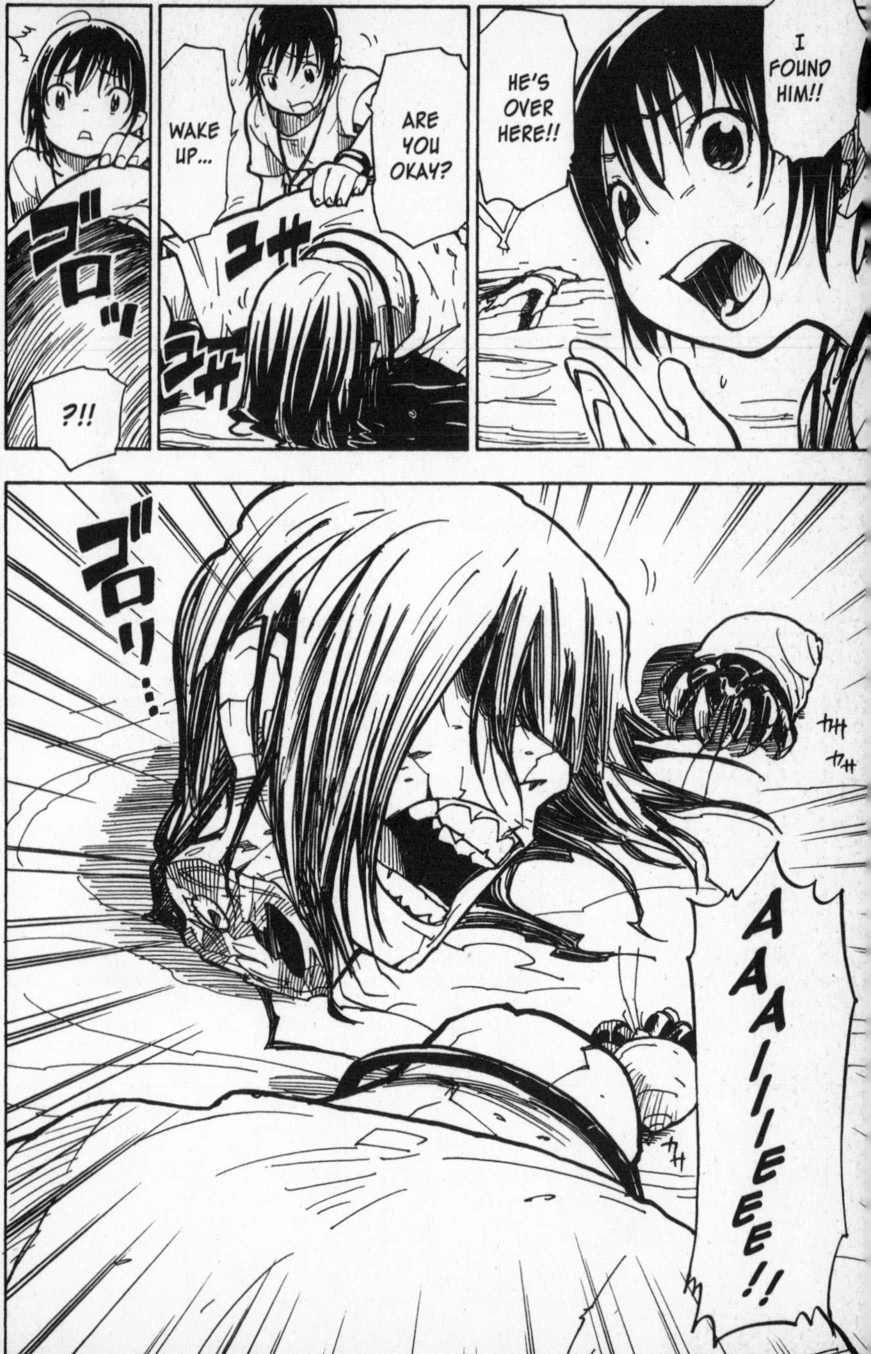
I FOUND HIM!!
HE'S OVER HERE!!
ARE YOU OKAY?
WAKE UP...
ユサ
ユサ
ゴロッ
?!!
ゴロリ...
カサ
カサ
カサ
AAAIIIEEE!!

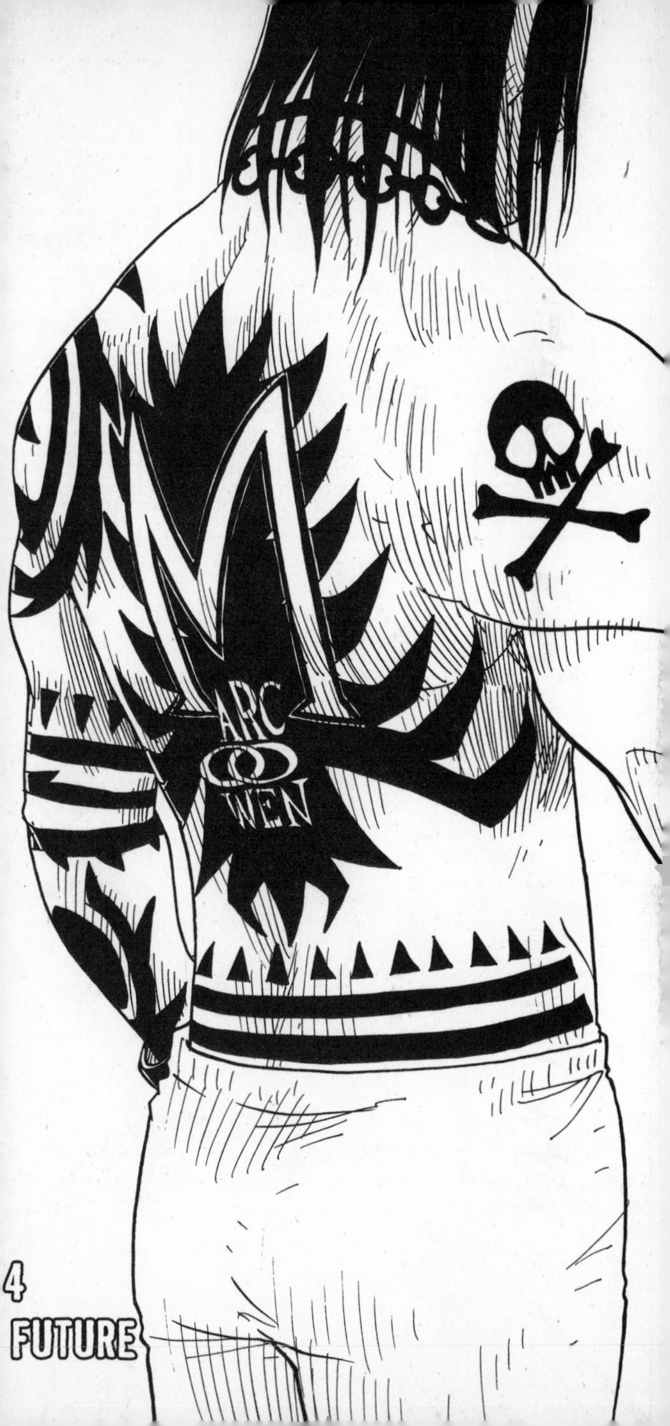
ARC
WEN

4
FUTURE

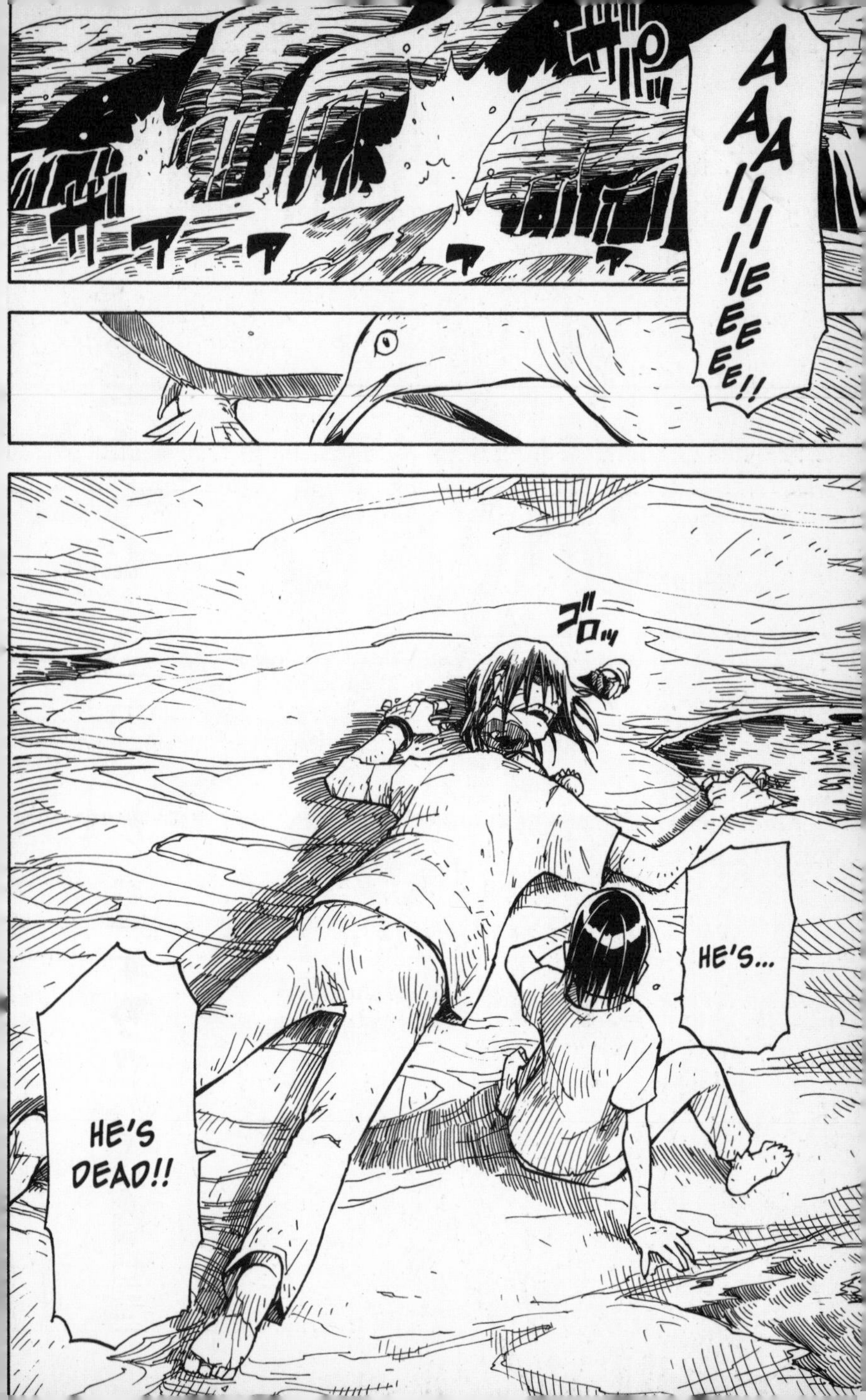
AAAIIIIEEEEE!!
HE'S...
HE'S DEAD!!

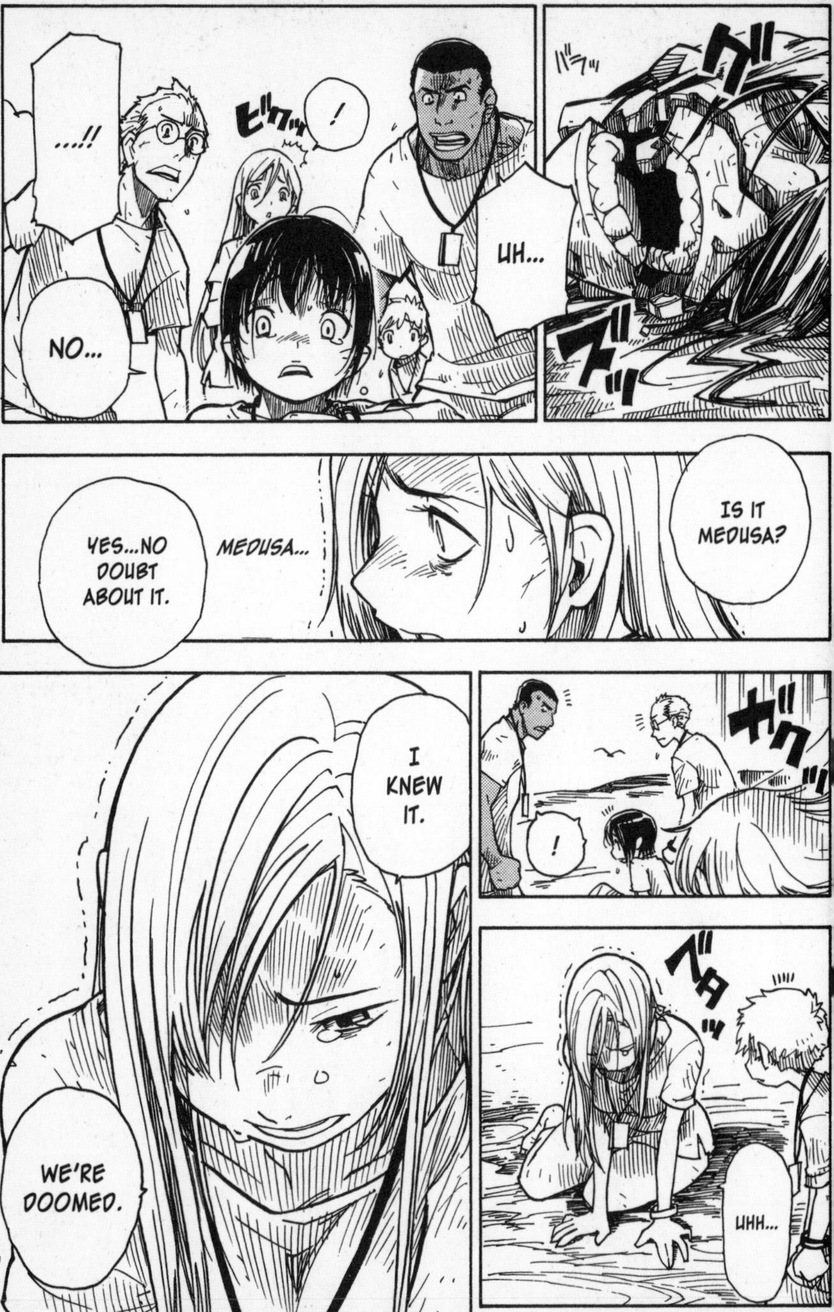
UH...
!
...!!
NO...
IS IT MEDUSA?
MEDUSA...
YES...NO DOUBT ABOUT IT.
!
UHH...
I KNEW IT.
WE'RE DOOMED.

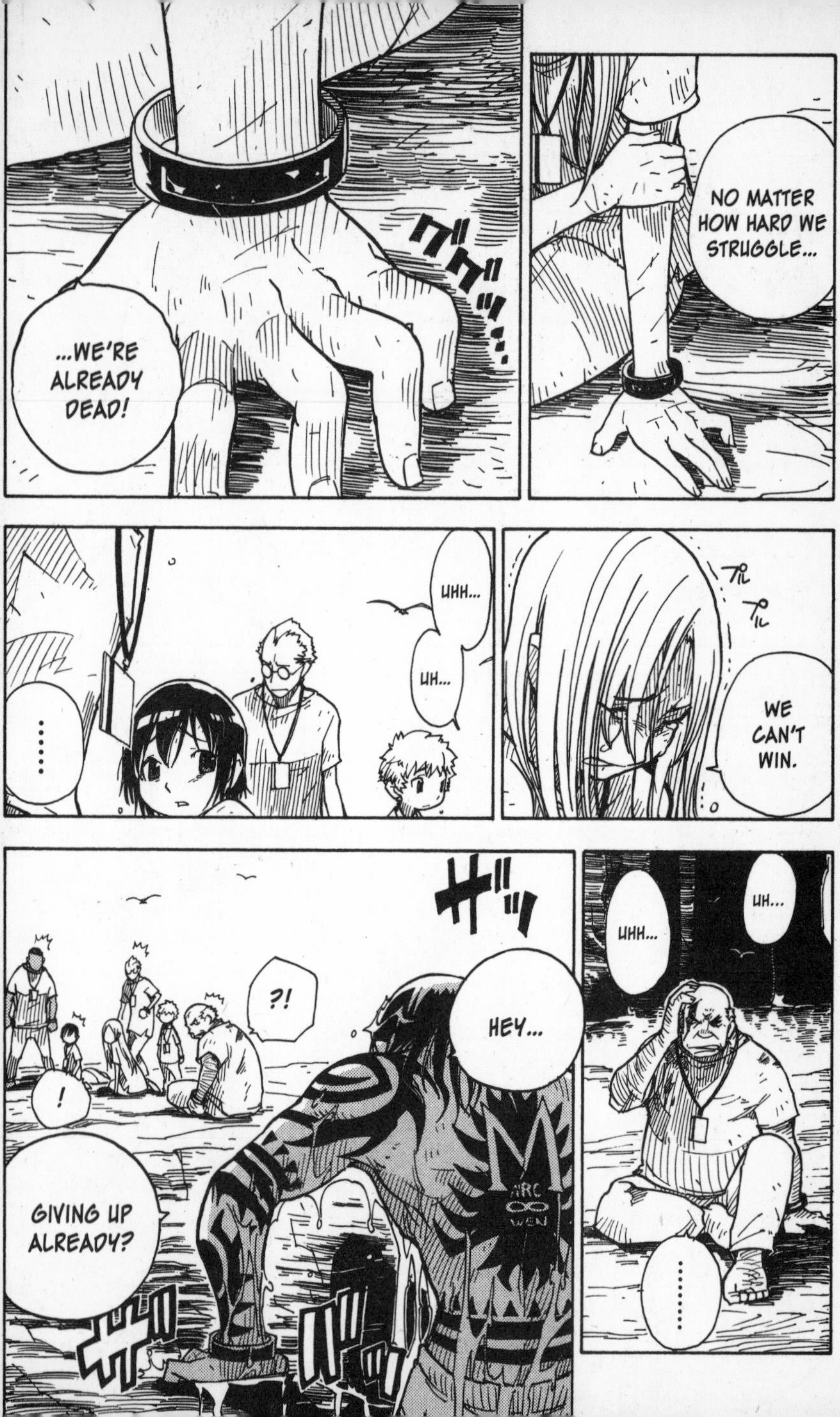
NO MATTER HOW HARD WE STRUGGLE...
...WE'RE ALREADY DEAD!
プル
プル
WE CAN'T WIN.
UHH...
UH...
......
UH...
UHH...
......
ザッ
HEY...
GIVING UP ALREADY?
?!
!

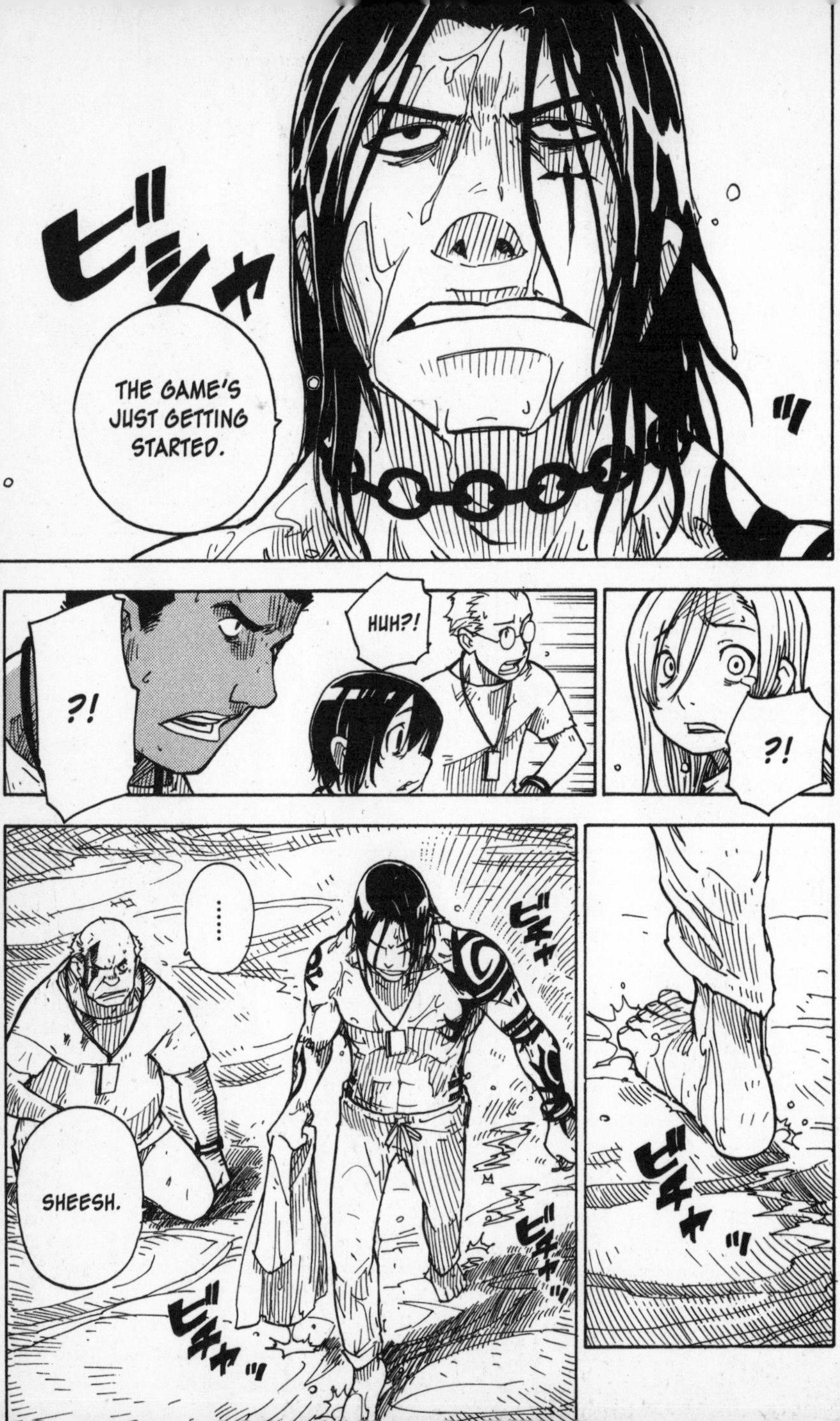
ビシャ
THE GAME'S JUST GETTING STARTED.
ッ
?!
HUH?!
?!
ビチャッ
ビチャ
......
ビチャッ
SHEESH.
ビチャッ

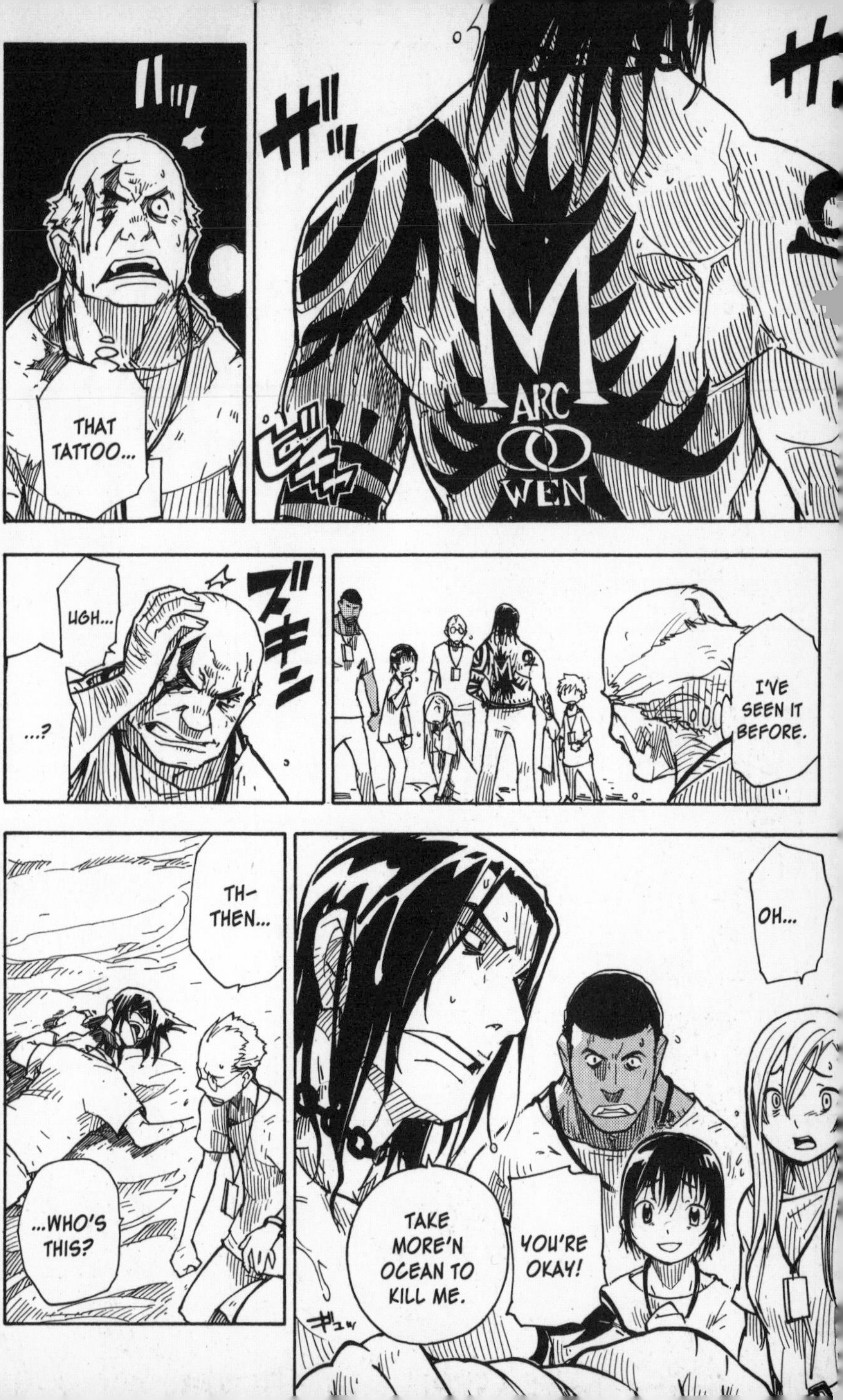
M
ARC
WEN
THAT TATTOO...
I'VE SEEN IT BEFORE.
UGH...
...?
OH...
YOU'RE OKAY!
TAKE MORE'N OCEAN TO KILL ME.
TH-THEN...
...WHO'S THIS?

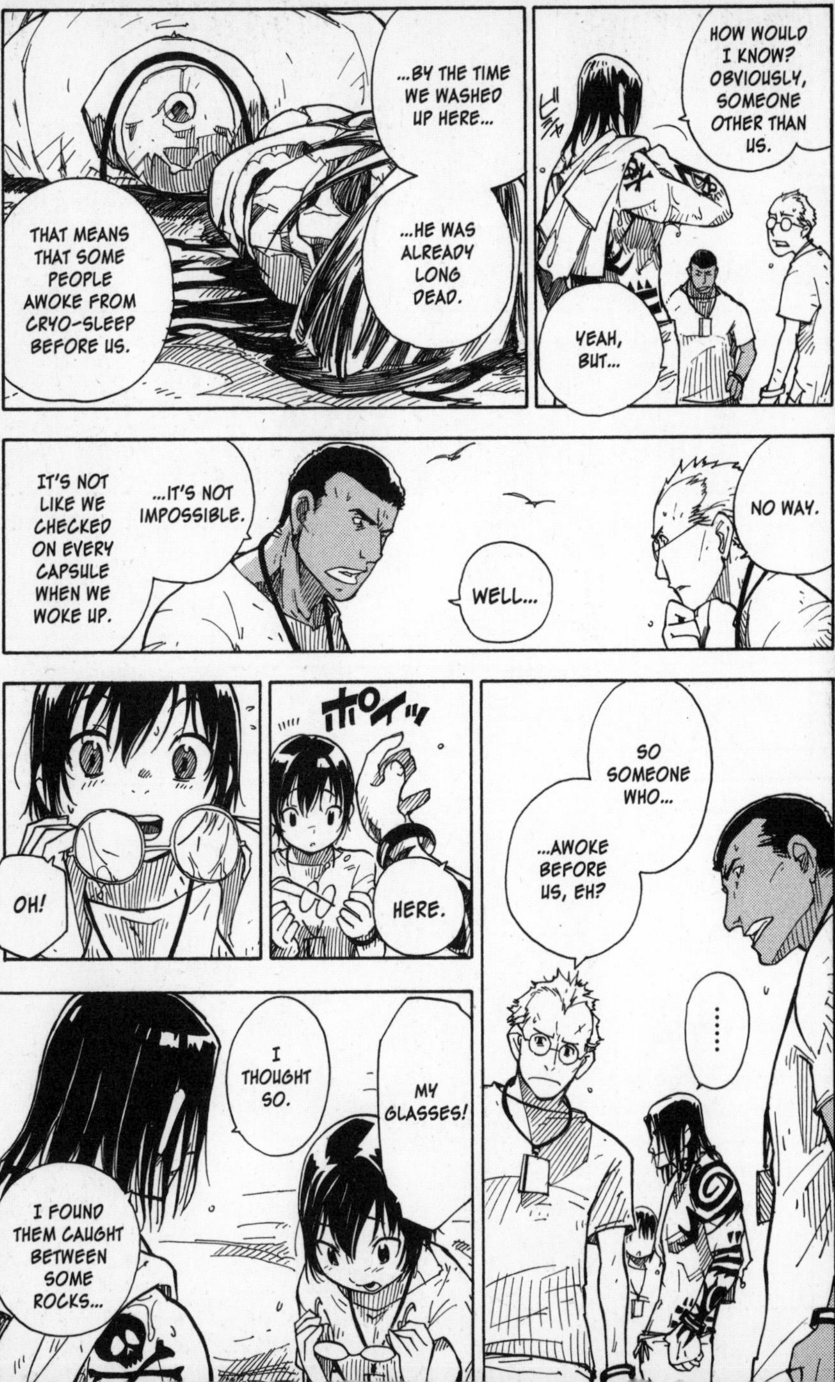
HOW WOULD I KNOW? OBVIOUSLY, SOMEONE OTHER THAN US.
YEAH, BUT...
...BY THE TIME WE WASHED UP HERE...
...HE WAS ALREADY LONG DEAD.
THAT MEANS THAT SOME PEOPLE AWOKE FROM CRYO-SLEEP BEFORE US.
NO WAY.
WELL...
...IT'S NOT IMPOSSIBLE.
IT'S NOT LIKE WE CHECKED ON EVERY CAPSULE WHEN WE WOKE UP.
SO SOMEONE WHO...
...AWOKE BEFORE US, EH?
......
ホイッ
HERE.
OH!
MY GLASSES!
I THOUGHT SO.
I FOUND THEM CAUGHT BETWEEN SOME ROCKS...

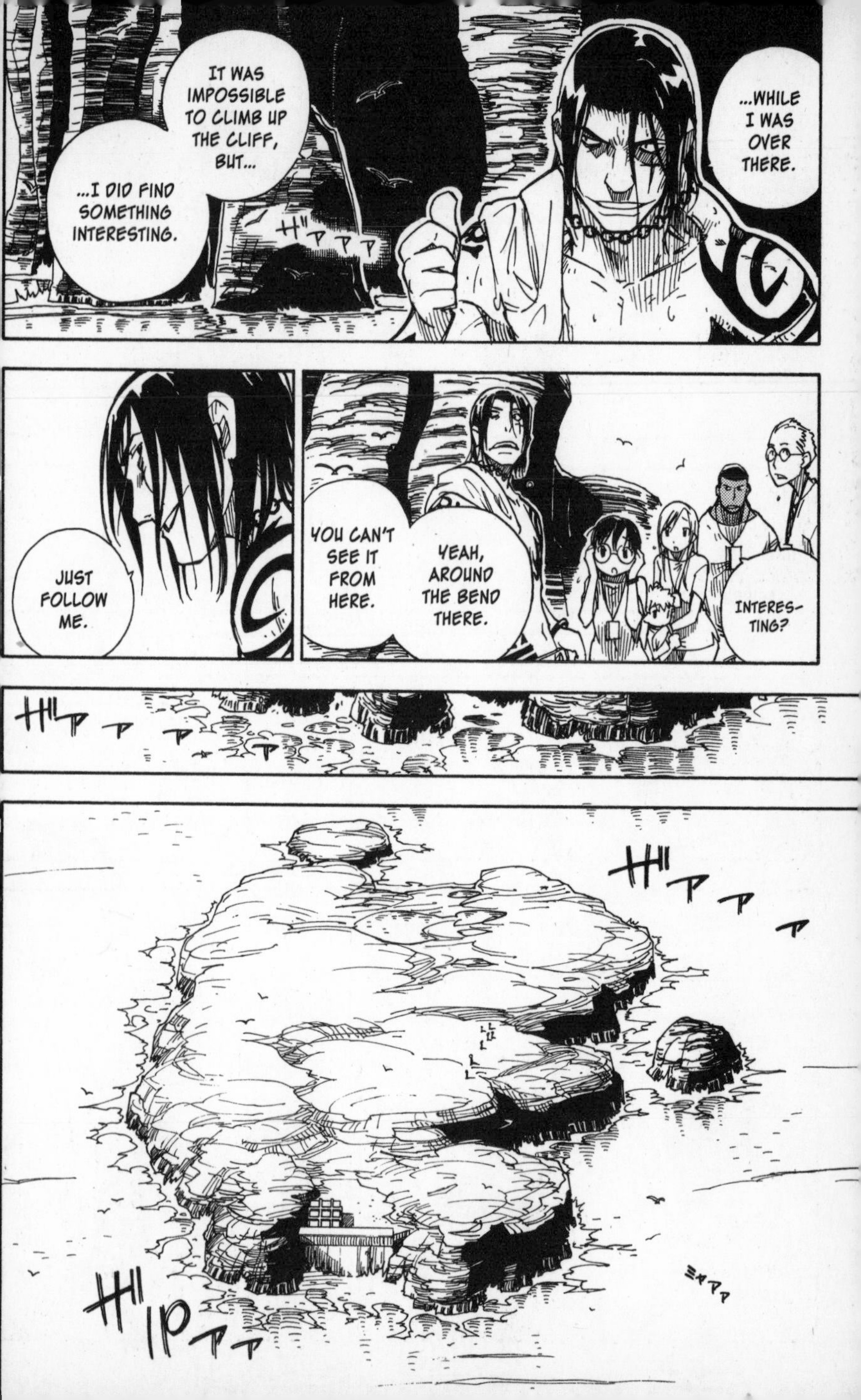
...WHILE I WAS OVER THERE.
IT WAS IMPOSSIBLE TO CLIMB UP THE CLIFF, BUT...
...I DID FIND SOMETHING INTERESTING.
INTERESTING?
YEAH, AROUND THE BEND THERE.
YOU CAN'T SEE IT FROM HERE.
JUST FOLLOW ME.

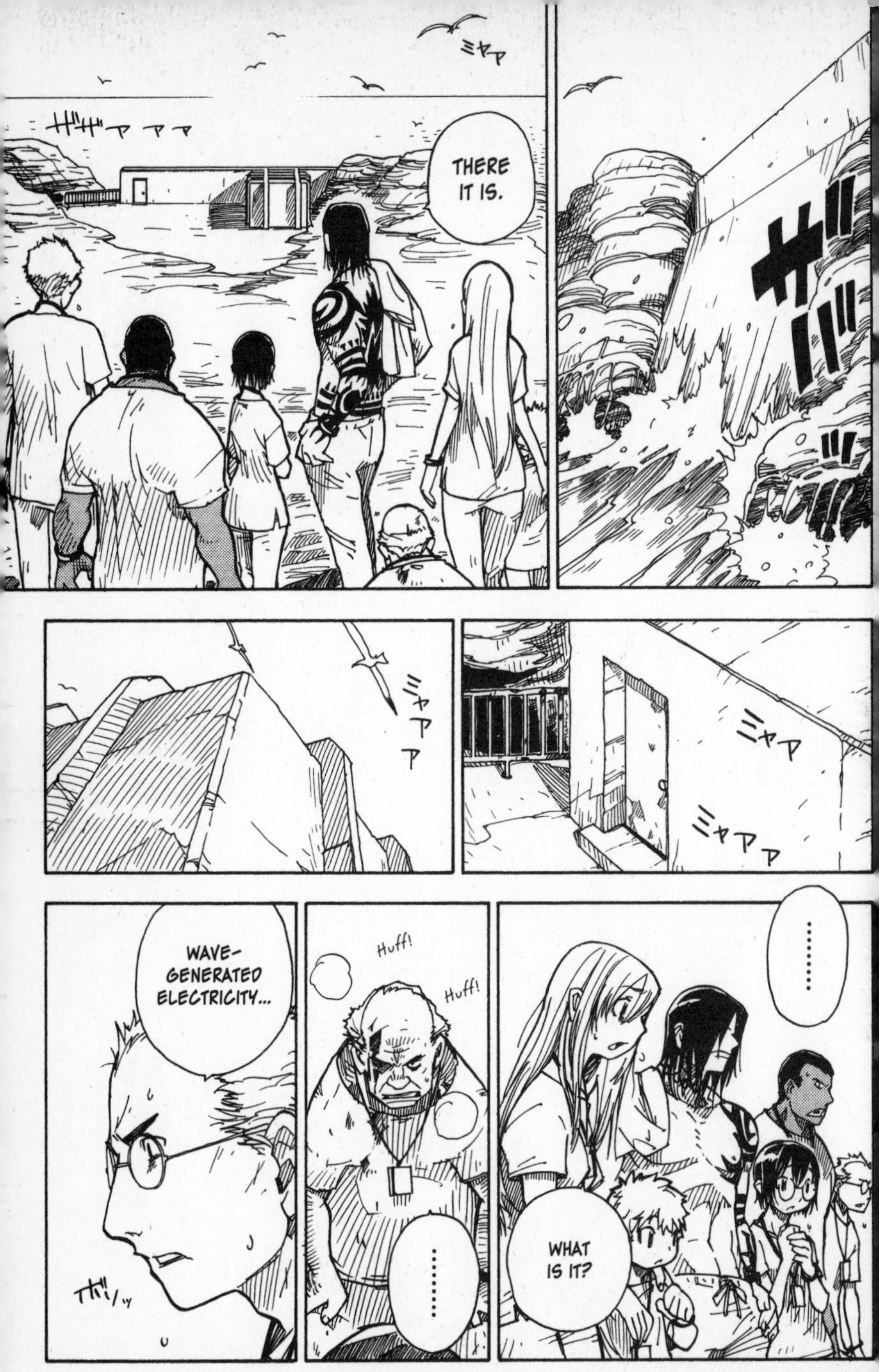
ミャア
THERE IT IS.
ミャアア
ミャア
ミャアア
ミャアア
......
WHAT IS IT?
Huff!
Huff!
......
WAVE-GENERATED ELECTRICITY...

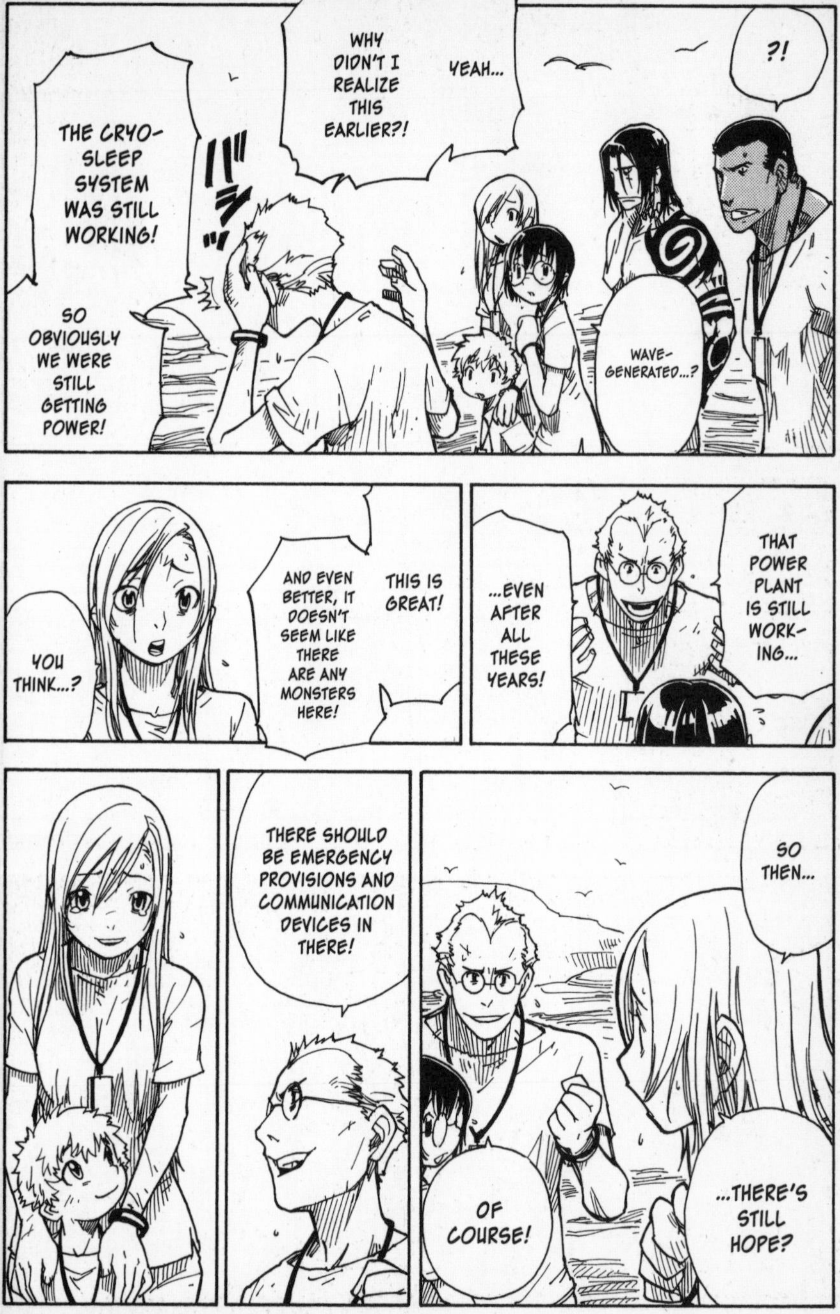
?!
YEAH...
WHY DIDN'T I REALIZE THIS EARLIER?!
WAVE-GENERATED...?
THE CRYO-SLEEP SYSTEM WAS STILL WORKING!
SO OBVIOUSLY WE WERE STILL GETTING POWER!
THAT POWER PLANT IS STILL WORKING...
...EVEN AFTER ALL THESE YEARS!
THIS IS GREAT!
AND EVEN BETTER, IT DOESN'T SEEM LIKE THERE ARE ANY MONSTERS HERE!
YOU THINK...?
SO THEN...
...THERE'S STILL HOPE?
OF COURSE!
THERE SHOULD BE EMERGENCY PROVISIONS AND COMMUNICATION DEVICES IN THERE!

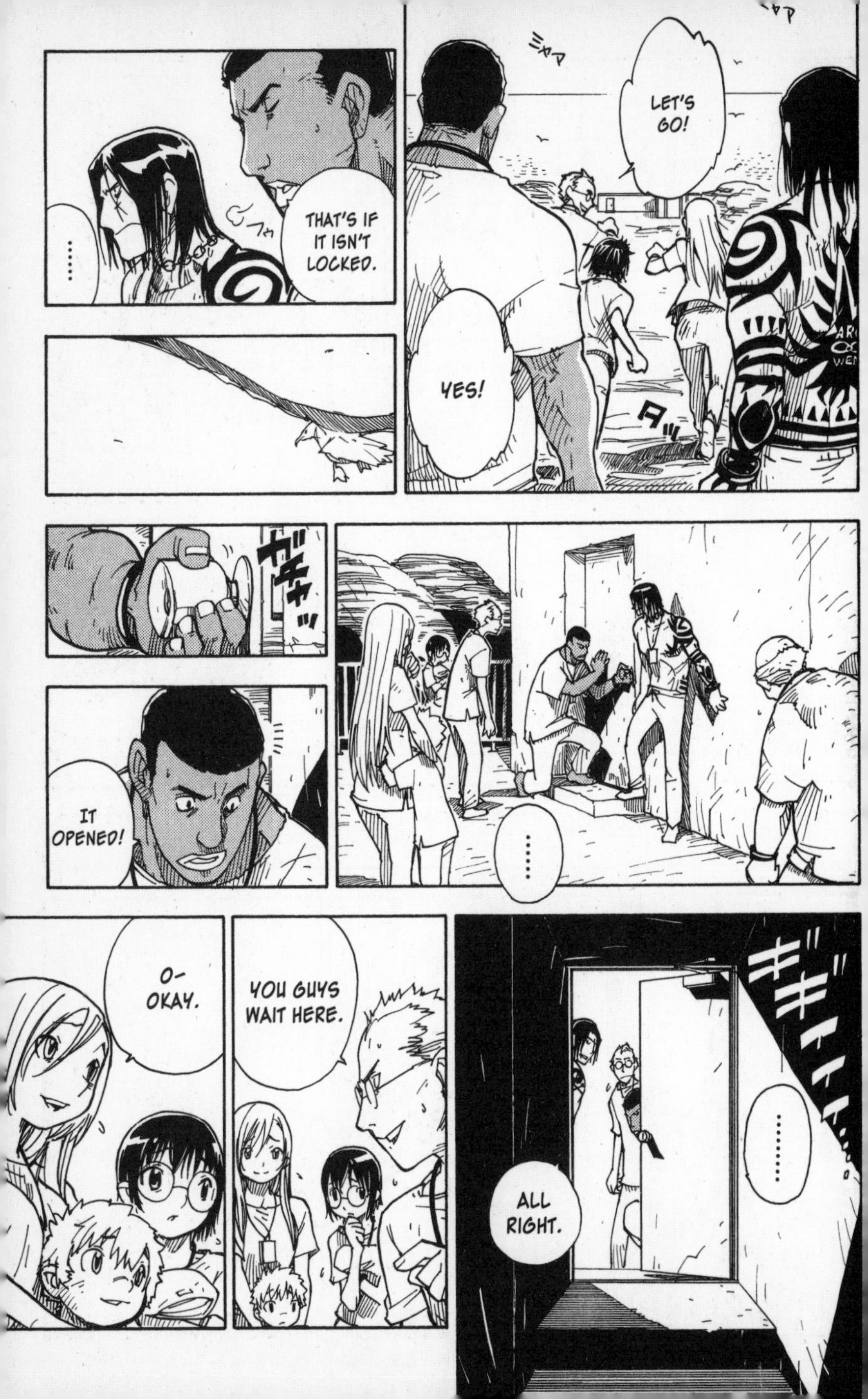
LET'S GO!
YES!
THAT'S IF IT ISN'T LOCKED.
......
......
IT OPENED!
......
ALL RIGHT.
YOU GUYS WAIT HERE.
O- OKAY.

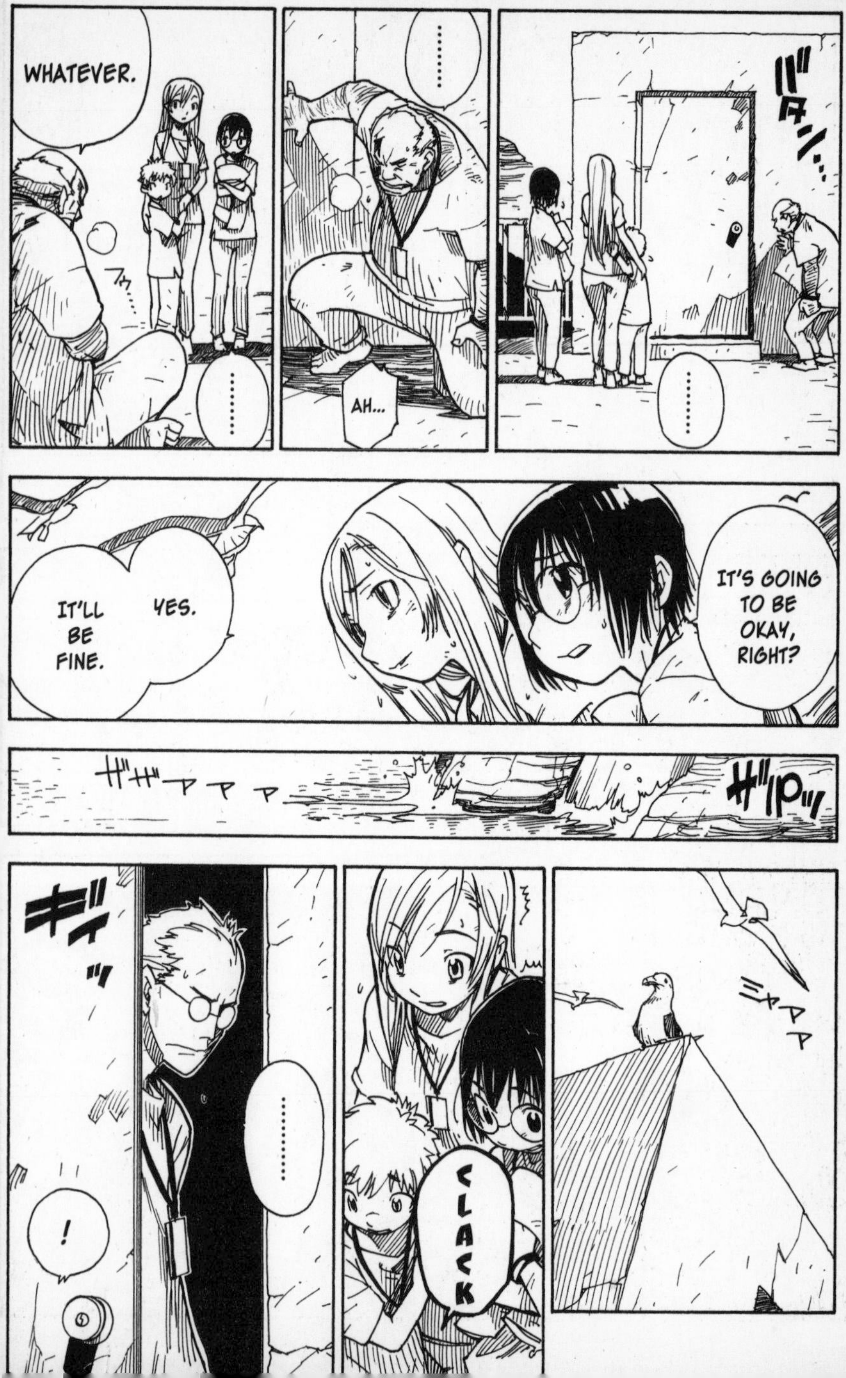

バタン…
……
……
AH...
WHATEVER.
フゥ…
……
IT'S GOING TO BE OKAY, RIGHT?
YES.
IT'LL BE FINE.
ザパッ
ザザァァァ
ミャアア
CLACK
ギィッ
……
!

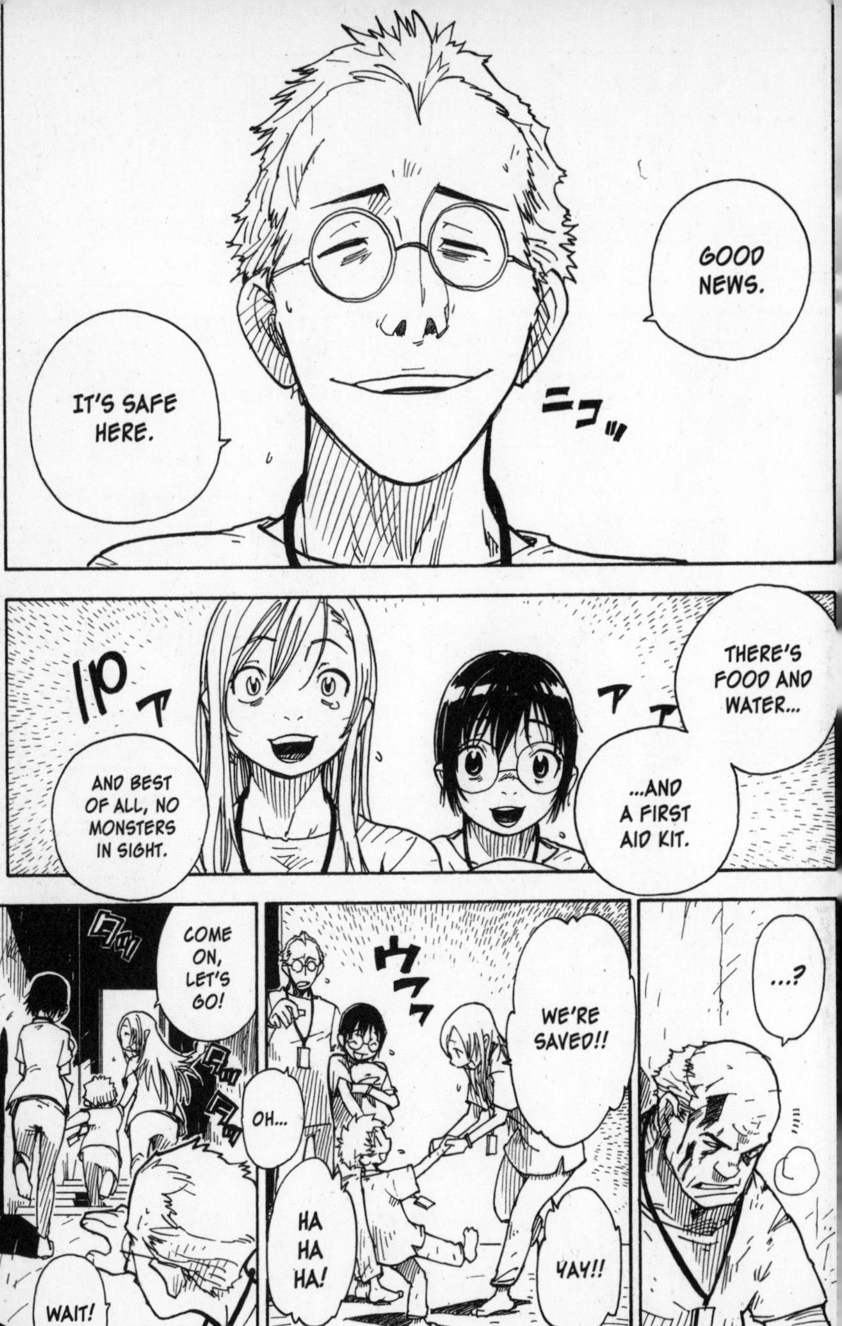
GOOD NEWS.
IT'S SAFE HERE.
ニコッ
THERE'S FOOD AND WATER...
...AND A FIRST AID KIT.
AND BEST OF ALL, NO MONSTERS IN SIGHT.
...?
WE'RE SAVED!!
OH...
HA HA HA!
YAY!!
COME ON, LET'S GO!
WAIT!

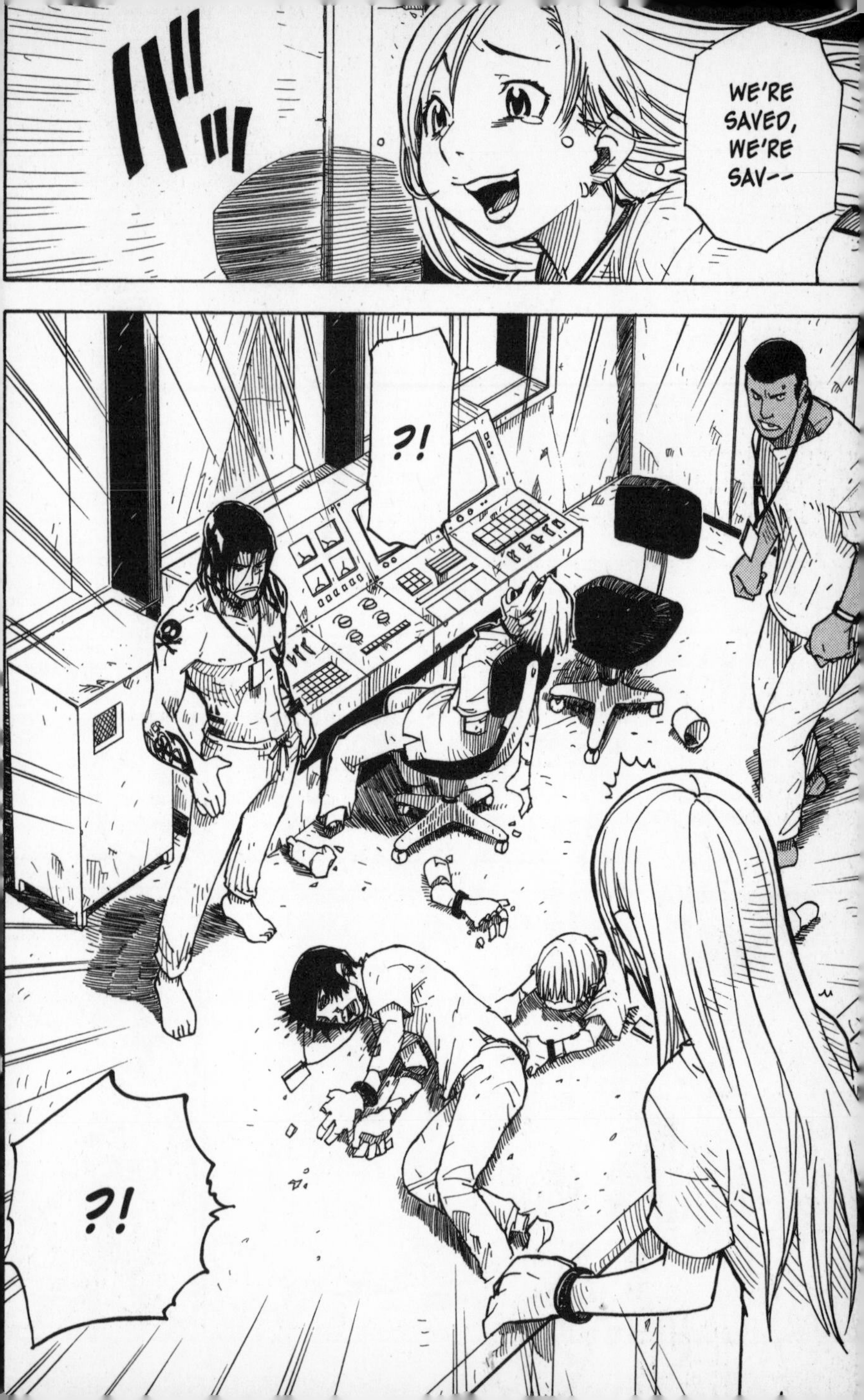
WE'RE SAVED, WE'RE SAV--
?!
?!

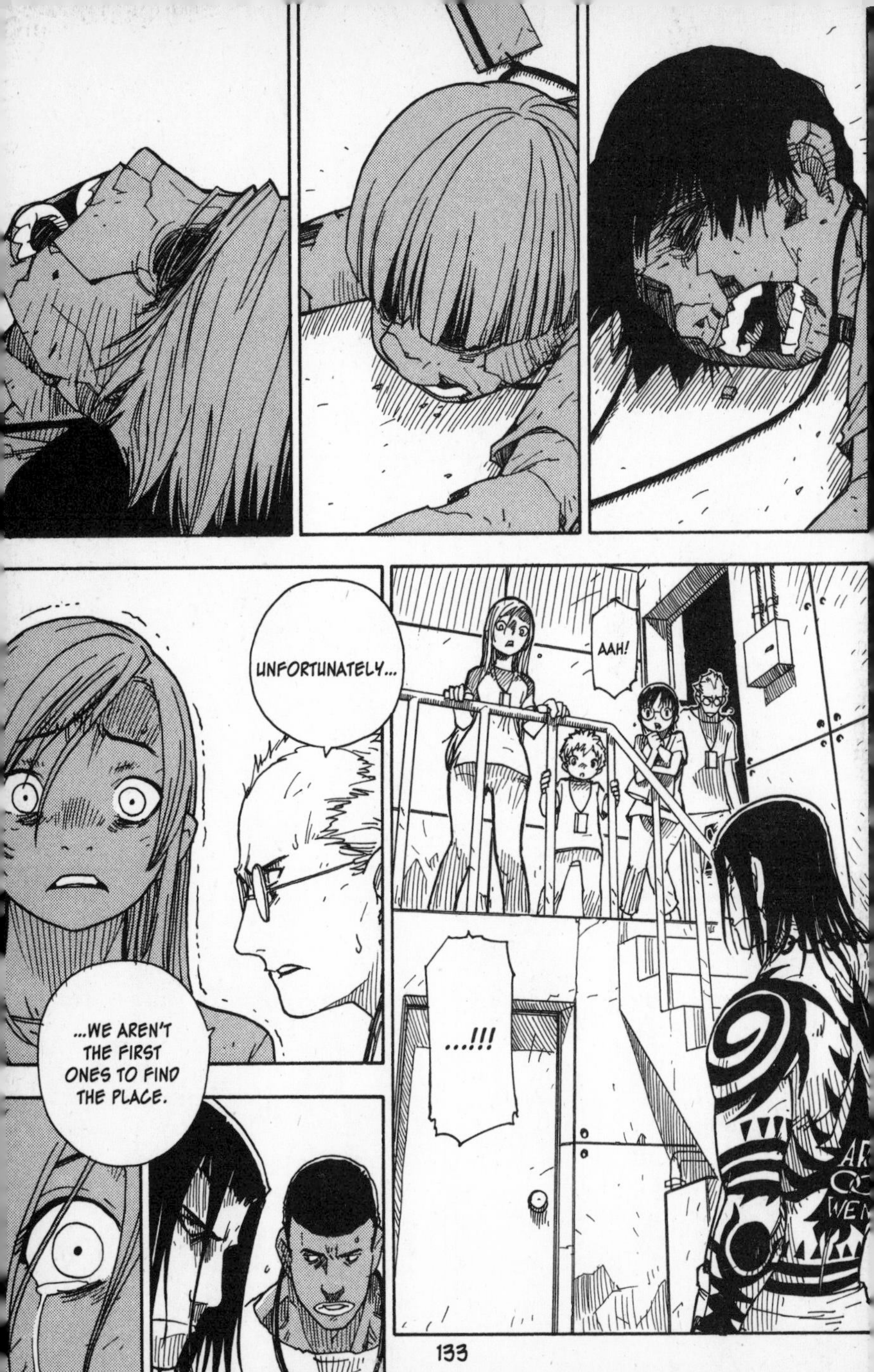
AAH!
UNFORTUNATELY...
...!!!
...WE AREN'T THE FIRST ONES TO FIND THE PLACE.

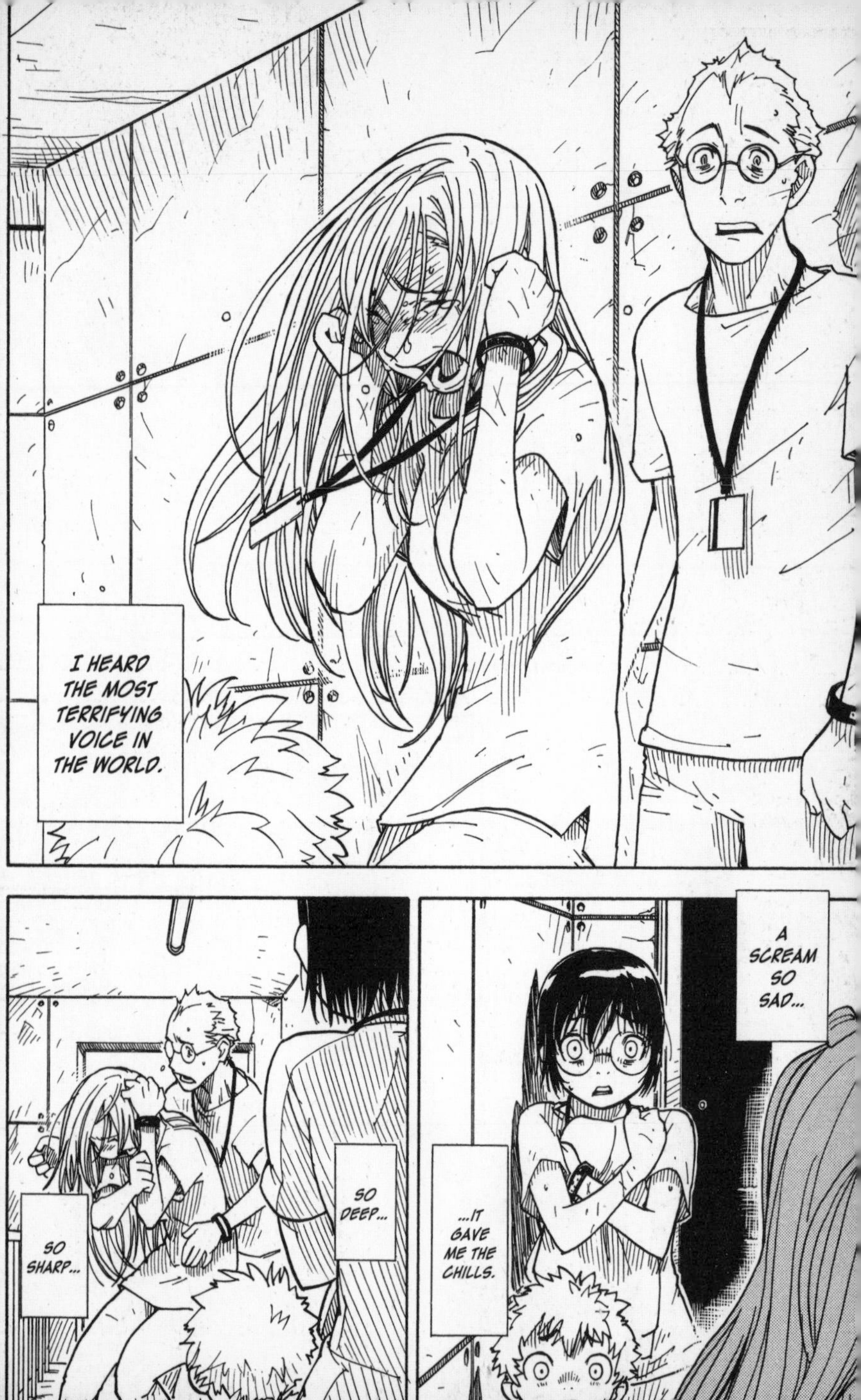
I HEARD THE MOST TERRIFYING VOICE IN THE WORLD.
A SCREAM SO SAD...
...IT GAVE ME THE CHILLS.
SO DEEP...
SO SHARP...

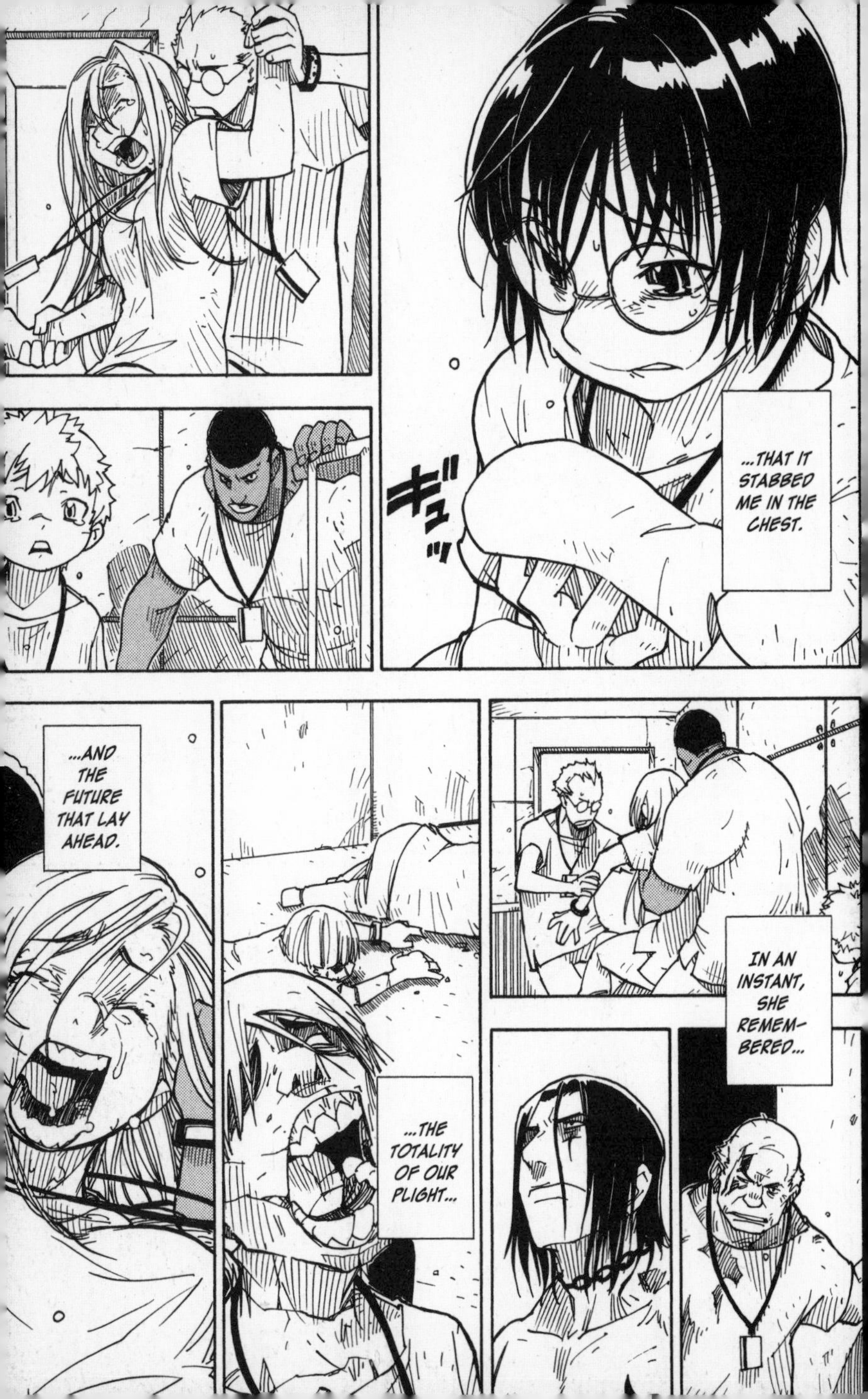
...THAT IT STABBED ME IN THE CHEST.
ギュッ
IN AN INSTANT, SHE REMEMBERED...
...THE TOTALITY OF OUR PLIGHT...
...AND THE FUTURE THAT LAY AHEAD.

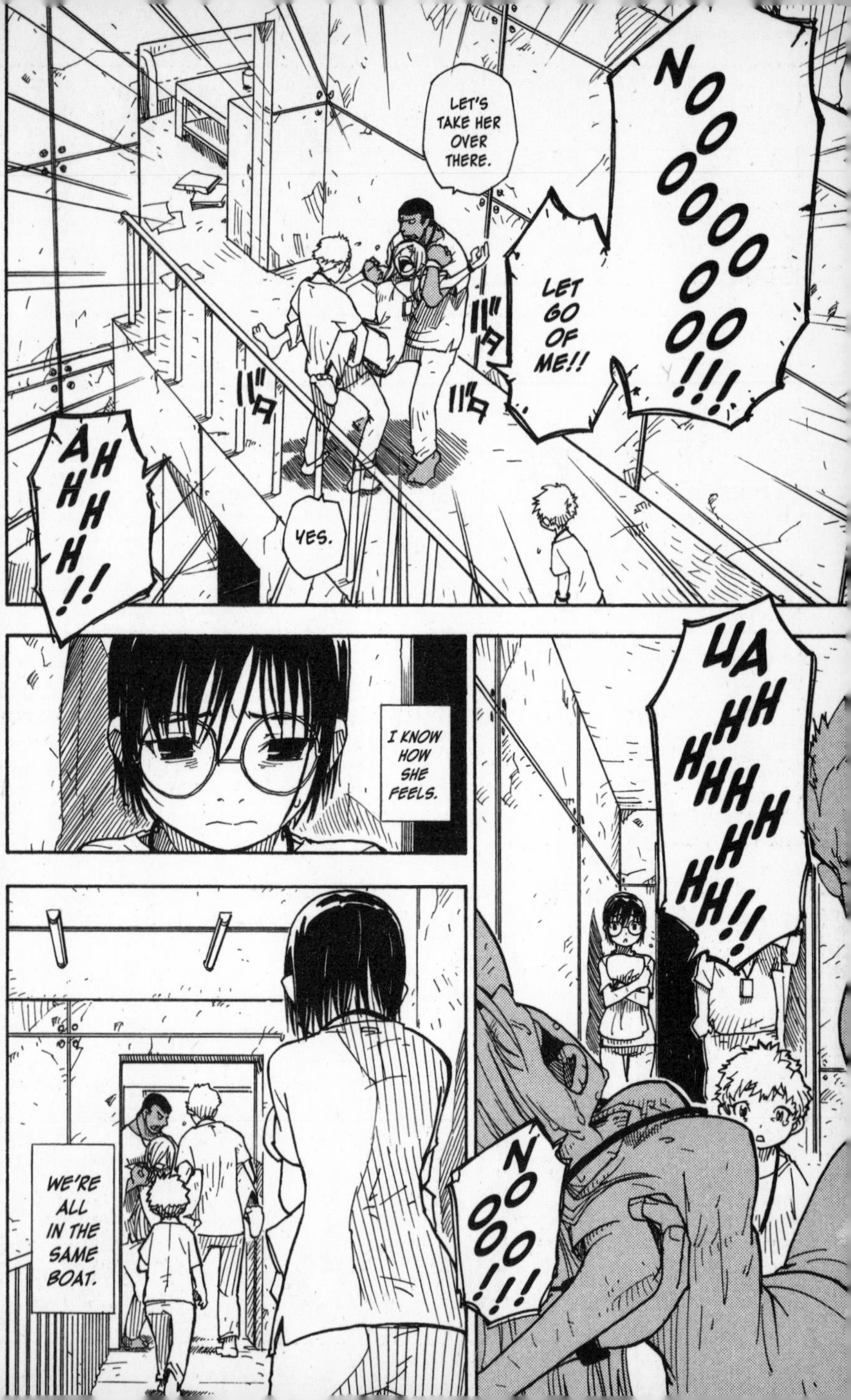

NOOOOOOOOOO!!!
LET'S TAKE HER OVER THERE.
LET GO OF ME!!
バタ
バタ
バタ
AHHHH!!
YES.
UAHHHHHHHHHH!!
NOOOOO!!!
I KNOW HOW SHE FEELS.
WE'RE ALL IN THE SAME BOAT.

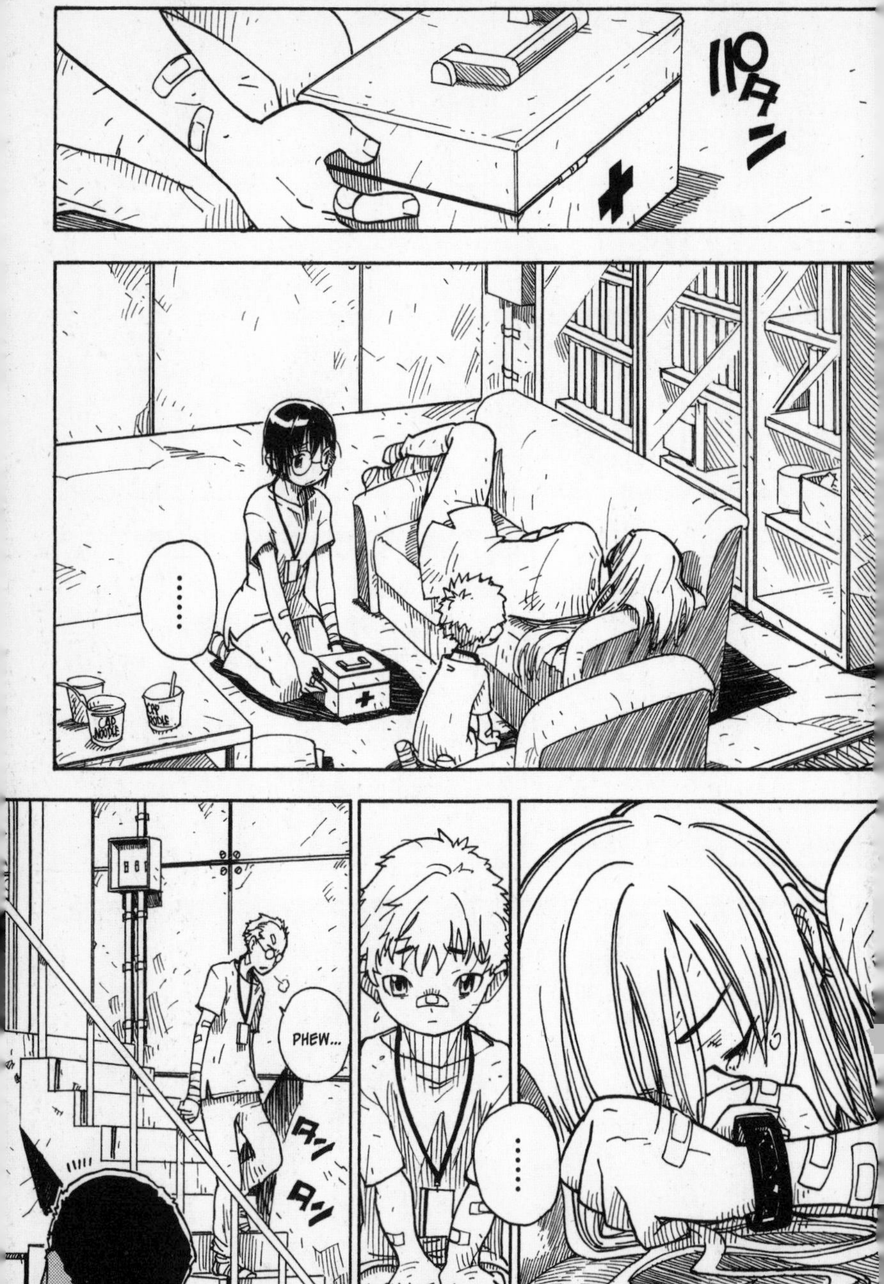
パタン
......
......
PHEW...
タッ
タッ
!!!

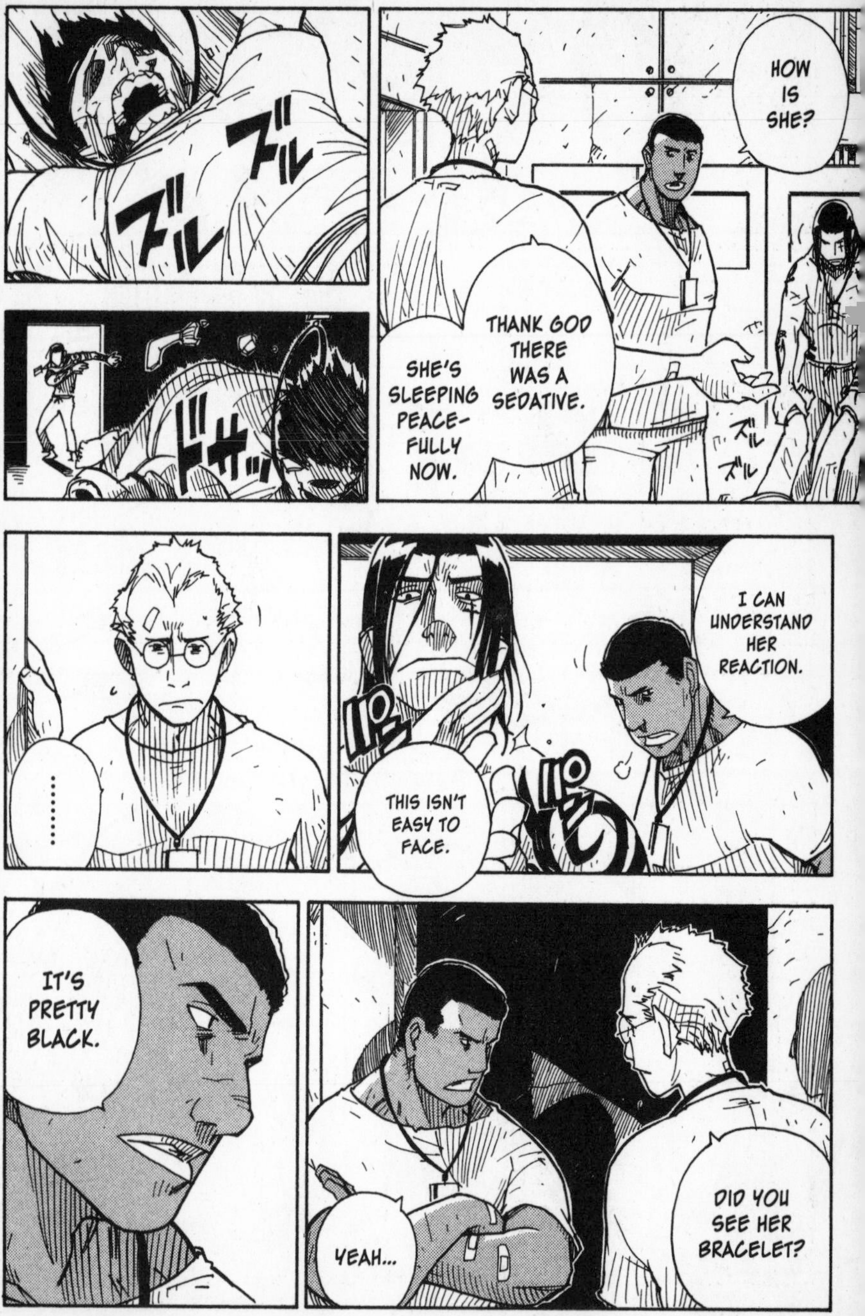
HOW IS SHE?
THANK GOD THERE WAS A SEDATIVE.
SHE'S SLEEPING PEACE-FULLY NOW.
ズル
ズル
ズル
ズル
ドサッ
I CAN UNDERSTAND HER REACTION.
THIS ISN'T EASY TO FACE.
......
DID YOU SEE HER BRACELET?
YEAH...
IT'S PRETTY BLACK.

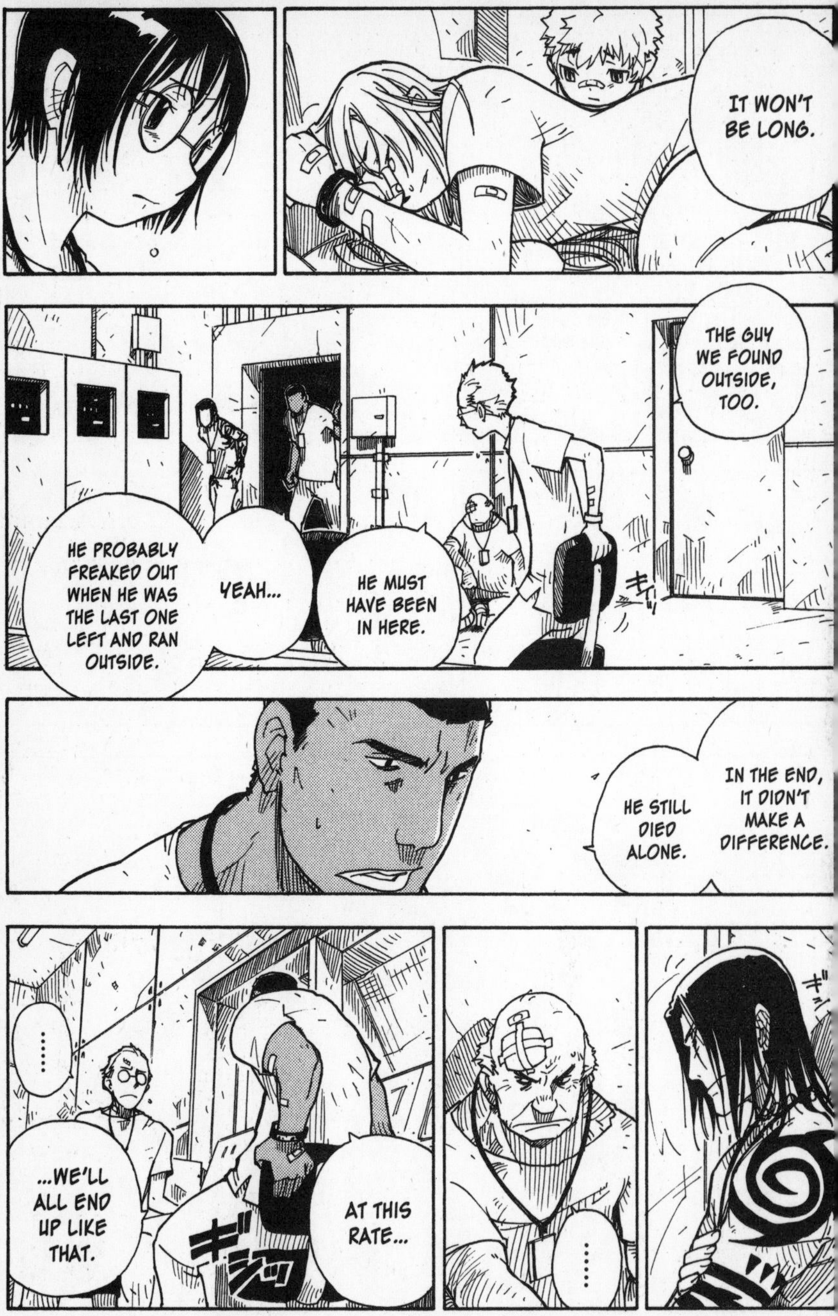
IT WON'T BE LONG.
THE GUY WE FOUND OUTSIDE, TOO.
HE MUST HAVE BEEN IN HERE.
YEAH...
HE PROBABLY FREAKED OUT WHEN HE WAS THE LAST ONE LEFT AND RAN OUTSIDE.
IN THE END, IT DIDN'T MAKE A DIFFERENCE.
HE STILL DIED ALONE.
......
......
AT THIS RATE...
...WE'LL ALL END UP LIKE THAT.

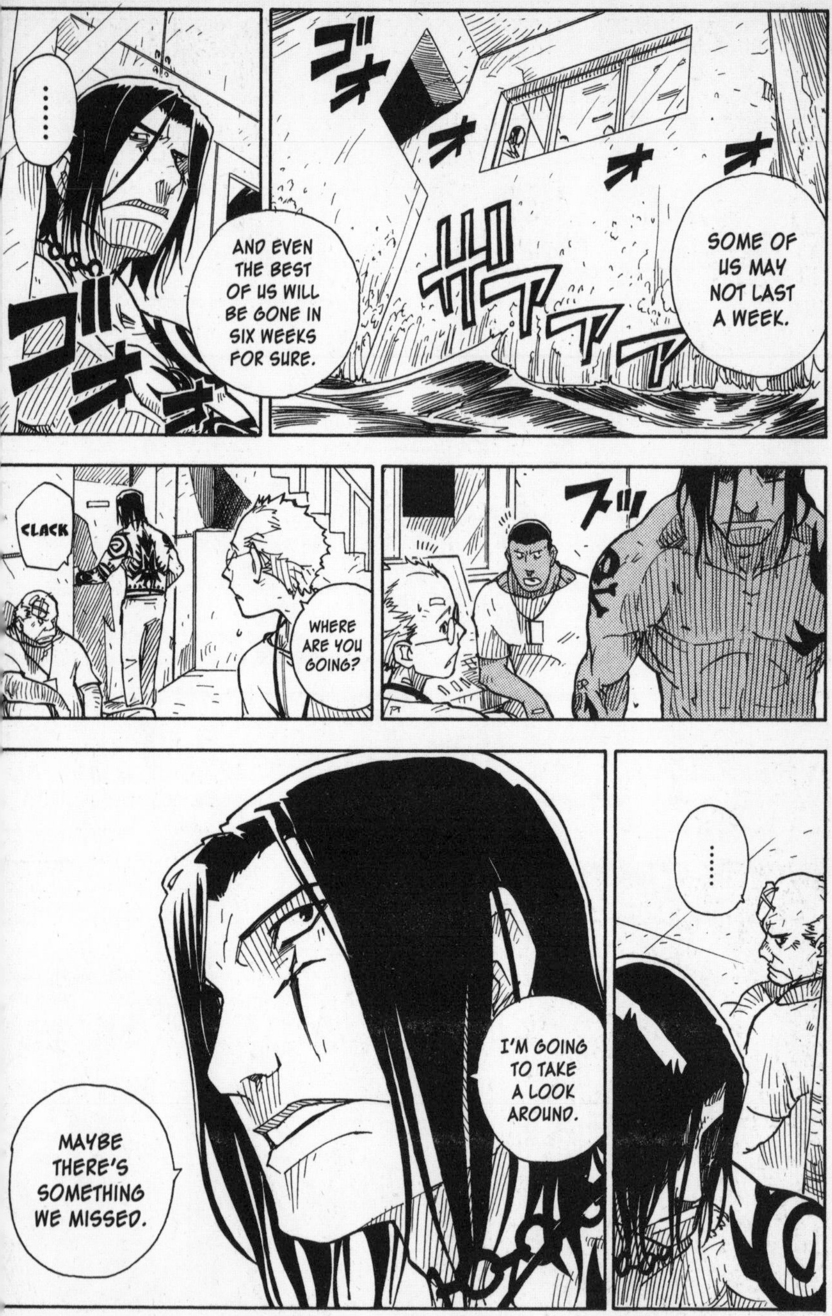
SOME OF US MAY NOT LAST A WEEK.
ゴオオオオ
ザァァァ
……
AND EVEN THE BEST OF US WILL BE GONE IN SIX WEEKS FOR SURE.
ゴオオ
ズッ
CLACK
WHERE ARE YOU GOING?
……
I'M GOING TO TAKE A LOOK AROUND.
MAYBE THERE'S SOMETHING WE MISSED.

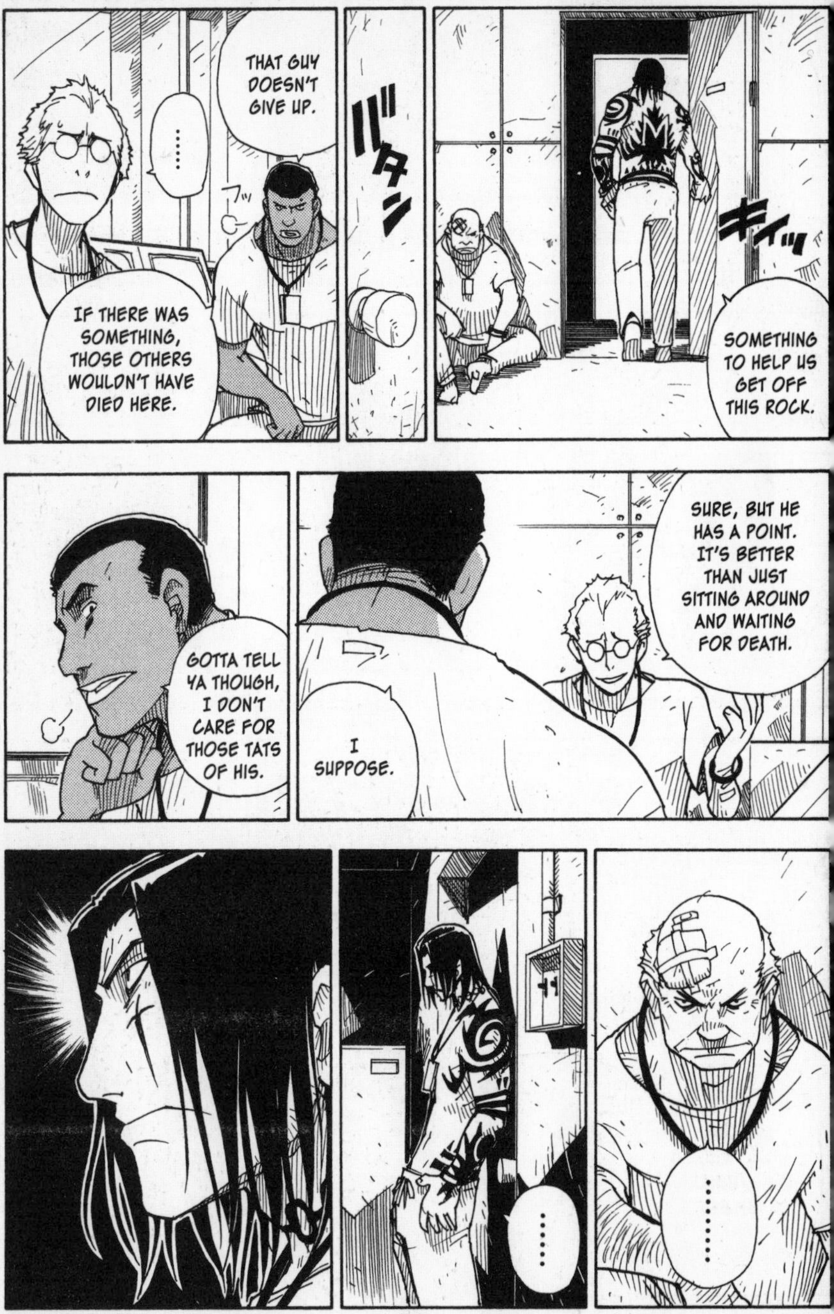
キィッ
SOMETHING TO HELP US GET OFF THIS ROCK.
バタン
THAT GUY DOESN'T GIVE UP.
......
フッ
IF THERE WAS SOMETHING, THOSE OTHERS WOULDN'T HAVE DIED HERE.
SURE, BUT HE HAS A POINT. IT'S BETTER THAN JUST SITTING AROUND AND WAITING FOR DEATH.
I SUPPOSE.
GOTTA TELL YA THOUGH, I DON'T CARE FOR THOSE TATS OF HIS.
....
......

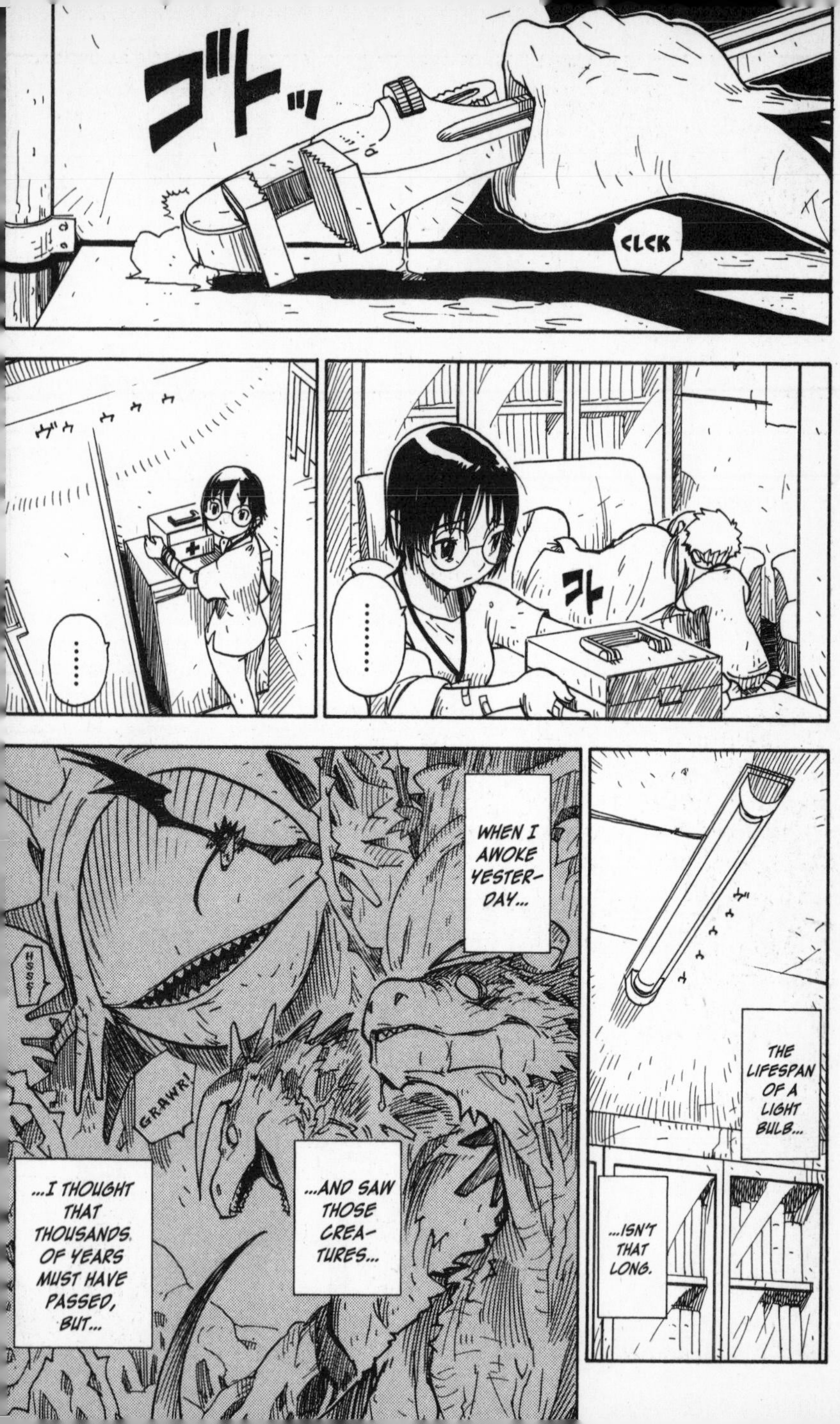
ゴトッ
CLCK
......
カ
......
WHEN I AWOKE YESTER-DAY...
...AND SAW THOSE CREA-TURES...
HSSS!
GRAWR!
...I THOUGHT THAT THOUSANDS OF YEARS MUST HAVE PASSED, BUT...
THE LIFESPAN OF A LIGHT BULB...
...ISN'T THAT LONG.

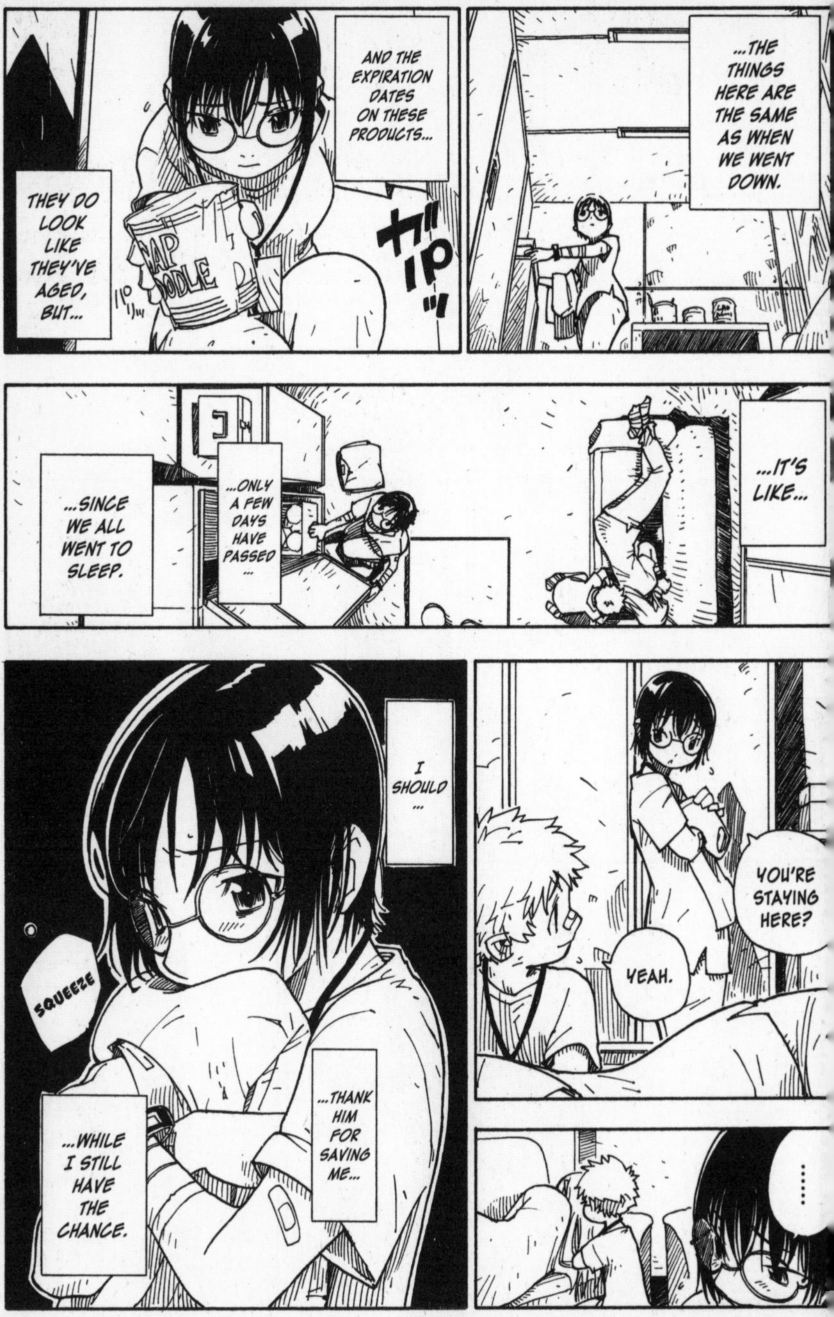
...THE THINGS HERE ARE THE SAME AS WHEN WE WENT DOWN.
AND THE EXPIRATION DATES ON THESE PRODUCTS...
THEY DO LOOK LIKE THEY'VE AGED, BUT...
...IT'S LIKE...
...ONLY A FEW DAYS HAVE PASSED...
...SINCE WE ALL WENT TO SLEEP.
YOU'RE STAYING HERE?
YEAH.
......
I SHOULD...
...THANK HIM FOR SAVING ME...
...WHILE I STILL HAVE THE CHANCE.
SQUEEZE

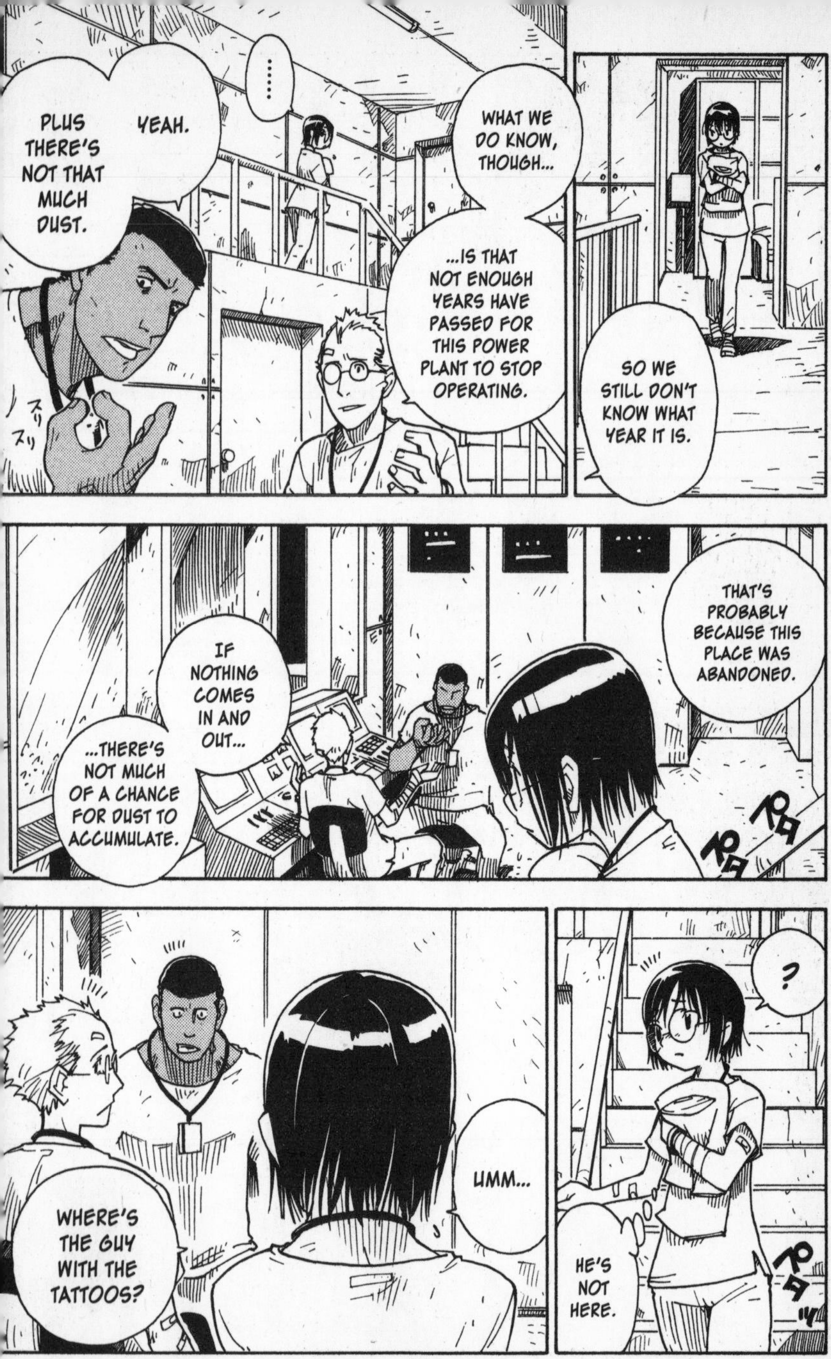
SO WE STILL DON'T KNOW WHAT YEAR IT IS.
WHAT WE DO KNOW, THOUGH...
...IS THAT NOT ENOUGH YEARS HAVE PASSED FOR THIS POWER PLANT TO STOP OPERATING.
......
YEAH.
PLUS THERE'S NOT THAT MUCH DUST.
スリ
スリ
THAT'S PROBABLY BECAUSE THIS PLACE WAS ABANDONED.
IF NOTHING COMES IN AND OUT...
...THERE'S NOT MUCH OF A CHANCE FOR DUST TO ACCUMULATE.
?
HE'S NOT HERE.
UMM...
WHERE'S THE GUY WITH THE TATTOOS?

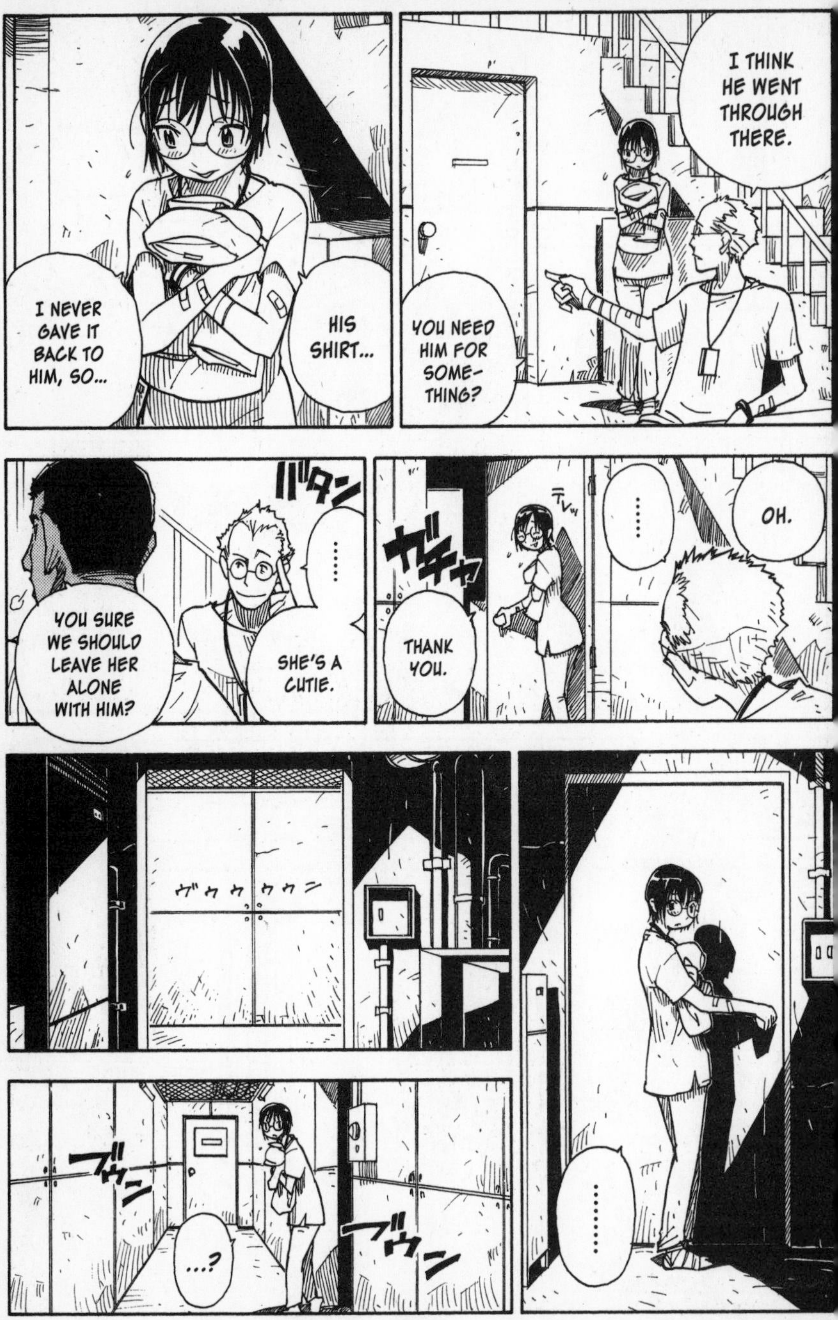
I THINK HE WENT THROUGH THERE.
YOU NEED HIM FOR SOMETHING?
HIS SHIRT...
I NEVER GAVE IT BACK TO HIM, SO...
OH.
......
ガチャ
THANK YOU.
バタン
......
SHE'S A CUTIE.
YOU SURE WE SHOULD LEAVE HER ALONE WITH HIM?
....
ヴゥゥゥウン
ブゥン
...?
ブゥン

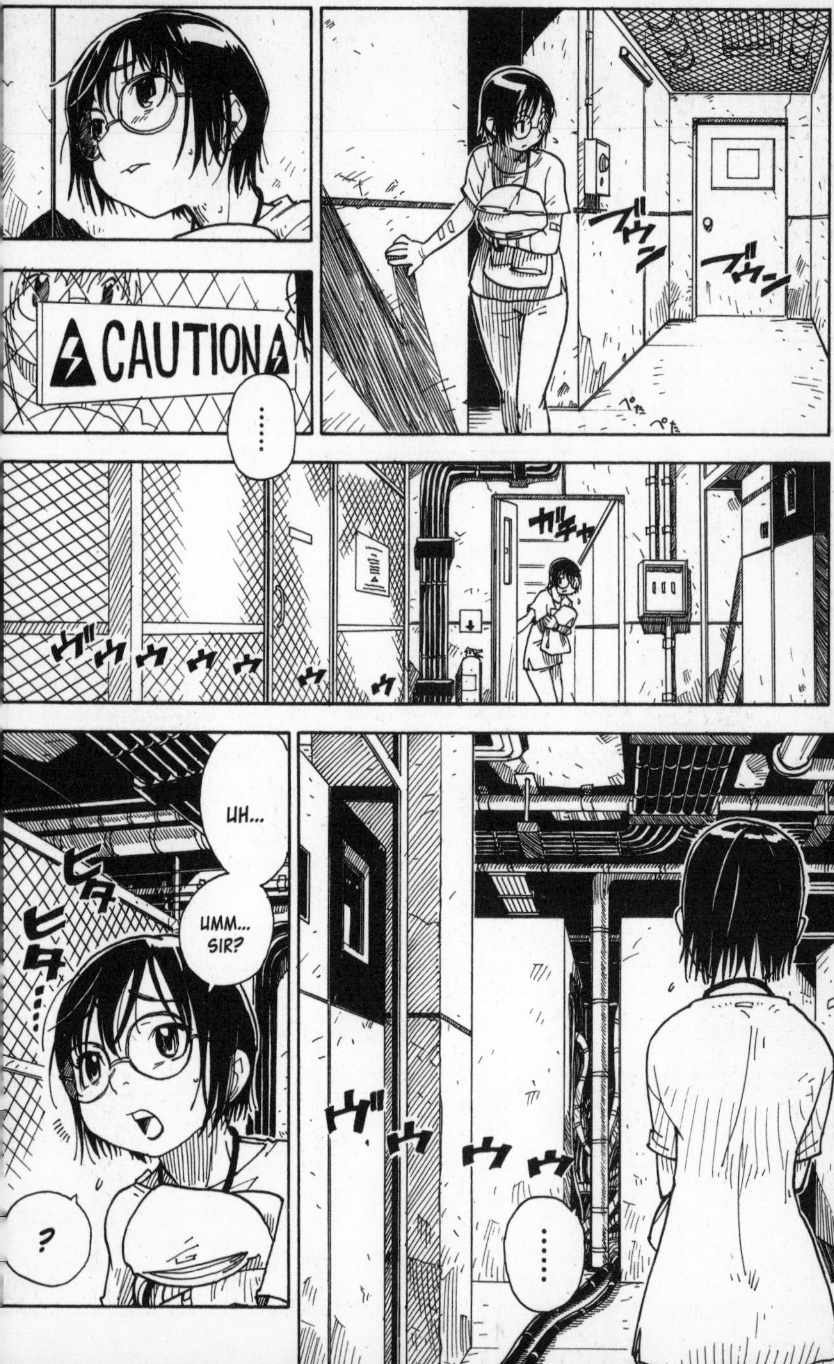

ブゥン
ブゥン
ぺた
ぺた
CAUTION
......
ガチャ
ヴゥゥゥゥゥゥ
ヴゥゥゥ
......
ゥ
UH...
UMM... SIR?
ヒタ ヒタ......
?

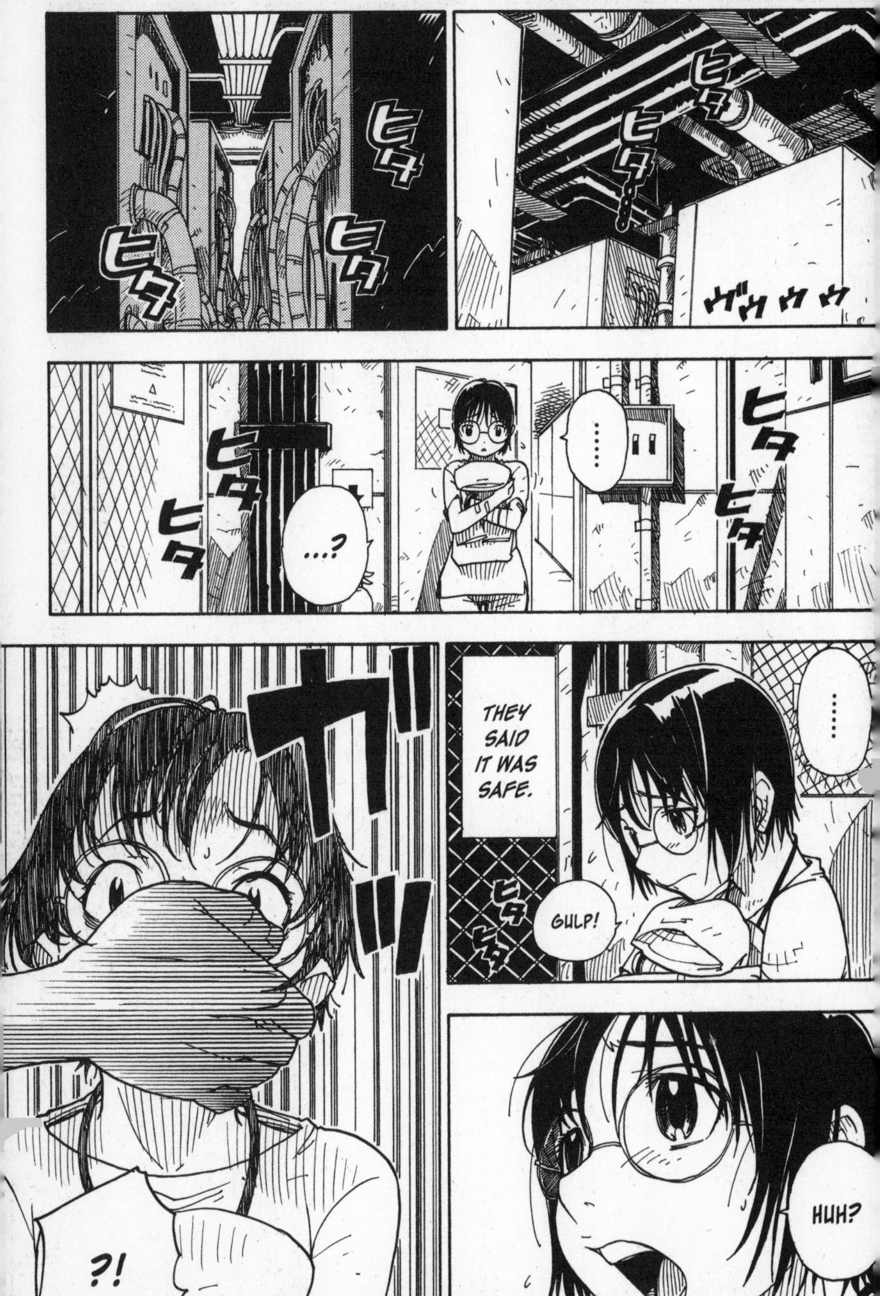
ヒタ
ヒタ
ヴゥゥゥ
ヒタ
ヒタ
ヒタ
ヒタ
ヒタ
......
...?
ヒタ
ヒタ
......
THEY SAID IT WAS SAFE.
GULP!
ヒタ
ヒタ
HUH?
ガ
?!

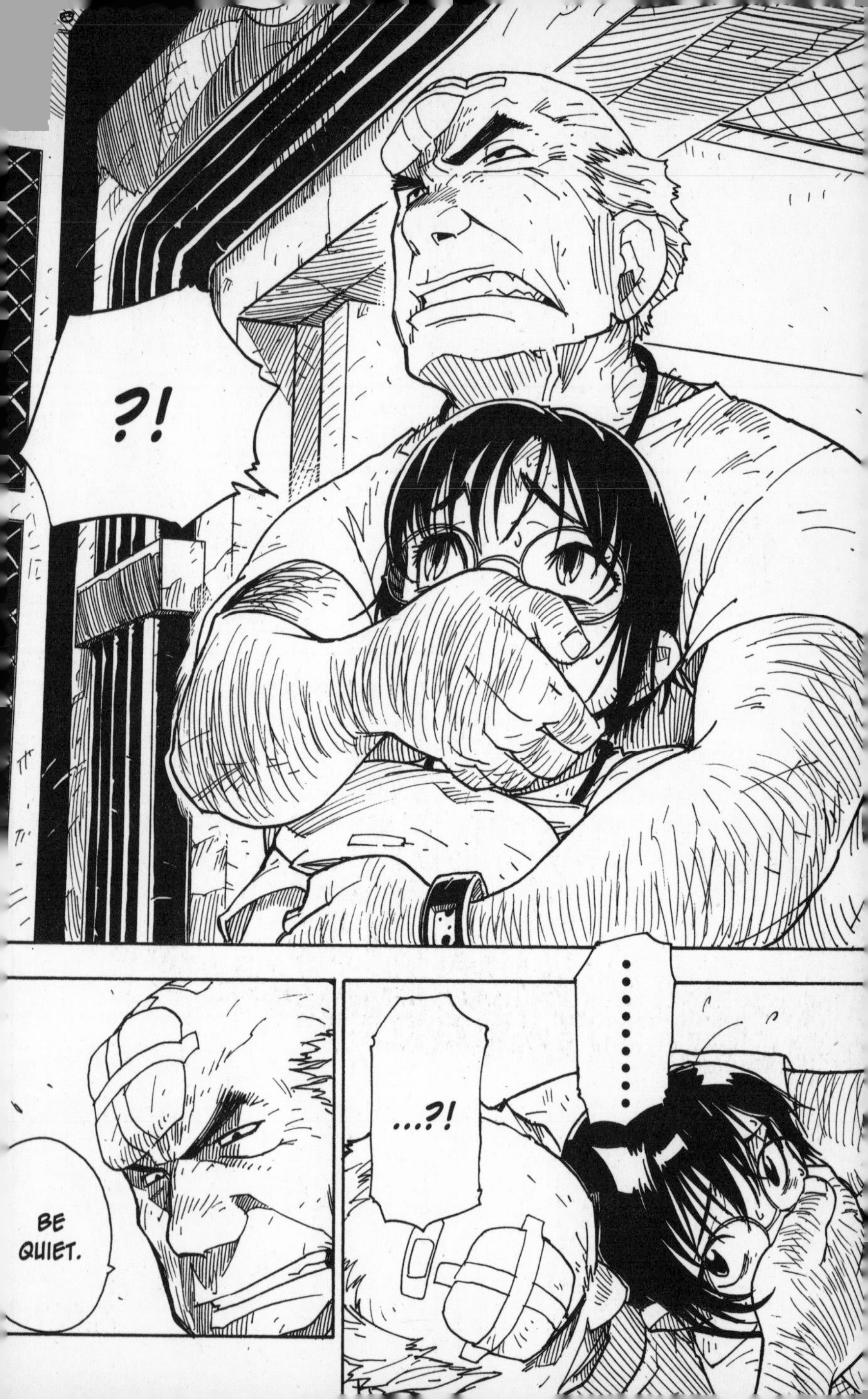
?!
......
...?!
BE QUIET.

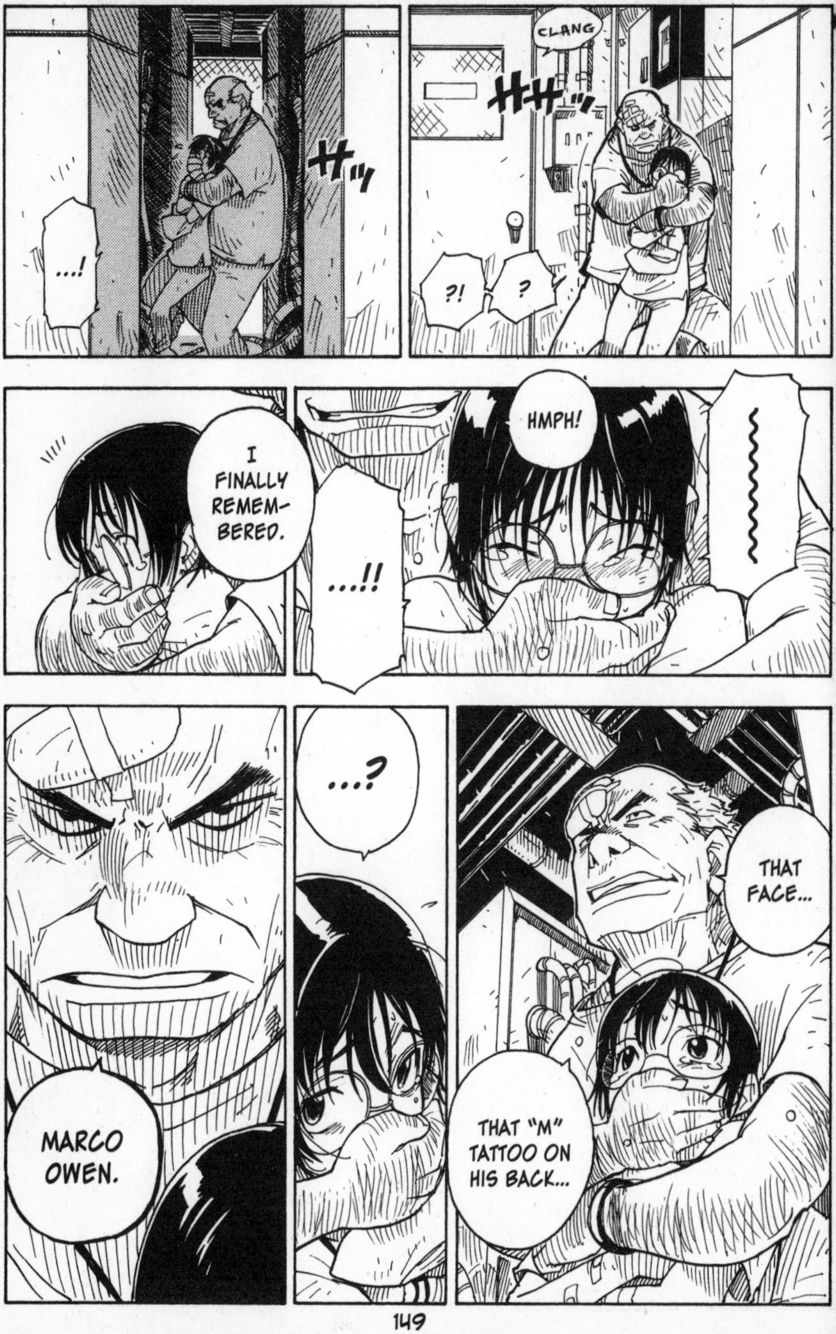
CLANG
ザザッ
?!
?
ザッ
...!
HMPH!
...!!
I FINALLY REMEMBERED.
THAT FACE...
THAT "M" TATTOO ON HIS BACK...
...?
MARCO OWEN.

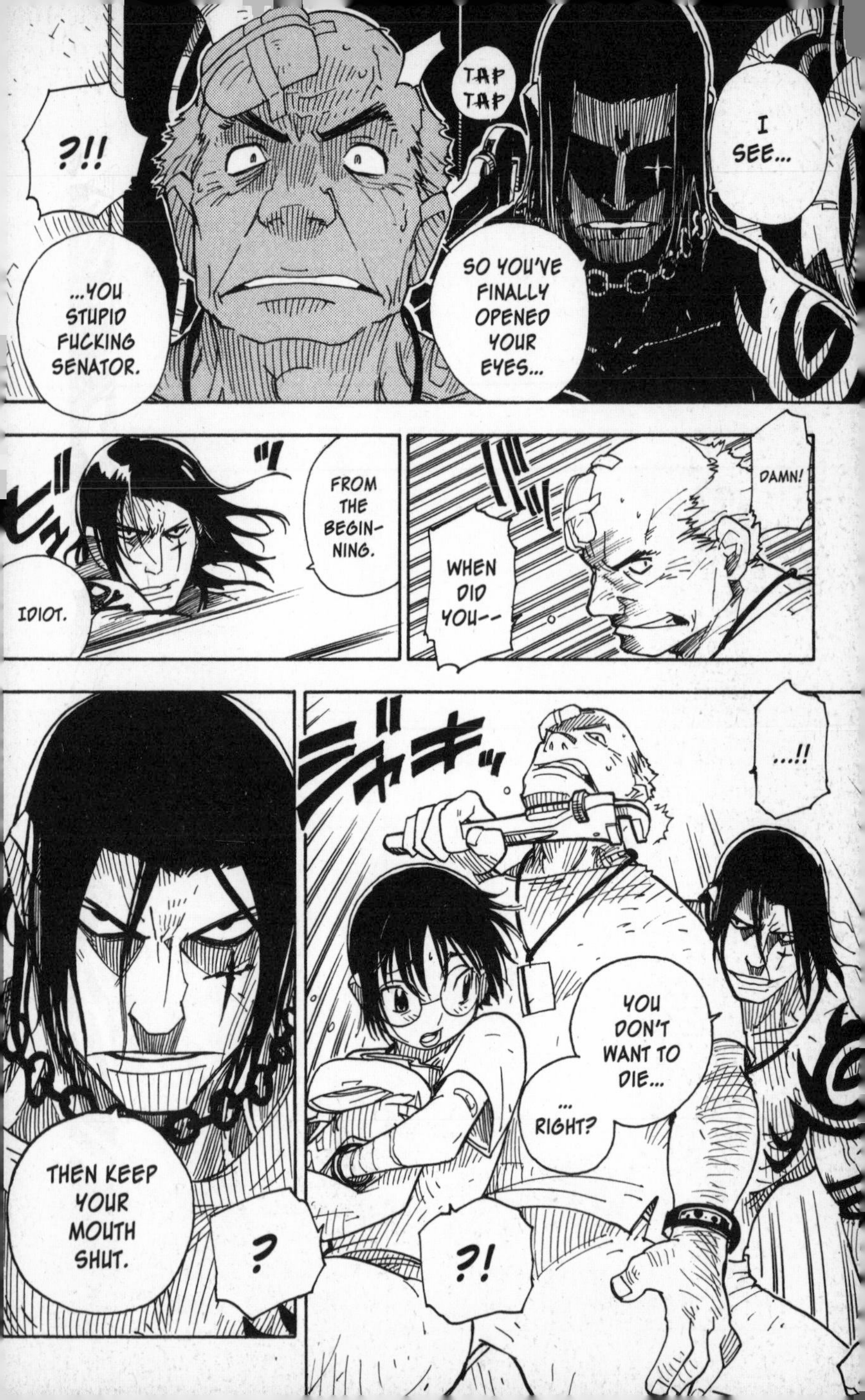
I SEE...
TAP TAP
SO YOU'VE FINALLY OPENED YOUR EYES...
?!!
...YOU STUPID FUCKING SENATOR.
DAMN!
WHEN DID YOU--
FROM THE BEGIN-NING.
IDIOT.
...!!
YOU DON'T WANT TO DIE...
... RIGHT?
?!
THEN KEEP YOUR MOUTH SHUT.
?

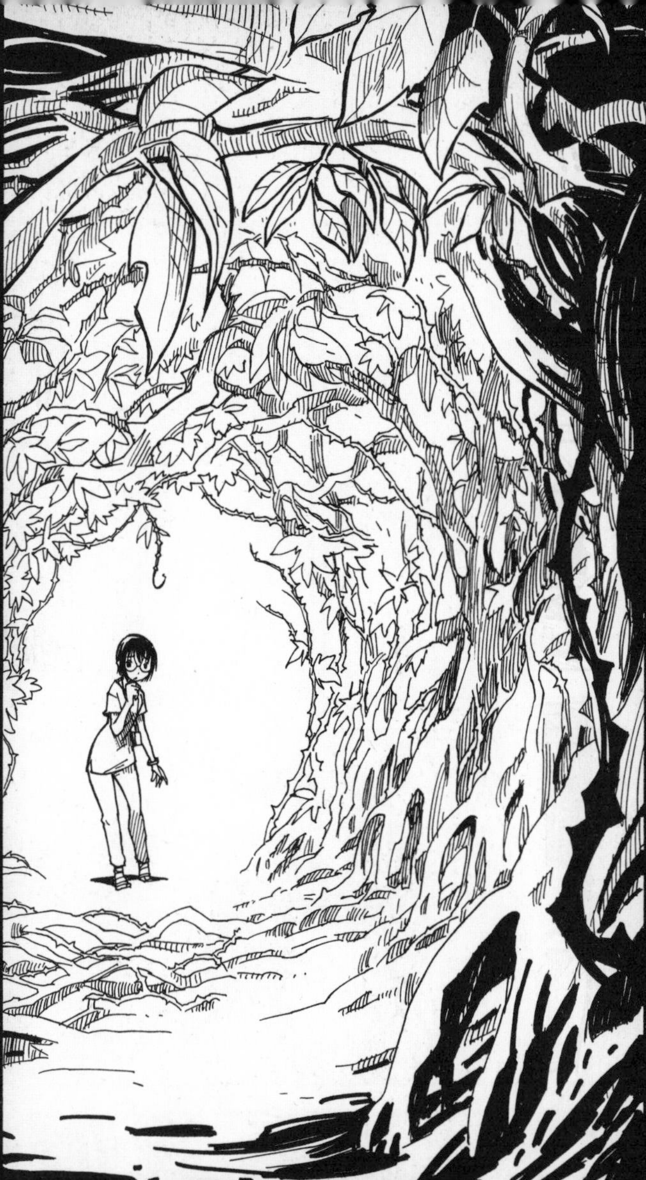

CHAPTER 5
THE THORN GIRL

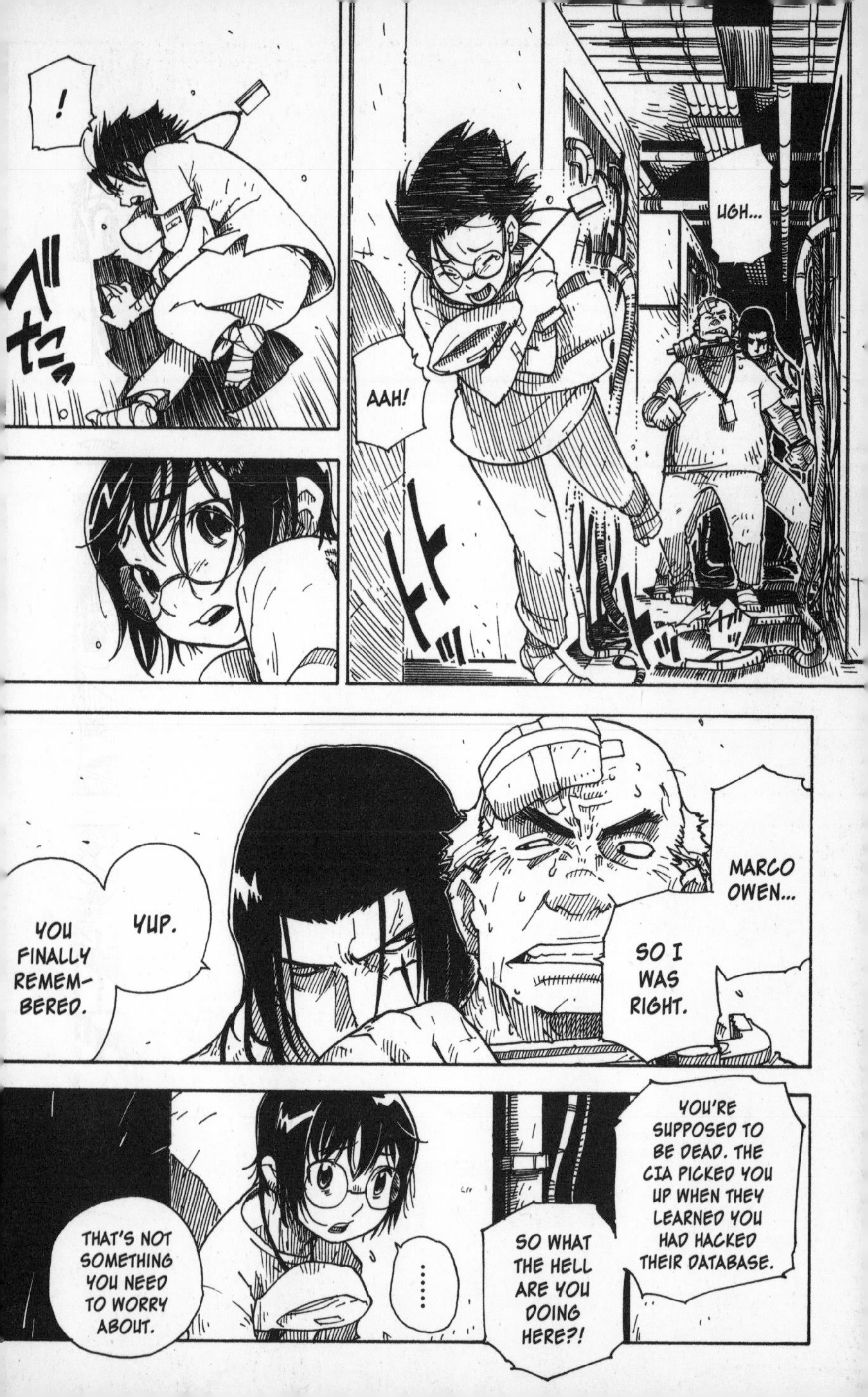
UGH...
AAH!
!
MARCO OWEN...
SO I WAS RIGHT.
YUP.
YOU FINALLY REMEMBERED.
YOU'RE SUPPOSED TO BE DEAD. THE CIA PICKED YOU UP WHEN THEY LEARNED YOU HAD HACKED THEIR DATABASE.
SO WHAT THE HELL ARE YOU DOING HERE?!
......
THAT'S NOT SOMETHING YOU NEED TO WORRY ABOUT.

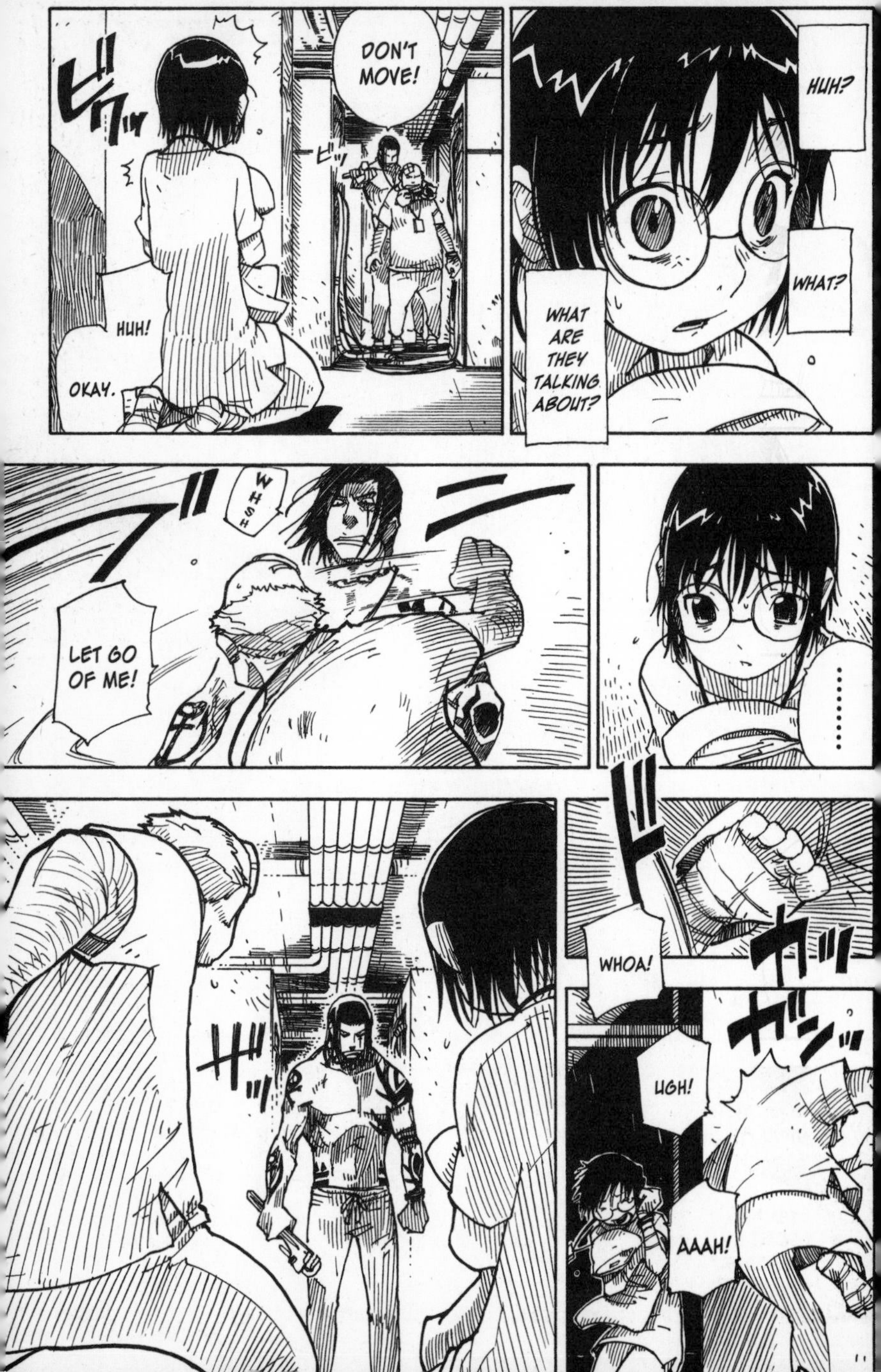
HUH?
WHAT?
WHAT ARE THEY TALKING ABOUT?
DON'T MOVE!
HUH!
OKAY.
......
WHSH
LET GO OF ME!
WHOA!
UGH!
AAAH!

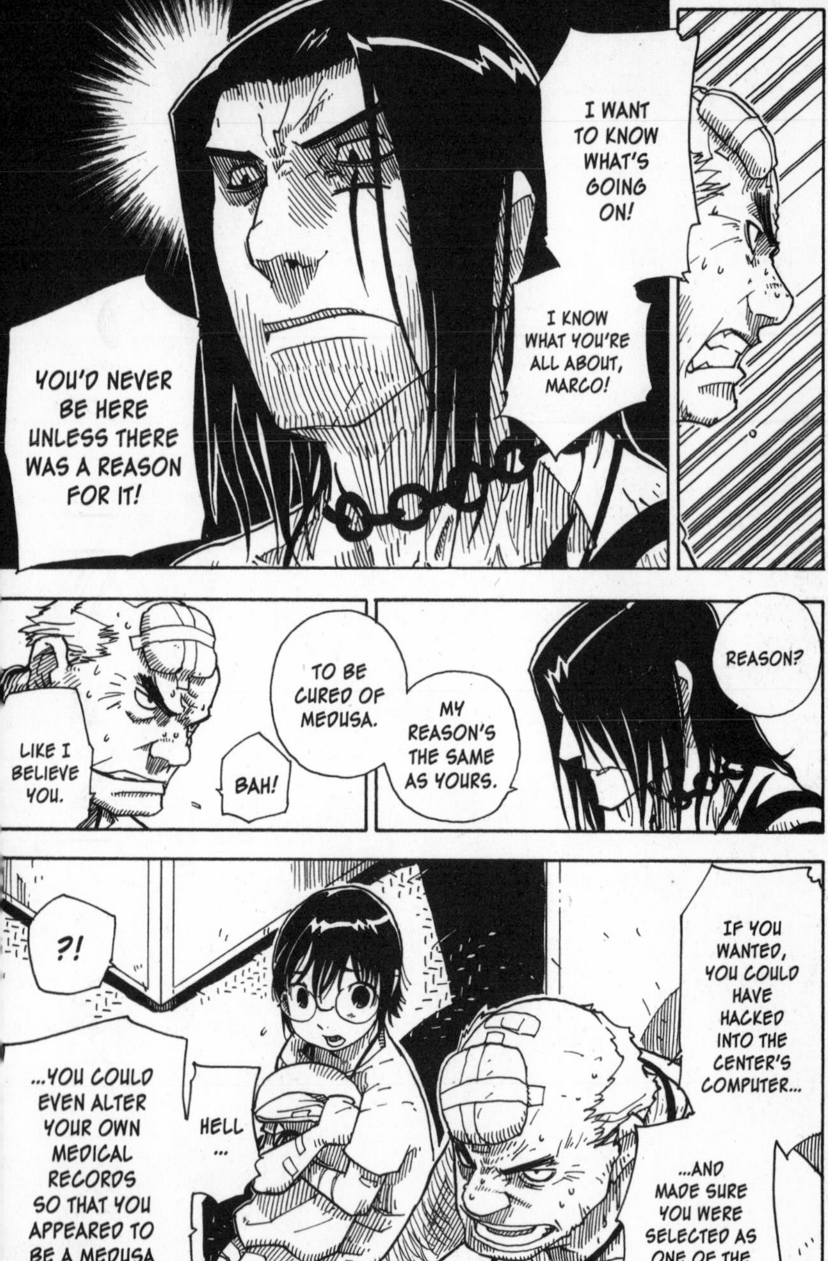
I WANT TO KNOW WHAT'S GOING ON!
I KNOW WHAT YOU'RE ALL ABOUT, MARCO!
YOU'D NEVER BE HERE UNLESS THERE WAS A REASON FOR IT!
REASON?
MY REASON'S THE SAME AS YOURS.
TO BE CURED OF MEDUSA.
BAH!
LIKE I BELIEVE YOU.
IF YOU WANTED, YOU COULD HAVE HACKED INTO THE CENTER'S COMPUTER...
...AND MADE SURE YOU WERE SELECTED AS ONE OF THE 160 PEOPLE.
?!
HELL ...
...YOU COULD EVEN ALTER YOUR OWN MEDICAL RECORDS SO THAT YOU APPEARED TO BE A MEDUSA PATIENT.

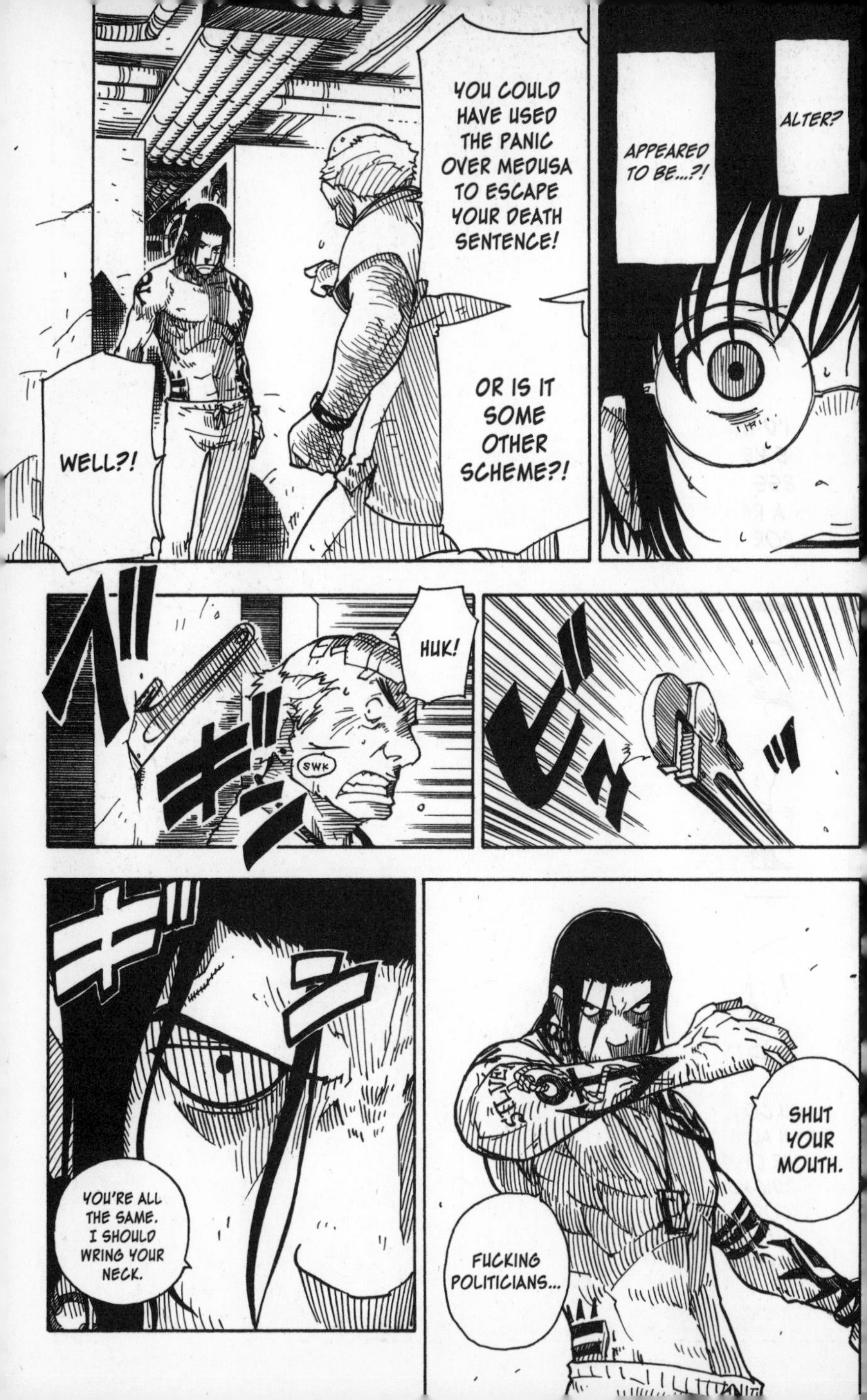
ALTER?
APPEARED TO BE...?!
YOU COULD HAVE USED THE PANIC OVER MEDUSA TO ESCAPE YOUR DEATH SENTENCE!
OR IS IT SOME OTHER SCHEME?!
WELL?!
HUK!
SWK
SHUT YOUR MOUTH.
FUCKING POLITICIANS...
YOU'RE ALL THE SAME. I SHOULD WRING YOUR NECK.

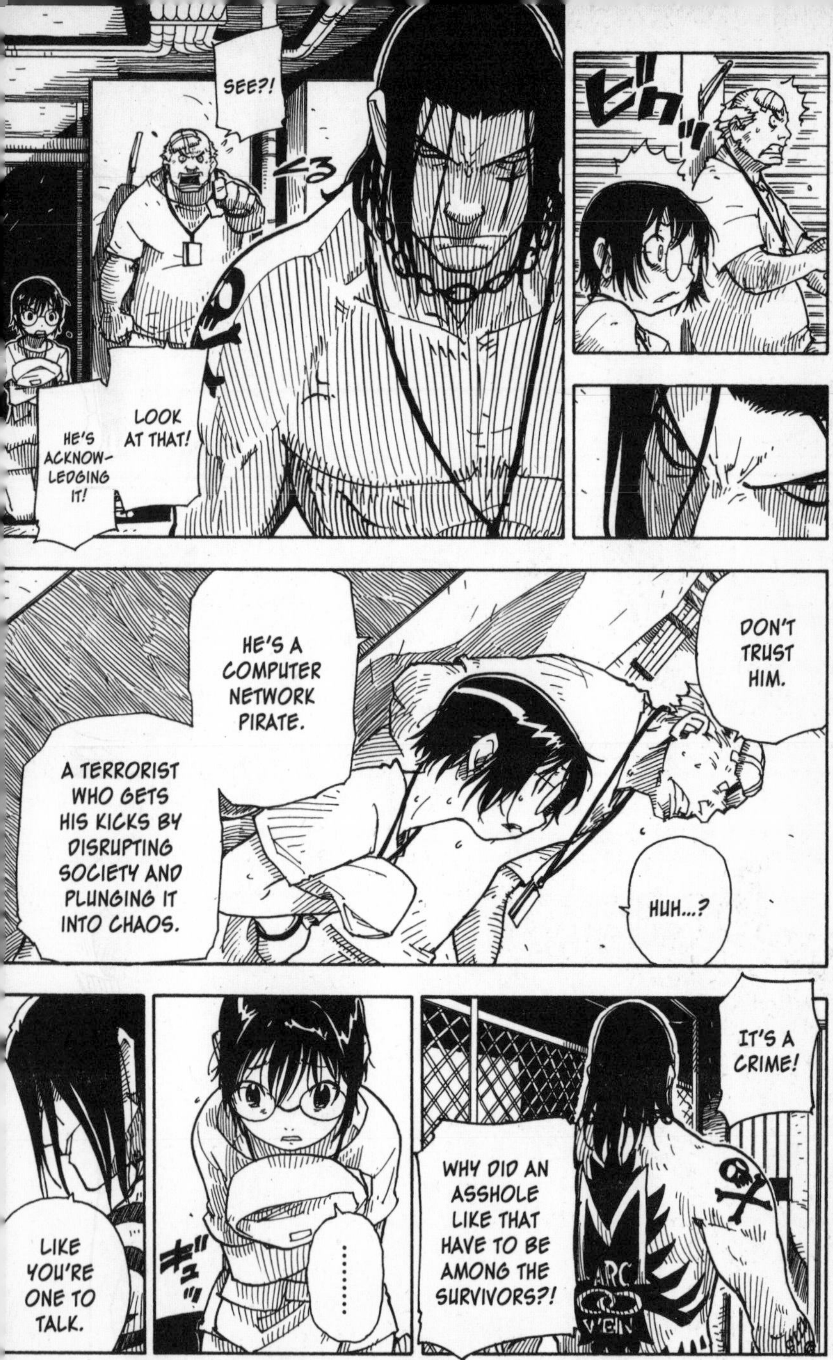

ビクッ
SEE?!
くる
LOOK AT THAT!
HE'S ACKNOWLEDGING IT!
DON'T TRUST HIM.
HE'S A COMPUTER NETWORK PIRATE.
A TERRORIST WHO GETS HIS KICKS BY DISRUPTING SOCIETY AND PLUNGING IT INTO CHAOS.
HUH...?
IT'S A CRIME!
WHY DID AN ASSHOLE LIKE THAT HAVE TO BE AMONG THE SURVIVORS?!
ARC VEIN
ギュ
......
LIKE YOU'RE ONE TO TALK.

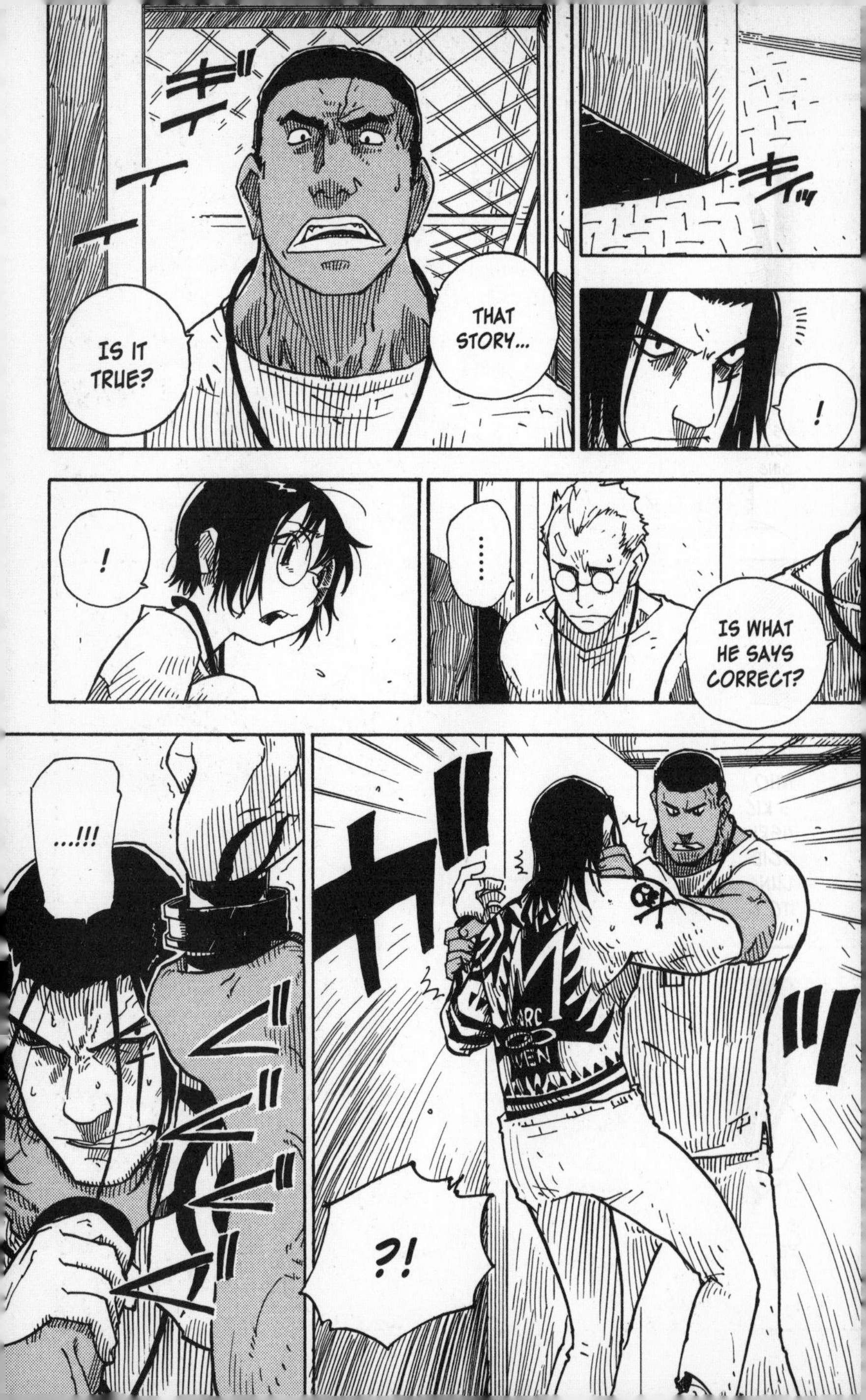
!
THAT STORY...
IS IT TRUE?
......
IS WHAT HE SAYS CORRECT?
!
?!
...!!!

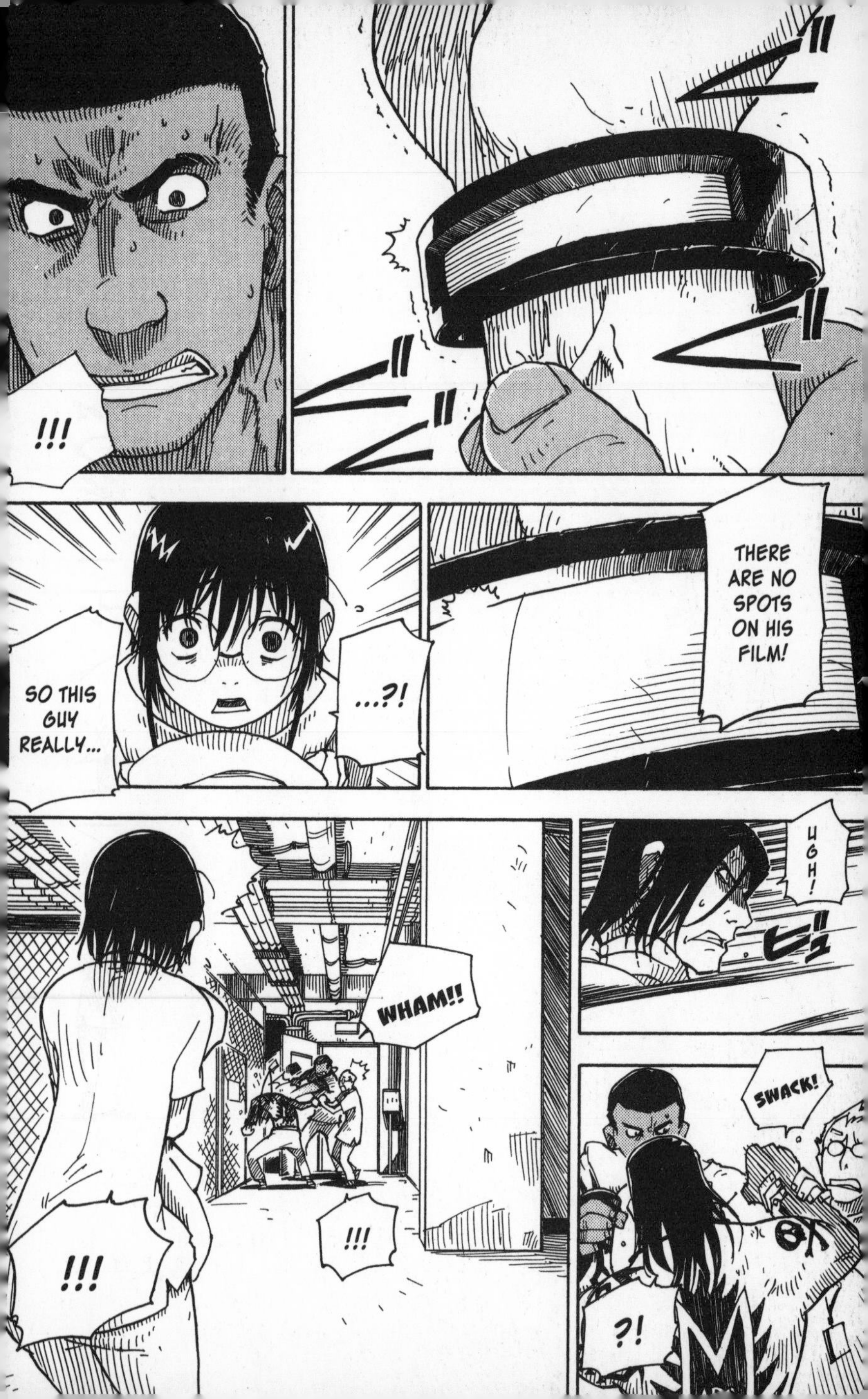
!!!
THERE ARE NO SPOTS ON HIS FILM!
...?!
SO THIS GUY REALLY...
UGH!
SWACK!
?!
WHAM!!
!!!
!!!

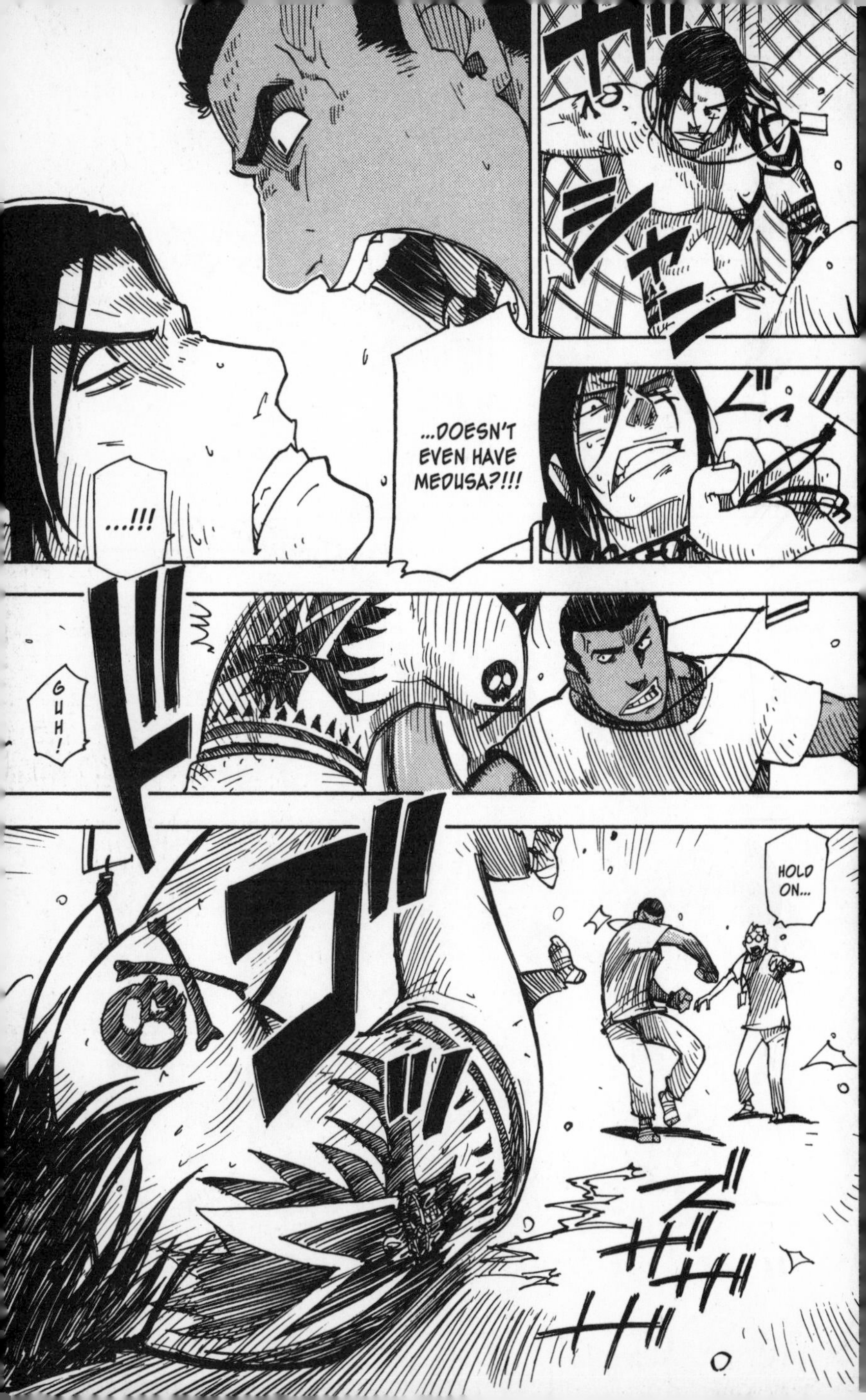
...DOESN'T EVEN HAVE MEDUSA?!!!
...!!!
GUH!
HOLD ON...

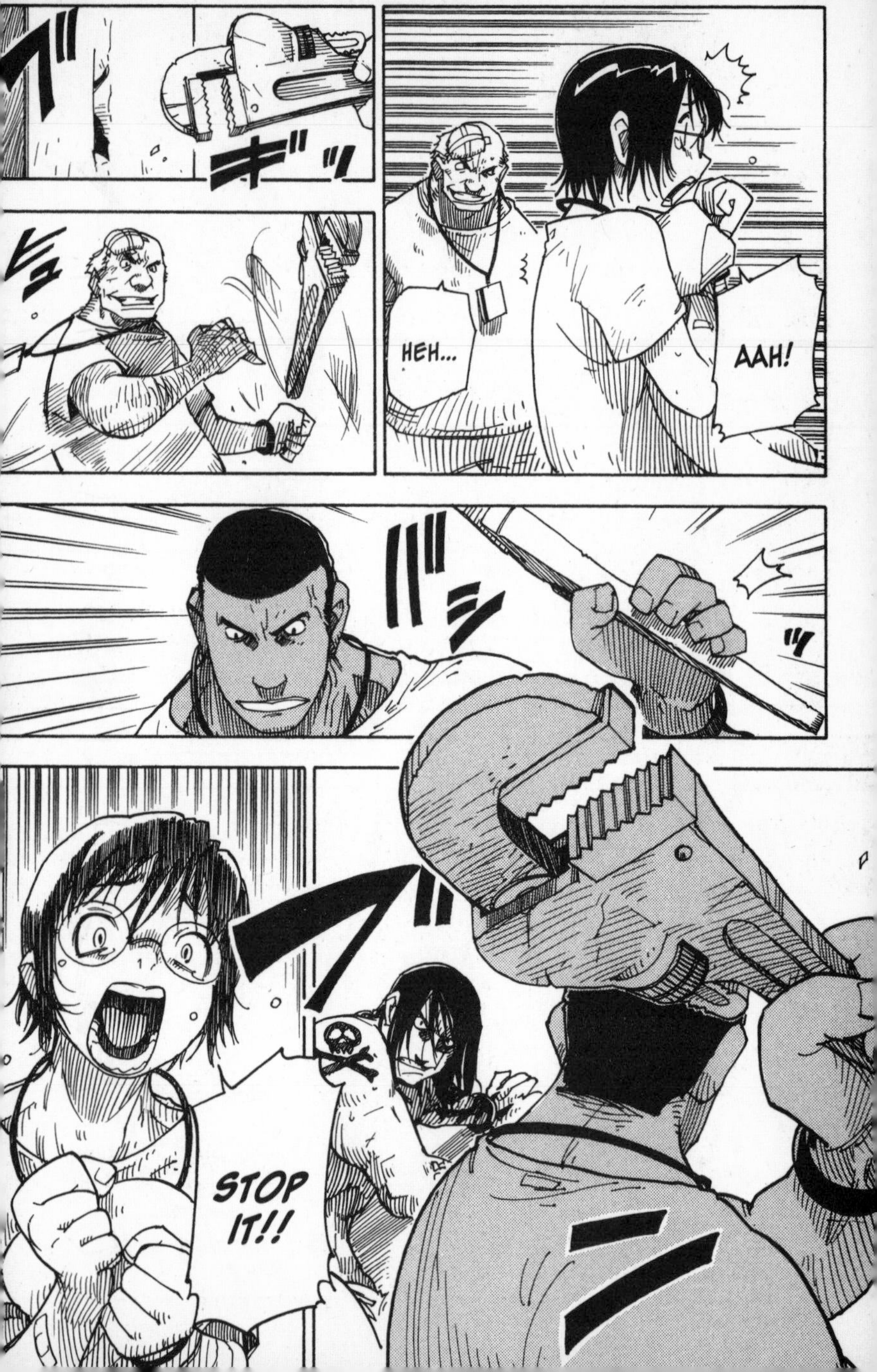
AAH!
HEH...
ブ
ギッ
ヒュ
バシッ
STOP IT!!

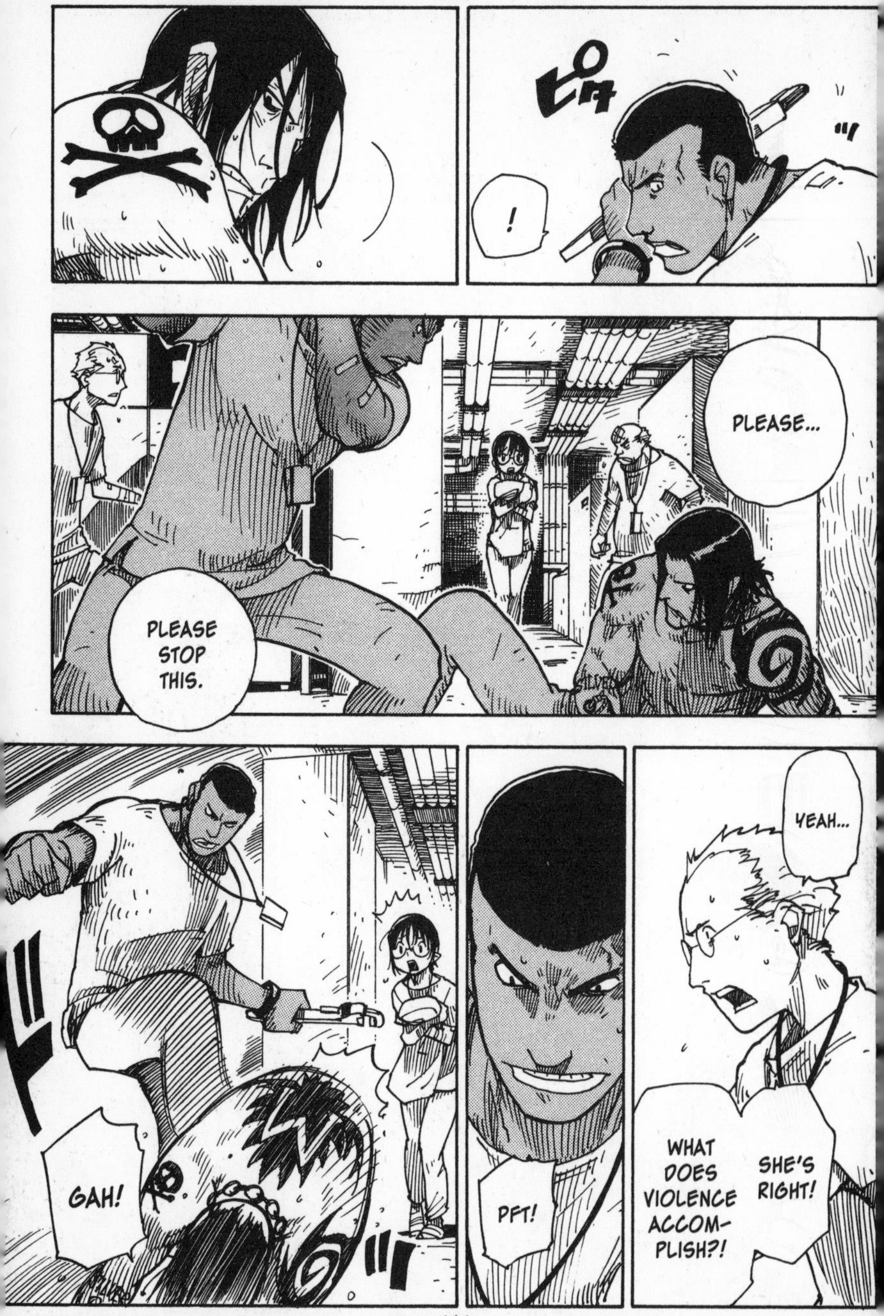
ピク
!
PLEASE...
PLEASE STOP THIS.
YEAH...
SHE'S RIGHT!
WHAT DOES VIOLENCE ACCOM-PLISH?!
PFT!
GAH!

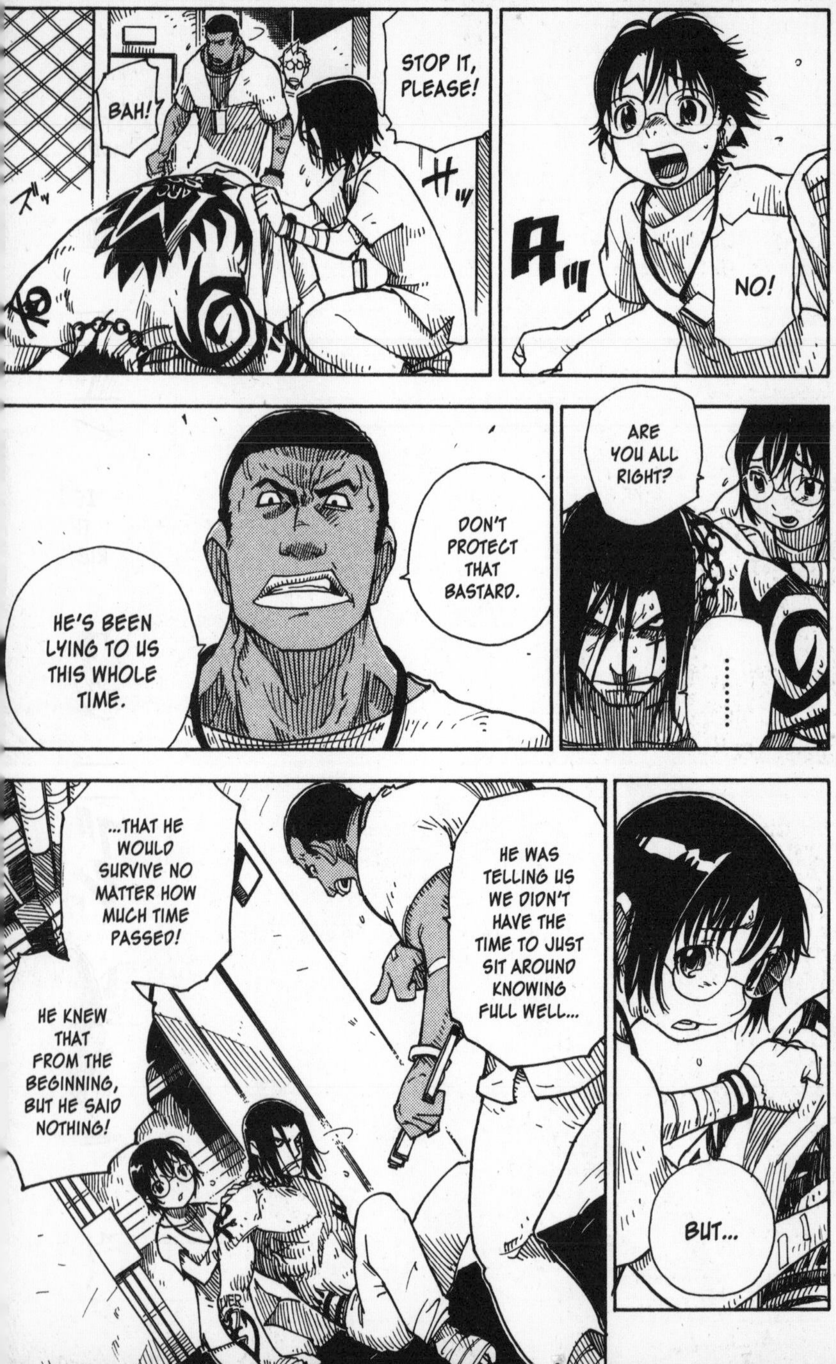
NO!
STOP IT, PLEASE!
BAH!
ARE YOU ALL RIGHT?
......
DON'T PROTECT THAT BASTARD.
HE'S BEEN LYING TO US THIS WHOLE TIME.
BUT...
HE WAS TELLING US WE DIDN'T HAVE THE TIME TO JUST SIT AROUND KNOWING FULL WELL...
...THAT HE WOULD SURVIVE NO MATTER HOW MUCH TIME PASSED!
HE KNEW THAT FROM THE BEGINNING, BUT HE SAID NOTHING!

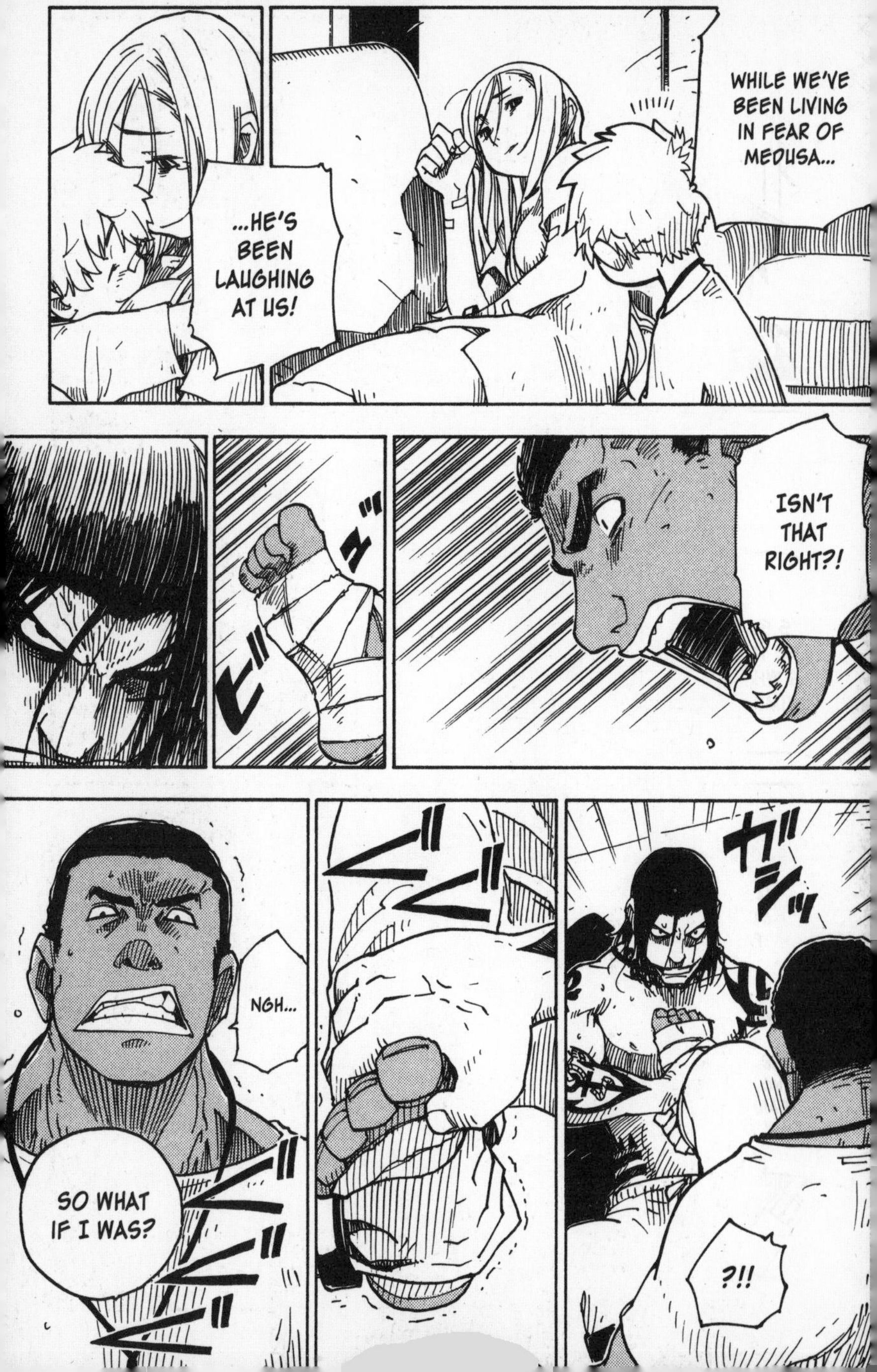
WHILE WE'VE BEEN LIVING IN FEAR OF MEDUSA...
...HE'S BEEN LAUGHING AT US!
ISN'T THAT RIGHT?!
?!!
NGH...
SO WHAT IF I WAS?

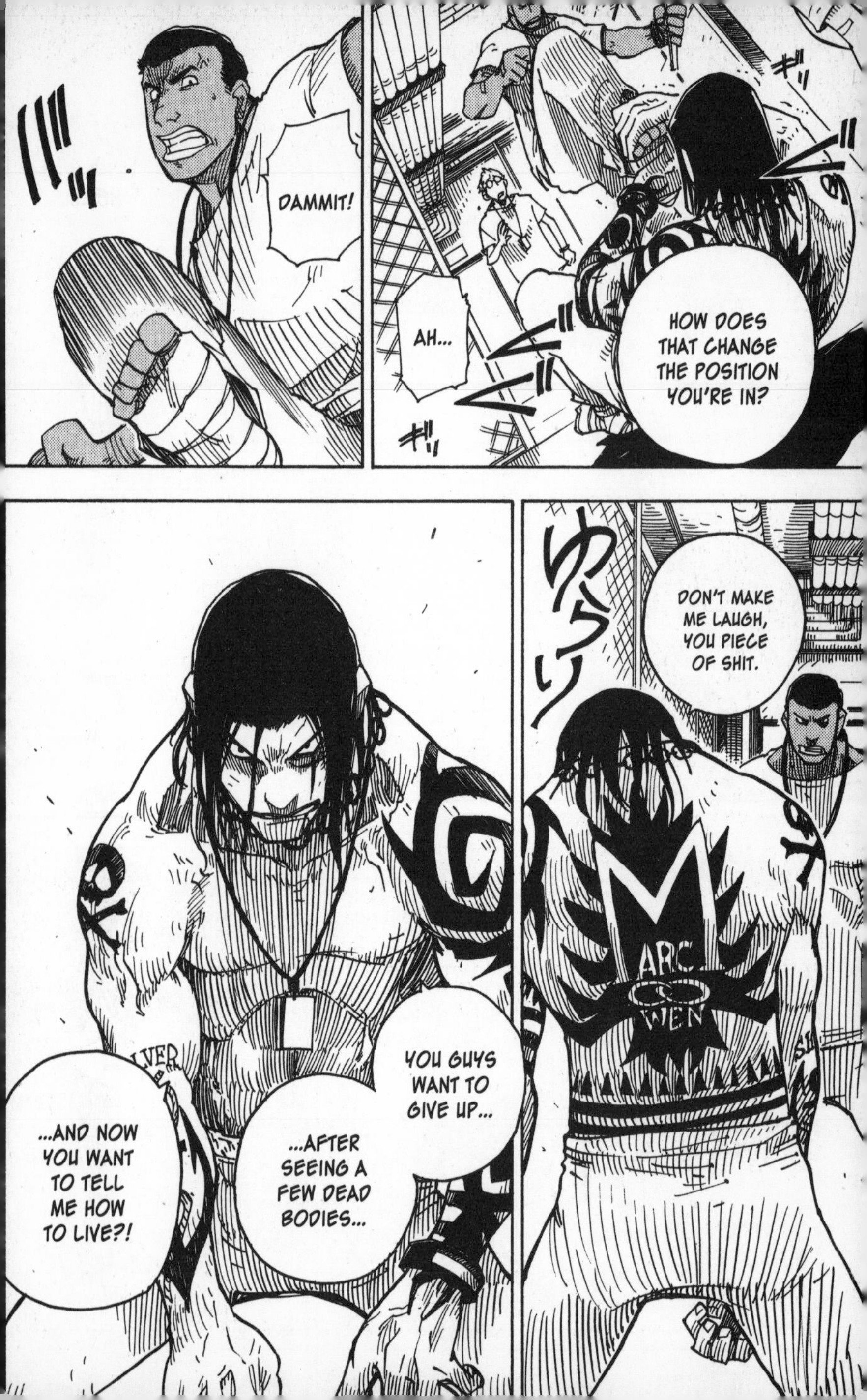
HOW DOES THAT CHANGE THE POSITION YOU'RE IN?
AH...
DAMMIT!
ゆらり
DON'T MAKE ME LAUGH, YOU PIECE OF SHIT.
YOU GUYS WANT TO GIVE UP...
...AFTER SEEING A FEW DEAD BODIES...
...AND NOW YOU WANT TO TELL ME HOW TO LIVE?!

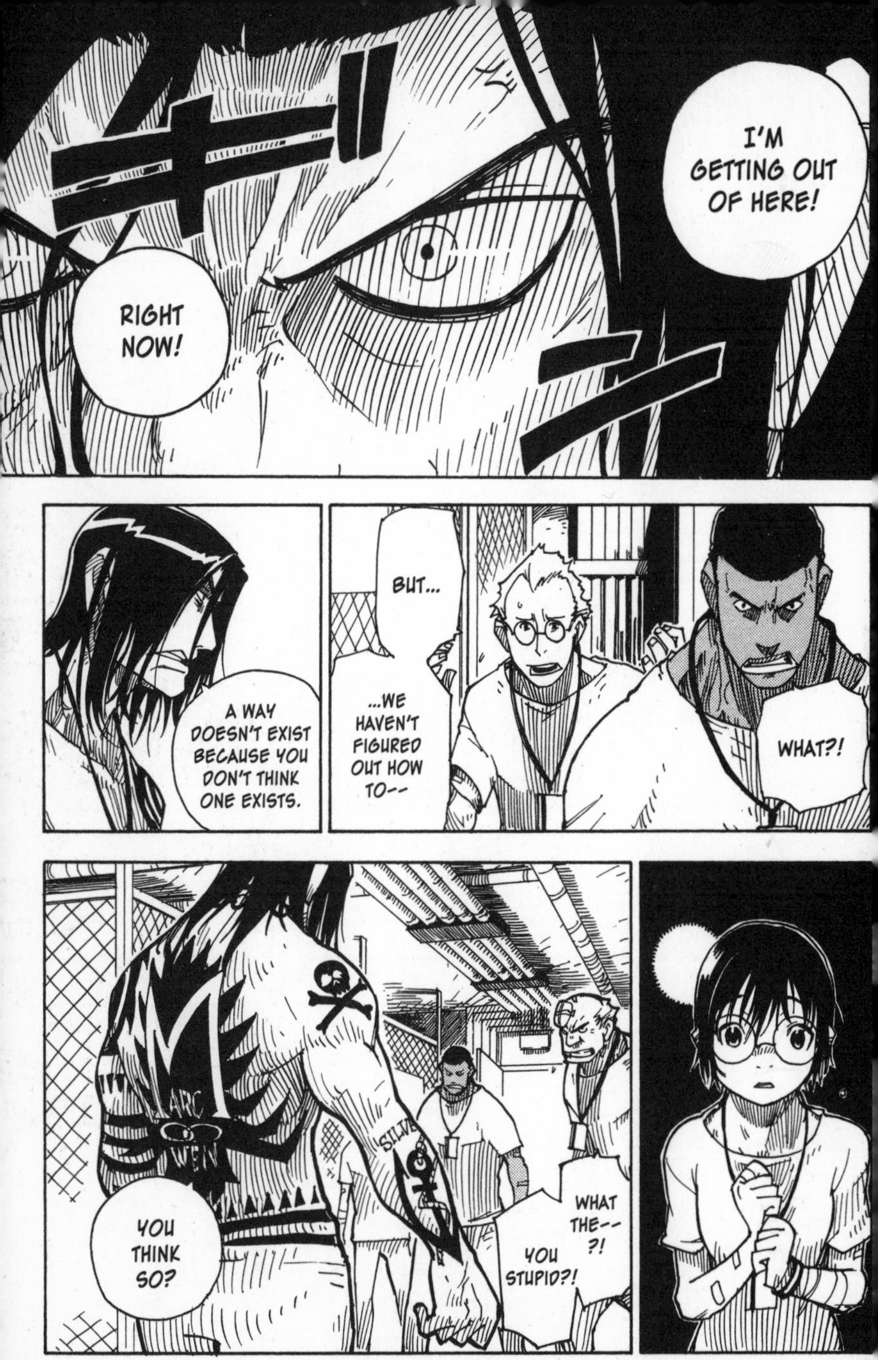
I'M GETTING OUT OF HERE!
RIGHT NOW!
WHAT?!
BUT...
...WE HAVEN'T FIGURED OUT HOW TO--
A WAY DOESN'T EXIST BECAUSE YOU DON'T THINK ONE EXISTS.
WHAT THE--?!
YOU STUPID?!
YOU THINK SO?

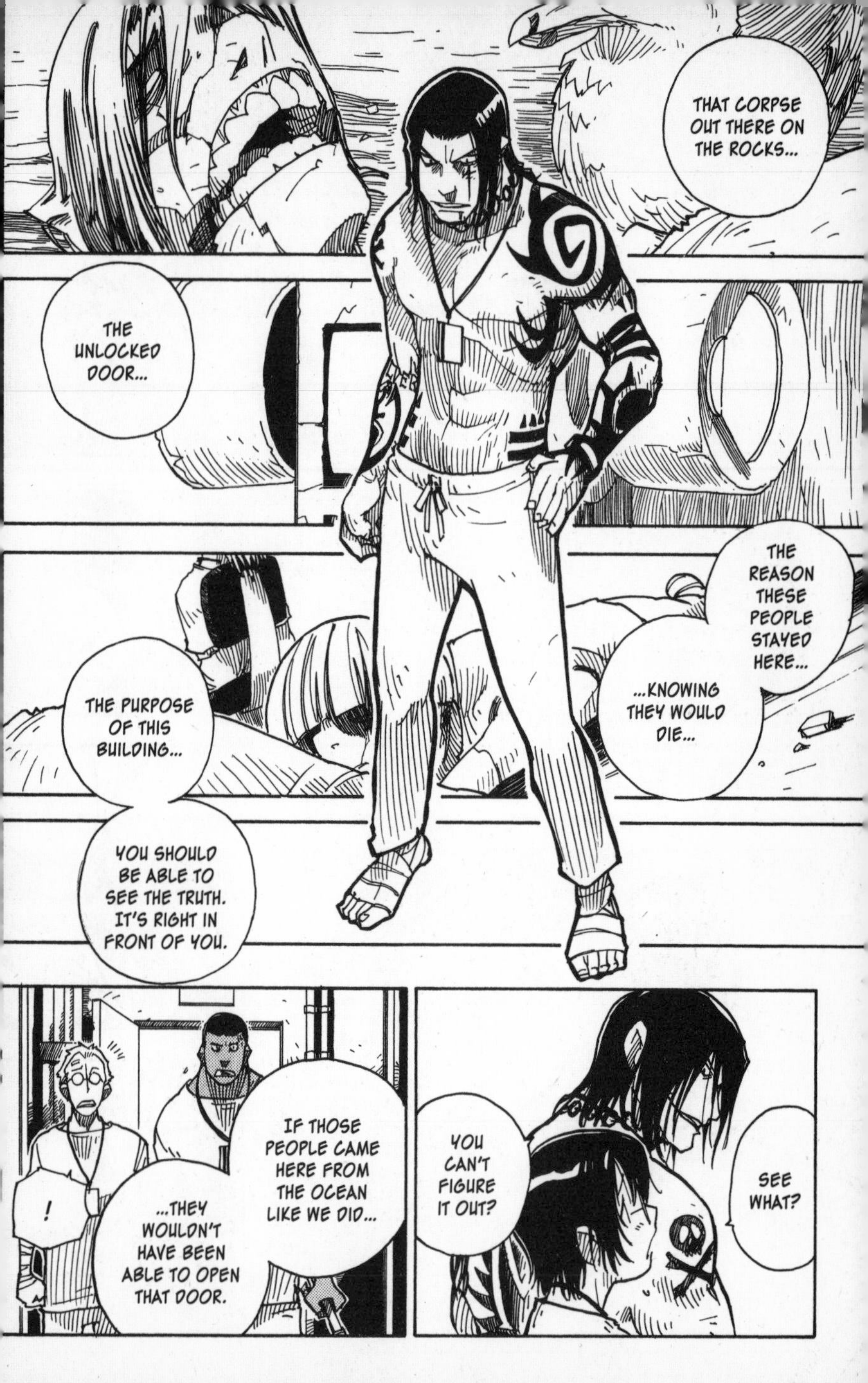
THAT CORPSE OUT THERE ON THE ROCKS...
THE UNLOCKED DOOR...
THE REASON THESE PEOPLE STAYED HERE...
...KNOWING THEY WOULD DIE...
THE PURPOSE OF THIS BUILDING...
YOU SHOULD BE ABLE TO SEE THE TRUTH. IT'S RIGHT IN FRONT OF YOU.
SEE WHAT?
YOU CAN'T FIGURE IT OUT?
IF THOSE PEOPLE CAME HERE FROM THE OCEAN LIKE WE DID...
...THEY WOULDN'T HAVE BEEN ABLE TO OPEN THAT DOOR.
!

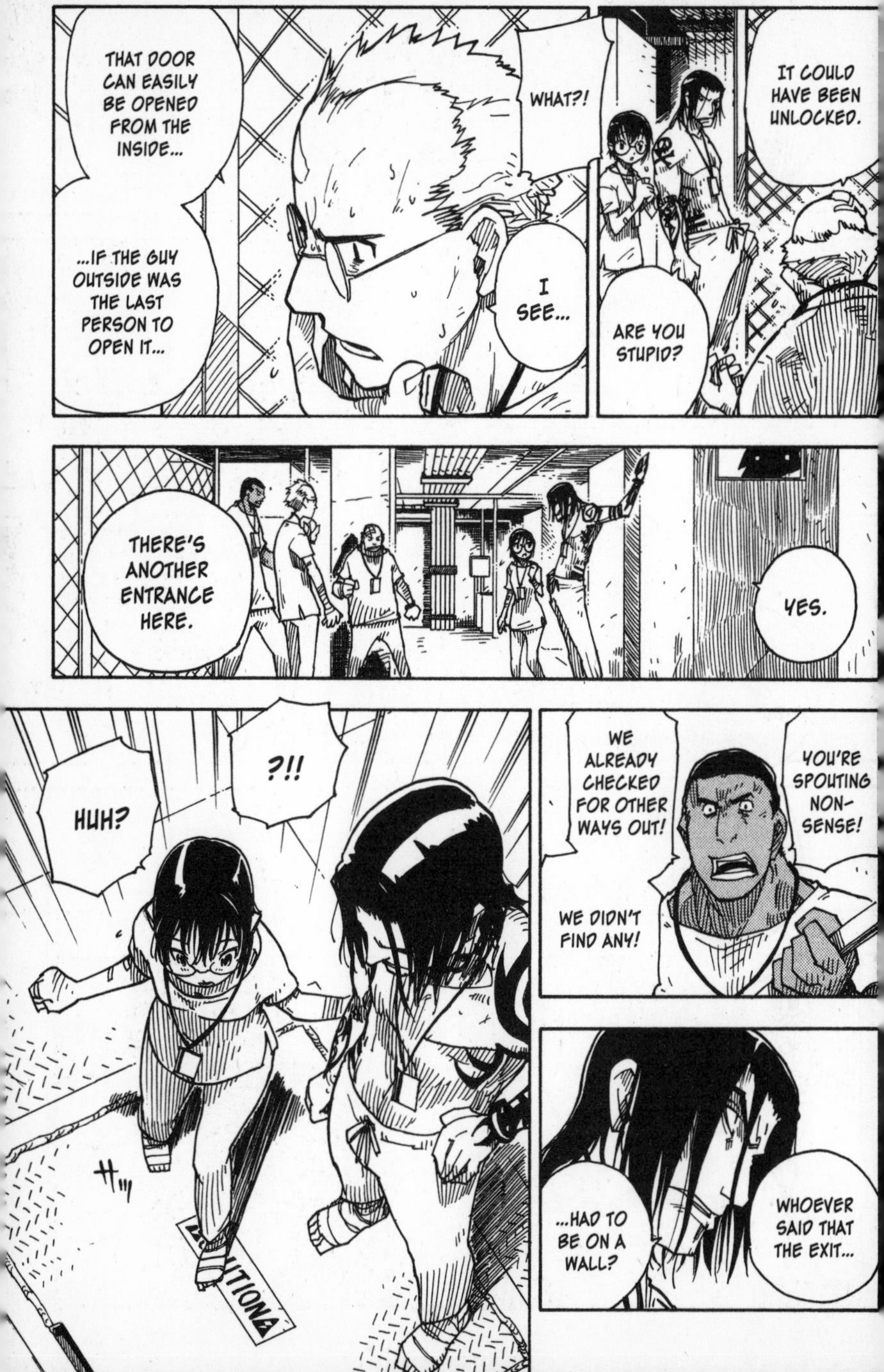
IT COULD HAVE BEEN UNLOCKED.
ARE YOU STUPID?
WHAT?!
THAT DOOR CAN EASILY BE OPENED FROM THE INSIDE...
I SEE...
...IF THE GUY OUTSIDE WAS THE LAST PERSON TO OPEN IT...
YES.
THERE'S ANOTHER ENTRANCE HERE.
YOU'RE SPOUTING NON-SENSE!
WE ALREADY CHECKED FOR OTHER WAYS OUT!
WE DIDN'T FIND ANY!
WHOEVER SAID THAT THE EXIT...
...HAD TO BE ON A WALL?
?!!
HUH?

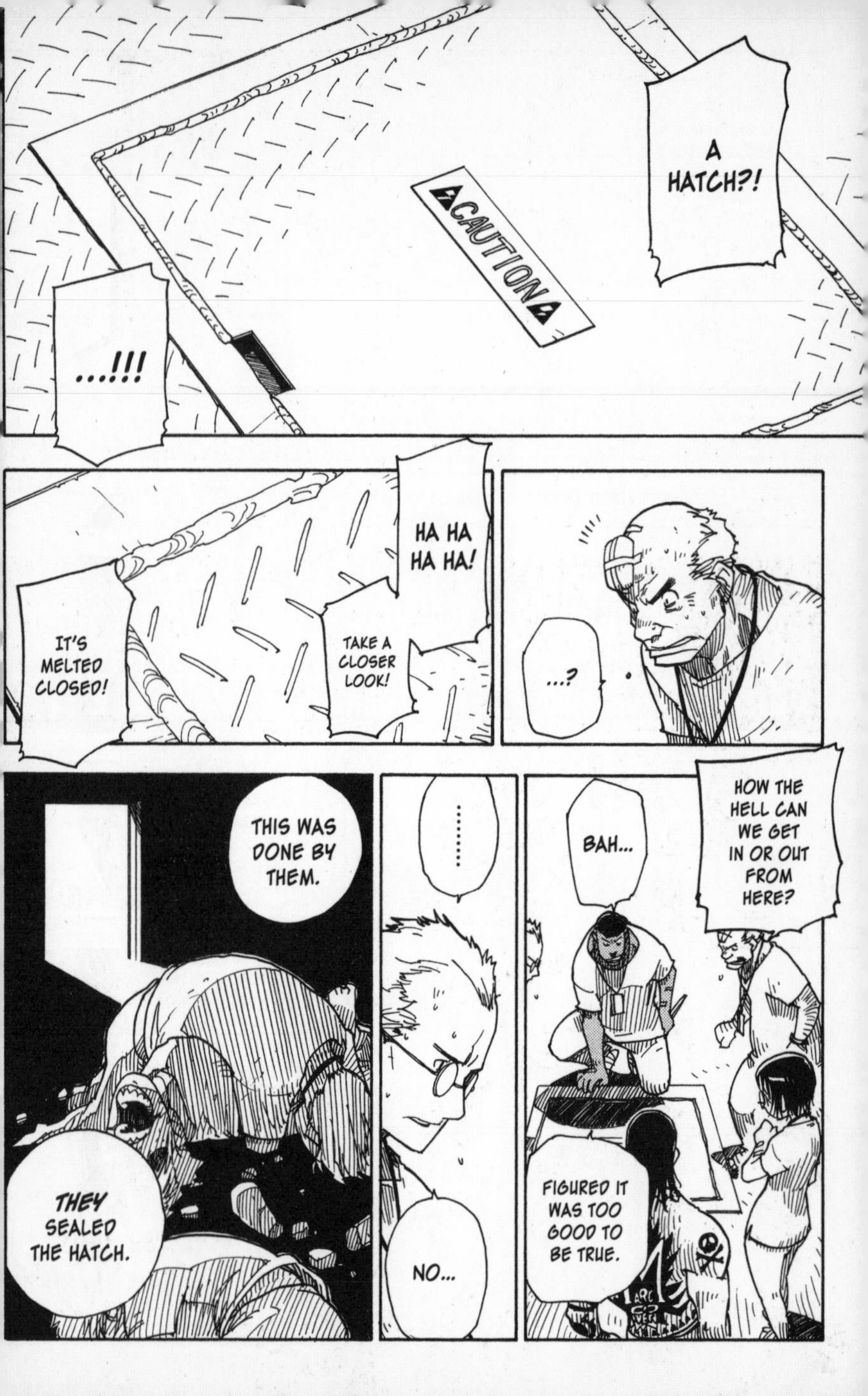
A HATCH?!
CAUTION
...!!!
...?
HA HA HA HA!
TAKE A CLOSER LOOK!
IT'S MELTED CLOSED!
HOW THE HELL CAN WE GET IN OR OUT FROM HERE?
BAH...
FIGURED IT WAS TOO GOOD TO BE TRUE.
....
NO...
THIS WAS DONE BY THEM.
THEY SEALED THE HATCH.

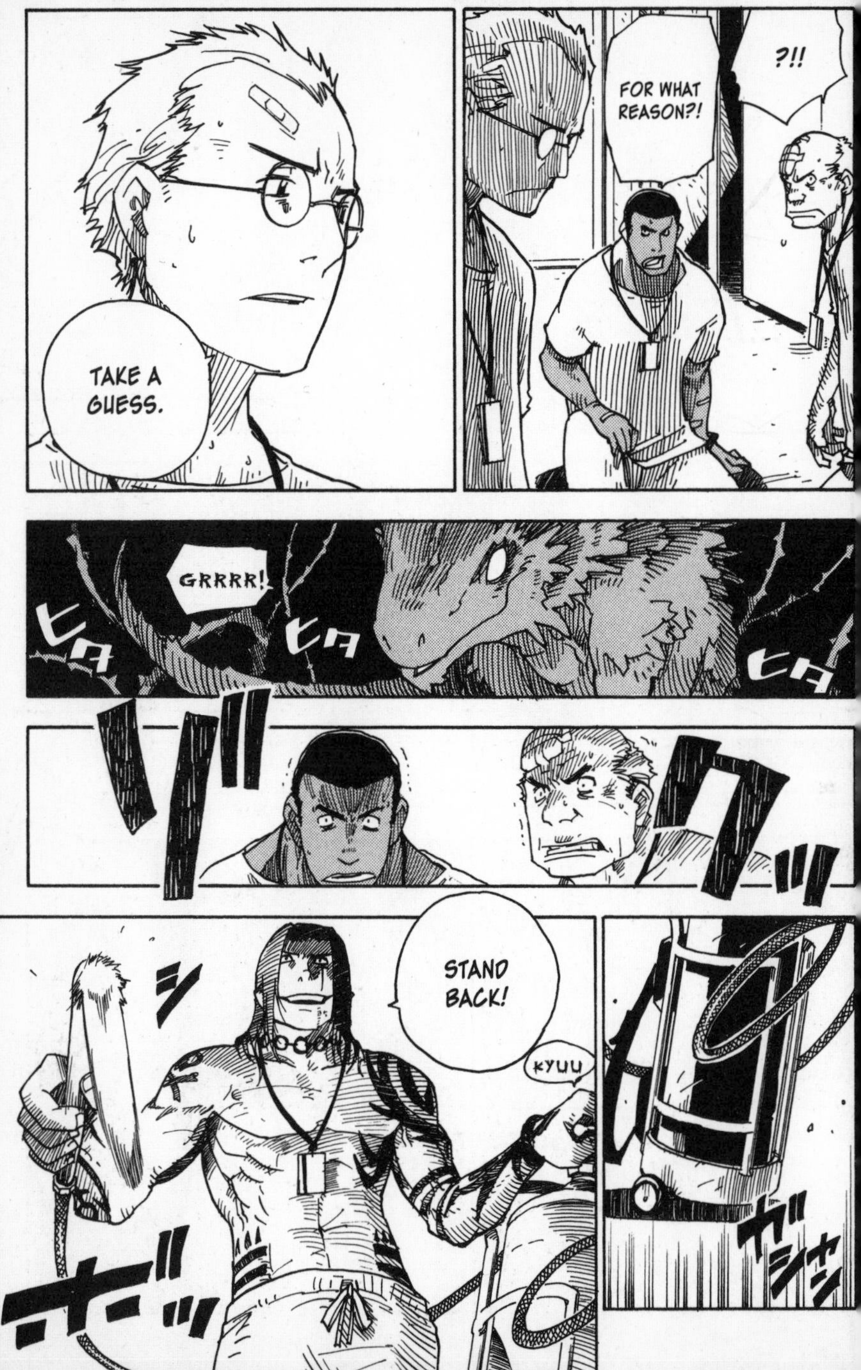
?!!
FOR WHAT REASON?!
TAKE A GUESS.
GRRRR!
ヒタ
ヒタ
ヒタ
KYUU
STAND BACK!

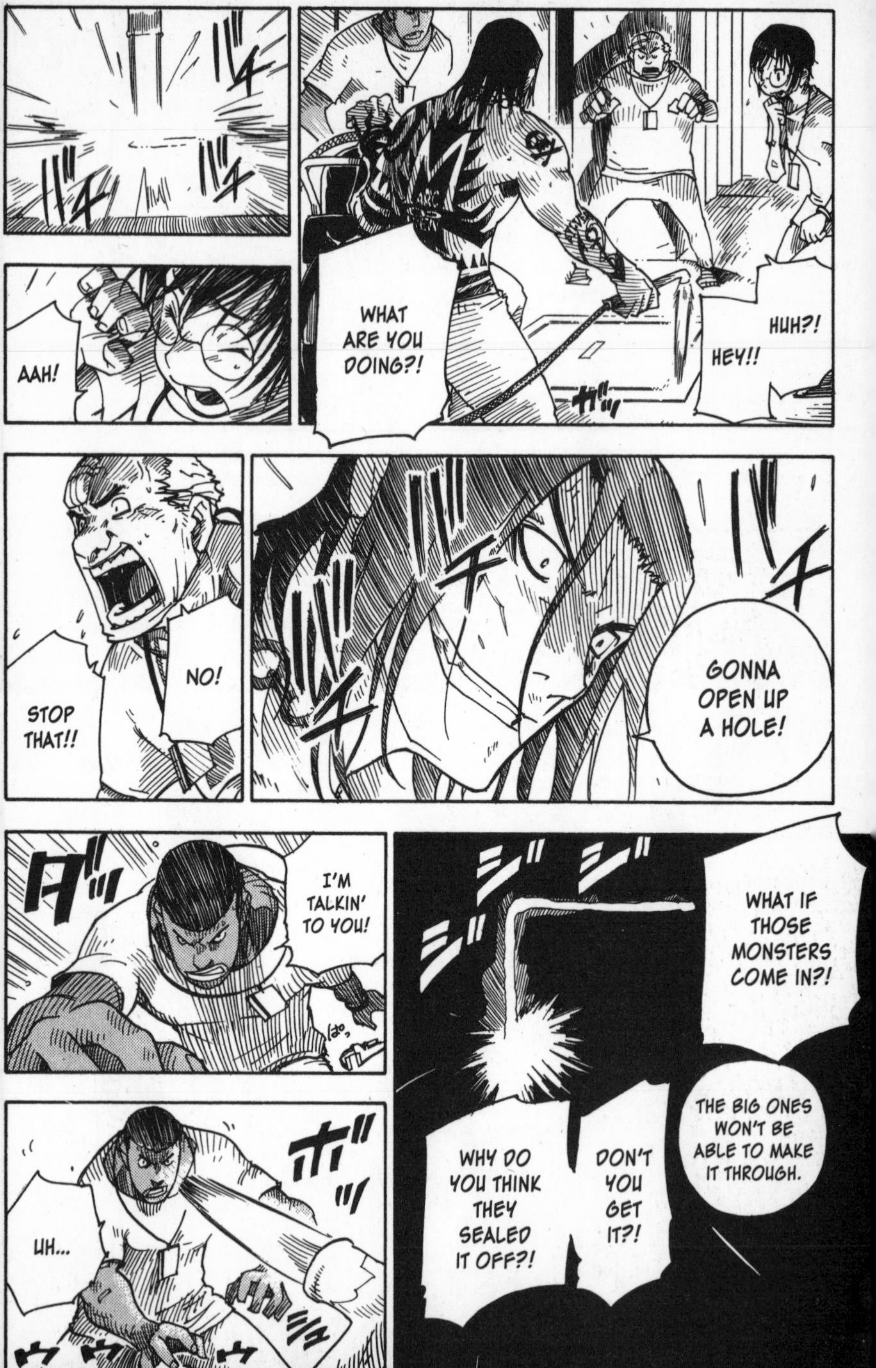
HUH?!
HEY!!
WHAT ARE YOU DOING?!
AAH!
GONNA OPEN UP A HOLE!
NO!
STOP THAT!!
WHAT IF THOSE MONSTERS COME IN?!
THE BIG ONES WON'T BE ABLE TO MAKE IT THROUGH.
DON'T YOU GET IT?!
WHY DO YOU THINK THEY SEALED IT OFF?!
I'M TALKIN' TO YOU!
UH...

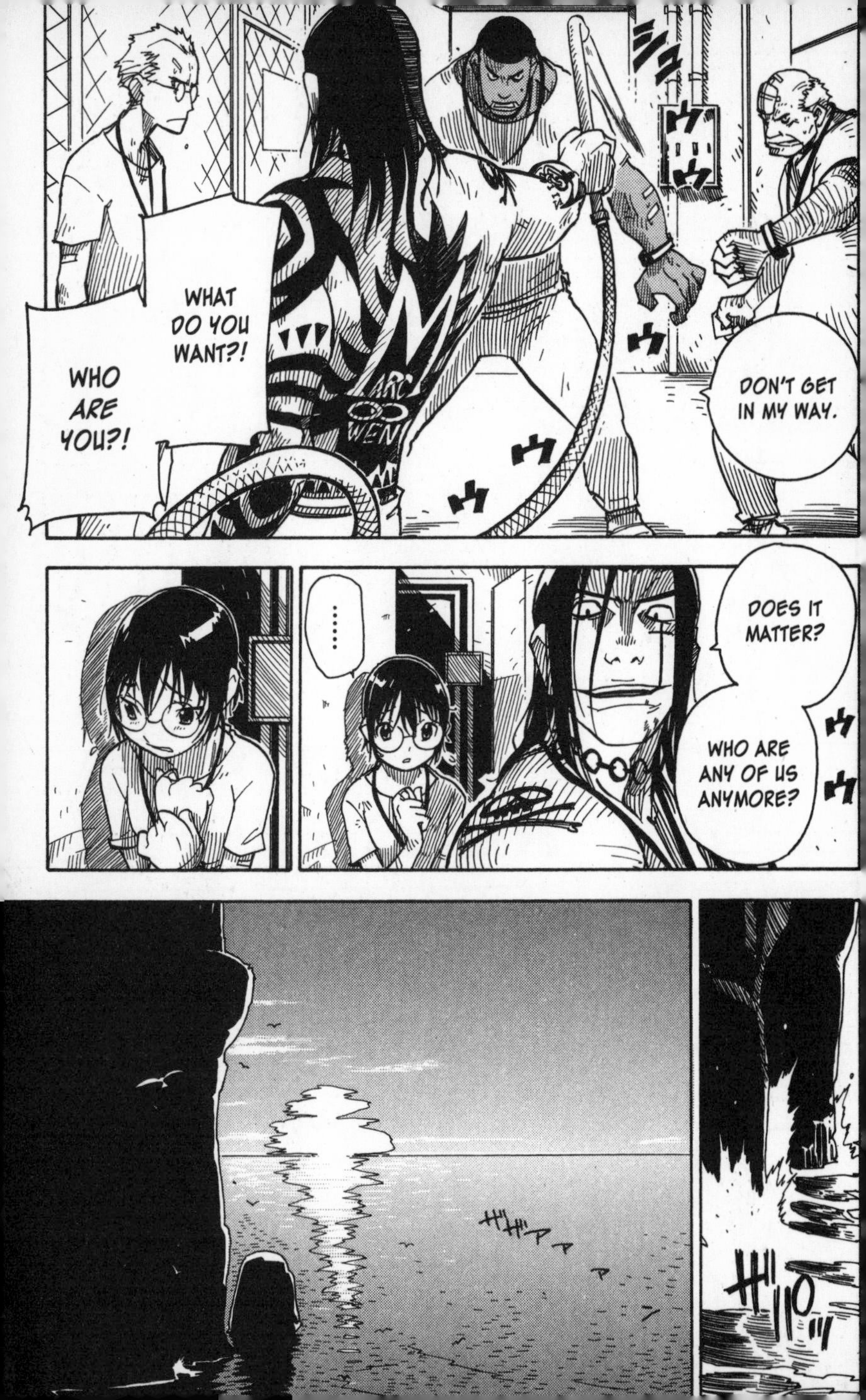
シュ
ウ
ウ
DON'T GET IN MY WAY.
ウ
ウ
WHAT DO YOU WANT?!
WHO ARE YOU?!
DOES IT MATTER?
WHO ARE ANY OF US ANYMORE?
ウ
ウ
……
ザパッ
ザザァァァ

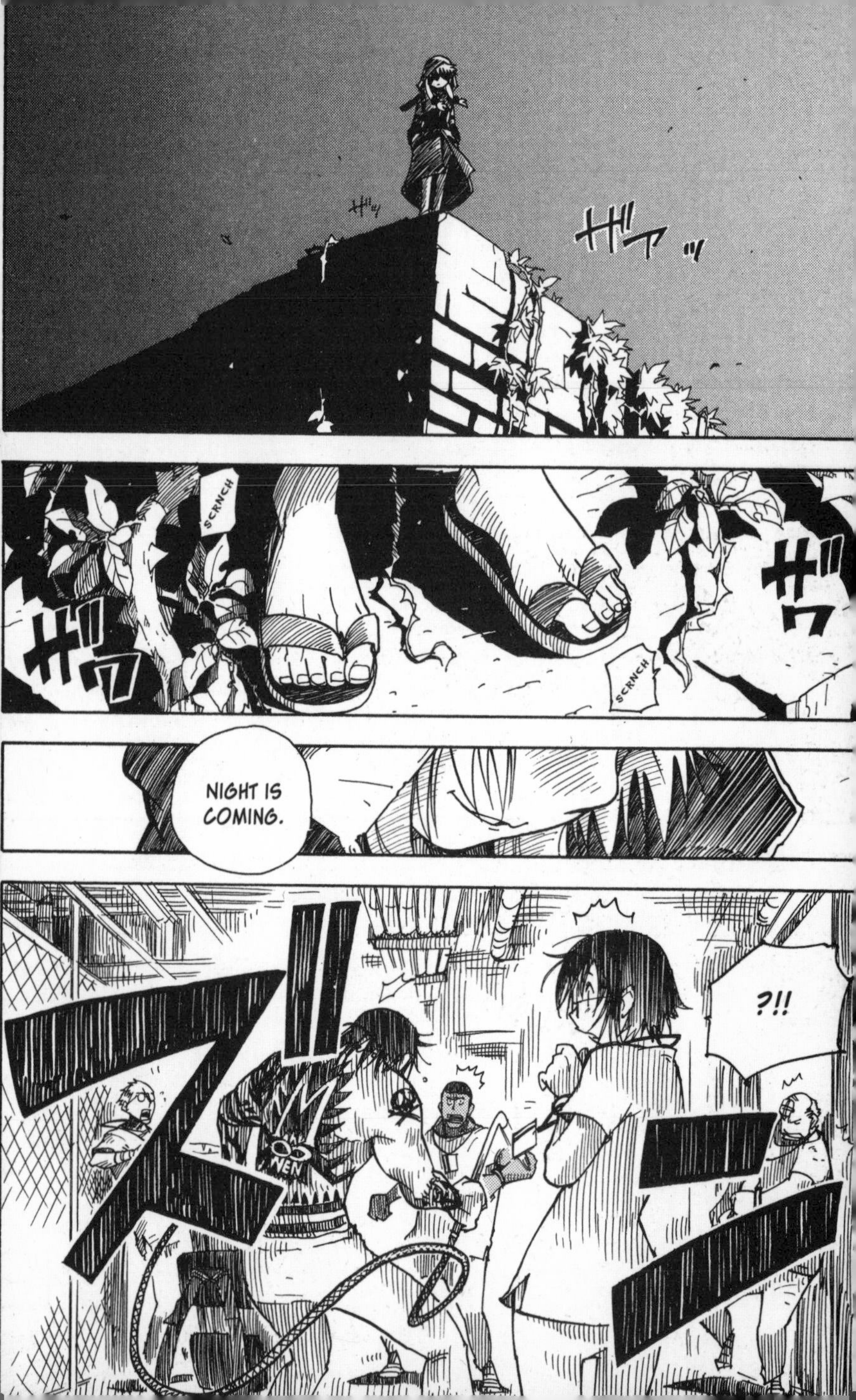
SCRNCH
SCRNCH
NIGHT IS COMING.
?!!

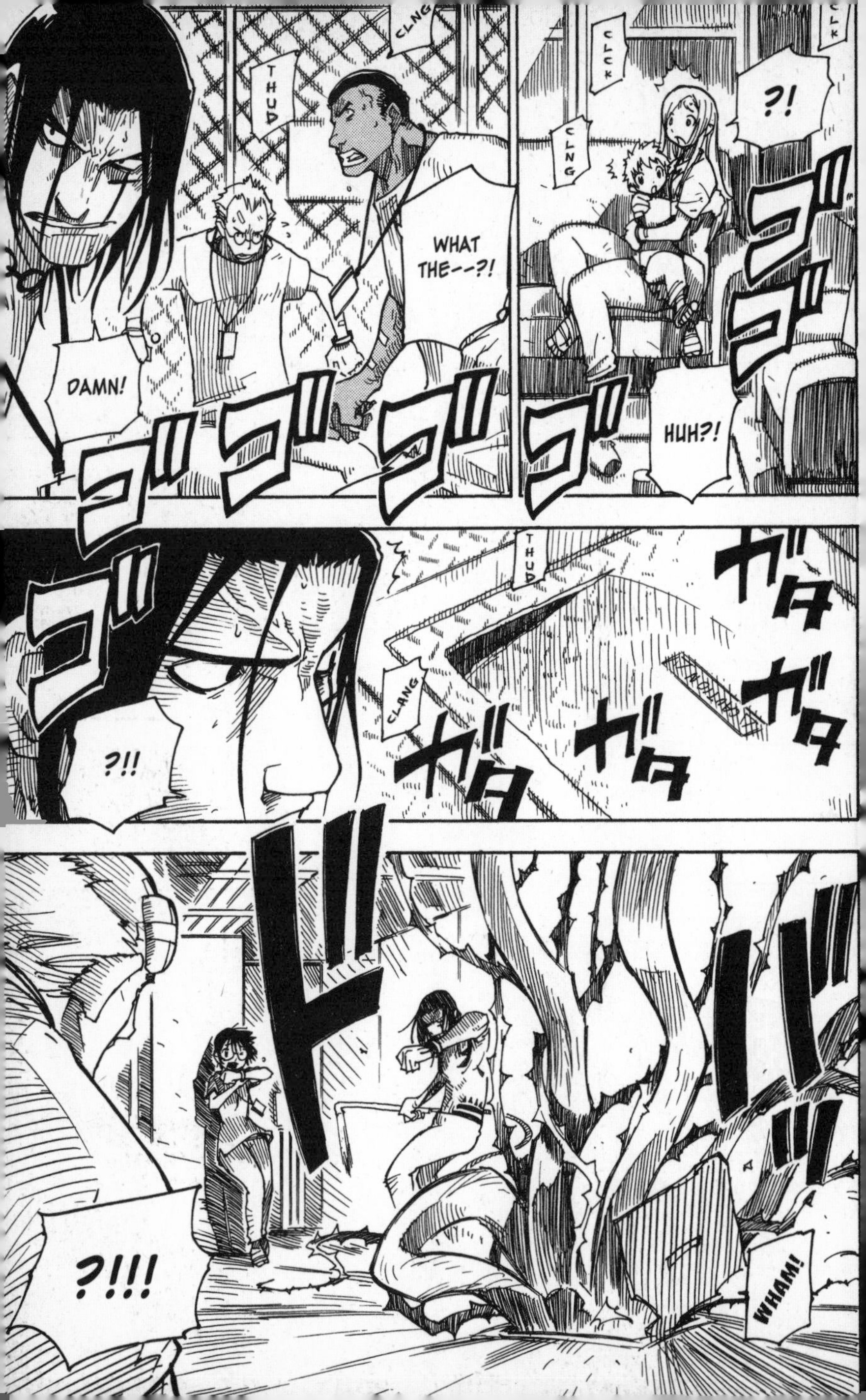
CLK
?!
CLCK
CLNG
ゴゴゴ
HUH?!
CLNG
THUD
WHAT THE--?!
DAMN!
ゴゴゴゴ
THUD
ガタガタ
CLANG
ガタガタ
?!!
ドドド
WHAM!
?!!!

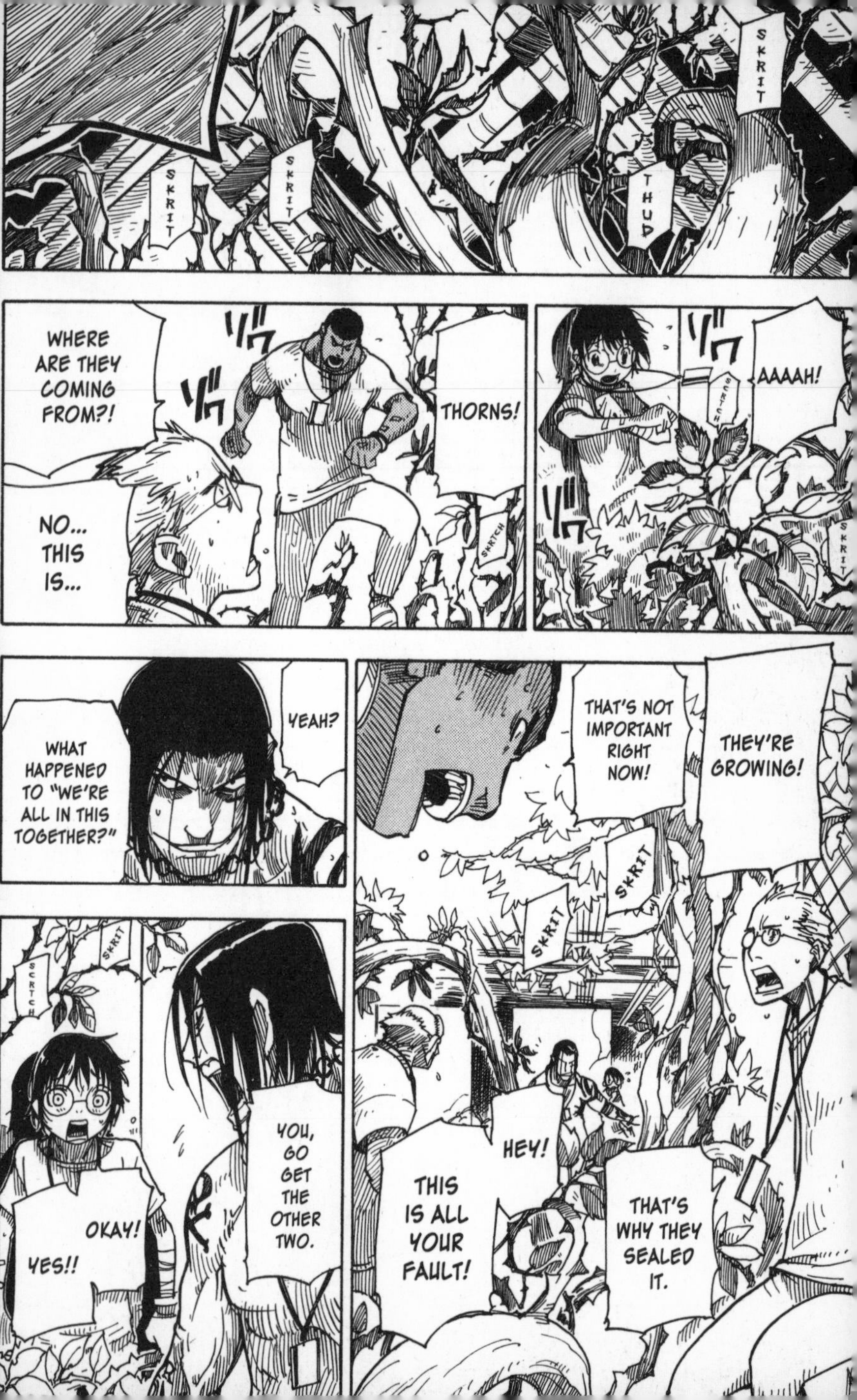
SKRIT
THUD
SKRIT
SKRIT
AAAAH!
SCRTCH
ゾワ
ゾワ
SKRIT
THORNS!
WHERE ARE THEY COMING FROM?!
ゾワ
ゾワ
NO... THIS IS...
SKRTCH
THEY'RE GROWING!
THAT'S NOT IMPORTANT RIGHT NOW!
SKRIT
SKRIT
HEY!
THAT'S WHY THEY SEALED IT.
THIS IS ALL YOUR FAULT!
YEAH?
WHAT HAPPENED TO "WE'RE ALL IN THIS TOGETHER?"
SKRIT
SCRTCH
YOU, GO GET THE OTHER TWO.
OKAY!
YES!!

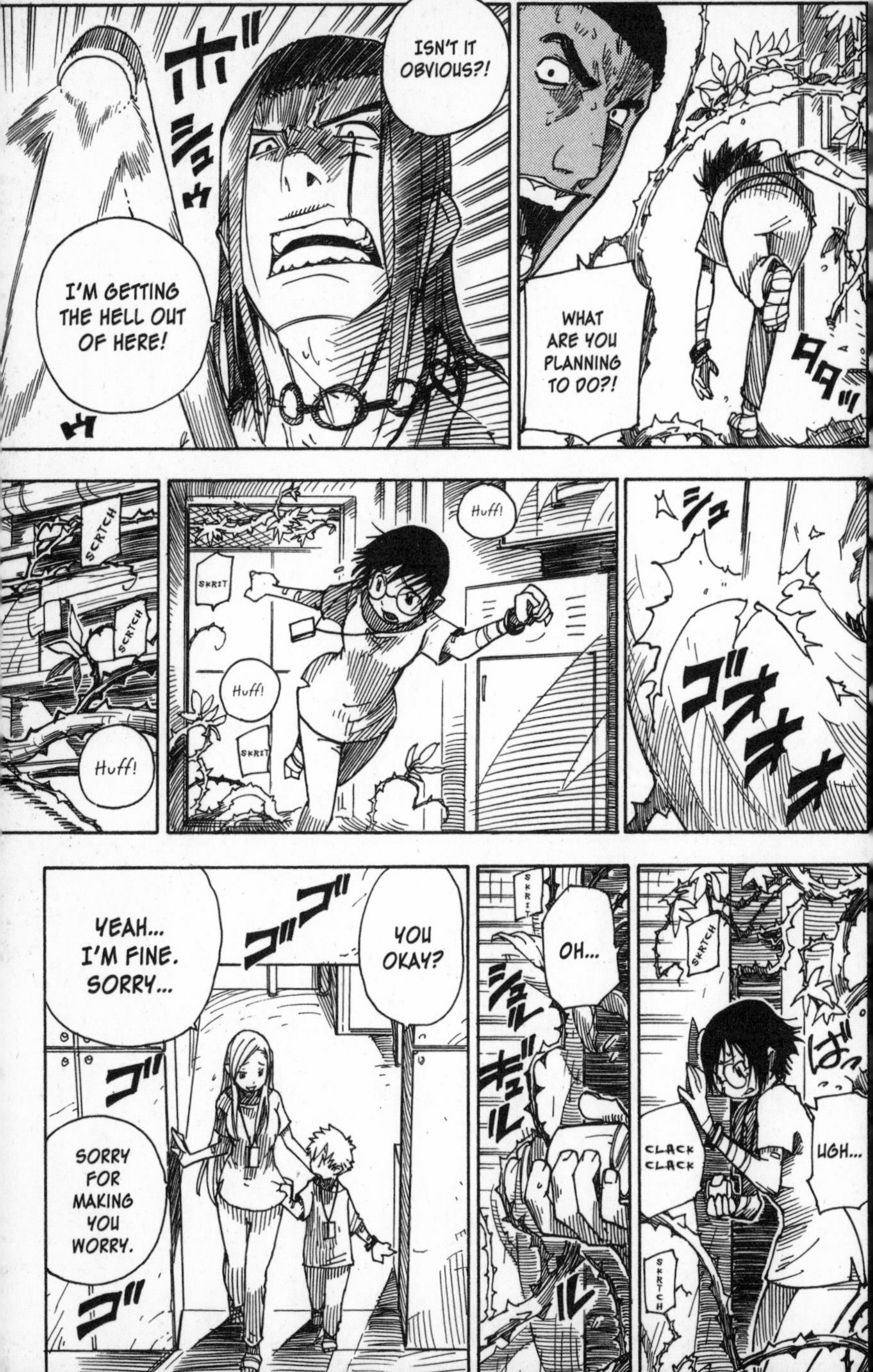
WHAT ARE YOU PLANNING TO DO?!
タタッ
ISN'T IT OBVIOUS?!
ホシュウ
I'M GETTING THE HELL OUT OF HERE!
シュ
ゴオオオ
Huff!
SKRIT
Huff!
SKRIT
SCRTCH
SCRTCH
Huff!
SKRTCH
ばっ
UGH...
CLACK CLACK
SKRTCH
SKRIT
OH...
シュル
ギュル
ル
ゴゴ
YOU OKAY?
YEAH... I'M FINE. SORRY...
ゴ
SORRY FOR MAKING YOU WORRY.
ゴ

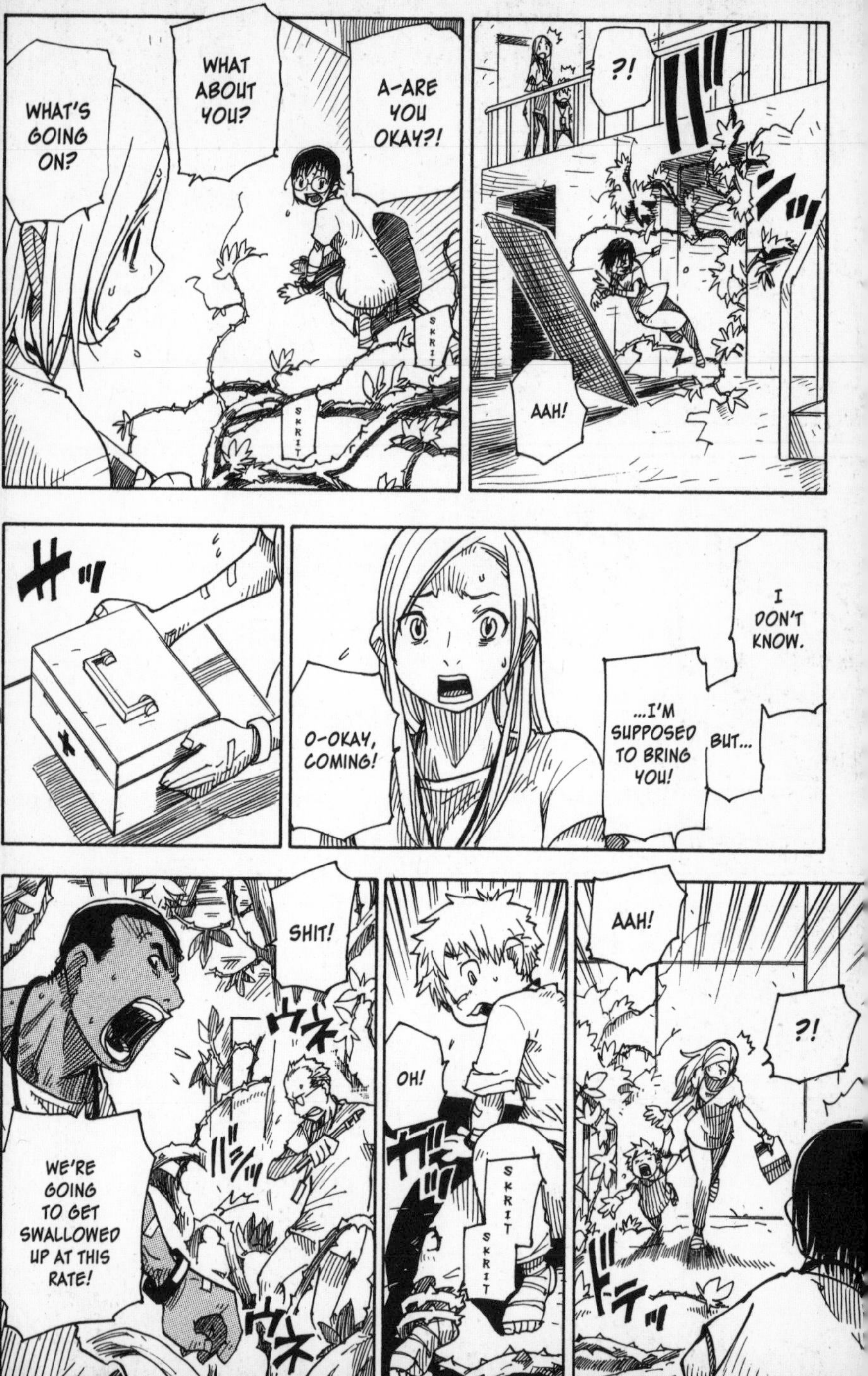
?!
AAH!
A-ARE YOU OKAY?!
WHAT ABOUT YOU?
WHAT'S GOING ON?
SKRIT
SKRIT
I DON'T KNOW.
BUT...
...I'M SUPPOSED TO BRING YOU!
O-OKAY, COMING!
AAH!
?!
OH!
SKRIT
SKRIT
SHIT!
WE'RE GOING TO GET SWALLOWED UP AT THIS RATE!

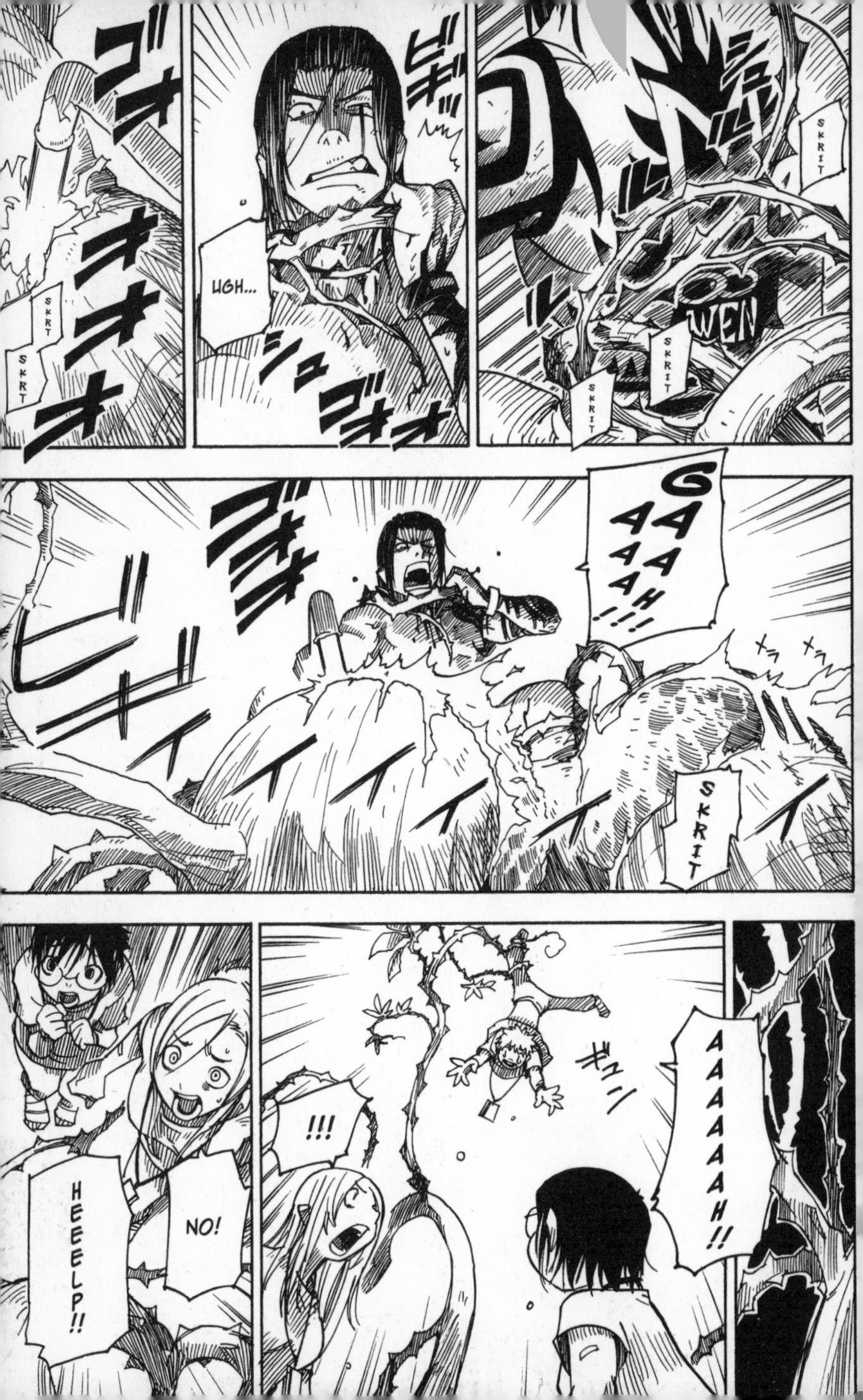
SKRIT
WEN
SKRIT
SKRIT
UGH...
SKRT
SKRT
GAAAAAAH!!!!
SKRIT
AAAAAAAH!!
!!!
NO!
HEEEELP!!

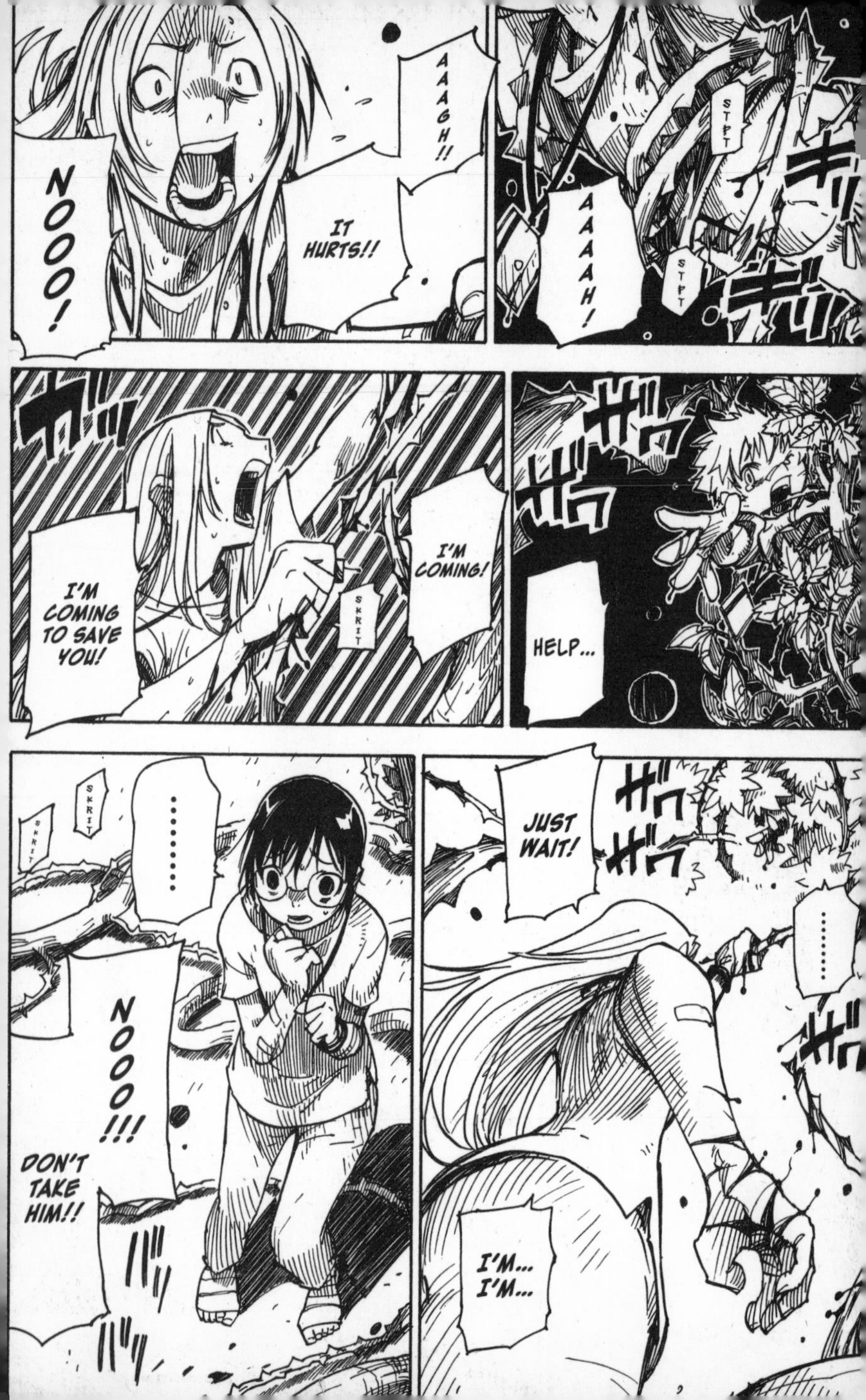
STPT
AAAAAH!
STPT
AAAGH!!
IT HURTS!!
NOOOO!
HELP...
I'M COMING!
SKRIT
I'M COMING TO SAVE YOU!
JUST WAIT!
......
I'M... I'M...
SKRIT
SKRIT
......
NOOOO!!!
DON'T TAKE HIM!!

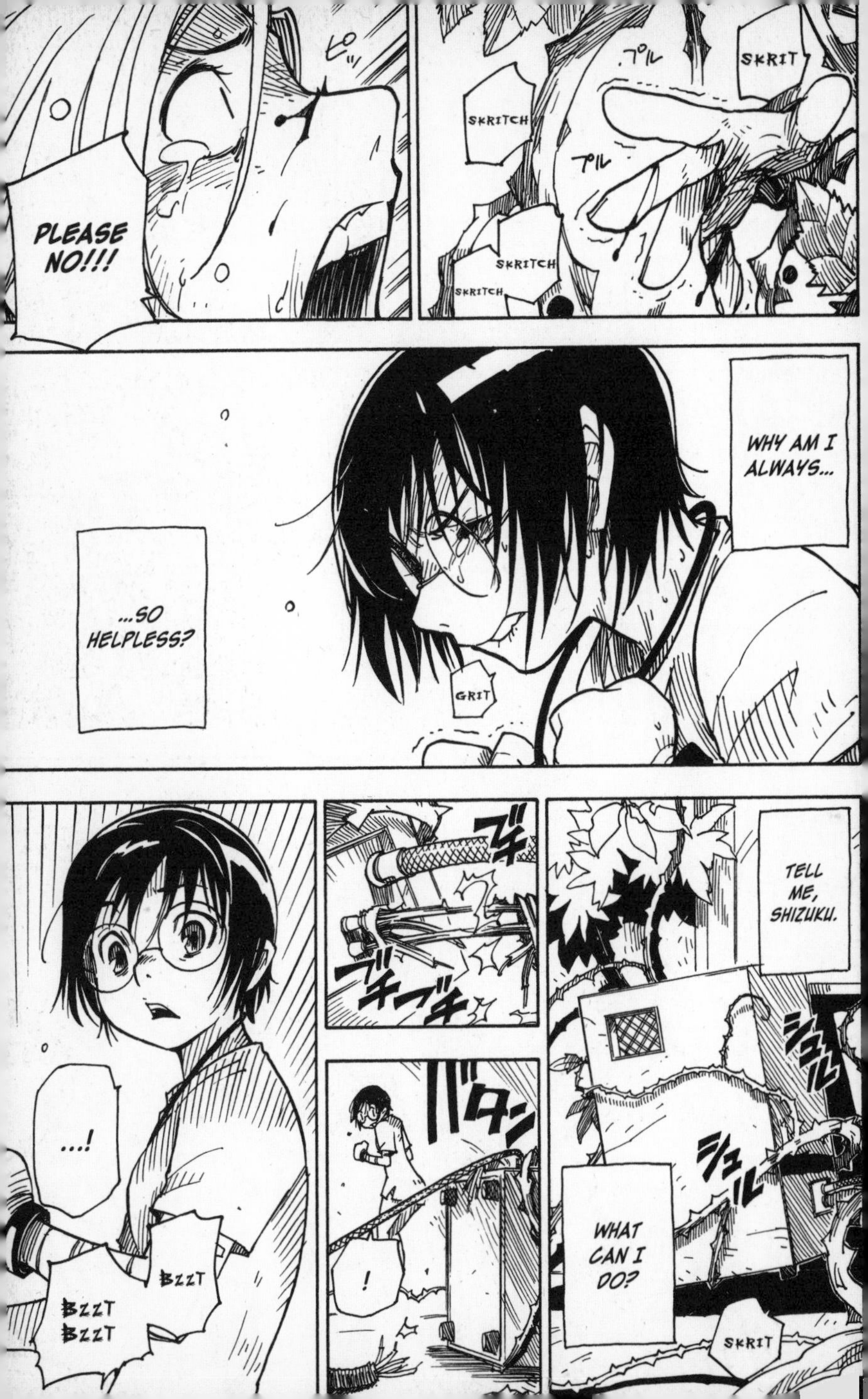
SKRIT
プル
SKRITCH
プル
SKRITCH
SKRITCH
ピッ
PLEASE NO!!!
WHY AM I ALWAYS...
GRIT
...SO HELPLESS?
TELL ME, SHIZUKU.
シュル
シュル
WHAT CAN I DO?
SKRIT
ブチ
ブチブチ
バタン
!
...!
BZZT
BZZT
BZZT

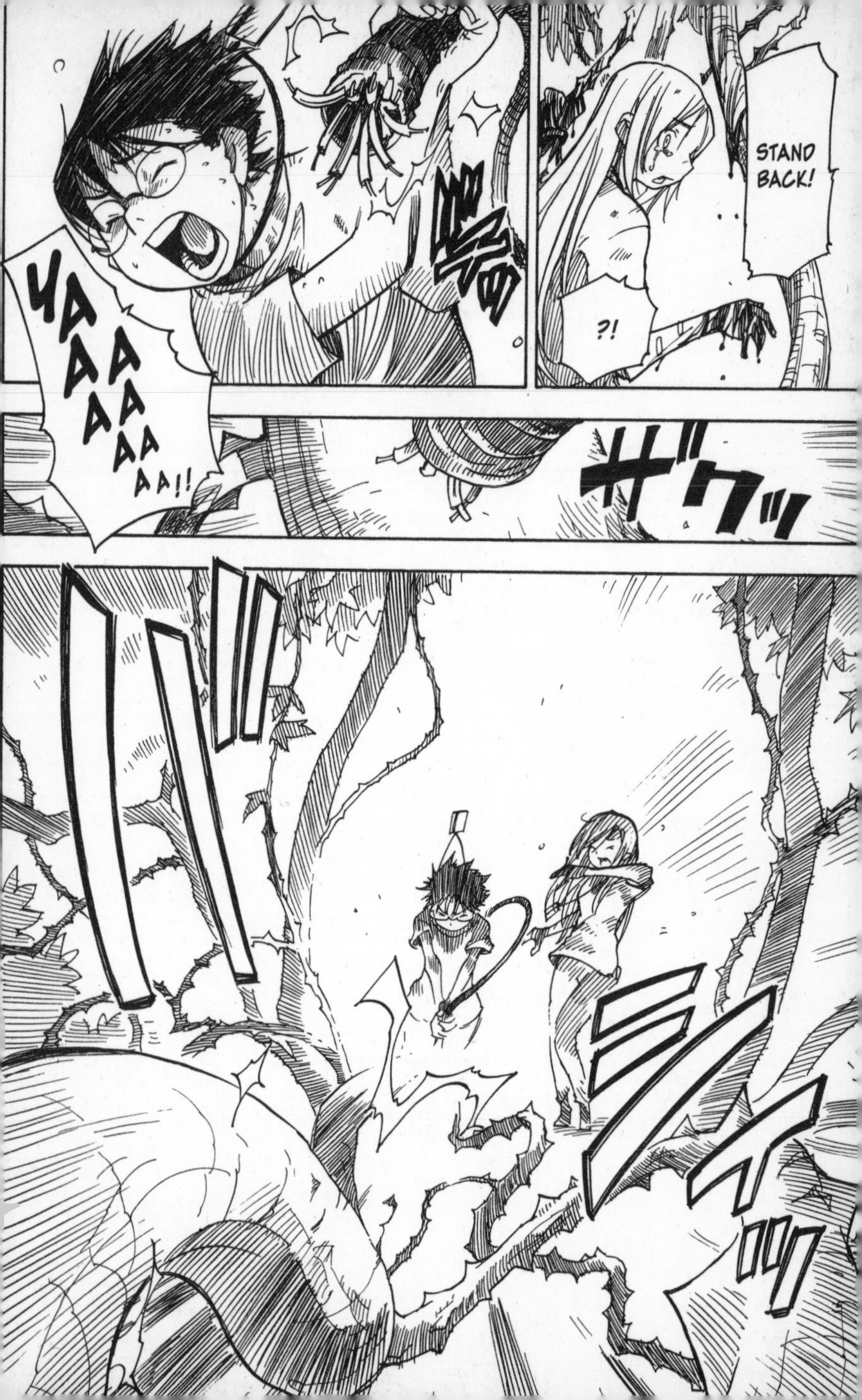
STAND BACK!
?!
YAAAAAAAAA!!
ザクッ

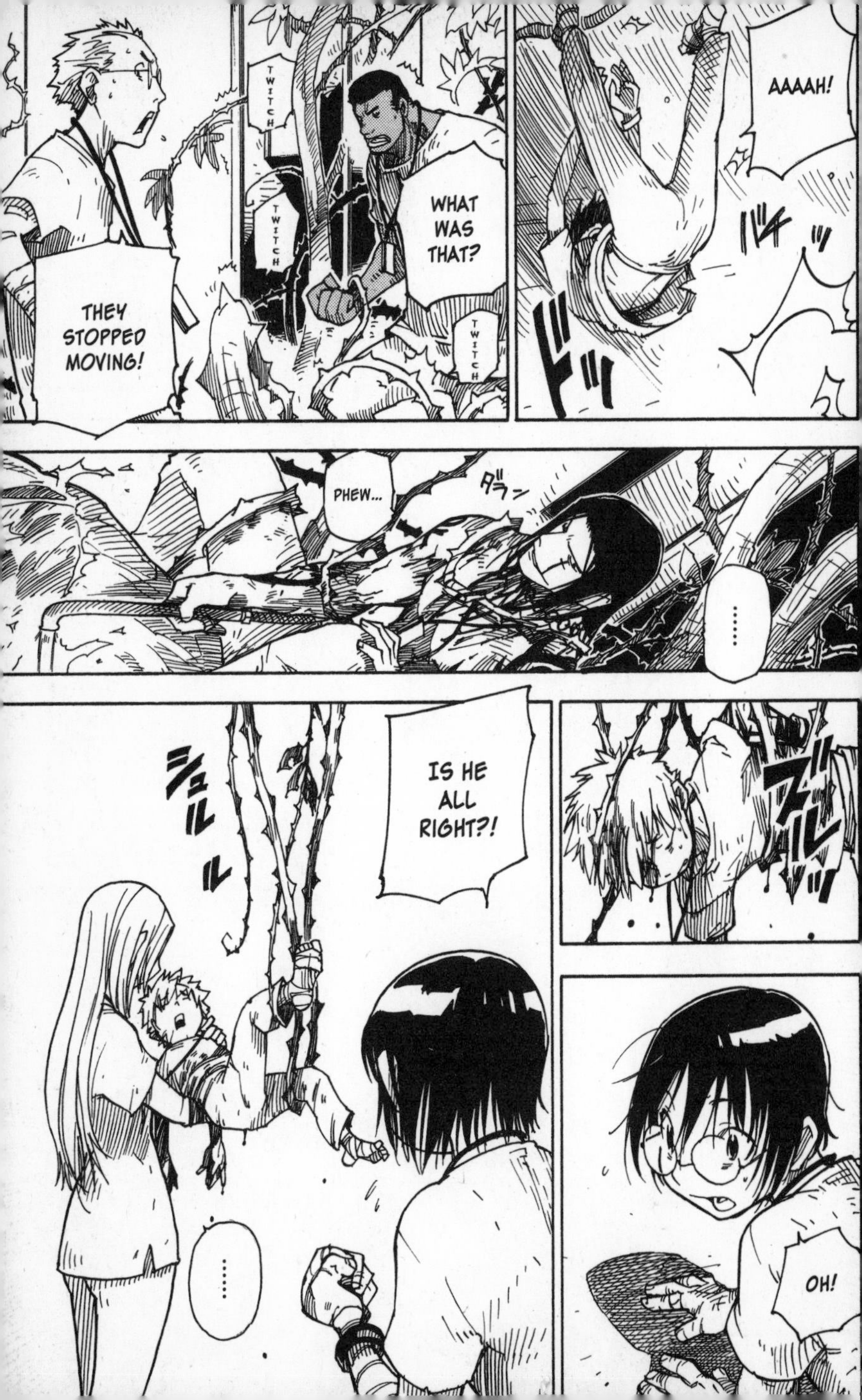
AAAAH!
バッ
ドッ
WHAT WAS THAT?
TWITCH
TWITCH
TWITCH
THEY STOPPED MOVING!
ダラン
PHEW...
......
ズルッ
OH!
IS HE ALL RIGHT?!
シュルル
......

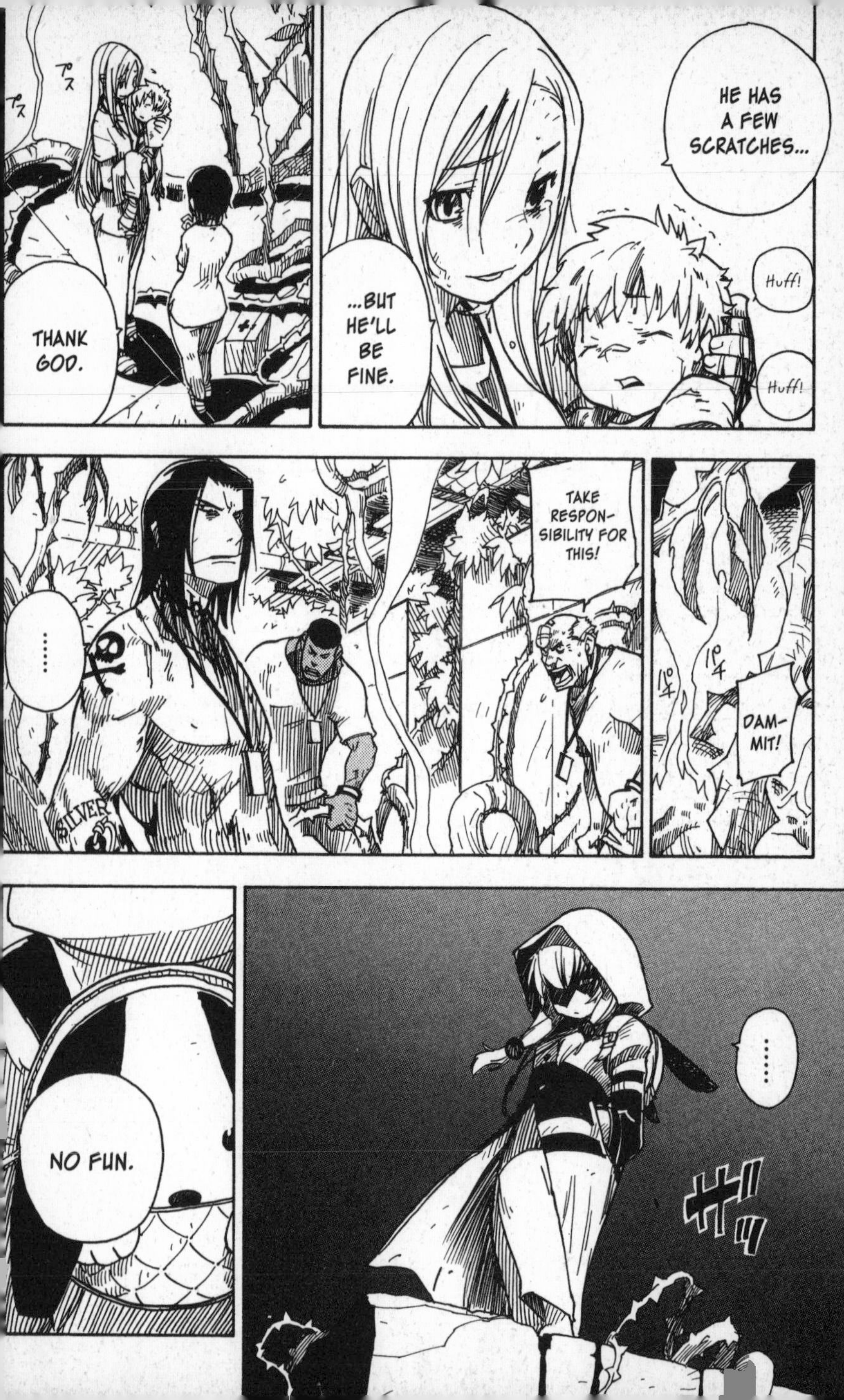
HE HAS A FEW SCRATCHES...
...BUT HE'LL BE FINE.
Huff!
Huff!
THANK GOD.
DAM-MIT!
TAKE RESPON-SIBILITY FOR THIS!
......
SILVER
......
NO FUN.

To be continued...

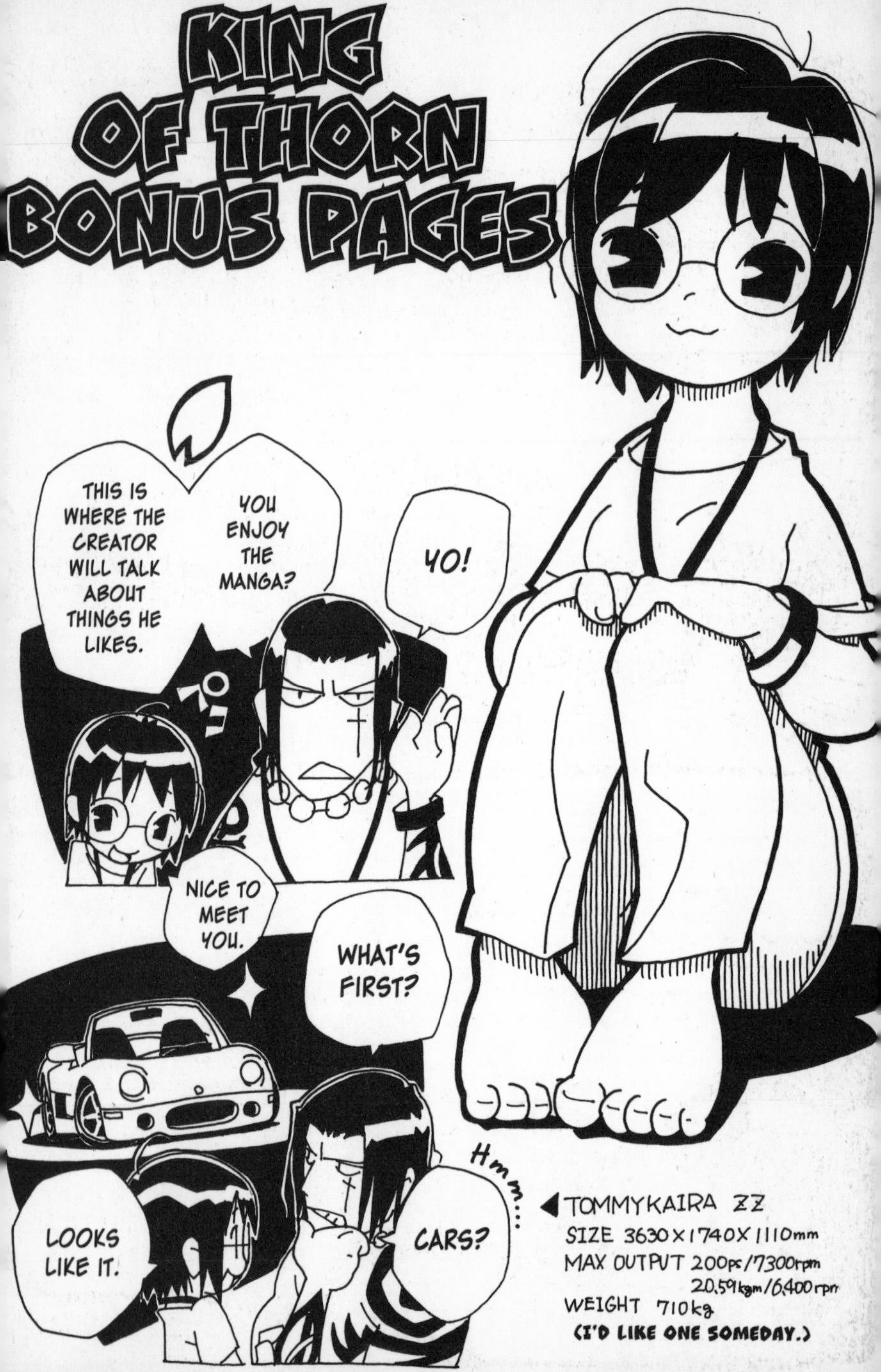
KING OF THORN BONUS PAGES
YO!
YOU ENJOY THE MANGA?
THIS IS WHERE THE CREATOR WILL TALK ABOUT THINGS HE LIKES.
NICE TO MEET YOU.
WHAT'S FIRST?
Hmm...
CARS?
LOOKS LIKE IT.
◀TOMMYKAIRA ZZ
SIZE 3630×1740×1110mm
MAX OUTPUT 200ps/7300rpm
20.59kgm/6400rpm
WEIGHT 710kg
(I'D LIKE ONE SOMEDAY.)

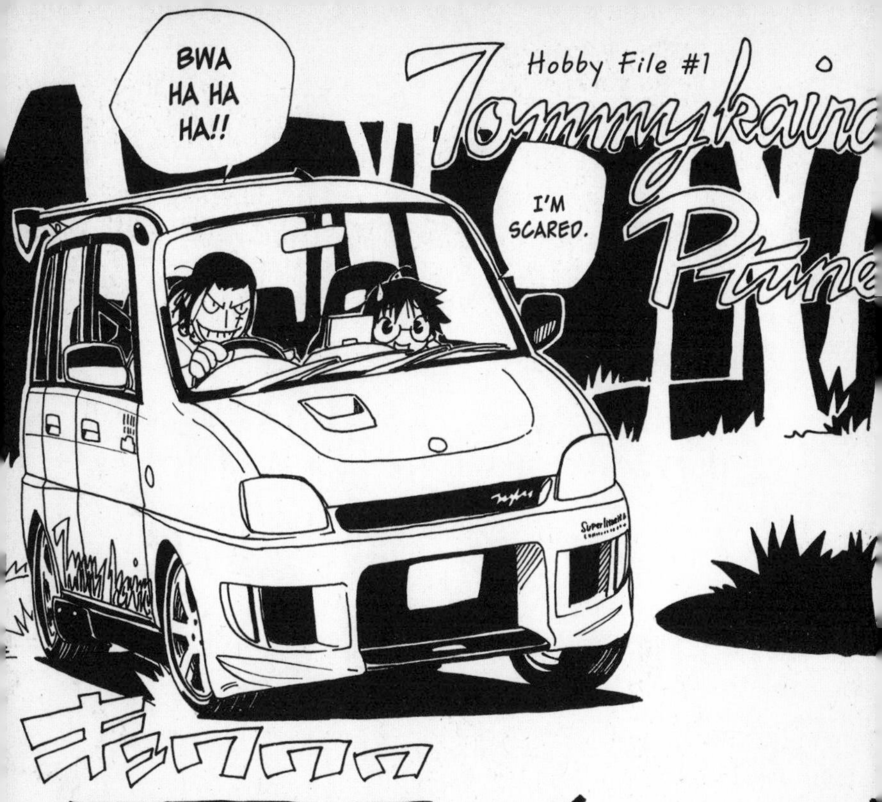
Hobby File #1
I'M SCARED.
BWA HA HA HA!!

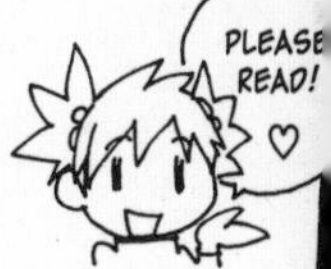
PLEASE READ! ♡

This is a car I bought for myself as a gift while working hard on my previous series, *Chikyu Misaki*. It was my first ever car and while it was expensive, I figured I'd need it for work-related things, too. It's a light Subaru "Preo" that's been tuned by Tommy Kaira of Kyoto. The coloring is similar to the WRC Impreza. I love how it handles! Plus, it can carry four people!

I've been too busy to do it lately, but what I look forward to most in life is going up to a natural hot spring in the mountains and just relaxing and thinking about new ideas and plots for my manga. The roads are so narrow that it's scary in a larger car, but I love driving there as fast as I can. As I drive around those curves, it makes me feel really happy that I finally got myself a car.

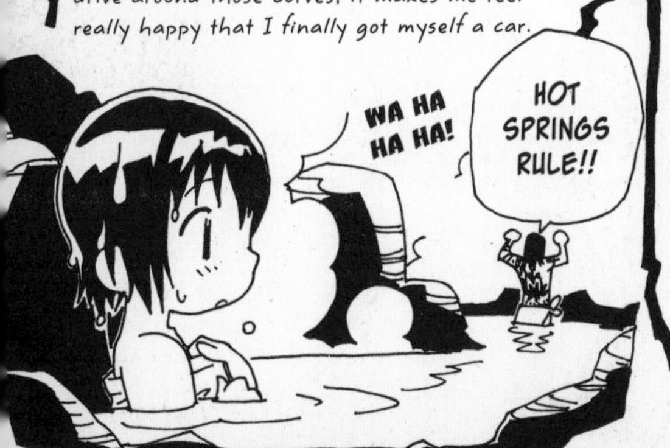
HOT SPRINGS RULE!!
WA HA HA HA!

I wanted to talk more but I'm out of time. Sorry!

In the next...

KING of THORN™

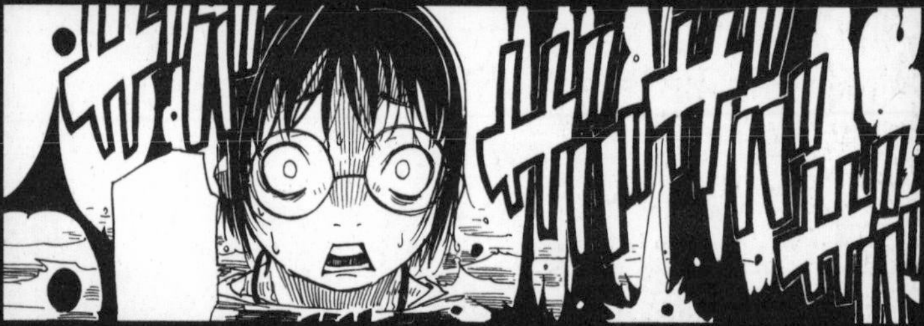

The hatch has been opened, but where does it lead? An underwater tunnel will take our group of survivors to a familiar place, but what new horrors await them there? Slowly, the survivors begin to fall, and all the while, an unfamiliar face watches from afar. Who is this mysterious girl? And what is the secret behind the Medusa virus? Answers and excitement await in Vol. 2 of King of Thorn!

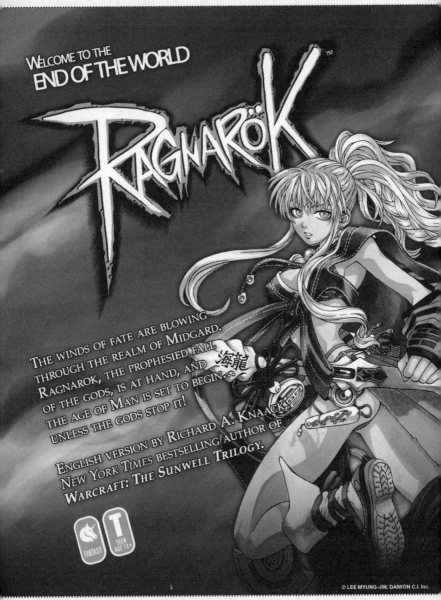

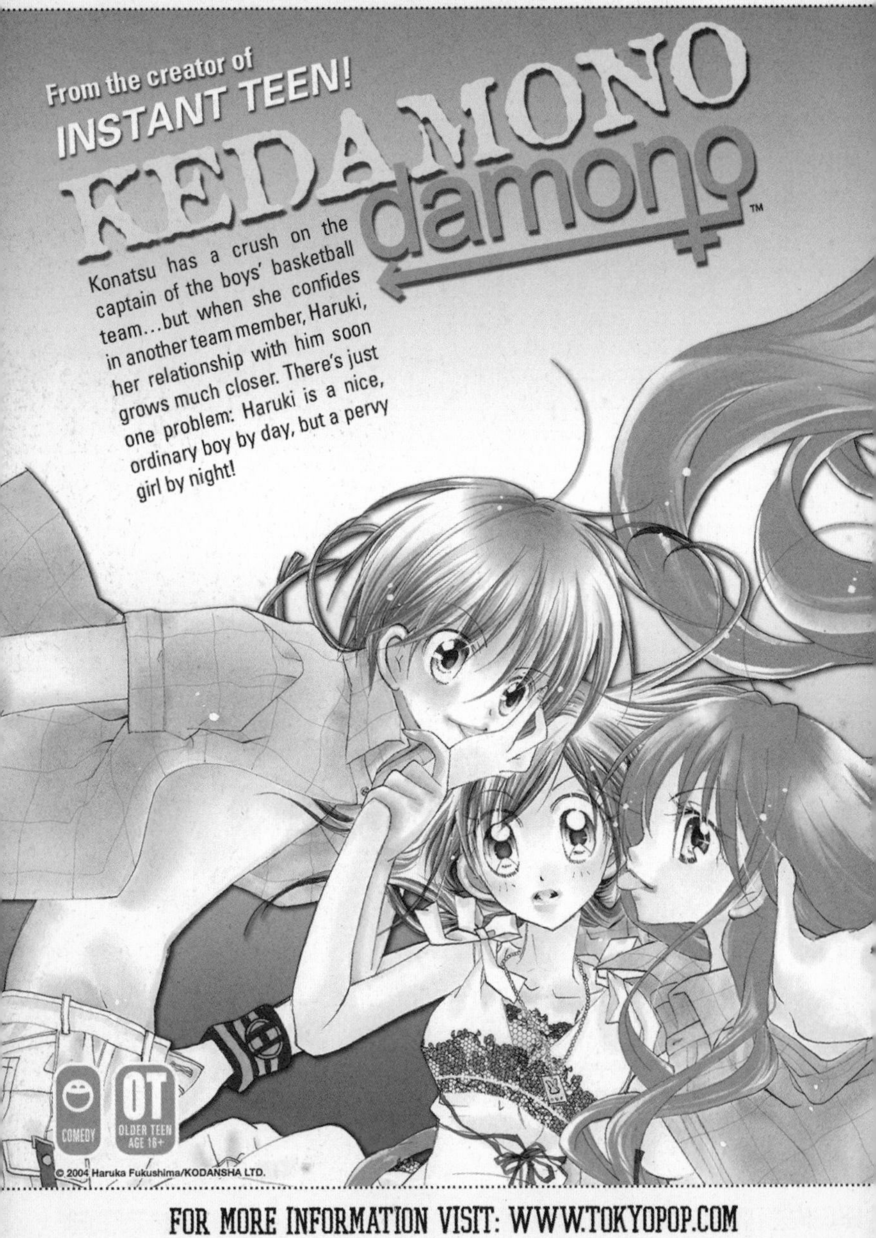
From the creator of
INSTANT TEEN!
KEDAMONO damono™
Konatsu has a crush on the captain of the boys' basketball team...but when she confides in another team member, Haruki, her relationship with him soon grows much closer. There's just one problem: Haruki is a nice, ordinary boy by day, but a pervy girl by night!
COMEDY
OT
OLDER TEEN AGE 16+
© 2004 Haruka Fukushima/KODANSHA LTD.

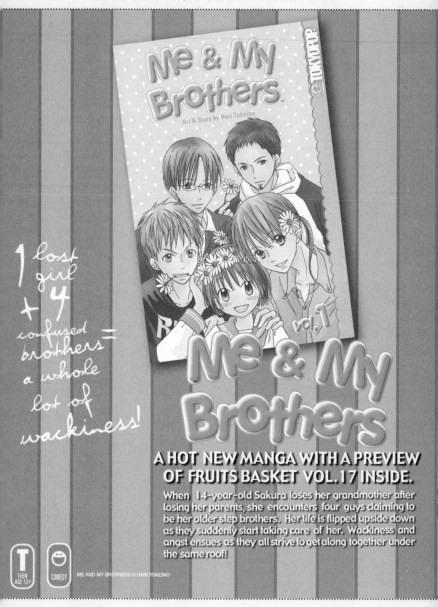

STOP!

This is the back of the book.
You wouldn't want to spoil a great ending!

This book is printed "manga-style," in the authentic Japanese right-to-left format. Since none of the artwork has been flipped or altered, readers get to experience the story just as the creator intended. You've been asking for it, so TOKYOPOP® delivered: authentic, hot-off-the-press, and far more fun!

DIRECTIONS

If this is your first time reading manga-style, here's a quick guide to help you understand how it works.

It's easy... just start in the top right panel and follow the numbers. Have fun, and look for more 100% authentic manga from TOKYOPOP®!